FUNDAMENTALS OF BANKRUPTCY LAW

American Law Institute
American Bar Association
Committee on Continuing
Professional Education

As of March 29, 1989

FUNDAMENTALS OF
BANKRUPTCY LAW

SECOND EDITION

GEORGE M. TREISTER
of the California Bar

J. RONALD TROST
of the California,
District of Columbia,
and Texas Bars

LEON S. FORMAN
of the Pennsylvania Bar

KENNETH N. KLEE
of the California and
District of Columbia Bars

RICHARD B. LEVIN
of the California and
District of Columbia Bars

**AMERICAN LAW INSTITUTE-AMERICAN BAR ASSOCIATION
COMMITTEE ON CONTINUING PROFESSIONAL EDUCATION**
4025 CHESTNUT STREET • PHILADELPHIA • PENNSYLVANIA 19104

Library of Congress Catalog Number: 88-070141

© 1988 by The American Law Institute. All rights reserved

Printed in the United States of America

Second Printing 1989

ISBN: 0-8318-0504-8

Carolyn Muldoon and Thea R. Clark
of the ALI-ABA staff supervised the
production of this book

Foreword

For many years the authors of this book have collaborated in the presentation of basic and advanced ALI-ABA Courses of Study on bankruptcy law. Their written materials for attendees have been of a quality and character that made them useful in the law office. In 1986, the materials were published in book form—after extensive updating and the addition of indexes by subject, case, and statute for easy reference—under the title *Fundamentals of Bankruptcy Law*. This second edition of the work incorporates the 1986 amendments to the Bankruptcy Code and the 1987 revisions to the Bankruptcy Rules, as well as decisions in numerous important cases before the federal courts during the intervening years.

Readers will find this text an easily assimilable explanation of a complex and difficult area of the law. The understanding of the subject, which is, to a large degree, determined by statutory prescription, is facilitated by the format of the volume: complete statutory language appears on the left-hand pages adjacent to the textual discussions on the right-hand pages, whenever pertinent.

Through the spoken and written efforts of the authors of *Fundamentals of Bankruptcy Law*, thousands of lawyers have been able to expand their knowledge of bankruptcy law. This book affords the authors an opportunity to reach an even larger audience. ALI-ABA is grateful to George M. Treister, J. Ronald Trost, Leon S. Forman, Kenneth N. Klee, and Richard B. Levin for unselfishly sharing their expertise and experience with the bar.

Paul A. Wolkin
Executive Director
American Law Institute-American Bar Association
Committee on Continuing Professional Education

April 5, 1988

[vii]

Preface

Bankruptcy law is widely regarded as a difficult subject. Although this reputation is not entirely warranted, the Bankruptcy Code is indeed a lengthy, technical statute. Moreover, the meaning of many of its sections is obscured by the fact that language derived from the former Bankruptcy Act is often carried forward into the Code laden with a considerable judicial gloss.

Another obstacle to understanding results from the congressional policy of separating substantive bankruptcy law from the implementing procedural provisions. The Code itself contains mainly matters of substance; procedure by and large is governed by a separate package of Bankruptcy Rules promulgated pursuant to the Supreme Court's rule-making power. To read the Code's substantive sections before becoming familiar with the procedural glue that holds them together and makes them work is likely to be confusing. On the other hand, reading the Rules before becoming familiar with the substantive provisions they are designed to implement also is confusing, if not fruitless.

Perhaps what is most disconcerting about an initial approach to bankruptcy law is the highly interrelated nature of the various statutory provisions. Many sections are understandable only in the context of the overall Bankruptcy Code. A real grasp of the part can be achieved only after there is a grasp of the whole, which in turn depends upon learning the parts.

In any event, it seems useful to begin the study with a broad-brushed, relatively quick general orientation. This book is intended to serve that purpose. As sometime teachers, we were motivated to write it because of a felt need for this kind of resource in our continuing legal education courses in bankruptcy and business reorganization law, sponsored by ALI-ABA primarily for general practitioners and others who do not specialize in the insolvency field. We emphasize that the book is a primer, not a research tool, although perhaps for some it may serve as a starting point for serious research. The book deals mainly with fundamentals, but refinements are discussed at various places when they are necessary to an understanding of the big picture or to the way the bankruptcy system actually functions. There are relatively few case citations; no attempt has been made to cite all or even a significant portion of the hundreds of important judicial decisions that have interpreted the Bankruptcy Code since it became effective in 1979. We think that such detail would tend to obscure the overview we want to achieve.

Although our effort is to explain simply and accurately the basic meaning of the Bankruptcy Code, the beginning student cannot proceed confidently without a focus on the statute itself. The book is intended as an aid to the study of the Code, not as a substitute for it. The desirability of careful attention to the language of the statute explains the somewhat unusual format of the book. The text is printed only on the right-hand, or odd-numbered, pages, so that the important Code sections under discussion can be reproduced close-by on the facing pages. Thus comparison of the precise statutory wording with what we have to say about it should be facilitated.

Finally, an acknowledgment is in order. We deeply appreciate the invaluable editorial assistance we received from Sally A. Ulrich of the ALI-ABA staff in preparing the manuscript for publication. Her help certainly has made this book better than it otherwise would have been.

GEORGE M. TREISTER
J. RONALD TROST
LEON S. FORMAN
KENNETH N. KLEE
RICHARD B. LEVIN

We dedicate this book to our friend

Alex Hart.

His care for our personal comfort and

attention to every administrative detail

have made participation in the

ALI-ABA bankruptcy programs

a pleasure for all of us.

Contents

1

Introduction and Overview

§ 1.01 THE NEED FOR REVISION OF BANKRUPTCY LAWS IN 1978

The present bankruptcy laws are, for the most part, the result of legislation originally passed by Congress in 1978 and amended in 1984 and 1986. The 1978 statute, Pub. L. No. 95–598, 92 Stat. 2549 — sometimes referred to unofficially as the Bankruptcy Reform Act of 1978 — became effective, in general, for cases filed on or after October 1, 1979. The former Bankruptcy Act (sometimes referred to as the 1898 Act) remained applicable to cases then pending.

A consideration of the history of the 1978 legislation probably should begin with the study of bankruptcy and bankruptcy administration made by the Brookings Institution in the late 1960s. The "Brookings Report" (D. STANLEY, M. GIRTH, ET AL., BANKRUPTCY: PROBLEM, PROCESS, REFORM) was published in 1971. The previous year Congress had established the Commission on the Bankruptcy Laws of the United States to "study, analyze, evaluate, and recommend changes" in the Bankruptcy Act and the system of bankruptcy administration. Pub. L. No. 91–354, 84 Stat. 468, 468. The Commission consisted of nine members — three appointed by the President and two each by and from the Senate, House, and Judiciary — and employed a total staff of 27 during its lifetime.

During its two-year existence the Commission conducted public hearings, gathered evidence, and, as had Brookings, generally studied the operation of the existing bankruptcy system. Its findings were similar to Brookings' (although Brookings recommended quite different solutions). Because Public Law No. 95–598, ultimately enacted in 1978, was the recognizable descendant of the statute proposed by the Commission in July 1973, the Commission's Report merits discussion.

The even-numbered pages
are reserved for
reproduction of the
appropriate statutory language.
See, for instance, page 18.

The Commission's Report to Congress in July 1973 was in two parts. Part I was a narrative of the Commission's findings and recommendations. H.R. Doc. No. 137, 93d Cong., 1st Sess., part I (1973) [hereinafter cited as "Report"]. Part II consisted of the proposed text of a new bankruptcy code that would have effected the Commission's recommendations. H.R. Doc. No. 137, 93d Cong., 1st Sess., part II (1973) [hereinafter cited as "Commission's Bill"].

The Commission concluded that the bankruptcy statute and system needed reform for a number of reasons. The "rising tide of consumer bankruptcies" since World War II had placed a severe strain on the existing bankruptcy system. Report at 2. Moreover, a substantial portion of the costs of operating the bankruptcy system was devoted to cases that produced little or no benefit to creditors, and the adversary process used to resolve those matters was inappropriate. Report at 3. In addition, the bankruptcy laws were found not to be uniformly applied. For example, wage-earner plans under Chapter XIII of the former Bankruptcy Act were employed frequently in many parts of the country but were never used in other geographic areas. Report at 4.

A different type of problem arose from the Supreme Court's promulgation of the Rules of Bankruptcy Procedure during the 1970s. The result was a comprehensive revision of practice and procedure in the bankruptcy court. At the same time the Rules had a significant impact on the Bankruptcy Act itself. Under the federal statute pursuant to which the Rules were originally promulgated, former 28 U.S.C. § 2075, a rule superseded any inconsistent provision in the Bankruptcy Act as long as the rule dealt with a matter that was one of "practice and procedure." Since a considerable portion of that Act was in the nature of "practice and procedure," many of its provisions were, in effect, repealed by the Bankruptcy Rules, although the repealed provisions were not actually removed from the statute. The courts and lawyers were left to determine for themselves which portions of the Act were "substantive" and therefore still effective.

Although the procedural provisions governing bankruptcy administration had recently been revised and updated by the Bankruptcy Rules of the 1970s, the substantive provisions were, for the

most part, at least 40 years old. *See* Countryman, *The New Dis-chargeability Law*, 45 AM. BANKR. L.J. 1 (1971). In the Bankruptcy Act Congress had left for determination by state law much of what is substantive in bankruptcy. *See* Countryman, *The Use of State Law in Bankruptcy Cases (Part II)*, 47 N.Y.U. L. REV. 631 (1972). State law, particularly in the area of the competing rights of secured and unsecured creditors, had changed significantly since the Chandler Act of 1938, the last comprehensive revision of the 1898 Act. Yet no wholesale reexamination of the bankruptcy law had taken place to determine whether the dual bankruptcy principles of fairness in the treatment of creditors and the grant of a fresh start to the debtor were being served by the use of state substantive provisions. Moreover, the former Bankruptcy Act was a hodgepodge; sections were out of order as well as out of date.

The organic bankruptcy court system had simply evolved up to 1978 without legislative definition, and it was inadequate. As originally contemplated, the referee in bankruptcy was an administrative assistant to the United States district judge. The referee's duty was to conduct the administration of bankruptcy cases under the general supervision of the district judge. In matters of litigation the referee was to report findings of fact and conclusions of law to the district court. But especially during the four decades following the 1938 Chandler amendments, the referee's role grew. The referee in bankruptcy became a "bankruptcy judge" (*see* former Bankruptcy Rule 901(7)) and exercised virtually all the original jurisdiction of the bankruptcy court. The bankruptcy judge thus had come to exercise the judicial power to decide disputes as a court of original jurisdiction but still was responsible for supervising the administration of bankruptcy cases.

The dual role of the referee, or bankruptcy judge, was, in the opinion of many, the most glaring defect in the former bankruptcy system. Informal contacts between the bankruptcy judge and lawyers and others participating in bankruptcy administration were encouraged, if not required, by the very nature of the many administrative duties imposed on the court by the Bankruptcy Act. In supervising the administration of the bankruptcy estate, the bankruptcy judge appointed the receiver or trustee and approved the employment of counsel; often countersigned checks; approved

the sale of property and the borrowing of money; and, in reorganization cases, received operating reports for use in determining whether the business operation should continue. The Report of the Bankruptcy Commission observed that "[t]he involvement of the referee in the administration of estates entails numerous conferences and communications that are informal and *ex parte*." Report at 93. Consequently, the Commission concluded on pages 93–94 of the Report that

> making an individual [the bankruptcy judge] responsible for conduct of both administrative and judicial aspects of a bankruptcy case is incompatible with the proper performance of the judicial function. Even if a paragon of integrity were sitting on the bench and could keep his mind and feelings insulated from influences which arise from his previous official connections with the case before him and with one of the parties to it, he probably could not dispel the appearance of a relationship which might compromise his judicial objectivity.

The method of appointment of bankruptcy judges, their dependence on the district judges, and the length of their terms of office were also criticized. Under the Bankruptcy Act the district judges appointed the referees, or bankruptcy judges, for relatively short, six-year terms. The referees' dependence upon district judges for their reappointment created an obviously subservient relationship between the two levels of the judiciary; it detracted from the dignity, stability, and public acceptance of the referee's office and tended to discourage highly qualified lawyers from aspiring to positions on the bankruptcy bench.

With respect to rehabilitation cases the Commission concluded that the separate statutory vehicles for business reorganization under Chapters X, XI, and XII of the Bankruptcy Act created inflexibility and wasteful litigation and that, accordingly, the rehabilitation chapters should be unified. The Commission also found a number of glaring deficiencies in the way the former statute worked in consumer cases.

For these and other reasons the Commission proposed a pervasive revision of the bankruptcy system and the substantive law (summarized at pages 5–31 of the Report) and submitted a complete proposed statute embodying the recommended reforms.

§ 1.02 THE PROGRESS OF THE REFORM MOVEMENT

The 94th Congress, in 1975, was the first to give serious consideration to the proposed reforms. It considered not only the legislative equivalent of the Commission's Bill (H.R. 31, 94th Cong., 1st Sess. (1975)) but also a bill introduced at the request of the National Conference of Bankruptcy Judges. H.R. 32, 94th Cong., 1st Sess. (1975) [hereinafter cited as "Judges' Bill"]. The Judges' Bill adopted large portions of the Commission's recommendations and draftsmanship but deviated from the Commission's Bill in significant respects. (A careful and detailed comparison between the Commission's Bill and the Judges' Bill may be found in *Hearings on H.R. 31 and H.R. 32 Before the Subcomm. on Civil and Constitutional Rights of the House Comm. on the Judiciary,* 94th Cong., 1st & 2d Sess., ser. 27, Appendix (1975–1976).)

Following the issuance of the Commission's Report and during the course of the congressional hearings, the National Bankruptcy Conference,[1] an unofficial organization composed of law professors, bankruptcy judges, and practicing lawyers, thoroughly considered both the Commission's and the Judges' proposals. At the urging of Congressman Don Edwards, Chairman of the House Judiciary Subcommittee, to which H.R. 31 and H.R. 32 were referred, representatives of the National Bankruptcy Conference and of the National Conference of Bankruptcy Judges met on various occasions and attempted to reach agreement on the most important features of the bankruptcy reform legislation. Those meetings resulted in a series of joint recommendations to Congress. *Hearings on H.R. 31 and H.R. 32 Before the Subcomm. on Civil and Constitutional Rights of the House Comm. on the Judiciary,* 94th Cong., 2d Sess., ser. 27, part 3, 1938–41 (1976).

After Chairman Edwards' subcommittee had again considered the Commission's recommendations and the consensus changes suggested by the National Bankruptcy Conference and the National Conference of Bankruptcy Judges, it applied its own analysis and style and drafted H.R. 6, which was introduced in January 1977. H.R. 6, 95th Cong., 1st Sess. (1977). In March 1977, the

---

[1]Since it was formed in the 1930s, the National Bankruptcy Conference has been a significant factor in bankruptcy reform legislation.

subcommittee produced a revised version of H.R. 6, known as H.R. 7330. H.R. 7330, 95th Cong., 1st Sess. (1977). About four months later, H.R. 8200, embodying further refinements, was introduced. H.R. 8200, 95th Cong., 1st Sess. (1977).

While these developments were going on in the House, the Senate also held hearings and considered bankruptcy reform legislation, although the Senate tended to follow the House's lead until S. 2266 was introduced in the fall of 1977. S. 2266, 95th Cong., 1st Sess. (1977). Although organized along the lines of H.R. 8200 and containing many of the same provisions, this bill differed in a number of significant respects from the House version.

H.R. 8200 first passed in the House in February 1978. S. 2266 passed in the Senate in September 1978, during the closing days of the 95th Congress. A flurry of last-minute compromises reconciled the different versions of the legislation. The final product—known as H.R. 8200, as amended—emerged and was passed by both the House and the Senate. President Carter signed the bill, which then was designated Pub. L. No. 95-598, 92 Stat. 2549, on November 6, 1978.

As noted earlier, most of the provisions of the new law became effective for cases filed on or after October 1, 1979.[2]

§ 1.03 THE CONSTITUTIONAL SETBACK OF 1982 AND THE 1984 AMENDMENTS

As is discussed in more detail later, pp. 23–25, *infra*, the 1978 legislation established a bankruptcy court system that was intended, inter alia, to upgrade the judicial office, but it did not give Article III constitutional status to the bankruptcy judges. That is,

---

[2]Originally, it had been contemplated that the new law would apply to transactions or events whenever they occurred, either before or after 1978, provided that the bankruptcy petition was filed after October 1, 1979. In United States v. Security Indus. Bank, 459 U.S. 70 (1982), however, the Supreme Court held that if retroactive application of the 1978 Act would eliminate a lien or property right (as distinguished from a contract right) that had vested before enactment of the law on November 6, 1978, the Act should be construed not to apply to this preenactment property right so as to avoid a difficult Fifth Amendment taking clause issue.

rather than providing for their appointment to serve during good behavior, the statute contemplated that these judges, beginning in 1984, would be appointed by the President, subject to Senate confirmation, to serve 14-year terms. But as had been anticipated during the legislative process (see, e.g., H.R. REP. No. 595, 95th Cong., 1st Sess. 23–39 (1977)), there was promptly raised the constitutional question whether, consistently with Article III, untenured federal judges could exercise the broad jurisdiction conferred upon them in 1978. In June 1982, the Supreme Court held they could not, in essence invalidating, prospectively only, the entire statutory grant of jurisdiction to the bankruptcy judges. *Northern Pipeline Constr. Co. v. Marathon Pipe Line Co.*, 458 U.S. 50 (1982). The effective date of the decision, however, was stayed by the Court, ultimately to December 24, 1982, to permit Congress to repair the damage by enacting a bankruptcy court system that would pass constitutional muster.

When Congress failed to respond by the expiration of this stay period, the Judicial Branch attempted to fill the breach. At the prompting of the Judicial Conference of the United States, the various circuit councils recommended to the district courts that they promulgate so-called local Emergency Rules within the respective federal districts. As adopted, these rules varied only in minor details from district to district. They were premised on the assumption that the Supreme Court's decision, although invalidating the jurisdictional grant to the bankruptcy courts, had left the Article III district courts with full bankruptcy jurisdiction. Essentially, the rules provided, pursuant to the rule-making authority of the district courts, for the delegation of most of that jurisdiction to the bankruptcy judges.

The Emergency Rules in the various districts were superseded when Congress subsequently passed, and the President signed on July 10, 1984, the Bankruptcy Amendments and Federal Judgeship Act of 1984, Pub. L. No. 98–353, 98 Stat. 333. This legislation, among other things, created a bankruptcy jurisdictional scheme that resembled the one established by the Emergency Rules. In addition, as a result of the urgings of a number of pressure groups, the new law amended the substantive provisions of the 1978 Bankruptcy Code in a variety of ways. Among the more

publicized substantive amendments were many provisions concerning consumer cases; changes in the provisions concerning executory contracts, particularly collective bargaining agreements, leases of nonresidential real estate, and time-share contracts; provisions concerning grain storage facility bankruptcies; and some changes in the trustee's avoiding powers.

The 1984 legislation became effective immediately upon its enactment on July 10 with respect to the court system changes; the substantive amendments, for the most part, became effective for cases filed on or after October 8, 1984. Pub. L. No. 98–353, §§ 122(a), 553(a), 98 Stat. 346, 392.

Two years later, Congress passed the Bankruptcy Judges, United States Trustees, and Family Farmer Bankruptcy Act of 1986, which was signed by the President on October 27. Pub. L. No. 99-554. It provides for, among other things, a permanent nationwide United States trustee system housed in the Justice Department and a new Chapter 12, a form of relief for the so-called family farmers. The 1986 law also repealed former Chapter 15, a set of provisions that were necessary to accommodate the United States trustee system when it was only a pilot or experimental program in limited areas before being made permanent and extended nationwide.

§ 1.04 OVERVIEW OF THE PRESENT LAW

Bankruptcy legislation, as amended, is now codified in two places in the United States Code. Title 28, the Judicial Code, contains the provisions on bankruptcy jurisdiction, the bankruptcy judges and the "bankruptcy court," venue and transfer, and the structure of the United States trustee system. Title 11, the Bankruptcy Code, contains both substantive and procedural law for bankruptcy liquidation and rehabilitation cases; Congress, however, left most procedural detail for the Supreme Court to supply pursuant to its rule-making power.

The Bankruptcy Code is divided into eight chapters (Chapters 1, 3, 5, 7, 9, 11, 12, and 13), which are further divided into subchapters. There are five potential kinds of cases, or types of relief available, under the Bankruptcy Code, depending on the

debtor's eligibility (*see* Bankruptcy Code § 109, 11 U.S.C. § 109 [hereinafter, citations to section numbers refer to sections of the Bankruptcy Code unless otherwise indicated]) and on what is sought to be accomplished. Each type of case or relief is the subject of one of the Chapters 7, 9, 11, 12, or 13.[3]

1. Chapter 7 is "Liquidation," sometimes colloquially referred to under the former Bankruptcy Act as "straight bankruptcy." Its purpose is to achieve a fair distribution to creditors of whatever nonexempt property the debtor has and to give the individual debtor a fresh start through the discharge in bankruptcy.

2. Chapter 9 deals with the "Adjustment of Debts of a Municipality"; it is too specialized to be within the coverage of this book.

3. Chapter 11 is a unified set of provisions for all kinds of "Reorganization," usually for debtors engaged in business, including individuals, partnerships, and corporations, and for both public and closely held companies. Its goal ordinarily is to rehabilitate a business as a going concern rather than to liquidate it. The debtor is given a fresh start through the binding effect on all concerned of the order of confirmation of a reorganization plan. (There is a special subchapter for "Railroad Reorganization.")

4. Chapter 12, enacted in 1986, is designed to give special relief to a "family farmer with regular annual income," a defined term. Individuals, partnerships, and corporations are potentially eligible so long as the debtor's total indebtedness does not exceed $1.5 million. Chapter 12 is intended as a temporary measure; the assumption is that this special form of relief will be unnecessary after the crisis in the farm economy of the mid-1980's has passed. Accordingly, Section 302(f) of Public Law 99-554 provides for the sunset, or expiration, of the chapter on October 1, 1993. Because of its specialized nature, Chapter 12 will not receive detailed attention in this book. In general, its provisions are patterned on Chapter 13.

5. Chapter 13, a rehabilitation vehicle for an "individual with

---

[3] In addition, Section 304 provides for cases ancillary to or in aid of foreign bankruptcy or insolvency proceedings, a subject beyond the scope of this book.

11 U.S.C. § 105. Power of court

(a) The court may issue any order, process, or judgment that is necessary or appropriate to carry out the provisions of this title. . . .

regular income" whose debts do not exceed specified amounts, typically is used to budget some of the debtor's future earnings under a plan through which creditors are paid in whole or in part. The fresh start comes from the discharge granted at the end of the case; the debtor's incentive to propose a plan rather than use Chapter 7 comes from the sometimes more favorable or powerful provisions found in Chapter 13.

Chapters 1, 3, and 5 of the Code contain provisions of general applicability. Among other things, Chapter 1 contains the definition section, sets forth some rules of construction, specifies who may be a debtor in different kinds of cases under the Bankruptcy Code, has a waiver of sovereign immunity section, and includes a frequently relied upon section (Section 105(a)) that is comparable to an "all writs" statute.

Chapter 3, entitled "Case Administration," covers how a case is begun (voluntary and involuntary petitions); deals with officers and their compensation; and contains various administrative provisions and the very important "Administrative Powers," including the automatic stay (Section 362), the use, sale, and lease of property (Section 363), the obtaining of credit (Section 364), and the assumption or rejection of executory contracts (Section 365).

Chapter 5 contains much of the bankruptcy substantive law, including "Creditors and Claims," the "Debtor's Duties and Benefits," what property constitutes the estate, and the trustee's avoiding powers.

The reader should always bear in mind that under Section 103, the provisions of Chapters 1, 3, and 5 apply in any kind of case under the Bankruptcy Code, whether it be liquidation under Chapter 7 or rehabilitation under Chapter 11, 12, or 13. Chapter 9 has its own provision, Section 901, specifying which provisions in the other chapters apply in a Chapter 9 case. In contrast, the provisions found in Chapters 7, 9, 11, 12, and 13 are not generally applicable; they apply only to cases brought under their particular chapter.

28 U.S.C. § 2075. Bankruptcy rules

The Supreme Court shall have the power to prescribe by general rules, the forms of process, writs, pleadings, and motions, and the practice and procedure in cases under Title 11.

Such rules shall not abridge, enlarge, or modify any substantive right.

Such rules shall not take effect until they have been reported to Congress by the Chief Justice at or after the beginning of a regular session thereof but not later than the first day of May and until the expiration of ninety days after they have been thus reported.

§ 1.05 PROCEDURAL RULES

In bankruptcy, as in federal practice generally, matters of procedure are for the most part the subject of rules promulgated by the Supreme Court rather than of provisions incorporated into the statute itself. The bankruptcy rule-making enabling statute is 28 U.S.C. § 2075. It authorizes the Supreme Court to prescribe rules for practice and procedure in bankruptcy. If Congress fails, within 90 days after the rules are submitted to it, to pass a law amending the rules or preventing them from becoming effective, they take effect and have the force of law so long as they are not inconsistent with the Bankruptcy Code or with other statutes. There is relatively little of a bankruptcy procedural nature in the Code or in Title 28; Congress purposely left a wide field for the exercise of the rule-making power without the inhibition of inconsistent statutory provisions. (Before 1978, the rule-making authority under 28 U.S.C. § 2075 was broader. Rules inconsistent with the former Bankruptcy Act in matters of practice and procedure then could be promulgated by the Supreme Court, and these rules had the effect of superseding the statutory provisions.)

Rules that were written for the 1978 court system were adopted in 1983 and were amended in 1987, principally to take account of the current, or 1984, court structure. They may be found in the appendix to Title 11.

2

The Bankruptcy System

§ 2.01 THE BANKRUPTCY COURT

§ 2.01(a) Introduction

The bankruptcy court system enacted by the Bankruptcy Amendments and Federal Judgeship Act of 1984 ("BAFJA"), Pub. L. No. 98–353, 98 Stat. 333, is a mixture of compromises and a product of its tortuous history. Before 1978, bankruptcy courts were staffed by "referees," renamed "bankruptcy judges" by the 1973 Bankruptcy Rules, who were appointed by the district courts for 6-year terms. Although the powers and jurisdiction of bankruptcy judges had grown over the 80-year history from their establishment under the Bankruptcy Act of 1898, their jurisdiction continued to be limited by outmoded concepts of possession and consent, and their powers and status were limited by their roles as subordinate functionaries of the district courts.

The 1978 Bankruptcy Reform Act attempted to upgrade the jurisdiction, powers, and status of bankruptcy judges. It did not, however, adopt the approach of the original House Bill, H.R. 8200, which would have established Article III bankruptcy courts[1] with judges who enjoyed the full powers of a federal trial court. Nevertheless, the 1978 Act went a long way toward achieving the goal of improving the bankruptcy system. It created bankruptcy courts, nominally referred to as adjuncts of the district courts but in fact virtually independent of them. The concept of "adjunct"

---

[1]Article III of the Constitution requires judges exercising the judicial power of the United States to be appointed to serve during good behavior, sometimes referred to as life tenure, and to be protected against salary reduction. Since the 1978 Act provided 14-year terms rather than life tenure for the bankruptcy judges, they were not Article III judges.

was never defined or explained. The judges were to be appointed by the President, by and with the advice and consent of the Senate, to serve for 14-year terms and were given broad powers. The former limitations on the jurisdiction of the bankruptcy judges were mostly eliminated. Bankruptcy judges were able to hear all Title 11 cases and all proceedings "arising under title 11 or arising in or related to cases under title 11." Former 28 U.S.C. § 1471(b). The bankruptcy judges had plenary powers, except that they could not punish a criminal contempt not committed in the presence of the court and could not enjoin another court. The bankruptcy court could hold jury trials and could enter final judgments, including in personam judgments, in any proceeding within its jurisdiction.

To give Congress time to determine the number of new judges that would be required and the President and Senate the opportunity to complete the appointments process, a five-year transition period was to precede implementation of the new court system. In the meantime, former bankruptcy judges were continued in office for the transition period and were immediately given the broad jurisdiction and powers of the new court. The system appeared to be working very well until it encountered an obstacle that was not altogether unexpected.

In the legislative debates leading to the enactment of the 1978 Act, the House Judiciary Committee had argued, and the House of Representatives had apparently agreed, that the broad new powers and jurisdiction given to the bankruptcy courts could be exercised only by judges who enjoyed Article III protections. Although the Senate acknowledged that the broader powers and jurisdiction were critical to improving the bankruptcy system, it could not be persuaded of the need to provide Article III protections for the judges who exercised those powers. As a result, the 1978 legislation compromised the system and created non-Article III courts. Thus the issue of the constitutional propriety of the 1978 court system was framed.

As noted in Chapter 1, the Supreme Court in June 1982 rendered its decision in *Northern Pipeline Constr. Co. v. Marathon Pipe Line Co.,* 458 U.S. 50 (1982), which invalidated the entire grant of jurisdiction to the bankruptcy courts. The Court's decision did not produce a majority opinion, and therein lies much of the uncer-

tainty concerning its effect. Mr. Justice Brennan, writing for a plurality of four Justices, ruled broadly that the creation of non-Article III bankruptcy courts to handle the wide range of matters comprehended by the jurisdictional provisions of the 1978 Bankruptcy Reform Act could not come within any of the previously permitted exceptions, including the "public rights" exception, to the requirement that the federal judiciary be tenured "during good Behaviour" under Article III, Section 1, of the Constitution. Because, under the statutory scheme, the bankruptcy courts were quite independent of the Article III district courts, the so-called adjunct relationship between them did not overcome the constitutional defect. Mr. Justice Brennan then concluded that the jurisdictional grant was not severable, or more properly, not divisible, since Congress intended a unified system of bankruptcy jurisdiction. Consequently, even though the plurality opinion recognized that certain aspects of the bankruptcy jurisdiction might constitutionally be exercised by nontenured judges, it invalidated the entire grant of jurisdiction to the non-Article III bankruptcy courts, not merely the portion that was beyond the capability of nontenured judges.

Mr. Justice Rehnquist, writing for himself and Mme. Justice O'Connor, concurred on the narrower ground that the trial of the *Marathon* contract dispute action, brought by the debtor in possession against a defendant who had no other connection with the bankruptcy case, was the kind of traditional common law suit that, in the federal judiciary, could be brought only in an Article III court with tenured judges. While limiting his concurrence to the specific kind of lawsuit involved in *Marathon*, he agreed with the plurality that Congress intended the jurisdictional grant to be nonseverable and therefore concurred in the judgment invalidating the grant in its entirety.

Three dissenting Justices, namely, the Chief Justice and Justices White and Powell, would have upheld the constitutionality of the jurisdictional grant. But in a somewhat unusual action, the Chief Justice wrote an additional separate dissent, attempting to suggest the narrow limits of the *Marathon* holding and what Congress could do to overcome the problem. He suggested that Congress provide for a "rerouting" of traditional common law matters to the federal

district courts, leaving everything else within the jurisdiction of the bankruptcy courts. Mr. Justice Brennan's opinion took sharp issue with the Chief Justice's characterization of the plurality's position and with his suggestion concerning congressional reformulation of the bankruptcy court's jurisdiction, but Mr. Justice Rehnquist's opinion did not. Thus any broad effect of the case is uncertain at best. Technically, however, the Chief Justice seems correct in his view that the holding is limited to the precise kind of lawsuit involved in the *Marathon* case.[2] Moreover, his suggestion for reformulation of the system represents a fair approximation of the jurisdictional scheme that Congress ultimately adopted.

The Supreme Court stayed the *Marathon* decision for over three months to allow Congress to respond by restructuring either the courts or their jurisdiction. Congress did not act within that time, and the Court extended the stay for another three months. Finally, upon the expiration of the second stay, the ruling took effect. Since Congress still had not acted, the courts devised their own interim solution to the problem. The Judicial Conference of the United States recommended to all the judicial councils of the circuits that they approve and recommend for adoption by the district courts a model Emergency Rule to govern the operation of the bankruptcy court system until Congress acted. All districts adopted the Rule with only minor variations in its provisions.

The Emergency Rule was drafted on the premise that under *Marathon* the Article III district courts retained the entire bankruptcy jurisdiction, notwithstanding the invalidation of the grant to the bankruptcy courts. (In form the 1978 legislation conferred the bankruptcy jurisdiction in the first instance on the district courts. Former 28 U.S.C. § 1471(a), (b). Former Section 1471(c) then provided that all this jurisdiction "shall" be exercised by the bankruptcy courts.) The Rule authorized the district courts to re-

---

[2]In the subsequent decision in Thomas v. Union Carbide Agr. Prods. Co., 473 U.S. 568, 584 (1985), five Justices joined an opinion that emphasized this narrow limitation:

> The Court's holding in that [*Marathon*] case establishes only that Congress may not vest in a non-Article III court the power to adjudicate, render final judgment, and issue binding orders in a traditional contract action arising under state law, without consent of the litigants, and subject only to ordinary appellate review.

fer any or all bankruptcy cases and proceedings to bankruptcy judges for hearing. It then introduced a distinction that is the forerunner of the distinction contained in the 1984 BAFJA. The Rule characterized certain kinds of proceedings, such as the common law action involved in *Marathon,* as "related proceedings." The distinction arose from the language of the jurisdictional grant in former Section 1471(b): "jurisdiction of all civil proceedings [1] arising under title 11 or [2] arising in or [3] *related to* cases under title 11" (emphasis added). The drafters of the Rule characterized the *Marathon* action as one falling solely within the third category — hence the "related proceedings" nomenclature.

Under the Emergency Rule bankruptcy judges could both hear and determine — that is, make final dispositive orders with respect to — all disputes and controversies in matters other than related proceedings. These other matters, which consisted of proceedings arising under Title 11 or arising in a case under Title 11, were termed "core proceedings," a phrase adopted from Justice Brennan's observation that "the restructuring of debtor-creditor relations . . . is at the core of the federal bankruptcy power." 458 U.S. at 71. In related proceedings the Rule permitted bankruptcy judges only to hear the matter and recommend findings, conclusions, and a proposed order. The matter then went to the district court for de novo review and entry of an appropriate order. If the parties consented, however, the bankruptcy judge could enter a final order or judgment in a related proceeding.

The constitutionality and legal propriety of this patchwork system of bankruptcy courts, essentially an implementation of the recommendation in the Chief Justice's dissent in *Marathon,* was upheld by virtually all the courts of appeals. The Supreme Court twice denied certiorari in cases challenging the validity of the Rule and once denied a petition for a writ of mandamus. Thus the system seemed secure.

Meanwhile, Congress continued its efforts to reformulate the bankruptcy court system. A substantial body of opinion favored the original House approach of establishing Article III bankruptcy courts to enable them to handle the full jurisdiction granted under the 1978 Act. That view did not prevail, however, and Congress adopted instead a court system modeled closely on the Emergency

28 U.S.C. § 151. Designation of bankruptcy courts

In each judicial district, the bankruptcy judges in regular active service shall constitute a unit of the district court to be known as the bankruptcy court for that district. Each bankruptcy judge, as a judicial officer of the district court, may exercise the authority conferred under this chapter with respect to any action, suit, or proceeding and may preside alone and hold a regular or special session of the court, except as otherwise provided by law or by rule or order of the district court.

28 U.S.C. § 152. Appointment of bankruptcy judges

(a)(1) The United States court of appeals for the circuit shall appoint bankruptcy judges for the judicial districts established in paragraph (2) in such numbers as are established in such paragraph. Such appointments shall be made after considering the recommendations of the Judicial Conference submitted pursuant to subsection (b). Each bankruptcy judge shall be appointed for a term of fourteen years, subject to the provisions of subsection (e). Bankruptcy judges shall serve as judicial officers of the United States district court established under Article III of the Constitution.

Rule. The law was enacted on July 10, 1984, and became effective immediately, even for pending cases (with one exception relating to jury trials).

§ 2.01(b) The BAFJA Bankruptcy Court System

BAFJA vests the district courts, as Article III courts, with primary bankruptcy jurisdiction. 28 U.S.C. § 1334. The statute authorizes the appointment of bankruptcy judges in each judicial district. The bankruptcy judges "constitute a unit of the district court to be known as the bankruptcy court for that district." 28 U.S.C. § 151. The bankruptcy judges are appointed by the courts of appeals for their respective circuits for 14-year terms. § 152(a)(1). They are subject to removal during their term of office "only for incompetence, misconduct, neglect of duty, or physical or mental disability and only by the judicial council of the circuit." § 152(e). Congress establishes the number of bankruptcy judges under Section 152(a)(2). The judges are entitled to staff, including a secretary and a law clerk. With the approval of the Director of the Administrative Office of the United States Courts, the bankruptcy judges in a particular district may appoint their own bankruptcy clerk, who may employ deputy clerks. § 156.

In short, the bankruptcy unit of the district court, known as the "bankruptcy court," looks very much like an ordinary court. But the statute does not designate it as a court, except in name, nor is there any explanation in the statute or the legislative history of the precise relationship between the district court and the "unit of the district court." The bankruptcy judges are to "serve as judicial officers of the United States district court," § 152(a)(1), but that designation does little to explain the relationship.

What is important is that the relationship, whatever it may be, is probably close enough (at least Congress assumes so) to satisfy the requirement of *Marathon* and of *United States v. Raddatz,* 447 U.S. 667 (1980) (upholding the Magistrates Act against Article III challenge), that any officer of an Article III court who performs judicial functions must be closely supervised and regulated by the Article III court. The "unit" concept is probably best described as an antidote to the independence of the "adjunct" bankruptcy court as it was established in 1978. As will be seen later, the relationship

28 U.S.C. § 1334. Bankruptcy cases and proceedings

(a) Except as provided in subsection (b) of this section, the district courts shall have original and exclusive jurisdiction of all cases under title 11.

(b) Notwithstanding any Act of Congress that confers exclusive jurisdiction on a court or courts other than the district courts, the district courts shall have original but not exclusive jurisdiction of all civil proceedings arising under title 11, or arising in or related to cases under title 11.

(d) The district court in which a case under title 11 is commenced or is pending shall have exclusive jurisdiction of all of the property, wherever located, of the debtor as of the commencement of such case, and of property of the estate.

and closeness of supervision is accomplished by the statute more
through limits on the bankruptcy court's powers and through the
ability of the district court to control what the bankruptcy judges
may hear than through the "unit," or structural, relationship between the bankruptcy judges and the district court.

§ 2.01(c) The Pervasive Bankruptcy Subject-Matter Jurisdiction

Section 1334 of Title 28 vests all the original bankruptcy jurisdiction in the United States district courts. There are three different, but occasionally overlapping, aspects of this jurisdiction: jurisdiction over cases, § 1334(a); over civil proceedings, § 1334(b); and
over property, § 1334(d).

§ 2.01(c)(1) Jurisdiction over Cases

§ 2.01(c)(1)(A)   *Exclusive Jurisdiction*. Section 1334(a) of Title 28
vests "original and exclusive jurisdiction of all cases under title 11"
in the United States district courts. A case under Title 11 is commenced by the filing of a bankruptcy petition. Bankruptcy Code
§§ 301–304. As the district court has exclusive jurisdiction over
the case, a bankruptcy petition may be filed only there; it may not
be filed in a state court. *See Gonzales v. Parks*, 830 F.2d 1033 (9th
Cir. 1987) (exclusive bankruptcy jurisdiction over case deprived
state court of subject matter jurisdiction to determine that filing of
petition constituted abuse of process as a matter of state law).

§ 2.01(c)(1)(B)   *What Constitutes a "Case"?* Because the original
jurisdiction of the district court is exclusive for "cases" but not
exclusive for "civil proceedings," as discussed later, the distinction
between the two categories is a matter of theoretical interest. To
date, however, the courts have not had to consider the distinction
to any significant extent. Undoubtedly, the petition and the proceedings on the petition itself, such as the trial of an involuntary bankruptcy petition or a motion to dismiss the petition, constitute part of
the "case." Beyond this, the meaning of "case" is entirely debatable. *See
Matter of Wood*, 825 F.2d 90 (5th Cir. 1987) ("case" refers merely to the
bankruptcy petition itself). Whether, as a practical matter, there will

28 U.S.C. § 1334. Bankruptcy cases and proceedings

(b) Notwithstanding any Act of Congress that confers exclusive jurisdiction on a court or courts other than the district courts, the district courts shall have original but not exclusive jurisdiction of all civil proceedings arising under title 11, or arising in or related to cases under title 11.

be a need in the future to refine the case/proceeding distinction remains to be seen.

§ 2.01(c)(2) Jurisdiction over Civil Proceedings

§ 2.01(c)(2)(A) Nonexclusive Jurisdiction. Under Section 1334(b) of Title 28, the district courts are given "original *but not exclusive* jurisdiction of all civil proceedings arising under title 11, or arising in or related to cases under title 11" (emphasis added). This language is the same as that used in the jurisdictional grant of the 1978 Act. In general, it overrides any other statutory grant of exclusive jurisdiction to any other court. Moreover, the bankruptcy jurisdictional grant is a pervasive one, and even when it is nonexclusive, it is generally paramount to the jurisdiction of any competing court.

Because the jurisdiction over civil proceedings is nonexclusive, other federal and state courts are not deprived of jurisdiction over matters to which this pervasive bankruptcy jurisdiction extends. It is frequently desirable to permit bankruptcy litigation to proceed elsewhere even though the bankruptcy court has jurisdiction to hear it. Thus, as discussed later, the district court or the bankruptcy court may for various reasons choose (or may occasionally be required) to abstain from hearing a particular proceeding, may remand an action removed to it, or may authorize an action to be filed originally in some other trial court. Were the bankruptcy jurisdiction over civil proceedings made exclusive, other courts, at least arguably, would be denied jurisdiction over matters that might be left to them. On the other hand, the grant in Section 1334(d) of exclusive jurisdiction over the estate's and the debtor's property, discussed later, has never been thought to deprive other courts of jurisdiction over disputes about this property when the bankruptcy court chooses to abstain. *See, e.g., Cournoyer v. Town of Lincoln,* 790 F.2d 971, 974 (1st Cir. 1986).

In any event, there should be no doubt that the bankruptcy jurisdiction, though nonexclusive, nevertheless is paramount. Litigation in other courts is generally stayed automatically by the filing of a bankruptcy petition, Bankruptcy Code § 362, or may be enjoined by an affirmative injunction issued under Bankruptcy Code § 105(a). Actions in other courts may be removed to the

28 U.S.C. § 1334. Bankruptcy cases and proceedings

(b) Notwithstanding any Act of Congress that confers exclusive jurisdiction on a court or courts other than the district courts, the district courts shall have original but not exclusive jurisdiction of all civil proceedings arising under title 11, or arising in or related to cases under title 11.

district court sitting in bankruptcy. 28 U.S.C. § 1452. The decision to abstain or to remand or not to remand a removed action is not reviewable. 28 U.S.C. §§ 1334(c)(2), 1452(b).

§ 2.01(c)(2)(B) Categories of "Civil Proceedings." The language of 28 U.S.C. § 1334(b) is derived from the original language of the House bill that became the 1978 Act. *See* former 28 U.S.C. § 1471(b). The legislative history of the meaning of "proceedings" and of the distinctions among proceedings that arise under Title 11, those that arise in a case under Title 11, and those that are related to such a case was contained in the House Judiciary Committee Report that accompanied the bill:

> The bill uses the term "proceeding" instead of the current "matters and proceedings" found in the Bankruptcy Act and Rules. The change is intended to conform the terminology of title 28, under which anything that occurs within a case is a proceeding. Thus, proceeding here is used in its broadest sense, and would encompass what are now called contested matters, adversary proceedings, and plenary actions under the current bankruptcy law. It also includes any disputes related to administrative matters in a bankruptcy case.
>
> The use of the term "proceeding," though, is not intended to confine the bankruptcy case. Very often, issues will arise after the case is closed, such as over the validity of a purported reaffirmation agreement . . . , the existence of prohibited post-bankruptcy discrimination . . . , the validity of securities issued under a reorganization plan, and so on. The bankruptcy courts will be able to hear these proceedings because they arise under title 11.
>
> The phrase "arising under" has a well defined and broad meaning in the jurisdictional context. By a grant of jurisdiction over all proceedings arising under title 11, the bankruptcy courts will be able to hear any matter under which a claim is made under a provision of title 11. For example, a claim of exemptions under 11 U.S.C. 522 would be cognizable by the bankruptcy court, as would a claim of discrimination in violation of 11 U.S.C. 525. Any action by the trustee under an avoiding power would be a proceeding arising under title 11, because the trustee would be claiming based on a right given by one of the sections in subchapter III of chapter 5 of title 11. Many of these claims would also be claims arising under or

related to a case under title 11. Indeed, because title 11, the bankruptcy code, only applies once a bankruptcy case is commenced, any proceeding arising under title 11 will be in some way "related to" a case under title 11. In sum, the combination of the three bases for jurisdiction, "arising under title 11," "arising under a case under title 11," and "related to a case under title 11," will leave no doubt as to the scope of the bankruptcy court's jurisdiction over disputes.

H.R. REP. No. 595, 95th Cong., 1st. Sess. 445–46 (1977) [hereinafter cited in this chapter as "House Report"].

Thus the original congressional concept of the jurisdictional grant did not involve any clear distinctions among the three categories of civil proceedings covered by the grant. In other words, there was at best only a blurred understanding of the differences among (1) a proceeding that arose under Title 11, (2) a proceeding that arose in a case under Title 11, and (3) a proceeding that was related to a Title 11 case. Nor, before the *Marathon* decision, was there any practical need to make the distinctions.

After that decision, however, courts and commentators, the Emergency Rule, and now BAFJA came to describe the *Marathon* type of lawsuit as a "related" matter, thus distinguishing this kind of civil proceeding, which untenured judges could not finally decide, from the other categories, which, according to the Chief Justice's view, could constitutionally be left to non-Article III judges. This distinction will be discussed later in connection with the powers bankruptcy judges may exercise in matters referred to them.

Whether or not the lines separating the three categories of proceedings are difficult to ascertain, there can be no doubt that Section 1334(b), taken as a whole, constitutes an extraordinarily broad grant of jurisdiction to the Article III district court. Both the statutory language and the legislative history indicate that the jurisdictional grant covers virtually all litigation in which the debtor or the estate could be expected to have any interest. True, the district court (and the bankruptcy court) cannot grant a debtor a divorce, handle a probate proceeding, or otherwise act with respect to a debtor's personal relationships that do not affect the

28 U.S.C. § 1334. Bankruptcy cases and proceedings

(d) The district court in which a case under title 11 is commenced or is pending shall have exclusive jurisdiction of all of the property, wherever located, of the debtor as of the commencement of such case, and of property of the estate.

bankruptcy; nor, probably, can either court decide disputes between third parties in which the estate has no interest. *See, e.g., Matter of Xonics, Inc.,* 813 F.2d 127 (7th Cir. 1987). But except at these outer reaches, there should be no legitimate question about the legislative intent to vest the court with a complete, or pervasive, jurisdiction over all matters that have to do with a bankruptcy case or that have any significant bearing upon it. *E.g., Pacor, Inc. v. Higgins,* 743 F.2d 984, 994 (3d Cir. 1984) (a matter is "related to" the bankruptcy case if "*the outcome of that proceeding could conceivably have any effect on the estate being administered*" or if it "could alter the debtor's rights, liabilities, options, or freedom of action") (emphasis in original).

§ 2.01(c)(3) Jurisdiction over Property

Section 1334(d) of Title 28 grants the district court "exclusive jurisdiction of all of the property, wherever located, of the debtor as of the commencement of such case, and of property of the estate." The purpose of this section is to make clear that a bankruptcy proceeding continues, in large measure, to be an in rem action, with one of its primary purposes the collection, liquidation, and distribution of an estate. To this end, the court is given exclusive jurisdiction of all the indicated property and of all disputes about ownership or lien interests in that property and about its disposition. In general, the property is brought *in custodia legis* and accorded the court's protection, even if it was subject to the jurisdiction of another court at the time the bankruptcy petition was filed.

Given the broad grants of jurisdiction over "cases" and "proceedings" in Section 1334(a) and (b), the grant of jurisdiction over "property" in subsection (d) probably adds little, if anything, to the subject-matter jurisdiction of the court. Any dispute about property probably already falls within the concept of case or proceeding. The specific grant of jurisdiction over property perhaps helps to carry out the automatic stay of Bankruptcy Code § 362 and emphasizes that no other court may exercise in rem jurisdiction over property of a bankruptcy estate, at least not without leave of the district or bankruptcy court.

28 U.S.C. § 157. Procedures

(a) Each district court may provide that any or all cases under title 11 and any or all proceedings arising under title 11 or arising in or related to a case under title 11 shall be referred to the bankruptcy judges for the district.

§ 2.01(d) Who Exercises the Bankruptcy Jurisdiction?

§ 2.01(d)(1) General Reference

Although Congress vested all the bankruptcy jurisdiction in the United States district courts, it did not intend (nor was it possible as a practical matter) that the judges of the district courts actually exercise that jurisdiction. Rather, Congress contemplated that the district courts could and would delegate the bankruptcy jurisdiction, at least for the most part, to their "units" known as bankruptcy courts and that the bankruptcy judges would act in nearly all bankruptcy matters as the trial courts in fact. Although the district courts theoretically retain unlimited powers, in practice they exercise them on relatively infrequent occasions only in particular cases. In the congressional view the system passes constitutional muster under *Marathon* because the Article III district courts have the power to control what is referred and because of certain limitations on the bankruptcy judges' authority over *Marathon*-type, or "related," matters, discussed later.

Section 157 of Title 28, entitled "Procedures," implements the reference system and prescribes the powers of the bankruptcy judges with respect to the matters delegated to them. It begins by permitting the district courts (if they so choose) to refer the entire subject-matter jurisdiction conferred by Section 1334(a) and (b). Although Section 157(a) does not explicitly authorize reference of the district courts' "exclusive jurisdiction of . . . property" conferred by Section 1334(d), this apparent legislative oversight has no practical consequence because the jurisdiction over property is undoubtedly already included within the general grant of jurisdiction over cases and proceedings contained in subsections (a) and (b).

In fact, every district court in the country has adopted a policy of virtually complete reference pursuant to Section 157(a). There may be some minor local variations in very limited classes of matters, but, by and large, bankruptcy judges are now performing the trial court function except when the statute itself specifically limits that role and reserves certain powers to the district court.

28 U.S.C. § 157. Procedures

(b)(1) Bankruptcy judges may hear and determine all cases under title 11 and all core proceedings arising under title 11, or arising in a case under title 11, referred under subsection (a) of this section, and may enter appropriate orders and judgments, subject to review under section 158 of this title.

11 U.S.C. § 105. Power of court

(a) The court may issue any order, process, or judgment that is necessary or appropriate to carry out the provisions of this title. No provision of this title providing for the raising of an issue by a party in interest shall be construed to preclude the court from, sua sponte, taking any action or making any determination necessary or appropriate to enforce or implement court orders or rules, or to prevent an abuse of process.

(c) The ability of any district judge or other officer or employee of a district court to exercise any of the authority or responsibilities conferred upon the court under this title shall be determined by reference to the provisions relating to such judge, officer, or employee set forth in title 28. This subsection shall not be interpreted to exclude bankruptcy judges and other officers or employees appointed pursuant to chapter 6 of title 28 from its operation.

28 U.S.C. § 157. Procedures

(c)(1) A bankruptcy judge may hear a proceeding that is not a core proceeding but that is otherwise related to a case under title 11. In such proceeding, the bankruptcy judge shall submit proposed findings of fact and conclusions of law to the district court, and any final order or judgment shall be entered by the district judge after considering the bankruptcy judge's proposed findings and conclusions and after reviewing de novo those matters to which any party has timely and specifically objected.

(2) Notwithstanding the provisions of paragraph (1) of this subsection, the district court, with the consent of all the parties to the proceeding, may refer a proceeding related to a case under title 11 to a bankruptcy judge to hear and determine and to enter appropriate orders and judgments, subject to review under section 158 of this title.

§ 2.01(d)(2) Powers of Bankruptcy Judges in Referred Matters

The extent of the bankruptcy judges' power to act in referred matters turns on whether the matter is classified as a "case" or as a "core" or "noncore" proceeding. (More technically, Section 157 of Title 28 distinguishes between "core proceedings," § 157(b), and "a proceeding that is not a core proceeding but that is otherwise related to a case under title 11." § 157(c).) In cases and in core proceedings bankruptcy judges may "hear and determine," § 157(b)(1); that is, they may conduct the entire proceeding and may enter the final or dispositive order or judgment (as well as interlocutory orders), subject only to a timely appeal. *(See also* Section 105 of Title 11, granting power to make all appropriate orders.) The district court's role when there has been a general reference of a case or core proceeding is that of an appellate tribunal.

In noncore proceedings, on the other hand, bankruptcy judges may not make final orders except with the parties' consent. Rather, their function is similar to that of special masters or magistrates; they submit proposed findings and conclusions, and the dispositive orders are made by the district courts. § 157(c)(1). Bankruptcy judges may, however, make interlocutory orders in noncore proceedings. And with the parties' consent, they may exercise the full trial court power as if a matter were a core proceeding. § 157(c)(2). The statute does not define what constitutes consent for this purpose. The Bankruptcy Rules applicable to adversary proceedings, however, provide that such consent must be expressed in the pleadings and that consent in this context is not to be implied from a failure to affirmatively object to the bankruptcy judge's making a dispositive order. *See* Bankruptcy Rules 7008(a), 7012(b), and Committee Notes thereto. In any event, the conduct of a noncore proceeding by a bankruptcy judge up to the time he reaches a decision should not differ from the way he would conduct a core proceeding; whether the distinction between actually making a dispositive order and merely recommending one to the district court will turn out to be of much practical significance remains to be seen.

Although appeals of bankruptcy court orders in core proceedings are discussed in more detail *infra,* pp. 77–81, it is useful to

28 U.S.C. § 157. Procedures

(b)(1) Bankruptcy judges may hear and determine all cases under title 11 and all core proceedings arising under title 11, or arising in a case under title 11, referred under subsection (a) of this section, and may enter appropriate orders and judgments, subject to review under section 158 of this title.

(2) Core proceedings include, but are not limited to—

(A) matters concerning the administration of the estate;

(B) allowance or disallowance of claims against the estate or exemptions from property of the estate, and estimation of claims or interests for the purposes of confirming a plan under chapter 11, 12, or 13 of title 11 but not the liquidation or estimation of contingent or unliquidated personal injury tort or wrongful death claims against the estate for purposes of distribution in a case under title 11;

note here the different standards of review that apply in core and noncore proceedings. As an appellate court with respect to a core proceeding (or to a "case"), the district court reviews the bankruptcy judge's findings of fact according to the "clearly erroneous" standard: "Findings of fact, whether based on oral or documentary evidence, shall not be set aside unless clearly erroneous, and due regard shall be given to the opportunity of the bankruptcy court to judge the credibility of the witnesses." Bankruptcy Rule 8013. In contrast, the proposed findings in noncore proceedings are subject to de novo review to the extent that any party has timely and specifically objected to them. § 157(c)(1). But this does not imply that the district court must conduct a further trial or receive additional evidence if offered. In a case construing the de novo review standard of the Emergency Rule, it was held that the district court need only pass an independent judgment; if the court so chooses, the record before the bankruptcy judge may be relied upon and the proposed findings may be adopted. *Moody v. Amoco Oil Co.,* 734 F.2d 1200 (7th Cir. 1984). Bankruptcy Rule 9033(d) apparently adopts this view.

§ 2.01(d)(2)(A) What Is a Core Proceeding? Most important matters that occur during a case under the Code will either be part of the "case" or fall within the classification of core proceeding. Fifteen overlapping subparagraphs of 28 U.S.C. § 157(b)(2) illustrate a wide variety of core matters, and the list explicitly is not intended to be exclusive. That state law is involved is not determinative of whether a proceeding is a core matter. § 157(b)(3).

Subparagraph (A) of Section 157(b)(2) refers to "matters concerning the administration of the estate." This broad category apparently encompasses many of the other items designated as core proceedings in later subparagraphs. It seems to include such matters as assembling the assets of the estate, the abandonment of property, the assumption or rejection of executory contracts, the employment of professionals and the determination of their compensation, and virtually all the matters covered by subchapters II and III (Sections 321–350) of Chapter 3 of the Bankruptcy Code.

Allowance and disallowance of claims and exemptions are also core proceedings, with one notable exception. § 157(b)(2)(B). The liquidation or estimation of personal injury and wrongful death

28 U.S.C. § 157. Procedures

> (b)(5) The district court shall order that personal injury tort and wrongful death claims shall be tried in the district court in which the bankruptcy case is pending, or in the district court in the district in which the claim arose, as determined by the district court in which the bankruptcy case is pending.

28 U.S.C. § 157. Procedures

> (b)(2) Core proceedings include, but are not limited to—
>
> (C) counterclaims by the estate against persons filing claims against the estate;

claims against the estate *for distribution purposes* is specifically designated a noncore proceeding. This exception, together with Section 157(b)(5), is intended to insure that these claims are tried before a district judge. For purposes other than distribution, however—for example, voting upon or confirming a plan—the determination or estimation of personal injury and wrongful death claims is a core proceeding within the bankruptcy judge's dispositive power. Even for distribution purposes, proceedings preliminary to the trial itself may be handled by the bankruptcy judge.

The claims allowance process, all of which is core with the noted exception, covers the entire range of matters governed by subchapter I (Sections 501–510) of Chapter 5 of the Bankruptcy Code, including the determination of administrative expense claims under Section 503, the determination of tax claims under Section 505, the determination of secured status under Section 506, and the resolution of questions about priority and the subordination of claims under Sections 507 and 510.

Subparagraph (B) also defines as core all matters relating to the debtor's exemptions under Section 522 of the Bankruptcy Code. Jurisdiction over exemptions and exempt property does not depend on whether the property is in the actual or constructive possession of the debtor or the estate. Moreover, even after a determination that property is exempt, disputes about that property are included within the scope of core proceedings.

"[C]ounterclaims by the estate against persons filing claims against the estate" are core proceedings under Section 157-(b)(2)(C). Thus a cause of action that might be noncore if brought originally by the trustee becomes core when asserted by way of counterclaim to a proof of claim filed by a creditor. To some extent this provision reflects the decision in *Katchen v. Landy,* 382 U.S. 323 (1966), which held that a counterclaim by the trustee for recovery of a preference against a creditor who had filed a proof of claim was within the summary jurisdiction of the bankruptcy court under the former Bankruptcy Act. In effect, the policy of Section 157(b)(2)(C) is that, by filing a proof of claim or commencing an action in the bankruptcy court, the creditor is deemed to consent or submit to final disposition of all issues by the bankruptcy judge,

28 U.S.C. § 157. Procedures

> (b)(2) Core proceedings include, but are not limited to —
> (D) orders in respect to obtaining credit;

28 U.S.C. § 157. Procedures

> (b)(2) Core proceedings include, but are not limited to —
> (E) orders to turn over property of the estate;

28 U.S.C. § 157. Procedures

> (b)(2) Core proceedings include, but are not limited to —
> (F) proceedings to determine, avoid, or recover preferences;
> (H) proceedings to determine, avoid, or recover fraudulent conveyances;

28 U.S.C. § 157. Procedures

> (b)(2) Core proceedings include, but are not limited to —
> (G) motions to terminate, annul or modify the automatic stay;

28 U.S.C. § 157. Procedures

> (b)(2) Core proceedings include, but are not limited to —
> (I) determinations as to the dischargeability of particular debts;
> (J) objections to discharges;

28 U.S.C. § 157. Procedures

> (b)(2) Core proceedings include, but are not limited to —
> (K) determinations of the validity, extent, or priority of liens;

including disposition of any claim that the estate may have against the creditor.

Subparagraph (D) covers "orders in respect to obtaining credit" under Bankruptcy Code § 364.

Core proceedings also include "orders to turn over property of the estate" under Sections 542 and 543 of the Bankruptcy Code. 28 U.S.C. § 157(b)(2)(E). When the turnover proceeding involves a specific res — for example, the debtor's automobile — the congressional intention to classify the matter as a core proceeding seems clear. It has been suggested, however, that an action to recover a liquidated obligation owing to the estate under Bankruptcy Code § 542(b) also is a core turnover proceeding. It is too soon to tell how in personam actions to collect matured liquidated debts will be classified. The *Marathon* lawsuit itself, a kind of action that Congress apparently meant to classify as a "related," or noncore, matter, involved an unliquidated cause of action.

"[P]roceedings to determine, avoid, or recover preferences . . . or fraudulent conveyances" are core proceedings. 28 U.S.C. § 157(b)(2)(F), (H). The theory of a fraudulent transfer suit — that is, whether the suit is based on Section 548 of the Bankruptcy Code, or on state law and Section 544(b) — should make no difference for the purpose of classification as core. *In re Mankin*, 823 F.2d 1296 (9th Cir. 1987). Indeed, Section 157(b)(3) specifically provides that "[a] determination that a proceeding is not a core proceeding shall not be made solely on the basis that its resolution may be affected by State law."

All matters concerning the automatic stay of Section 362 and the codebtor stay of Section 1301 of the Bankruptcy Code are included within core proceedings. 28 U.S.C. § 157(b)(2)(G). These matters include proceedings to determine whether a particular action is covered by the automatic stay, to enforce the automatic stay, and to obtain relief from the automatic stay.

All matters concerning discharge and the dischargeability of particular claims are included within core proceedings by Section 157(b)(2)(I) and (J).

Subparagraph (K) includes as core proceedings "determinations of the validity, extent, or priority of liens." This category covers not

28 U.S.C. § 157. Procedures

> (b)(2) Core proceedings include, but are not limited to —
>
> (L) confirmations of plans;

28 U.S.C. § 157. Procedures

> (b)(2) Core proceedings include, but are not limited to —
>
> (M) orders approving the use or lease of property, including the use of cash collateral;
>
> (N) orders approving the sale of property other than property resulting from claims brought by the estate against persons who have not filed claims against the estate;

28 U.S.C. § 157. Procedures

> (b)(2) Core proceedings include, but are not limited to —
>
> (O) other proceedings affecting the liquidation of the assets of the estate or the adjustment of the debtor-creditor or the equity security holder relationship, except personal injury tort or wrongful death claims.

only determinations of the secured status of claims under Section 506(c) and (d) of the Bankruptcy Code but also any issue concerning the trustee's or debtor's ability to invalidate liens through an avoiding power or on the ground of the unenforceability of a lien under nonbankruptcy law.

Subparagraph (L) provides that confirmations of reorganization or repayment plans (under Chapters 9, 11, 12, and 13 of the Bankruptcy Code) are core proceedings.

All matters governed by Section 363 of the Bankruptcy Code, which regulates the use, sale, or lease of property of the estate, are also core proceedings under Section 157(b)(2)(M) and (N) of Title 28. The use of cash collateral is specifically mentioned in subparagraph (M); also included are all other aspects of use, sale, and lease — for example, sales free and clear of other interests and conditions or limitations on the use of property to meet the requirements of the concept of adequate protection. Specifically excluded from classification as core proceedings in Section 157(b)(2)(M) are "orders approving the sale of property . . . resulting from claims brought by the estate against persons who have not filed claims against the estate." The meaning of this language is obscure; in any event, it is not likely that the exclusion will have much practical significance.

The last enumerated category of core proceedings is a broad catchall, namely, "other proceedings affecting the liquidation of the assets of the estate or the adjustment of the debtor-creditor or the equity security holder relationship." § 157(b)(2)(O). This category seems to cover virtually all proceedings that have to do with the conduct of the bankruptcy case or that involve the rights, powers, duties, or responsibilities set forth in the various sections of the Bankruptcy Code.

§ 2.01(d)(2)(B) What Is a Related, or Noncore, Proceeding? The statute contains no affirmative definition of what constitutes a related, or noncore, proceeding. Section 157(c)(1) of Title 28 refers only to "a proceeding that is not a core proceeding but that is otherwise related to a case under title 11." As noted, the existence of state law issues does not control the distinction between core and noncore. § 157(b)(3). Because Section 157(b)(2)(B) excludes from the core proceeding category personal injury and wrongful death claims for

28 U.S.C. § 157. Procedures

(b)(3) The bankruptcy judge shall determine, on the judge's own motion or on timely motion of a party, whether a proceeding is a core proceeding under this subsection or is a proceeding that is otherwise related to a case under title 11. A determination that a proceeding is not a core proceeding shall not be made solely on the basis that its resolution may be affected by State law.

the purpose of distribution, it is plain that the determination of these claims for this purpose is noncore. It also seems clear that Congress intended the *Marathon* type of lawsuit to be classified as a related, or noncore, matter. This kind of action may be described as an in personam cause of action, not created by the Bankruptcy Code, that the debtor possessed at the time of the petition and that thus became part of the estate under Bankruptcy Code § 541(a)(1) or (2). (Whether it makes any difference for this purpose that the claim is liquidated or unliquidated, or matured or unmatured, remains to be seen.) Finally, it seems likely that the noncore category includes a suit between third parties to which neither the estate nor the debtor is a party but which is within the pervasive jurisdictional grant because it indirectly affects the estate and thus is related to it — for example, a suit by a creditor against a guarantor of the debtor's obligation. But at least arguably, everything within the bankruptcy jurisdiction other than these few limited types of matters is a core proceeding. (In *In re Arnold Print Works, Inc.*, 815 F.2d 165 (1st Cir. 1987), the court held that "core proceeding" should be generously construed, suggesting that the category encompassed any litigation that a non-Article III judge may constitutionally decide. Specifically, a suit by the estate to recover under a contract made postpetition should be classified as core. On the other hand, in *In re Castlerock Properties*, 781 F.2d 159 (9th Cir. 1986), it was held that in situations in which the classification is unclear under the statute and designating a proceeding as core might raise a serious constitutional issue, the matter should be treated as noncore so as to avoid that problem.)

§ *2.01(d)(2)(C) Who Determines Core or Noncore Status?* A bankruptcy judge is empowered to determine whether a particular proceeding referred to him is core or not. This determination may be made on the judge's own motion or on the timely motion of a party. 28 U.S.C. § 157(b)(3). A bankruptcy judge's determination that a proceeding is core — either express or implied from his entering a final order — is presumably subject to review on appeal. But unless it is timely appealed and reversed, the final judgment or order will bind the parties, even though the matter was truly noncore.

§ *2.01(d)(2)(D) Contempt Power and Power to Impose Sanctions.* Whether the bankruptcy judge has the power of civil or criminal

11 U.S.C. § 105. Power of court

(a) The court may issue any order, process, or judgment that is necessary or appropriate to carry out the provisions of this title. No provision of this title providing for the raising of an issue by a party in interest shall be construed to preclude the court from, sua sponte, taking any action or making any determination necessary or appropriate to enforce or implement court orders or rules, or to prevent an abuse of process.

(c) The ability of any district judge or other officer or employee of a district court to exercise any of the authority or responsibilities conferred upon the court under this title shall be determined by reference to the provisions relating to such judge, officer, or employee set forth in title 28. This subsection shall not be interpreted to exclude bankruptcy judges and other officers or employees appointed pursuant to chapter 6 of title 28 from its operation.

contempt in core or noncore proceedings has not yet been decided authoritatively. Section 105(a) and (c) of the Bankruptcy Code and Section 157(b) of Title 28 can be read as broad enough to delegate the contempt power to the bankruptcy judge as a statutory matter, but there is disagreement on this point in the lower courts. One Court of Appeals has held that Congress did not intend to confer the contempt power on bankruptcy judges in the 1984 BAFJA legislation and that a non-Article III judge has no inherent power of contempt. *In re Sequoia Auto Brokers, Ltd., Inc.,* 827 F.2d 1281 (9th Cir. 1987). Moreover, courts to date have disagreed about the constitutional ability of untenured judges to exercise this power. (For example, *compare In re Omega Equipment Corp.,* 51 Bankr. 569 (D.D.C. 1985) (non-Article III judge cannot make contempt order) *with Better Homes of Virginia v. Budget Service Co.,* 52 Bankr. 426 (E.D. Va. 1985) (bankruptcy judge may make civil but not criminal contempt order), *aff'd on other grounds, Budget Service Co. v. Better Homes of Virginia, Inc.,* 804 F.2d 289 (4th Cir. 1986).) The Committee Note to Bankruptcy Rule 9020 regards the question as an open one. The Rule nevertheless provides that the bankruptcy judge may summarily determine a contempt committed in his presence, and may determine other contempts after a hearing upon notice. The order of contempt must specify whether the contempt is civil or criminal. The order, however, does not become effective until 10 days after service on the contemnor. If within this period there is a timely objection to the bankruptcy judge's order, the district court reviews it de novo, pursuant to the procedure prescribed by Bankruptcy Rule 9033, whether the contempt was committed in or related to a core or noncore proceeding. Bankruptcy Rule 9020(c).

Although the bankruptcy judge's general contempt power remains in doubt, his power to impose "sanctions" that are specifically provided by statute or rule seems to be recognized. *See Budget Service Co. v. Better Homes of Virginia, Inc.,* 804 F.2d 289 (4th Cir. 1986) (bankruptcy judge may impose sanctions for violation of automatic stay under Section 362(h)); *In re Arkansas Communities, Inc.,* 827 F.2d 1219 (8th Cir. 1987); *Gonzales v. Parks,* 830 F.2d 1033, 1036 n. 7 (9th Cir. 1987) (bankruptcy judge may impose sanctions for violation of Bankruptcy Rule 9011).

28 U.S.C. § 157. Procedures

(d) The district court may withdraw, in whole or in part, any case or proceeding referred under this section, on its own motion or on timely motion of any party, for cause shown. The district court shall, on timely motion of a party, so withdraw a proceeding if the court determines that resolution of the proceeding requires consideration of both title 11 and other laws of the United States regulating organizations or activities affecting interstate commerce.

§ 2.01(d)(3) Withdrawal of Reference

The district court's position of control in the bankruptcy system stems not only from its power to refer to, or to withhold reference from, bankruptcy judges in the first instance, 28 U.S.C. § 157(a), but also from its power to withdraw in whole or in part matters that have been referred. § 157(d). The power to withdraw extends to both core and noncore proceedings as well as to "cases." Withdrawal of reference ordinarily is discretionary, but in one situation it is mandatory. "[F]or cause shown," the district court *may* withdraw the reference of all or part of any referred matter on its own motion or on the timely motion of any party. *Id.* The district court is unlikely to exercise this discretionary power very often; it will be most likely to do so in a noncore proceeding in which the bankruptcy judge is limited to proposing findings and conclusions (particularly when there is a right to jury trial and a timely demand has been made).

On timely motion withdrawal of reference is mandatory if "resolution of the proceeding requires consideration of both title 11 and other laws of the United States regulating organizations or activities affecting interstate commerce." *Id.* It is unclear whether this clause refers to laws that actually affect interstate commerce or to laws that were enacted under the commerce clause of the Constitution. For example, tax laws arguably may regulate organizations or activities affecting interstate commerce, but they are not ordinarily enacted under the commerce clause. Nor does the quoted provision indicate whether the mere presence of two related bankruptcy and interstate commerce issues is adequate to trigger mandatory withdrawal or whether a balancing of a potential conflict of policies between the two laws is what is required. *See, e.g., NLRB v. Bildisco v. Bildisco,* 465 U.S. 513 (1984). The case authority to date suggests that withdrawal is not mandatory unless it appears clear that the court will have to decide substantial questions under *both* the Bankruptcy Code and nonbankruptcy federal law. It is not enough that the litigation merely involves the two sets of statutes. *See, e.g., In re Anthony Tammers, Inc.,* 56 Bankr. 999 (D.N.J. 1986); *In re White Motor Corp.,* 42 Bankr. 693 (N.D. Ohio 1984). (And, at least literally, it is not enough that the litigation involves a substantial question under only the nonbankruptcy federal statute.) Regu-

28 U.S.C. § 1334. Bankruptcy cases and proceedings

(c)(1) Nothing in this section prevents a district court in the interest of justice, or in the interest of comity with State courts or respect for State law, from abstaining from hearing a particular proceeding arising under title 11 or arising in or related to a case under title 11.

(2) Upon timely motion of a party in a proceeding based upon a State law claim or State law cause of action, related to a case under title 11 but not arising under title 11 or arising in a case under title 11, with respect to which an action could not have been commenced in a court of the United States absent jurisdiction under this section, the district court shall abstain from hearing such proceeding if an action is commenced, and can be timely adjudicated, in a State forum of appropriate jurisdiction. Any decision to abstain made under this subsection is not reviewable by appeal or otherwise. This subsection shall not be construed to limit the applicability of the stay provided for by section 362 of title 11, United States Code, as such section applies to an action affecting the property of the estate in bankruptcy.

latory action against a Code debtor under a federal environmental protection statute is the type of situation that might implicate the mandatory withdrawal provision. *See, e.g., United States v. ILCO, Inc.,* 48 Bankr. 1016 (N.D. Ala. 1985).

A motion to withdraw a reference should be filed with the bankruptcy clerk if one has been appointed for the district, but the motion is heard and ruled upon by the district judge. Bankruptcy Rule 5011(a) and Committee Note.

§ 2.01(e) Abstention

By creating the present pervasive bankruptcy jurisdictional scheme, Congress intended to eliminate the time-consuming and costly litigation over jurisdiction that occurred under the former Bankruptcy Act when the bankruptcy court was a court of limited jurisdiction. But some of the matters that are now covered by the jurisdictional grant are not really of a bankruptcy nature; sometimes they would be better left to other courts. Although under general federal principles a federal court with jurisdiction over a matter or proceeding must exercise that jurisdiction except under unusual circumstances, the provisions for abstention in 28 U.S.C. § 1334(c) relieve the district or bankruptcy courts of this strict obligation in the context of the bankruptcy jurisdiction.

(Abstention under Section 1334(c) from hearing a particular civil proceeding should be distinguished from abstention under Bankruptcy Code § 305 from hearing the entire case. The latter provision involves a finding that the interests of both the creditors and the debtor will be served by a dismissal of the petition.)

Since Section 1334 is structured as a grant of jurisdiction to the district court, subsection (c) speaks in terms of abstention by that court. The Bankruptcy Rules, however, logically provide that when there has been a reference to the bankruptcy judge, he should initially hear a motion to abstain in the matter pending before him. But he does not make the order with respect to abstention; rather, the bankruptcy judge reports and recommends a disposition of the motion to the district court. Bankruptcy Rule 5011(b). The prescribed procedure avoids a potential problem under Section 1334(c)(2), which makes nonreviewable a decision to

28 U.S.C. § 1334. Bankruptcy cases and proceedings

(c)(1) Nothing in this section prevents a district court in the interest of justice, or in the interest of comity with State courts or respect for State law, from abstaining from hearing a particular proceeding arising under title 11 or arising in or related to a case under title 11.

(2) Upon timely motion of a party in a proceeding based upon a State law claim or State law cause of action, related to a case under title 11 but not arising under title 11 or arising in a case under title 11, with respect to which an action could not have been commenced in a court of the United States absent jurisdiction under this section, the district court shall abstain from hearing such proceeding if an action is commenced, and can be timely adjudicated, in a State forum of appropriate jurisdiction. Any decision to abstain made under this subsection is not reviewable by appeal or otherwise. This subsection shall not be construed to limit the applicability of the stay provided for by section 362 of title 11, United States Code, as such section applies to an action affecting the property of the estate in bankruptcy.

abstain. If this provision is read as applying to a bankruptcy judge's order of abstention, a procedure authorizing him to make such an order (as distinguished from recommending one) would result in an unreviewable discretion that would be inconsistent with plenary district court control over the bankruptcy judge. *See also In re Corporacion de Servicios Medicos Hosp.*, 805 F.2d 440 (1st Cir. 1986).

Abstention in a civil proceeding in a bankruptcy case ordinarily is discretionary with the court. The standard is merely the flexible one of "interest of justice" or comity with state courts or state law. § 1334(c)(1). When the lawsuit is a traditional matter for the civil courts or involves issues about which bankruptcy judges lack special expertise, a decision to abstain would be appropriate, particularly if the litigation would be predictably lengthy, the bankruptcy court's regular calendar were currently crowded, and a reasonably prompt disposition by the state court could be expected.

In certain limited situations abstention is mandatory upon timely motion with respect to a noncore proceeding based on a cause of action created by state law. § 1334(c)(2). A requirement, however, is that "an action is commenced, and can be timely adjudicated, in a State forum of appropriate jurisdiction." *Id.* The present tense in this clause suggests that a state court lawsuit must be actually pending before the mandatory abstention motion will lie. Moreover, the calendar of the state court must be relatively clear. In any event, the class of cases covered by the mandatory abstention provision seems very narrow.

§ 2.01(f) Personal Jurisdiction

In personam jurisdiction over a defendant in a proceeding subject to the bankruptcy jurisdiction is governed by Bankruptcy Rule 7004. Among other things, the rule provides for nationwide service of process by mail. The "minimum contacts" doctrine or other rules limiting personal jurisdiction over defendants who have no contact with the forum state are inapplicable here. *E.g. Hogue v. Milondon Engineering*, 736 F.2d 989 (4th Cir. 1984) (Bankruptcy Act case involving predecessor to Rule 7004). *See also In re Park Nursing Center, Inc.*, 766 F.2d 261 (6th Cir. 1985) (service by mail does not violate due process). Rule 7004 also governs service of process on a

28 U.S.C. § 1408. Venue of cases under Title 11

Except as provided in section 1410 of this title, a case under title 11 may be commenced in the district court for the district—

(1) in which the domicile, residence, principal place of business in the United States, or principal assets in the United States, of the person or entity that is the subject of such case have been located for the one hundred and eighty days immediately preceding such commencement, or for a longer portion of such one-hundred-and-eighty-day period than the domicile, residence, or principal place of business, in the United States, or principal assets in the United States, of such person were located in any other district; or

(2) in which there is pending a case under title 11 concerning such person's affiliate, general partner, or partnership.

debtor in the context of an involuntary petition. *See* Bankruptcy Rule 1010.

§ 2.01(g) Venue and Transfer

§ 2.01(g)(1) Cases

The proper place to file a petition under the Bankruptcy Code is in the district where the debtor's domicile, residence, principal place of business, or principal American assets have existed for a greater part of the preceding 180 days than these contacts have existed with respect to any other district. A proper venue also exists in any district where a case involving the debtor's affiliate, general partner, or partnership is pending. 28 U.S.C. § 1408.

Notwithstanding the venue provision, the court may transfer the case to another district in the interest of justice and for the convenience of the parties, whether or not the transferee district is a proper venue. § 1412. Although the statute speaks in terms of transfer by the district court, it would seem that the bankruptcy judge is also authorized to order a transfer of a case referred to him. *See* Bankruptcy Rules 1014(a), 9001(4).

§ 2.01(g)(2) Civil Proceedings

With the extraordinarily broad subject matter jurisdiction of the bankruptcy court over civil proceedings arising under Title 11 and arising in or related to cases under Title 11 and with the availability of nationwide service of process, the jurisdictional system would be incomplete without some provisions for protecting litigants against the estate from being forced to trial at a remote, inconvenient, or unfair location. As a dramatic example, the trustee in an Alaska bankruptcy might sue in the Alaska bankruptcy court to recover an account receivable owed to the debtor by a Florida defendant and serve the defendant by mail.

The bankruptcy law relies more on liberal transfer provisions than on venue provisions to assure a fair place of trial. The basic rule is that the court where the bankruptcy case is pending—that is, the primary district or bankruptcy court—is a proper venue for any litigation brought by or against the debtor or the estate. 28

28 U.S.C. § 1409. Venue of proceedings arising under Title 11 or arising in or related to cases under Title 11

(a) Except as otherwise provided in subsections (b) and (d), a proceeding arising under title 11 or arising in or related to a case under title 11 may be commenced in the district court in which such case is pending.

(b) Except as provided in subsection (d) of this section, a trustee in a case under title 11 may commence a proceeding arising in or related to such case to recover a money judgment of or property worth less than $1,000 or a consumer debt of less than $5,000 only in the district court for the district in which the defendant resides.

(c) Except as provided in subsection (b) of this section, a trustee in a case under title 11 may commence a proceeding arising in or related to such case as statutory successor to the debtor or creditors under section 541 or 544(b) of title 11 in the district court for the district where the State or Federal court sits in which, under applicable nonbankruptcy venue provisions, the debtor or creditors, as the case may be, may have commenced an action on which such proceeding is based if the case under title 11 had not been commenced.

(d) A trustee may commence a proceeding arising under title 11 or arising in or related to a case under title 11 based on a claim arising after the commencement of such case from the operation of the business of the debtor only in the district court for the district where a State or Federal court sits in which, under applicable nonbankruptcy venue provisions, an action on such claim may have been brought.

(e) A proceeding arising under title 11 or arising in or related to a case under title 11, based on a claim arising after the commencement of such case from the operation of the business of the debtor, may be commenced against the representative of the estate in such case in the district court for the district where the State or Federal court sits in which the party commencing such proceeding may, under applicable nonbankruptcy venue provisions, have brought an action on such claim, or in the district court in which such case is pending.

U.S.C. § 1409(a). But "in the interest of justice or for the convenience of the parties," the court in which the action is brought may
transfer it to another district. § 1412. As previously noted in connection with the transfer of cases, the section speaks in terms of the
district court's ordering a transfer. However, it would seem that the
bankruptcy judge is also empowered to order the transfer of proceedings referred to him. *See* Bankruptcy Rules 7087, 9001(4). Of
course, there may be an abstention under Section 1334(c) instead.
Thus the statute generally relies upon the primary court to be fair-
minded in deciding transfer motions. The congressional intent is
that undue weight should not be given to the desire of the trustee
or the debtor in possession to litigate close to home.

In two situations, however, venue is not automatically proper in
the primary court. First, in small actions, in which the trustee sues
for less than $1,000 or to recover on a consumer debt of less than
$5,000, venue is proper only in the district or bankruptcy court for
the district where the defendant resides. § 1409(b). Second, a suit
on a claim that arises out of the operation of the debtor's business
after the bankruptcy petition must be brought by the representative of the estate in a district or bankruptcy court prescribed by
applicable nonbankruptcy venue provisions. § 1409(d).

There are also two alternative venue provisions. First, the
trustee, when suing as a statutory successor of the debtor or of
creditors, may properly lay venue not only in the primary court
but also in any district where the debtor or creditors to whose
rights the trustee succeeds could have sued under applicable nonbankruptcy venue rules. § 1409(c). Second, someone suing the estate on a postpetition claim arising out of the operation of the
debtor's business may sue not only in the primary court but also in
the bankruptcy court for any district that would have been a
proper venue under applicable nonbankruptcy law. § 1409(e).

Although a proceeding that is filed in either a proper or improper venue may be transferred by the court to any other district,
whether or not venue would have been proper in the transferee
district, § 1412, there no longer is statutory authority for retain-
ing, over timely objection, a proceeding brought in an improper
venue in the first instance. The 1978 legislation did provide for
that retention, *see* former 28 U.S.C. § 1477, but apparently the court

28 U.S.C. § 1412. Change of venue

A district court may transfer a case or proceeding under title 11 to a district court for another district, in the interest of justice or for the convenience of the parties.

28 U.S.C. § 1406. Cure or waiver of defects

(a) The district court of a district in which is filed a case laying venue in the wrong division or district shall dismiss, or if it be in the interest of justice, transfer such case to any district or division in which it could have been brought.

28 U.S.C. § 1452. Removal of claims related to bankruptcy cases

(a) A party may remove any claim or cause of action in a civil action other than a proceeding before the United States Tax Court or a civil action by a governmental unit to enforce such governmental unit's police or regulatory power, to the district court for the district where such civil action is pending, if such district court has jurisdiction of such claim or cause of action under section 1334 of this title.

must now dismiss the proceeding or perhaps transfer it to a proper venue. *Cf.* 28 U.S.C. § 1406(a). As venue is not jurisdictional, however, if venue is improperly laid and no timely objection is made, the proceeding may go forward in the improper venue.

§ 2.01(h) Removal

In some instances a civil action will be pending by or against the debtor in a nonbankruptcy forum when the bankruptcy case is commenced, or litigation may be brought after bankruptcy by or against the estate in a nonbankruptcy forum, perhaps in connection with matters arising out of the conduct of the business of the estate or against those involved in the administration of the estate. In any of these instances either the plaintiff or the defendant may remove the action to the district court, 28 U.S.C. § 1452, and, through the general reference, to the bankruptcy court for trial. (The Bankruptcy Rules provide for filing the application for removal directly with the clerk of the bankruptcy court if one has been appointed. Rule 9027(a)(1), 9001(1), (3).) The statute prohibits the removal of an action from the United States Tax Court or of an action brought by a governmental unit to enforce its police or regulatory powers. Otherwise, the only limitation on removability is that the action must be within the original jurisdictional grant of Section 1334. Although the statute permits removal by any party, it is unlikely that the courts would permit removal by a plaintiff who, after bankruptcy, had commenced a cause of action in a nonbankruptcy forum. The Rules seem to support this conclusion. *See* Bankruptcy Rule 9027(a)(3). But if the action were filed before bankruptcy, then removal by the plaintiff might well be appropriate.

Removal under Section 1452(a) is to the district or bankruptcy court for the district where the removed action was pending, not for the district where the bankruptcy case is pending if that is elsewhere.

Bankruptcy Rule 9027, which deals with removal, in general requires a removal application to be filed within 90 days after the order for relief in the bankruptcy case if the action was pending at the time the petition was filed (or if the action was subject to the automatic stay, within 30 days after the stay is lifted), or 30 days after service if the action was commenced after the bankruptcy

28 U.S.C. § 1452. Removal of claims related to bankruptcy cases

(b) The court to which such claim or cause of action is removed may remand such claim or cause of action on any equitable ground. An order entered under this subsection remanding a claim or cause of action, or a decision to not remand, is not reviewable by appeal or otherwise.

case was filed. The bankruptcy court apparently is authorized to extend these time periods under Bankruptcy Rule 9006(b).

The removal power should not be construed as a means of obtaining relief from the automatic stay. For example, if a creditor has sued the debtor before bankruptcy to collect a debt, the creditor should not be able to remove the action to the bankruptcy court and continue to judgment there. Once the bankruptcy is filed, the proper method of proceeding against the debtor on such a claim is by filing a proof of claim in the bankruptcy case.

The court may remand a removed action on any equitable ground. Section 1452(b). The bankruptcy judge ordinarily conducts the hearing on a motion to remand; he does not make the dispositive order, however, but merely recommends a disposition to the district court. Bankruptcy Rule 9027(e).

§ 2.01(i) Jury Trial

The subject of jury trials in bankruptcy cases and proceedings is barely treated by the 1984 bankruptcy amendments, and the case law interpreting the current statute is just beginning to develop. Thus only general statements can be made.

The right to a jury trial in a federal court is governed by the Seventh Amendment to the Constitution, which provides that "[i]n suits at common law, where the value in controversy shall exceed twenty dollars, the right of trial by jury shall be preserved." The Seventh Amendment has been interpreted to apply only to suits at common law, not to actions in equity or to those that seek equitable remedies. It has been held, for example, that in an action to avoid a preference (or perhaps a fraudulent transfer), when the prayer is for a money judgment, the right to a jury trial is preserved, *Schoenthal v. Irving Trust Co.*, 287 U.S. 92 (1932), but when the suit seeks to recover the property transferred, the action is in equity and there is no right to a jury. (*See In re Paula Saker & Co., Inc.*, 37 Bankr. 802 (Bankr. S.D.N.Y. 1984), for a more recent analysis of the distinction between law and equity in bankruptcy matters.) *But see In re Reda, Inc.*, 60 Bankr. 178 (Bankr. N.D. Ill. 1986) (no jury trial right in any core proceeding in bankruptcy court).

The allowance of claims against the estate and all matters con-

28 U.S.C. § 1411. Jury trials

(a) Except as provided in subsection (b) of this section, this chapter and title 11 do not affect any right to trial by jury that an individual has under applicable nonbankruptcy law with regard to a personal injury or wrongful death tort claim.

(b) The district court may order the issues arising under section 303 of title 11 to be tried without a jury.

28 U.S.C. § 157. Procedures

(b)(5) The district court shall order that personal injury tort and wrongful death claims shall be tried in the district court in which the bankruptcy case is pending, or in the district court in the district in which the claim arose, as determined by the district court in which the bankruptcy case is pending.

cerning the administration of the estate are equitable in nature, the theory being that the court is administering a res for the general benefit of the creditors. Most matters of this nature therefore do not give rise to a right to a jury trial. *See Katchen v. Landy,* 382 U.S. 323 (1966). Section 1411(a) of Title 28 specifically states, however, that the bankruptcy laws "do not affect any right to trial by jury that an individual has under applicable nonbankruptcy law with regard to a personal injury or wrongful death tort claim." Taken together with 28 U.S.C. § 157(b)(5), this section apparently embodies a congressional intention to preserve the right of jury trial in the district court for the specified kinds of claims against the estate. (Section 157(b)(2)(B) apparently suggests that there is no jury trial right with respect to estimation of these claims for purposes other than distribution.)

It seems clear that bankruptcy judges have the power to determine whether there is a right to a jury trial, subject to appeal on this issue to the district court. And this seems so even in noncore proceedings, in which bankruptcy judges, who may do everything but enter the final order, are likely to conduct all the pretrial matters. *See American Universal Ins. Co. v. Pugh,* 821 F.2d 1352 (9th Cir. 1987).

Whether bankruptcy judges themselves may conduct jury trials is not so clear an issue. The plurality opinion in *Marathon* suggested that conducting a jury trial is an essential attribute of the Article III judicial power. From this observation it might follow that untenured bankruptcy judges could not preside. On the other hand, United States Magistrates have been permitted to conduct jury trials.

The Emergency Rule that was promulgated in the wake of *Marathon* and that was in effect from late 1982 to mid-1984 explicitly prohibited a bankruptcy judge from conducting a jury trial. But there is nothing comparable in the 1984 legislation except the previously noted provision that jury trials of personal injury and wrongful death tort claims are to be before the district court.

The decisions to date, all in the lower courts, reach divergent conclusions as to the statutory and constitutional power of bankruptcy judges to conduct jury trials under the current law. This existing uncertainty (which, in the opinion of the Advisory Committee on Bankruptcy Rules, involves a matter of substantive right

28 U.S.C. § 158. Appeals

(a) The district courts of the United States shall have jurisdiction to hear appeals from final judgments, orders, and decrees, and, with leave of the court, from interlocutory orders and decrees, of bankruptcy judges entered in cases and proceedings referred to the bankruptcy judges under section 157 of this title. An appeal under this subsection shall be taken only to the district court for the judicial district in which the bankruptcy judge is serving.

(c) An appeal under subsections (a) and (b) of this section shall be taken in the same manner as appeals in civil proceedings generally are taken to the courts of appeals from the district courts and in the time provided by Rule 8002 of the Bankruptcy Rules.

so that its resolution lies beyond appropriate rulemaking) led to the abrogation of former Rule 9015 in the 1987 revision of the Rules. That Rule had prescribed the procedure· with respect to jury trials in the bankruptcy court; its existence tended to support an argument that the bankruptcy judge indeed could preside at such a trial. The note accompanying the Advisory Committee's proposal to abrogate the Rule indicates that any rule would be inappropriate while the issue remains undecided, and that amendment of the Rules will be in order if future decisions establish authoritatively the bankruptcy judge's power.

§ 2.02 APPELLATE JURISDICTION

§ 2.02(a) Appeal to the District Court

The district courts have jurisdiction to hear appeals from final judgments, orders, and decrees of the bankruptcy judges in cases and proceedings referred to them. 28 U.S.C. § 158(a). This jurisdiction is distinct from the district court's responsibility in those noncore proceedings in which the bankruptcy judge only proposes a final order and the district court actually signs it. In those instances the district court is acting as the court of original, not appellate, jurisdiction, and appeals from its judgments lie to the courts of appeals under 28 U.S.C. §§ 1291 and 1292.

The district courts also have discretionary jurisdiction over appeals from interlocutory orders and decrees of bankruptcy judges. § 158(a). In other words, this kind of appeal is not a matter of right but may be taken only with leave of the district court.

An appeal lies only to the district court for the district in which the bankruptcy judge who made the order is serving.

§ 2.02(a)(1) Final and Interlocutory Orders

Since the right to appeal depends on the finality of the order, the distinction between final and interlocutory orders can be important. The general concept of finality in civil cases, along with the various exceptions and expansions embodied in such cases as *Cohen v. Beneficial Indus. Loan Corp.*, 337 U.S. 541 (1949), and *Forgay v.*

Conrad, 47 U.S. (6 How.) 201 (1848), applies in bankruptcy cases. However, the special aspect of a bankruptcy case as a larger case in which numerous proceedings take place creates some unique problems of interpretation of the finality doctrine.

Generally speaking, finality is determined by reference to the proceeding in which the order is entered, rather than by reference to the bankruptcy case as a whole. In other words, the "unit of litigation" to which finality relates is a smaller unit, so that more orders will be treated as final. A striking example is *In re Mason,* 709 F.2d 1313 (9th Cir. 1983), in which the court held that an order for relief entered on an involuntary bankruptcy petition was a final order for purposes of appeal, even though that order actually caused the commencement of the administration of the case rather than representing its conclusion or determination. Already a substantial body of case law, often conflicting, considers whether particular kinds of orders are final for the purpose of a bankruptcy appeal.

Unlike the general interlocutory appeal section, 28 U.S.C. § 1292(b), which governs appeals to the courts of appeal from interlocutory orders of district courts in civil cases, Section 158(a) does not provide standards to guide or limit the district court's exercise of its discretion to hear an appeal from an interlocutory order. Nevertheless, some district courts have construed their discretion in harmony with Section 1292(b) and have permitted an appeal only when the interlocutory order involved either a controlling question of law, the determination of which would materially advance the progress of the proceeding, or a kind of order similar to the injunction and receivership orders listed in Section 1292(a). An example of the kind of interlocutory order for which leave to appeal generally will not be granted is one allowing or denying interim fees, as that order by its very nature may be subject to further consideration by the bankruptcy judge later in the case.

§ 2.02(a)(2) *Time for Taking Appeal*

Bankruptcy Rule 8002 specifies that an appeal must be taken within ten days after the order of the bankruptcy judge is entered. (Certain postjudgment motions have the effect of extending this time.) If the order is a final order, a notice of appeal is filed; if it is

28 U.S.C. § 158. Appeals

(b)(1) The judicial council of a circuit may establish a bankruptcy appellate panel, comprised of bankruptcy judges from districts within the circuit, to hear and determine, upon the consent of all the parties, appeals under subsection (a) of this section.

(2) No appeal may be referred to a panel under this subsection unless the district judges for the district, by majority vote, authorize such referral of appeals originating within the district.

(3) A panel established under this section shall consist of three bankruptcy judges, provided a bankruptcy judge may not hear an appeal originating within a district for which the judge is appointed or designated under section 152 of this title.

an interlocutory order, a notice of appeal and an application for leave must be filed, but the district court has discretion to permit late filing of the application for leave to appeal if the notice of appeal is properly and timely filed. Bankruptcy Rules 8001, 8003. A bankruptcy judge may extend to 30 days the time for filing a notice of appeal, but only if application for the extension is made within the original 10-day period or, if made after the initial 10 days, only if there has been excusable neglect. (Even if excusable neglect is shown, certain specified orders are not subject to the provision for late extension of the 10-day period.) Bankruptcy Rule 8002(c).

It is improper to appeal to the district court from a bankruptcy judge's *recommended* findings, conclusions, and order in a noncore proceeding, because nothing has been entered. However, Bankruptcy Rule 9033 provides a procedure similar to that of an appeal for bringing before the district court any objections to a recommended disposition. On the other hand, if a bankruptcy judge impliedly or expressly determines that a matter is a core proceeding and enters judgment, the 10-day time to appeal should govern even if that determination of core status is erroneous, since an order has been entered which will become effective and binding unless appealed. In other words, an erroneous determination that a matter is a core proceeding should not be subject to collateral attack in either the bankruptcy or district court or in another court.

§ 2.02(b) Appeal to the Bankruptcy Appellate Panels

As an alternative to the system of appeals to the district court, Section 158(b) of Title 28 contemplates the possibility that appeals from bankruptcy court orders may be heard by bankruptcy appellate panels. If the panel system is established by the judicial council of a circuit, the panels are composed of three sitting bankruptcy judges whom the council designates. The panels' jurisdiction is identical to the appellate jurisdiction of the district court. However, the district judges for the district in which the appeal arises must authorize, by majority vote, referral of appeals to the panels, and the parties to the appeal must consent. (To date, the appellate panel system has been established only in the Ninth Circuit.)

28 U.S.C. § 158. Appeals

(d) The courts of appeals shall have jurisdiction of appeals from all final decisions, judgments, orders, and decrees entered under subsections (a) and (b) of this section.

§ 2.02(c) Appeal to the Court of Appeals

The courts of appeals have jurisdiction over appeals from all final orders, judgments, and decrees of the district courts and of the bankruptcy appellate panels. 28 U.S.C. § 158(d). They are not granted jurisdiction over appeals of interlocutory orders. The problem of distinguishing final and interlocutory orders was referred to earlier in connection with appeals to the district court. See p. 77–79, *supra*.   An additional complication at the court of appeals level stems from that court's position as the second appellate tier in bankruptcy. For example, *In re Marin Motor Oil, Inc.*, 689 F.2d 445 (3d Cir. 1982), *cert. denied*, 495 U.S. 1207 (1983), involved a final order of the bankruptcy court that was reversed on appeal by the district court. The order of reversal, however, would have been classified as interlocutory had it been made by the district court as an original order. A further appeal was taken. The Third Circuit held that finality for the purpose of its jurisdiction turned on the character of the original order of the bankruptcy court. (*But see In re Brown*, 803 F.2d 120 (3d Cir. 1986).) There has been disagreement with this conclusion, however. Some other courts of appeals, perhaps a majority, apparently look to whether the district court's order, characterized independently, is final or not. *E.g., In re Riggsby*, 745 F.2d 1153 (7th Cir. 1984).

As previously noted, the appellate jurisdiction of a court of appeals derives from 28 U.S.C. §§ 1291 and 1292 when the district court is exercising its original bankruptcy jurisdiction, either because of withholding or withdrawing a reference or because the bankruptcy judge only proposed the order in a noncore proceeding.

Under Federal Rule of Appellate Procedure 4(a) and 28 U.S.C. § 2107, appeals to the courts of appeals from the district courts or the bankruptcy appellate panels must be taken within 30 days after entry of the order (subject to the tolling effect of a timely motion for rehearing under Bankruptcy Rule 8015). This rule is jurisdictional, and exceptions will not lie.

§ 2.02(d) Jurisdiction of the United States Supreme Court

The jurisdiction of the United States Supreme Court in bankruptcy matters is the same as its jurisdiction in ordinary civil actions.

The Court's jurisdiction is generally exercised by certiorari to review judgments of the courts of appeals, *see* 28 U.S.C. § 1254(1), but the other Supreme Court jurisdictional sections also apply.

§ 2.03 BANKRUPTCY ADMINISTRATION

§ 2.03(a) The Administrators

§ 2.03(a)(1) The United States Trustee

One of the primary reform goals of the 1978 Code was to separate the judicial and administrative functions that were performed by the bankruptcy judge under the former Bankruptcy Act. Although Congress was not persuaded originally that creation of an administrative apparatus outside the Judicial Branch was necessary, or even the desirable way to accomplish the separation, it did agree in 1978 to test that idea. Accordingly, the pilot project United States trustee system was enacted as a temporary experiment to be conducted in ten areas of the country comprising 18 judicial districts. (The automatic expiration or sunset date of the experiment, as subsequently extended, was to be September 30, 1986). Where the pilot project was in effect, responsibility for supervising most of the administration of bankruptcy estates was effectively shifted from the bankruptcy judge to the United States trustee, an official under the supervision of the Attorney General in the Executive Branch. (Chapter 15 of the Bankruptcy Code, now repealed, contained the various adjustments to the statute required to accommodate the experiment.) In the nonpilot areas of the country, responsibility for supervising bankruptcy administration remained with the court, although much of the actual administrative work was delegated to and performed by personnel within the clerk's office rather than by the bankruptcy judge himself.

By 1986 Congress had concluded that the pilot project was sufficiently successful to justify making the office of the United States trustee a permanent part of the bankruptcy system on a nationwide basis. The legislative decision is that, except in situations in which the Bankruptcy Code expressly requires a court order, matters of administration should be the responsibility of the United

28 U.S.C. § 586. Duties; supervision by Attorney General

(a) Each United States trustee, within the region for which such United States trustee is appointed, shall —

(1) establish, maintain, and supervise a panel of private trustees that are eligible and available to serve as trustees in cases under chapter 7 of title 11;

(2) serve as and perform the duties of a trustee in a case under title 11 when required under title 11 to serve as trustee in such a case;

(3) supervise the administration of cases and trustees in cases under chapter 7, 11, or 13 of title 11 by, whenever the United States trustee considers it to be appropriate —

(A) monitoring applications for compensation and reimbursement filed under section 330 of title 11 and, whenever the United States trustee deems it to be appropriate, filing with the court comments with respect to any of such applications;

[Continued]

States trustee, and the court's role should be limited to that of an arbiter of disputes.

For practical reasons, however, the 1986 legislation did not provide for the introduction of the new administrative apparatus into all the nonpilot districts at the same time. Rather, the effective dates of the 1986 law as it applies to different areas of the country are staggered; by the end of 1988, however, the United States trustee system should be in place throughout the United States except in the judicial districts in Alabama and North Carolina (where, as a matter of political compromise, it may be installed as late as October 1, 1992, depending on the local choice of the district).

The country is divided into 21 regions (composed of groups of federal judicial districts) for the purpose of the United States trustee system. 28 U.S.C. § 581(a). The Attorney General appoints a United States trustee for each region for a five-year term and has general supervisory power over him as well as the power of removal. § § 581(a)-(c); 586(c). Where necessary, the Attorney General may also appoint (and remove) assistant United States trustees. § 582.

The United States trustee (with an appropriate staff) has the initial responsibilities for appointing from the private sector the members of a panel of trustees, who actually administer bankruptcy cases. § 586(a)(1); *see also* Bankruptcy Code § 1302(a). Qualifications for membership on these panels are prescribed by the Attorney General. 28 U.S.C. § 586(d). In each Chapter 7 liquidation case the United States trustee appoints from the panel the person who is to serve as the trustee in that case (unless creditors elect someone else pursuant to Section 702 of the Bankruptcy Code). Bankruptcy Code § 701(a)(1). When no trustee from the private sector is available or desires to serve, the United States trustee — that is, a staff member — is permitted to act as trustee in the case. Bankruptcy Code § 701(a)(2). To date, however, funding limitations have prevented the United States trustee from serving in this capacity, and it has been that Office's policy always to find a private trustee.

In Chapter 11, the United States trustee appoints a private trustee if the court orders that there should be one in the case, but neither the United States trustee nor a staff member may serve in

28 U.S.C. § 586. Duties; supervision by Attorney General

(B) monitoring plans and disclosure statements filed in cases under chapter 11 of title 11 and filing with the court, in connection with hearings under sections 1125 and 1128 of such title, comments with respect to such plans and disclosure statements;

(C) monitoring plans filed under chapters 12 and 13 of title 11 and filing with the court, in connection with hearings under sections 1224, 1229, 1324, and 1329 of such title, comments with respect to such plans;

(D) taking such action as the United States trustee deems to be appropriate to ensure that all reports, schedules, and fees required to be filed under title 11 and this title by the debtor are properly and timely filed;

(E) monitoring creditors' committees appointed under title 11;

(F) notifying the appropriate United States attorney of matters which relate to the occurrence of any action which may constitute a crime under the laws of the United States and, on the request of the United States attorney, assisting the United States attorney in carrying out prosecutions based on such action;

(G) monitoring the progress of cases under title 11 and taking such actions as the United States trustee deems to be appropriate to prevent undue delay in such progress; and

(H) monitoring applications filed under section 327 of title 11 and, whenever the United States trustee deems it to be appropriate, filing with the court comments with respect to the approval of such applications;

11 U.S.C. § 307. United States trustee

The United States trustee may raise and may appear and be heard on any issue in any case or proceeding under this title but may not file a plan pursuant to section 1121(c) of this title.

that capacity in reorganizations. The appointed trustee in Chapter 11 need not be a member of the panel. Bankruptcy Code § 1104(c). In Chapters 12 and 13, the United States trustee may act as trustee or may choose to leave this role to a private standing trustee. Bankruptcy Code § 1202(a); § 1302(a); 28 U.S.C. § 586(b). As in Chapter 7 cases, all United States trustees have appointed private trustees in Chapter 13 (and no doubt will do so in Chapter 12).

Most important, as previously stated, the United States trustee is responsible for generally supervising the administration of all liquidation and Chapter 11 and 13 rehabilitation cases and for supervising the actions of the private trustee who may be serving in those and in Chapter 12 cases. 28 U.S.C. § 586(a)(3), (b). To fulfill this responsibility, he is specifically empowered to monitor applications for employment of professionals and applications for compensation and reimbursement of expenses; to monitor plans filed in rehabilitation cases and to monitor creditors' committees and disclosure statements in Chapter 11; to ensure that all required schedules and other papers and reports are timely and properly filed and that required filing or similar fees are paid. The statute further authorizes him to report to the court his views concerning all matters of administration and to take any necessary steps to ensure that cases under the Code progress expeditiously. § 586(a)(3)(A)-(H).

It should be emphasized that the United States trustee concept does not contemplate an official who has his own enforcement powers. He cannot make orders in the sense a court or even an administrative agency makes orders that require compliance with prescribed regulations. Rather, the influence of the United States trustee is exercised through his standing to file an appropriate motion, complaint, or objection that seeks a ruling by the bankruptcy court on a matter of administration as to which there has been no voluntary compliance. *See* § 307.

The United States trustee system is intended to be self-supporting. To this end Section 589a of Title 28 establishes a United States Trustee System Fund in the Treasury of the United States into which there are deposited portions of the bankruptcy filing fees in all cases other than those under Chapter 9, plus quar-

11 U.S.C. § 323. Role and capacity of Trustee

(a) The trustee in a case under title is the representative of the estate.

(b) The trustee in a case under this title has capacity to sue and be sued.

11 U.S.C. § 701. Interim trustee

(a) Promptly after the order for relief under this chapter, the United States trustee shall appoint one disinterested person that is a member of the panel of private trustees established under section 586(a)(1) of title 28 or that is serving as trustee in the case immediately before the order for relief under this chapter to serve as interim trustee in the case.

(b) The service of an interim trustee under this section terminates when a trustee elected or designated under section 702 of this title to serve as trustee in the case qualifies under section 322 of this title.

(c) An interim trustee serving under this section is a trustee in a case under this title.

11 U.S.C. § 702. Election of trustee

(b) At the meeting of creditors held under section 341 of this title, creditors may elect one person to serve as trustee in the case if election of a trustee is requested by creditors that may vote under subsection (a) of this section, and that hold at least 20 percent in amount of the claims specified in subsection (a)(1) of this section that are held by creditors that may vote under subsection (a) of this section.

(c) A candidate for trustee is elected trustee if—

(1) creditors holding at least 20 percent in amount of the claims of a kind specified in subsection (a)(1) of this section that are held by creditors that may vote under subsection (a) of this section vote; and

(2) such candidate receives the votes of creditors holding a majority in amount of claims specified in subsection (a)(1) of this section that are held by creditors that vote for a trustee.

(d) If a trustee is not elected under this section, then the interim trustee shall serve as trustee in the case.

terly assessments against Chapter 11 estates determined by a sliding scale of charges according to disbursements made in the case. *See also* 28 U.S.C. § 1930(a)(6).

§ 2.03(a)(2) Office of Receiver Abolished

The Bankruptcy Code abolished the office of receiver in bankruptcy, both for liquidation and reorganization cases. § 105(b). Instead, trustees and interim trustees are appointed.

§ 2.03(a)(3) The Trustee

The trustee is the representative of the estate and is the one who actually administers it. § 323. Promptly after the order for relief in a liquidation case, the United States trustee appoints an interim trustee from the panel of private trustees. At the meeting of creditors held early in the case pursuant to Section 341(a) of the Bankruptcy Code (Bankruptcy Rule 2003(a) requires the meeting ordinarily to be called within 20 to 40 days after the order for relief), unsecured creditors have the right to elect a qualified trustee by a majority vote if creditors holding at least 20 per cent of the amount of the outstanding unsecured claims call for the election. Bankruptcy Code § 702(c). An elected trustee need not be a member of the panel. But trustees are rarely elected, primarily because of the substantial creditor effort needed to meet the statutory requirements for an election. If no election takes place, the interim trustee continues to serve as the trustee for the Chapter 7 case. § 702(d). In Chapter 11 reorganizations a debtor in possession is the norm unless the court orders the appointment of a trustee for cause. The appointment in Chapter 11 may be ordered at any time up to confirmation of a plan. In Chapter 13, there ordinarily is at least one standing trustee in each district to whom all the cases under that chapter are assigned as the petitions are filed; the creditors have no opportunity to elect someone else. Bankruptcy Code §§ 1302.

§ 2.03(b) Employment of Professionals

Trustees, debtors in possession, and Chapter 11 committees may, with court authorization, employ attorneys, accountants, and

11 U.S.C. § 327. Employment of professional persons

(a) Except as otherwise provided in this section, the trustee, with the court's approval, may employ one or more attorneys, accountants, appraisers, auctioneers, or other professional persons, that do not hold or represent an interest adverse to the estate, and that are disinterested persons, to represent or assist the trustee in carrying out the trustee's duties under this title.

11 U.S.C. § 1107. Rights, powers, and duties of debtor in possession

(a) . . . [A] debtor in possession shall have all the rights . . . and powers, and shall perform all the functions and duties . . . of a trustee. . . .

(b) Notwithstanding section 327(a) of this title, a person is not disqualified for employment under section 327 of this title by a debtor in possession solely because of such person's employment by or representation of the debtor before the commencement of the case.

11 U.S.C. § 1103. Powers and duties of committees

(a) At a scheduled meeting of a committee appointed under section 1102 of this title, at which a majority of the members of such committee are present, and with the court's approval, such committee may select and authorize the employment by such committee of one or more attorneys, accountants, or other agents, to represent or perform services for such committee.

(b) An attorney or accountant employed to represent a committee appointed under section 1102 of this title may not, while employed by such committee, represent any other entity having an adverse interest in connection with the case. Representation of one or more creditors of the same class as represented by the committee shall not per se constitute the representation of an adverse interest.

11 U.S.C. § 327. Employment of professional persons

(d) The court may authorize the trustee to act as attorney or accountant for the estate if such authorization is in the best interest of the estate.

other professionals at the expense of the estate. §§ 327(a), 1103(a), 1107(a). A court order authorizing the employment before services are rendered is a prerequisite to an award of compensation, although occasionally some courts will make such an order nunc pro tunc. A debtor, as distinguished from a debtor in possession, apparently may employ counsel at the expense of the estate without court authorization, although this point may not be entirely free from doubt. *See, e.g., In re Triangle Chems., Inc.,* 697 F.2d 1280, 1289–90 (5th Cir. 1983).

Professional persons employed by the trustee or debtor in possession must be disinterested, as defined in Section 101(13), and free from adverse interests. § 327(a). An attorney or accountant employed by a Chapter 11 committee may not hold any adverse interest; although the statute, § 1103(b), does not in terms require disinterestedness, it is a requirement as a practical matter because lack of disinterestedness is a ground for denying compensation to a professional employed by a committee. § 328(c). A special counsel with some interest adverse to the estate may nevertheless be employed by the trustee or debtor in possession on a particular matter in which the attorney has no adverse interest. § 327(a), (e). Representing a creditor does not of itself disqualify an attorney or accountant from representing the trustee or a Chapter 11 creditors' committee if there is no actual conflict of interest. §§ 327(c), 1103(b). And, of course, employment by the debtor before the case was filed does not disqualify an attorney or accountant from employment by the debtor in possession in its capacity as representative of the estate. § 1107(b). Finally, the court may authorize a trustee to act as the estate's attorney or accountant and to be compensated for both types of services if this authorization is in the best interests of the estate. § 327(d).

§ 2.03(c) Compensation

§ 2.03(c)(1) Bankruptcy Judges

The annual compensation of bankruptcy judges is set under the general procedures for fixing most federal salaries—that is, by the Quadrennial Commission under Section 225 of the Federal Salary

11 U.S.C. § 101. Definitions

In this title—

(13) "disinterested person" means person that—

(A) is not a creditor, an equity security holder, or an insider;

(B) is not and was not an investment banker for any outstanding security of the debtor;

(C) has not been, within three years before the date of the filing of the petition, an investment banker for a security of the debtor, or an attorney for such an investment banker in connection with the offer, sale, or issuance of a security of the debtor;

(D) is not and was not, within two years before the date of the filing of the petition, a director, officer, or employee of the debtor or of an investment banker specified in subparagraph (B) or (C) of this paragraph; and

(E) does not have an interest materially adverse to the interest of the estate or of any class of creditors or equity security holders, by reason of any direct or indirect relationship to, connection with, or interest in, the debtor or an investment banker specified in subparagraph (B) or (C) of this paragraph, or for any other reason;

11 U.S.C. § 330. Compensation of officers

(a) After notice to any parties in interest and to the United States trustee and a hearing, and subject to sections 326, 328, and 329 of this title, the court may award to a trustee, to an examiner, to a professional person employed under section 327 or 1103 of this title, or to the debtor's attorney—

(1) reasonable compensation for actual, necessary services rendered by such trustee, examiner, professional person, or attorney, as the case may be, and by any paraprofessional persons employed by such trustee, professional person, or attorney, as the case may be, based on the nature, the extent, and the value of such services, the time spent on such services, and the cost of comparable services other than in a case under this title; and

(2) reimbursement for actual, necessary expenses.

(b) There shall be paid from the filing fee in a case under chapter 7 of this title $45 to the trustee serving in such case, after such trustee's services are rendered.

Act of 1967 (2 U.S.C. §§ 351–361), subject to annual cost-of-living adjustments under 28 U.S.C. § 461. *See* 28 U.S.C. § 153. During 1987, bankruptcy judges received salaries of approximately $72,500.

§ 2.03(c)(2) United States Trustees

The compensation of United States trustees and assistant United States trustees is fixed by the Attorney General pursuant to 28 U.S.C. § 587. Under that section the highest amount the Attorney General may fix is equal to the rate of basic compensation provided for Executive Level IV of the Executive Schedule, 5 U.S.C. § 5315. (In 1987, this compensation was $77,500 per year.) The statute anticipated that the Attorney General would vary the compensation for United States trustees and assistants based on factors of location, workload, and experience, much the same as is done in compensating United States attorneys and their assistants. (Any compensation collected out of the estate by a United States trustee who serves as trustee in the case is to be paid into the Treasury. Bankruptcy Code § 330(d).)

§ 2.03(c)(3) Private Trustees

Compensation of private trustees is governed by Sections 330 and 326 of the Bankruptcy Code. As a general matter, Section 330(a) entitles all officers of the estate and authorized professional persons to reasonable compensation from the estate for actual and necessary services rendered, based on the time, nature, extent, and value of the services and the cost of comparable services performed outside the bankruptcy context. In addition, all actual and necessary expenses may be reimbursed. The Code's compensation policy represents a sharp departure from the practice under the former Bankruptcy Act. That practice required the court in allowing professional and other fees to give due regard to the so-called economy principle, which emphasized conservation of the estate and the interests of creditors. The House Report makes clear at 329–30 that the former requirement was deleted intentionally in order to insure that compensation in a bankruptcy case will be commensurate with compensation for similar services rendered elsewhere. *Accord In re Nucorp Energy, Inc.,* 764 F.2d 655 (9th Cir. 1985).

11 U.S.C. § 326. Limitation on compensation of trustee

(a) In a case under chapter 7 or 11, the court may allow reasonable compensation under section 330 of this title of the trustee for the trustee's services, payable after the trustee renders such services, not to exceed fifteen percent on the first $1,000 or less, six percent on any amount in excess of $1,000 but not in excess of $3,000, and three percent on any amount in excess of $3,000, upon all moneys disbursed or turned over in the case by the trustee to parties in interest, excluding the debtor, but including holders of secured claims.

(b) In a case under chapter 12 or 13 of this title, the court may not allow compensation for services or reimbursement of expenses of the United States trustee or of a standing trustee appointed under section 586(b) of title 28, but may allow reasonable compensation under section 330 of this title of a trustee appointed under section 1202(a) or 1302(a) of this title for the trustee's services, payable after the trustee renders such services, not to exceed five percent upon all payments under the plan.

(c) If more than one person serves as trustee in the case, the aggregate compensation of such persons for such service may not exceed the maximum compensation prescribed for a single trustee by subsection (a) or (b) of this section, as the case may be.

(d) The court may deny allowance of compensation for services or reimbursement of expenses of the trustee if the trustee failed to make diligent inquiry into facts that would permit denial of allowance under section 328(c) of this title or, with knowledge of such facts, employed a professional person under section 327 of this title.

Though the general standard of compensation is set forth in Section 330(a), Section 326 places a ceiling on the amount that may be awarded to a trustee in a case under Chapter 7 or 11. A trustee's compensation may not exceed 15 per cent of the first $1,000, 6 per cent of the next $2,000, and 3 per cent of any amount in excess of $3,000 "upon all moneys disbursed or turned over in the case by the trustee to parties in interest, excluding the debtor, but including holders of secured claims." § 326(a). Although these percentages were intended as limits on reasonable compensation, in practice they sometimes work like commissions, except in very large cases. A fee of $45 per case, paid from the filing fee, is assured the Chapter 7 trustee by Section 330(b).

Section 326(c) limits the aggregate compensation of successive trustees in a case to that awarded a single trustee. In addition, the trustee may be denied compensation or reimbursement of expenses under Section 326(d) if he negligently or intentionally employs a professional person who is not disinterested. Further restrictions apply under Section 328(b) when the trustee serves as attorney or accountant in the case in addition to serving as trustee.

Different limitations apply to trustees in cases under Chapter 13. Section 326(b) limits the compensation of a nonstanding private trustee to 5 per cent of the payments made under the plan. A standing Chapter 13 trustee receives compensation, depending on variables, fixed by the Attorney General under 28 U.S.C. § 586(e). The maximum annual compensation that may be fixed by the Attorney General is limited to the lowest annual rate of basic pay in effect for Civil Service grade GS-16. However, instead of prescribing a guaranteed salary as is done for the United States trustee, the Attorney General specifies a maximum annual compensation for each standing trustee, together with a percentage fee to be charged against each Chapter 13 estate. The percentage fee may not exceed 10 per cent and must be based on the targeted maximum compensation plus projected expenses.

The standing trustee may pay office expenses and personal compensation from the percentage fee. However, compensation derived from the percentage fee may not exceed 5 per cent of all payments under the plans in cases in which the trustee serves. Thus there are alternative limits on the trustee's compensation: the

11 U.S.C. § 331. Interim compensation

A trustee, an examiner, a debtor's attorney, or any professional person employed under section 327 or 1103 of this title may apply to the court not more than once every 120 days after an order for relief in a case under this title, or more often if the court permits, for such compensation for services rendered before the date of such an application or reimbursement for expenses incurred before such date as is provided under section 330 of this title. After notice and a hearing, the court may allow and disburse to such applicant such compensation or reimbursement.

11 U.S.C. § 328. Limitation on compensation of professional persons

(a) The trustee, or a committee appointed under section 1102 of this title, with the court's approval, may employ or authorize the employment of a professional person under section 327 or 1103 of this title, as the case may be, on any reasonable terms and conditions of employment, including on a retainer, on an hourly basis, or on a contingent fee basis. Notwithstanding such terms and conditions, the court may allow compensation different from the compensation provided under such terms and conditions after the conclusion of such employment, if such terms and conditions prove to have been improvident in light of developments not capable of being anticipated at the time of the fixing of such terms and conditions.

limit fixed by the Attorney General (not to exceed the level of pay for grade GS-16 employees) and 5 per cent on plan payments made in the trustee's cases. The trustee must return to the Treasury any amount by which collections of the percentage fee exceed the compensation fixed by the Attorney General, as adjusted by the 5 per cent maximum and by actual office expenses.

In Chapter 13, no compensation will be paid to the United States trustee or to a designated assistant for service as trustee in the case. Bankruptcy Code § 326(b). In a Chapter 7 case in which the United States trustee serves as trustee, any allowable compensation under Section 330 must be paid into the Treasury. § 330(d).

§ 2.03(c)(4) Professionals

Professional persons, such as attorneys, accountants, and appraisers, are compensated under the general standard of Section 330(a) of the Bankruptcy Code. As previously noted, the Code intended to change the former practice of awarding compensation in bankruptcy at levels below those prevailing for comparable services elsewhere. *See* House Report at 329–30; *In re Nucorp Energy, Inc.*, 764 F.2d 655 (9th Cir. 1985). Section 331 furthers this goal by authorizing the court to allow professional persons interim compensation or reimbursement of expenses in cases under Title 11.

The Bankruptcy Code places some statutory limitations on the compensation of professionals. Section 328(a) authorizes the court to approve the employment of professionals by the trustee, or by committees in reorganization cases, on any reasonable terms, including employment on a retainer, on a contingent fee, or on an hourly basis. But the section further permits the court to adjust the compensation of professionals so employed if the compensation originally authorized turns out to have been unfair for reasons that could not have been anticipated at the time of the time of employment. If the professional is not disinterested, Section 328(c) permits the court to disallow compensation entirely, subject to two exceptions specified in subsections (c) and (e) of Section 327, which do not require disinterestedness.

Compensation of the debtor's attorney is regulated more closely than compensation of other officers. Section 329 and Bankruptcy

11 U.S.C. § 329. Debtor's transactions with attorneys

(a) Any attorney representing a debtor in a case under this title, or in connection with such a case, whether or not such attorney applies for compensation under this title, shall file with the court a statement of the compensation paid or agreed to be paid, if such payment or agreement was made after one year before the date of the filing of the petition, for services rendered or to be rendered in contemplation of or in connection with the case by such attorney, and the source of such compensation.

(b) If such compensation exceeds the reasonable value of any such services, the court may cancel any such agreement, or order the return of any such payment, to the extent excessive, to—

(1) the estate, if the property transferred—

(A) would have been property of the estate; or

(B) was to be paid by or on behalf of the debtor under a plan under chapter 11, 12, or 13 of this title; or

(2) the entity that made such payment.

11 U.S.C. § 321. Eligibility to serve as trustee

(b) A person that has served as an examiner in the case may not serve as trustee in the case.

11 U.S.C. § 327. Employment of professional persons

(f) The trustee may not employ a person that has served as an examiner in the case.

Rule 2016(b) require the debtor's attorney to file a statement of payments and agreements for payment for services rendered in contemplation of, or in connection with, the case if the payment or agreement was made after one year before the date of the filing of the petition. To the extent that any such payment or agreement is found unreasonable, there will be a surcharge or a cancellation of the promise. § 329(b).

§ 2.03(c)(5) Examiners

An examiner serving in a case under Chapter 11 is the only other officer of the estate entitled to compensation from the estate. Compensation of an examiner appointed under Bankruptcy Code § 1104 is governed by the general standard in Section 330(a). Interim compensation may be applied for under Section 331. No limit is placed on the maximum compensation of an examiner, but the nature of the office itself ordinarily is an adequate safeguard against abuse. Moreover, an examiner is prohibited from later serving as the trustee or as the attorney or accountant for the trustee. §§ 321(b), 327(f). It is unclear under the statute whether an examiner is authorized to employ attorneys, accountants, or other professionals at the expense of the estate. *But see, e.g., In re Tighe Mercantile, Inc.*, 62 Bankr. 995 (Bankr. S.D. Cal. 1986) (court may authorize examiner to employ counsel at expense of estate under authority of § 105(a)).

11 U.S.C. § 109. Who may be a debtor

(a) Notwithstanding any other provision of this section, only a person that resides or has a domicile, a place of business, or property in the United States, or a municipality, may be a debtor under this title.

(b) A person may be a debtor under chapter 7 of this title only if such person is not —

(1) a railroad;

(2) a domestic insurance company, bank, savings bank, cooperative bank, savings and loan association, building and loan association, homestead association, credit union, or industrial bank or similar institution which is an insured bank as defined in section 3(h) of the Federal Deposit Insurance Act (12 U.S.C. 1813(h)); or

(3) a foreign insurance company, bank, savings bank, cooperative bank, savings and loan association, building and loan association, homestead association, or credit union, engaged in such business in the United States.

(d) Only a person that may be a debtor under chapter 7 of this title, except a stockbroker or a commodity broker, and a railroad may be a debtor under chapter 11 of this title.

11 U.S.C. § 101. Definitions

In this title —

(35) "person" includes individual, partnership, and corporation, but does not include governmental unit, *Provided, however,* That any governmental unit that acquires an asset from a person as a result of operation of a loan guarantee agreement, or as receiver or liquidating agent of a person, will be considered a person for purposes of section 1102 of this title;

3

Commencement of the Case

§ 3.01 ELIGIBILITY FOR RELIEF UNDER THE CODE

Section 109 and, to some extent, Section 303(a) contain the eligibility requirements for relief under the Bankruptcy Code. In general, any "person," defined in Section 101(35) as any individual, partnership, or corporation, with a sufficient nexus to the United States—residence, domicile, place of business, or property in the United States—is eligible for Chapter 7 liquidation or Chapter 11 reorganization relief. § 109(a), (b), (d). "Corporation" is broadly defined in Section 101(8) to include virtually all kinds of limited liability organizations other than limited partnerships. For example, labor unions, cooperatives, real estate investment trusts, and other "business trusts" are corporations under this definition and thus are eligible Chapter 7 or 11 debtors. Ordinary private trusts, however, as distinguished from business trusts in which interests are held by investors, are not "persons" within the definition of Section 101(35) and thus are ineligible. Similarly, probate or decedent estates are ineligible. The debtor's death after the filing of a petition, however, does not abate a Chapter 7 case; Chapter 11 and 13 cases may also continue if that course is feasible under the circumstances. Bankruptcy Rule 1016.

Certain heavily regulated financial institutions, including banks, insurance companies, savings and loan associations, building and loan associations, homestead associations, and credit unions, are expressly made ineligible for relief. § 109(b)(2). In deciding whether a given debtor falls within one of these ineligible classes, the benchmark for the court is the debtor's classification under the state (or nonbankruptcy) regulatory statute governing that kind of company. But that law need not always be followed literally; the bankruptcy court will look to the spirit of the law in

11 U.S.C. § 101. Definitions

In this title—

(8) "corporation"—

(A) includes—

(i) association having a power or privilege that a private corporation, but not an individual or a partnership, possesses;

(ii) partnership association organized under a law that makes only the capital subscribed responsible for the debts of such association;

(iii) joint-stock company;

(iv) unincorporated company or association; or

(v) business trust; but

(B) does not include limited partnership;

11 U.S.C. § 303. Involuntary cases

(a) An involuntary case may be commenced only under chapter 7 or 11 of this title, and only against a person, except a farmer, family farmer, or a corporation that is not a moneyed, business, or commercial corporation, that may be a debtor under the chapter under which such case is commenced.

11 U.S.C. § 109. Who may be a debtor

(f) Only a family farmer with regular annual income may be a debtor under chapter 12 of this title.

11 U.S.C. § 109. Who may be a debtor

(e) Only an individual with regular income that owes, on the date of the filing of the petition, noncontingent, liquidated, unsecured debts of less than $100,000 and noncontingent, liquidated, secured debts of less than $350,000, or an individual with regular income and such individual's spouse, except a stockbroker or a commodity broker, that owe, on the date of the filing of the petition, noncontingent, liquidated, unsecured debts that aggregate less than $100,000 and noncontingent, liquidated, secured debts of less than $350,000 may be a debtor under chapter 13 of this title.

determining the debtor's classification and has some independent judgment on the issue of eligibility for relief under the Code. *See, e.g., In re Cash Currency Exch., Inc.,* 762 F.2d 542 (7th Cir. 1985). A parent or holding company is eligible even though its only or most important asset is the stock of a financial institution that itself is ineligible. The bankruptcy court having jurisdiction of such a parent debtor, however, must take special care not to interfere with the administration of the estate of the subsidiary over which it has no jurisdiction. *See, e.g., In re Bankers Trust Co.,* 566 F.2d 1281 (5th Cir. 1978) (case decided under the former Bankruptcy Act).

Railroads are eligible for relief under Chapter 11 but are not eligible for Chapter 7 liquidation. § 109(b)(1), (d). However, liquidation of a railroad is possible under Chapter 11. *See* § 1174. Subchapter IV of Chapter 11, §§ 1161–1174, specially covers railroad reorganizations, a subject beyond the scope of this book.

Stockbrokers and commodity brokers are eligible for liquidation under Chapter 7 but not for reorganization under Chapter 11 or Chapter 13. § 109(b), (d), (e).

Certain debtors are eligible only for voluntary bankruptcy. Thus farmers, as defined by Section 101(19) and (20) (whether they are individual, partnership, or corporate farmers), family farmers, as defined by Section 101(17), and corporations that are "moneyed, business, or commercial" companies are not amenable to an involuntary petition, *see* § 303(a), although they may file voluntarily under Chapter 7, 11, or 12 (and, in the case of an individual debtor farmer, perhaps under Chapter 13).

Only a "family farmer with regular annual income," § 109(f), whose debts do not exceed $1.5 million, is eligible for Chapter 12. The quoted term, defined elaborately in § 101(17) and (18), includes individuals, partnerships, and corporations.

Chapter 13 relief is available only for an individual debtor other than a stockbroker or commodity broker. The debtor must have "regular income"—that is, a source of revenue that is sufficiently reliable to enable him to perform under his plan. Additionally, his unsecured debts must be less than $100,000 and his secured debts must be less than $350,000. *See* §§ 109(e), 101(29); pp. 333–35, *infra.*

The 1984 amendments added a new ground of disqualification for

11 U.S.C. § 101. Definitions

In this title—

(29) "individual with regular income" means individual whose income is sufficiently stable and regular to enable such individual to make payments under a plan under chapter 13 of this title, other than a stockbroker or a commodity broker;

11 U.S.C. § 109. Who may be a debtor

(g) Notwithstanding any other provision of this section, no individual or family farmer may be a debtor under this title who has been a debtor in a case pending under this title at any time in the preceding 180 days if—

(1) the case was dismissed by the court for willful failure of the debtor to abide by orders of the court, or to appear before the court in proper prosecution of the case; or

(2) the debtor requested and obtained the voluntary dismissal of the case following the filing of a request for relief from the automatic stay provided by section 362 of this title.

11 U.S.C. § 301. Voluntary cases

A voluntary case under a chapter of this title is commenced by the filing with the bankruptcy court of a petition under such chapter by an entity that may be a debtor under such chapter. The commencement of a voluntary case under a chapter of this title constitutes an order for relief under such chapter.

relief under Chapters 7, 11, and 13, aimed at certain individuals who engage in abusive multiple filings. (The 1986 amendments extended this ground to Chapter 12.) § 109(g). Thus a petition will not lie if, within the preceding 180 days, an earlier case was dismissed for specified kinds of improper conduct by the debtor or if he voluntarily dismissed an earlier case following a request for relief from the automatic stay. *See also* § 707(b).

Chapter 9 relief is available only for municipalities, defined as political subdivisions, public agencies, or instrumentalities of a state. §§ 109(c), 101(34).

§ 3.02 THE PETITION

§ 3.02(a) In General

A case under the Code is commenced by the filing of a petition with the clerk of the court. *See* Bankruptcy Rules 1002(a); 9001(3), (1). In general, a petition is either voluntary (filed by the debtor, § 301), involuntary (filed against the debtor by creditors, § 303), joint (a single petition filed by an individual debtor and spouse, § 302), or ancillary to a foreign bankruptcy or similar proceeding, § 304, a topic beyond the scope of this book. The venue provisions that prescribe the judicial district in which a petition should be filed are contained in 28 U.S.C. § 1408 and have been discussed earlier at p. 67.

Cases under Chapters 9, 12, and 13 are voluntary only; Chapter 7 and 11 cases may be filed either voluntarily or involuntarily. §§ 301, 303(a).

A filing fee ordinarily must accompany the filing of the petition, as prescribed by 28 U.S.C. § 1930. *See* Bankruptcy Rule 1006. At present the fee is $90 for Chapter 7 and 13 cases, $500 for Chapter 11 cases involving debtors other than railroads, $1,000 for railroad cases, $200 for Chapter 12 cases, and $300 for Chapter 9 cases. An individual debtor who is unable to advance the filing fee for a voluntary case may be authorized to pay it in not more than four installments over a period not exceeding 120 days. But the general in forma pauperis provision of 28 U.S.C. § 1915 does not apply to

11 U.S.C. § 521. Debtor's duties

The debtor shall—

(1) file a list of creditors, and unless the court orders otherwise, a schedule of assets and liabilities, a schedule of current income and current expenditures, and a statement of the debtor's financial affairs;

11 U.S.C. § 707. Dismissal

(b) After notice and a hearing, the court, on its own motion or on a motion by the United States Trustee, but not at the request or suggestion of any party in interest, may dismiss a case filed by an individual debtor under this chapter whose debts are primarily consumer debts if it finds that the granting of relief would be a substantial abuse of the provisions of this chapter. There shall be a presumption in favor of granting the relief requested by the debtor.

filing fees in bankruptcy cases. The debtor's attorney may not be compensated until the installments are fully paid. Bankruptcy Rule 1006(b)(3).

§ 3.02(b) Voluntary Petitions

A voluntary petition may be filed by any eligible debtor. The allegations are simple and are set forth in Official Form No. 1. Undoubtedly, the debtor must owe some debts in order to seek voluntary relief under the Code, but no particular amount of money owed is a prerequisite. In particular, the statute does not require that the petition allege insolvency or that the debtor is unable to pay his debts. The petition ordinarily must be accompanied by schedules of assets and liabilities (or a Chapter 13 Statement), a statement of financial affairs, and certain other financial information, *see* Official Forms Nos. 6–10, although there is an automatic 15-day extension for filing these documents, and the time may be further extended by the court for cause. § 521; Bankruptcy Rule 1007. In cases of any complexity, particularly in Chapter 11, the debtor is routinely granted additional time to file the documents. When the required information is not filed with the petition, the petition must be accompanied by a list of creditors. Bankruptcy Rule 1007(a)(1).

The 1978 Code did not contain any express requirement that a voluntary petition be filed in "good faith." *Cf.* §§ 1129(a)(3), 1325(a)(3) (requiring *plans* to be proposed in good faith). A 1984 amendment added Section 707(b) to provide that a Chapter 7 petition, in the limited context of an individual consumer debtor, is subject to dismissal if the court perceives the filing to be a substantial abuse of the spirit of the law. (Only the court itself and the United States trustee have standing to raise this ground.) Even before 1984, however, a considerable body of case law had developed under the Code to the effect that the bankruptcy court has the inherent power to dismiss any voluntary petition filed in bad faith.

Most frequently, these dismissals of petitions for abusive filing have occurred in Chapter 11 cases. A familiar situation involves a manipulative prepetition transfer of property to the debtor, which then files a petition to obtain the benefits of the automatic stay.

11 U.S.C. § 303. Involuntary cases

(a) An involuntary case may be commenced only under chapter 7 or 11 of this title, and only against a person, except a farmer, family farmer, or a corporation that is not a moneyed, business, or commercial corporation, that may be a debtor under the chapter under which such case is commenced.

[Continued]

Perhaps the original transferor was itself ineligible for relief under the Code; more likely, the original owner transferred a troubled property to a corporation, which then became the debtor in order to obtain the benefits of the Code for that property without subjecting any other assets to the jurisdiction of the court. Many courts, although not all, have found this course of conduct an improper imposition upon the bankruptcy jurisdiction and have dismissed the petition, sometimes sua sponte.

Other kinds of situations have also been characterized as bad faith filings. For example, judicial opinions state occasionally that a petition filed for the sole purpose of staying a foreclosure or lien enforcement proceeding violates the spirit of Chapter 11 and should be dismissed. Taken literally, this view is overbroad, for many legitimate reorganization filings are triggered by just such a foreclosure threat. However, if understood to mean that it is improper to file to stop a foreclosure, without any intention to reorganize and save the property or the equity through a plan providing for refinancing, sale, or other arrangement, then the view is not unreasonable. *Cinema Service Corp. v. Edbee Corp.*, 774 F.2d 584 (3d Cir. 1985), for example, took this limited position. In any event, it is sometimes difficult to draw the line between a sincere effort to take advantage of the relief available under the Code — which ought to be a good faith filing, even when the case does not involve a traditional Chapter 11 fact situation — and those abusive filings that do not warrant the protection of the law. A number of the "good faith" decisions are collected and discussed in Ordin, *The Good Faith Principle in the Bankruptcy Code: A Case Study*, 38 BUS. LAW. 1795 (1983).

§ 3.02(c) Involuntary Petitions

§ 3.02(c)(1) Qualifications of Petitioning Creditors

A Chapter 7 or 11 petition may be filed by creditors against any debtor who is eligible for involuntary relief under those chapters. Typically, there must be at least three petitioning creditors whose

11 U.S.C. § 303. Involuntary cases

(b) An involuntary case against a person is commenced by the filing with the bankruptcy court of a petition under chapter 7 or 11 of this title—

(1) by three or more entities, each of which is either a holder of a claim against such person that is not contingent as to liability or the subject of a bona fide dispute, or an indenture trustee representing such a holder, if such claims aggregate at least $5,000 more than the value of any lien on property of the debtor securing such claims held by the holders of such claims;

(2) if there are fewer than 12 such holders, excluding any employee or insider of such person and any transferee of a transfer that is voidable under section 544, 545, 547, 548, 549, or 724(a) of this title, by one or more of such holders that hold in the aggregate at least $5,000 of such claims;

(3) if such person is a partnership—

(A) by fewer than all of the general partners in such partnership; or

(B) if relief has been ordered under this title with respect to all of the general partners in such partnership, by a general partner in such partnership, the trustee of such a general partner, or a holder of a claim against such partnership; or

(4) by a foreign representative of the estate in a foreign proceeding concerning such person.

claims are not contingent as to liability[1] and are not subject to bona fide dispute. Moreover, the claims must aggregate at least $5,000 over the value of any lien or security the creditor or creditors hold with respect to the debtor's property — that is, the petitioning creditors as a group must have at least $5,000 of unsecured claims. One or two fully secured creditors will suffice as long as the requisite $5,000 of unsecured claims exists among the three. An indenture trustee is counted as one creditor for this purpose. § 303(b)(1).

If the debtor's creditors total fewer than 12 in number, then 1 or 2 creditors will suffice for an involuntary petition, provided the claim or claims meet the noncontingent, nondisputed requirement and aggregate in amount the necessary $5,000 above liens. The statute excludes several types of claimants from the calculation of the number of creditors for this purpose, namely, employees and insiders of the debtor and those who have received avoidable transfers. § 303(b)(2). The latter category often disqualifies from the 12-count a considerable number of creditors, so that a petition filed by 1 or 2 creditors properly lies in many more cases than might be expected. Whether creditors holding relatively de minimis or recurring-type claims should also be excluded from the 12-count has been the subject of conflicting judicial decisions. Probably the majority view under the Code is that these creditors should be counted because the statute does not expressly exclude them. *E.g., In re Rassi,* 701 F.2d 627 (7th Cir. 1983). Creditors who are excluded by Section 303(b)(2) for the purpose of determining

---

[1] A "contingent" claim for this purpose, as distinguished from one that is unliquidated or unmatured or disputed, is a claim as to which there is some remaining condition precedent to liability. When all the facts necessary to liability have occurred, the claim is no longer contingent, even though the existence of those facts may still be unknown to or disputed by the parties. For example, a creditor's claim against a guarantor of an obligation is a contingent claim until the maturity of the debt; the guarantor is only contingently liable to the creditor until there is a dishonor or default by the primary obligor. On the other hand, the claim against the primary obligor is not contingent, although it is not yet due. If liability already exists, the fact that the amount owing is ascertainable only after a trial may make the claim unliquidated or disputed, but it does not make it contingent. *See generally In re* Dill, 731 F.2d 629 (9th Cir. 1984).

11 U.S.C. § 303. Involuntary cases

(c) After the filing of a petition under this section but before the case is dismissed or relief is ordered, a creditor holding an unsecured claim that is not contingent, other than a creditor filing under subsection (b) of this section, may join in the petition with the same effect as if such joining creditor were a petitioning creditor under subsection (b) of this section.

11 U.S.C. § 303. Involuntary cases

(h) If the petition is not timely controverted, the court shall order relief against the debtor in an involuntary case under the chapter under which the petition was filed. Otherwise, after trial, the court shall order relief against the debtor in an involuntary case under the chapter under which the petition was filed, only if—

(1) the debtor is generally not paying such debtor's debts as such debts become due unless such debts that are the subject of a bona fide dispute; or

(2) within 120 days before the date of the filing of the petition, a custodian, other than a trustee, receiver, or agent appointed or authorized to take charge of less than substantially all of the property of the debtor for the purpose of enforcing a lien against such property, was appointed or took possession.

the required number of petitioners are not disqualified from being petitioning creditors themselves.

At any time before the case is dismissed, creditors holding non-contingent, unsecured claims may intervene as of right in a pending involuntary petition, with the same effect as if they had originally joined. § 303(c). Thus a one- or two-creditor petition that is defective because three creditors are necessary may be cured by an appropriate intervention. (However, an intentional misstatement in the petition concerning the required number of petitioning creditors may preclude curing the deficiency by intervention. *See Basin Elec. Power Coop. v. Midwest Processing Co.,* 769 F.2d 483 (8th Cir. 1985).) The policy here is to prevent dismissals on technical grounds because of the importance of preserving the date of the original petition. Many of the powers of a trustee to reach back and undo or recover prepetition transfers depend upon, or are calculated with reference to, the date of the filing of the petition that commences the case. A dismissal that necessitates a refiling would work to change or postpone that date and thus could prejudice the estate. Accordingly, Bankruptcy Rule 1003(b) provides a procedure that facilitates the obtaining of interventions when the requisite number of petitioning creditors becomes an issue.

§ 3.02(c)(2) Grounds for Relief; Abstention

To withstand a motion to dismiss, an involuntary petition must allege one of the statutory grounds for relief. If the petition is not timely contested by answer or motion, however, the court enters an order for relief promptly after the time to answer expires. § 303(h); Bankruptcy Rule 1013(b). There are two alternative but overlapping grounds for relief when the petition is controverted. The first ground exists if "the debtor is generally not paying" undisputed debts as they become due. § 303(h)(1). Note that the statute speaks in the present tense; traditional insolvency in the equity sense, which involves a prediction that the debtor will be unable in the future to pay maturing debts, does not suffice, even if the potential default appears virtually certain. Similarly, a previous inability to pay maturing debts would not constitute a ground for relief if, by the time the petition is filed, the debtor has become current on his obligations. Indeed, Section 303(h)(1) does not focus on ability or inability to pay debts at all

11 U.S.C. § 305. Abstention

(a) The court, after notice and a hearing, may dismiss a case under this title, or may suspend all proceedings in a case under this title, at any time if—

(1) the interests of creditors and the debtor would be better served by such dismissal or suspension; or

(2)(A) there is pending a foreign proceeding; and

(B) the factors specified in section 304(c) of this title warrant such dismissal or suspension.

(c) An order under subsection (a) of this section dismissing a case or suspending all proceedings in a case, or a decision not so to dismiss or suspend, is not reviewable by appeal or otherwise.

but only on whether the debtor is actually paying at the time of the petition.

Moreover, the nonpayment of debts must be a "general" course of conduct, not merely isolated instances. Case law, however, apparently is establishing that either nonpayment of a number of small debts or nonpayment of one or a few debts that are large relative to the total indebtedness will meet the requirement of general nonpayment. *See, e.g., In re International Teldata Corp.*, 12 Bankr. 879 (Bankr. D. Nev. 1981). Ability to pay the debts is not a defense if in fact the debtor is generally not paying.

The second ground for relief is that within the preceding 120 days the debtor made a general assignment for the benefit of creditors or suffered the appointment of a receiver, or that a custodian, as defined in Section 101(10), was appointed or took possession of the debtor's property. Excluded from this ground are lien enforcement receiverships involving less than substantially all the debtor's property. § 303(h)(2).

Even though a petition is properly grounded, the court may choose to abstain or dismiss the case rather than enter an order for relief, if abstention or dismissal would better serve "the interests of creditors and the debtor." § 305(a)(1). This provision, although literally applicable to both voluntary and involuntary cases, is aimed basically at improperly motivated involuntary petitions, particularly at situations in which a few disgruntled creditors with ulterior motives are using the bankruptcy process to supersede either a legitimate general assignment for the benefit of creditors or another non-bankruptcy liquidation or work-out proceeding. Under these circumstances a court might well find that both the general creditor body and the debtor would benefit from bankruptcy abstention. In a voluntary case, however, it is not likely that the debtor would be better served by a dismissal of the petition, a finding that Section 305(a)(1) requires. A decision to abstain or not to abstain is not appealable or otherwise reviewable. § 305(c).

§ 3.02(c)(3) Standing To Answer an Involuntary Petition

Only the debtor (or in a partnership case, a general partner who did not join in the petition) may answer an involuntary petition.

11 U.S.C. § 303. Involuntary cases

(d) The debtor, or a general partner in a partnership debtor that did not join in the petition, may file an answer to a petition under this section.

11 U.S.C. § 303. Involuntary cases

(f) Notwithstanding section 363 of this title, except to the extent that the court orders otherwise, and until an order for relief in the case, any business of the debtor may continue to operate, and the debtor may continue to use, acquire, or dispose of property as if an involuntary case concerning the debtor had not been commenced.

11 U.S.C. § 303. Involuntary cases

(e) After notice and a hearing, and for cause, the court may require the petitioners under this section to file a bond to indemnify the debtor for such amounts as the court may later allow under subsection (i) of this section.

11 U.S.C. § 303. Involuntary cases

(i) If the court dismisses a petition under this section other than on consent of all petitioners and the debtor, and if the debtor does not waive the right to judgment under this subsection, the court may grant judgment—

(1) against the petitioners and in favor of the debtor for—

(A) costs;

(B) a reasonable attorney's fee; or

(2) against any petitioner that filed the petition in bad faith, for—

(A) any damages proximately caused by such filing; or

(B) punitive damages.

§ 303(d). In particular, creditors lack standing to contest it. The purpose is to avoid collateral litigation at the beginning of the case. If creditors were given standing to answer the petition, many would be tempted to do so for ulterior motives, especially when they have received avoidable transfers that are potentially recoverable by a trustee.

§ 3.02(c)(4) The Gap Period Between the Involuntary Petition and the Order for Relief

In the period between the filing of an involuntary petition and the order for relief or dismissal of the case, the debtor is authorized to continue its business and use and dispose of property as if no bankruptcy were pending, unless the court orders otherwise. § 303(f). General restrictions in Section 363 on the use, sale, or lease of property of the estate, discussed *infra,* at pp. 223–33, are not applicable to the debtor during this gap period because it has not yet been established that the bankruptcy filing is proper. Persons who receive transfers from the debtor during this time are protected to some extent by Section 549(b) against later actions by the trustee to avoid those transfers. See p. 187, *infra.*

When there is substantial risk that the assets of the estate will be jeopardized if the debtor remains in control of them, an interim Chapter 7 trustee or a Chapter 11 trustee may be appointed to preserve those assets during the gap period. §§ 303(g), 1104(a). For cause, the court may require the petitioning creditors to post a bond to indemnify the debtor against the possible damages discussed in the next section. § 303(e).

§ 3.02(c)(5) Dismissal of Involuntary Petition

The consequences of the dismissal of an improperly grounded involuntary petition can be costly to the petitioning creditors. The court may enter judgment against them and in favor of the debtor for attorney's fees and costs. § 303(i)(1). In addition, if the involuntary petition was filed in bad faith, the petitioners may be liable for damages proximately caused by the filing and for punitive damages. § 303(i)(2).

Because preserving the original date of the commencement of

11 U.S.C. § 303. Involuntary cases

(j) Only after notice to all creditors and a hearing may the court dismiss a petition filed under this section—

(1) on the motion of a petitioner;

(2) on consent of all petitioners and the debtor; or

(3) for want of prosecution.

11 U.S.C. § 348. Effect of conversion

(a) Conversion of a case from a case under one chapter of this title to a case under another chapter of this title constitutes an order for relief under the chapter to which the case is converted, but, except as provided in subsections (b) and (c) of this section, does not effect a change in the date of the filing of the petition, the commencement of the case, or the order for relief.

the case is important to the creditor body, restrictions are placed on the voluntary dismissal of an involuntary petition. Thus Section 303(j) requires notice to all creditors, so that they may have an opportunity to intervene or to oppose dismissal, before the court may dismiss an involuntary petition for reasons other than on the merits after a trial. *See also* §§ 707, 1112, 1208, 1307.

§ 3.03 CONVERSION TO ANOTHER CHAPTER

A case may proceed under a given chapter of the Code not only through the filing of an original petition under that chapter but also through the conversion of a case filed under some other chapter. Each of the chapters has a section authorizing conversion to a different chapter if the debtor is eligible for relief under that chapter. §§ 706, 1112, 1208, 1307. Under some specified circumstances the debtor's consent to a conversion is required. The conversion order constitutes an order for relief under the chapter to which the case is converted but does not change the date of the commencement of the case. § 348(a).

11 U.S.C. § 541. Property of the estate

(a) The commencement of a case under section 301, 302, or 303 of this title creates an estate. Such estate is comprised of all the following property, wherever located and by whomever held:

(1) Except as provided in subsections (b) and (c)(2) of this section, all legal or equitable interests of the debtor in property as of the commencement of the case.

(2) All interests of the debtor and the debtor's spouse in community property as of the commencement of the case that is—

(A) under the sole, equal, or joint management and control of the debtor; or

(B) liable for an allowable claim against the debtor, or for both an allowable claim against the debtor and an allowable claim against the debtor's spouse, to the extent that such interest is so liable.

4

The Estate

§ 4.01 PROPERTY OF THE ESTATE

§ 4.01(a) The Estate in General

The filing of a voluntary, involuntary, or joint petition creates an estate, which consists of the various categories of property interests listed in Section 541(a). Initially, the estate includes, subject to two exclusions mentioned later, all the debtor's legal or equitable interests in property as of the commencement of the case. § 541(a)(1). The concept of an "interest" for the purpose of this section is not limited. It may be title or the fee, if in nontechnical terms the debtor owns the property; a limited or life estate; a leasehold interest; a contract right; a lien, if the debtor is a secured creditor of someone else; a mere possessory right; or any other kind of interest that derives from the debtor's relationship to property. In other words, the estate by operation of law takes over the debtor's position with respect to all property, both exempt and nonexempt. An individual debtor, however, is entitled later to exempt from the estate certain property. *See* § 522(b); pp. 299–305, *infra.* Whether the debtor's interest in his books, papers, or other recorded information concerning his financial affairs is an interest in property for the purpose of Section 541(a)(1) is only of academic interest, for ordinarily this financial information must be turned over to the trustee under Section 542(e).

With respect to community property over which the debtor has any legal management power or control or that is subject to claims of the debtor's creditors (or the joint creditors of the husband and wife), the entire interest of both spouses in that property, not merely the debtor's interest, becomes part of the estate of the first spouse to be a debtor under the Code. § 541(a)(2).

123

11 U.S.C. § 541. Property of the estate

(a) The commencement of a case under section 301, 302, or 303 of this title creates an estate. Such estate is comprised of all the following property, wherever located and by whomever held:

(3) Any interest in property that the trustee recovers under section 329(b), 363(n), 543, 550, 553, or 723 of this title.

(4) Any interest in property preserved for the benefit of or ordered transferred to the estate under section 510(c) or 551 of this title.

(5) Any interest in property that would have been property of the estate if such interest had been an interest of the debtor on the date of the filing of the petition, and that the debtor acquires or becomes entitled to acquire within 180 days after such date—

(A) by bequest, devise, or inheritance;

(B) as a result of a property settlement agreement with the debtor's spouse, or of an interlocutory or final divorce decree; or

(C) as a beneficiary of a life insurance policy or of a death benefit plan.

(6) Proceeds, product, offspring, rents, or profits of or from property of the estate, except such as are earnings from services performed by an individual debtor after the commencement of the case.

(7) Any interest in property that the estate acquires after the commencement of the case.

Property recovered or preserved under any of the trustee's avoiding or recovery powers is also part of the estate, § 541(a)(3), (4), as are proceeds, rents, profits, and the like of the estate's property and any property interests the estate itself acquires after the filing of the petition. § 541(a)(6), (7). *United States v. Whiting Pools, Inc.,* 462 U.S. 198 (1983), illustrates how one of the trustee's powers can enhance the property of the estate beyond the interest held by the debtor. The Internal Revenue Service had seized the debtor's assets under a tax lien before the filing of the Chapter 11 case. At the time of the petition, therefore, the debtor, under the nonbankruptcy tax law, had no right to possession of the property, at least not without paying the taxes. Nevertheless, the Supreme Court held that by virtue of the turnover provisions of Section 542(a), the Chapter 11 estate included the possessory interest, although the Code's requirement for "adequate protection" of the tax lien had to be complied with.

Insofar as the estate is the statutory successor to the debtor, the petition as a general proposition marks a date of cleavage. What the debtor has as of the petition date belongs to the estate, together with whatever that property subsequently produces. Any property interests of a corporation or partnership debtor that are generated after bankruptcy typically (although perhaps not invariably) represent a change in the form of estate property or represent proceeds, profits, or the like of the estate's property; thus these interests become part of the estate. When an individual debtor acquires property after the commencement of the case, however, this property, as distinguished from property that the estate produces, belongs to the debtor. With certain exceptions mentioned later, it does not become part of the estate. A specific provision in Section 541(a)(6) emphasizes that an individual's postpetition earnings are not part of the estate.

Sometimes it is difficult to determine what is a prepetition property interest that passes to the estate and what is postpetition property. For example, in *Segal v. Rochelle,* 382 U.S. 375 (1966), decided under the former Bankruptcy Act, the Court held that a tax refund attributable to a tax loss carryback for the year in which the petition was filed was estate property, even though there was no statutory right to the refund on the date of the petition—that is, the

11 U.S.C. § 541. Property of the estate

(c)(1) Except as provided in paragraph (2) of this subsection, an interest of the debtor in property becomes property of the estate under subsection (a)(1), (a)(2), or (a)(5) of this section notwithstanding any provision in an agreement, transfer instrument, or applicable nonbankruptcy law—

(A) that restricts or conditions transfer of such interest by the debtor; or

(B) that is conditioned on the insolvency or financial condition of the debtor, on the commencement of a case under this title, or on the appointment of or taking possession by a trustee in a case under this title or a custodian before such commencement, and that effects or gives an option to effect a forfeiture, modification, or termination of the debtor's interest in property.

11 U.S.C. § 363. Use, sale, or lease of property

(*l*) Subject to the provisions of section 365, the trustee may use, sell, or lease property under subsection (b) or (c) of this section, or a plan under chapter 11, 12, or 13 of this title may provide for the use, sale, or lease of property, notwithstanding any provision in a contract, a lease, or applicable law that is conditioned on the insolvency or financial condition of the debtor, on the commencement of a case under this title concerning the debtor, or on the appointment of or the taking possession by a trustee in a case under this title or a custodian, and that effects, or gives an option to effect, a forfeiture, modification, or termination of the debtor's interest in such property.

refund depended in part on the nonprofitability of the debtor after bankruptcy. As another example, the future renewal commissions of a debtor insurance salesman, which were earned in a sense when the policies were sold before bankruptcy, but which do not accrue to him until old policies are renewed by the insureds after the petition, present a problem of allocating on some fair basis the prepetition and postpetition values. Usually the time required to be spent by the debtor after the petition in continuing to service the policies is an important factor in making the allocation. Arguably, the right of a permanently disabled professional athlete to future salary under a contract providing for compensation whether or not he can play presents a similar problem.

The so-called windfall clause, § 541(a)(5), is an exception to the rule that the petition date is the date of cleavage. Property that the debtor acquires within 180 days after the petition by bequest, devise, or inheritance, as a result of a property settlement or divorce decree, or as a beneficiary under a life insurance policy or death benefit plan becomes part of the estate. Prepetition planning designed to prevent these interests from vesting in the debtor within the six-month period ought to be effective to keep the property out of the estate.

Otherwise, subject to a single exception discussed later, no provision in a contract, in a deed, or in applicable law making the debtor's interest in property nontransferable or conditioning its transferability is effective to prevent that interest from passing into the estate. § 541(c)(1)(A). (Whether a given restriction is enforceable as against the estate when the trustee or debtor in possession subsequently attempts to transfer property out of the estate is a different question; the answer depends in part on the nature of the property and the restriction and on the provisions of Sections 363(f)–(h), (l) and 365(f). See discussion at pp. 229–33, 245–47, *infra.*) Similarly, insolvency, bankruptcy, or financial condition clauses—the so-called forfeiture provisions—are ineffective to keep property out of the estate or to enable another party to modify the nature of the debtor's property interest upon the filing of the petition. § 541(c)(1)(B); *see also* § 363(l).

It bears emphasizing that the estate as statutory successor to the debtor under Section 541(a)(1) takes no greater interest than the

11 U.S.C. § 541. Property of the estate

(a) The commencement of a case under section 301, 302, or 303 of this title creates an estate. Such estate is comprised of all the following property, wherever located and by whomever held:

(1) Except as provided in subsections (b) and (c)(2) of this section, all legal or equitable interests of the debtor in property as of the commencement of the case.

(d) Property in which the debtor holds, as of the commencement of the case, only legal title and not an equitable interest, such as a mortgage secured by real property, or an interest in such a mortgage, sold by the debtor but as to which the debtor retains legal title to service or supervise the servicing of such mortgage or interest, becomes property of the estate under subsection (a)(1) or (2) of this section only to the extent of the debtor's legal title to such property, but not to the extent of any equitable interest in such property that the debtor does not hold.

11 U.S.C. § 541. Property of the estate

(b) Property of the estate does not include—

(1) any power that the debtor may exercise solely for the benefit of an entity other than the debtor;

(2) any interest of the debtor as a lessee under a lease of nonresidential real property that has terminated at the expiration of the stated term of such lease before the commencement of the case under this title, and ceases to include any interest of the debtor as a lessee under a lease of nonresidental real property that has terminated at the expiration of the stated term of such lease during the case.

11 U.S.C. § 541. Property of the estate

(c)(2) A restriction on the transfer of a beneficial interest of the debtor in a trust that is enforceable under applicable nonbankruptcy law is enforceable in a case under this title.

debtor had immediately before bankruptcy. Thus if property is encumbered or subject to liens, the estate's interest under Section 541(a)(1) is only the equity. True, the avoiding powers or some other Code provision may enhance the estate's interest beyond the debtor's; but Section 541(a)(1) does not. If the debtor was the trustee of a trust, the estate's interest under Section 541(a)(1) is the mere legal title (and perhaps the debtor's right to accrued compensation for services rendered as trustee); but no interest in the corpus passes to the estate. *See also* § 541(d). If the debtor has a cause of action that, as of the time of the petition, is barred by the applicable statute of limitations, only an unenforceable claim becomes part of the estate. (If the statute of limitations has not expired before the petition, however, Section 108(a) might extend the period during which the trustee may sue.) If a lease under which the debtor is lessee terminates because of the expiration of its term, either before or after bankruptcy, it follows that the estate's interest in the lease under Section 541(a)(1) likewise expires. An unnecessary 1984 amendment adding Section 541(b)(2) repeated this principle as it applies to leases of nonresidential real estate.

§ 4.01(b) Exclusions from Property of the Estate

There are two exceptions to the rule that all property interests of the debtor at bankruptcy pass to the estate. First, any power that the debtor can exercise only for someone else's benefit — for example, a power of appointment under a will or other instrument that prohibits appointment to the debtor himself or to his estate — is excluded from the estate. § 541(b)(1). The effect is to preclude the trustee from exercising this kind of power. Second, under Section 541(c)(2), a restriction on the transfer of the debtor's beneficial interest in a trust is effective to keep the trust interest out of the Section 541 estate if the restriction is enforceable under applicable nonbankruptcy law. The language of Section 541(c)(2) is broad enough to cover the debtor's interest in an ERISA pension plan, which typically contains nontransferability and nonleviability provisions as provided in the federal statute. However, although the decisions are in conflict, the majority view to date at the appellate court level is that the Section 541(c)(2) exclusion is limited to traditional spendthrift trust interests that are recognized by state law.

E.g., In re Goff, 706 F.2d 574 (5th Cir. 1983); *In re Graham*, 726 F.2d 1268 (8th Cir. 1984). *Contra McLean v. Central States, S. & S. Areas Pen. Fund*, 762 F.2d 1204 (4th Cir. 1985). Since state law typically makes unenforceable a purported spendthrift interest created by the settlor directly or indirectly for his own benefit, it follows under this majority rule that the debtor's interest in an ERISA plan is not excluded from the estate.

§ 4.01(c) What Is a Property Interest and What Law Governs Its Nature?

The general policy of the Code, particularly Section 541(a)(1), is to bring into the estate (with the two exceptions just noted) all interests of the debtor that could conceivably be classified as property, especially any interest that has realizable value. Thus interests in any form of intangible property, as well as tangible property interests, are included within the concept of property as a matter of overriding federal policy. In this context a property right includes a contract right and any kind of cause of action that the debtor has at the time of bankruptcy. If state law, or even non-bankruptcy federal law, were to characterize some interest of value belonging to the debtor as nonproperty, that determination would not be binding in the application of Section 541(a). *See Chicago Bd. of Trade v. Johnson*, 264 U.S. 1 (1924) (case decided under the former Bankruptcy Act).

On the other hand, neither the Code nor the former Bankruptcy Act has attempted in any general way to define for bankruptcy purposes the nature of property interests held by debtors. With perhaps a few exceptions Congress has left the determination of the attributes of a given property interest to nonbankruptcy law, usually state law. *See Butner v. United States*, 440 U.S. 48 (1979). Thus, subject to specific provisions of the Code permitting lien avoidance, a determination of the extent and validity of a lien and, conversely, of the debtor's equity remaining after the lien, turns on applicable state law. Put another way, if under that law the debtor's property interest has a lien or some other interest carved out of it, the part carved out does not become property of the estate.

Chicago Bd. of Trade v. Johnson, supra, illustrates the point. In that case the debtor's membership seat on the Board of Trade could not

be transferred under the governing rules of the Board so long as the debtor was delinquent on his obligations to other members. The Court held that the membership was property — that, in the scheme of the present Code, would become part of the estate under Section 541(a)(1) and (c)(1)(A) — despite applicable state law that classified it as nonproperty. Nevertheless, the limitations on the property interest recognized by that law, namely, the requirement of satisfaction of debts owing to other members of the Board of Trade before the membership could be transferred, bound the trustee in his attempt to sell it.

Similarly, statutes regulating licenses to sell liquor sometimes require that state taxes, and perhaps claims of other specified creditors, must be paid as a condition of transferring the license. These provisions apparently work to limit the bankruptcy estate's property interest. The debtor's interest in the license is viewed as having carved out of it the interests that run in favor of the beneficiary creditors, just as if the state had expressly granted those creditors a statutory lien. *See, e.g., In re Anchorage Int'l Inn, Inc.,* 718 F.2d 1446 (9th Cir. 1983). From a different perspective, however, it would seem that state statutes which define property interests in this manner collide with, and should be overridden by, the federal bankruptcy law priority system and the other provisions of the Code that decree ratable distribution among general unsecured creditors.

§ 4.02 PROTECTION OF PROPERTY OF THE ESTATE; TURNOVER

Upon the filing of the petition, the automatic stay provision, Section 362, opens the bankruptcy umbrella over the property of the estate, protecting it from any unilateral action to interfere with its possession or to enforce any liens or other rights against it. The automatic stay is discussed at pp. 195–223, *infra.* Section 549, discussed at pp. 185–87, *infra,* also serves a protective function. In general, the provision enables the trustee to recover any postpetition transfer of estate property unless it was authorized by the court or by the Code.

To liquidate an estate in Chapter 7 or to proceed meaningfully in cases under the rehabilitation chapters, the trustee or debtor in possession typically must take possession of the property of the

11 U.S.C. § 542. Turnover of property to the estate

(a) Except as provided in subsection (c) or (d) of this section, an entity, other than a custodian, in possession, custody, or control, during the case, of property that the trustee may use, sell, or lease under section 363 of this title, or that the debtor may exempt under section 522 of this title, shall deliver to the trustee, and account for, such property or the value of such property, unless such property is of inconsequential value or benefit to the estate.

(b) Except as provided in subsection (c) or (d) of this section, an entity that owes a debt that is property of the estate and that is matured, payable on demand, or payable on order, shall pay such debt to, or on the order of, the trustee, except to the extent that such debt may be offset under section 553 of this title against a claim against the debtor.

(e) Subject to any applicable privilege, after notice and a hearing, the court may order an attorney, accountant, or other person that holds recorded information, including books, documents, records, and papers, relating to the debtor's property or financial affairs, to turn over or disclose such recorded information to the trustee.

11 U.S.C. § 521. Debtor's duties

The debtor shall —

(4) if a trustee is serving in the case, surrender to the trustee all property of the estate and any recorded information, including books, documents, records, and papers, relating to property of the estate, whether or not immunity is granted under section 344 of this title;

11 U.S.C. § 543. Turnover of property by a custodian

(a) A custodian with knowledge of the commencement of a case under this title concerning the debtor may not make any disbursement from, or take any action in the administration of, property of the debtor, proceeds, product, offspring, rents, or profits of such property, or property of the estate, in the possession, custody, or control of such custodian, except such action as is necessary to preserve such property.

estate. Two sections aid in obtaining assets in the possession of third parties when help from the statute is necessary. Section 542 covers anyone other than a custodian in possession of estate property. "Custodian" is defined in Section 101(10) to mean an assignee for the benefit of creditors, a receiver, or a similar official. A noncustodian must turn over property if it can be used by the trustee under Section 363 or can be exempted by the debtor under Section 522. § 542(a). Since the trustee's right of use is ordinarily conditional on furnishing adequate protection for whatever interest the one in possession may have, see pp. 223–29, *infra,* the turnover also is ordinarily subject to the requirement of providing adequate protection. *United States v. Whiting Pools, Inc.,* 462 U.S. 198 (1983), makes clear that turnover may be appropriately ordered, at least in a Chapter 11 case, even when the debtor itself had no possessory right in the property at the date of the petition and even as against a governmental entity. The *debtor,* however, cannot rely on the adequate protection requirement to resist a turnover under Section 542(a) to his own trustee. He has an independent, unconditional duty under Section 521(4) to turn over property of the estate.

Section 542(e) requires either turnover of the debtor's books, papers, and other recorded financial data or disclosure of the recorded information, subject to any applicable claim of privilege. The Supreme Court has held that the trustee of a debtor corporation has standing to waive the corporation's attorney-client privilege with respect to prepetition communications. *Commodity Futures Trading Comm'n v. Weintraub,* 471 U.S. 343 (1985). The opinion is expressly limited to cases involving a corporate debtor; it leaves open for another day the rule concerning waiver of the privilege in cases in which the debtor is an individual.

One who owes the debtor a matured obligation that becomes part of the estate must pay it to the representative of the estate or to the representative's order, except to the extent that a right of setoff exists under Section 553. § 542(b).

A custodian in possession of estate property may not deal with it after bankruptcy and, ordinarily, must turn it over to the trustee or debtor in possession. § 543(a), (b). Under Section 543, this right to obtain turnover is not limited to property that the trustee may use under Section 363. The issue of adequate protection thus

11 U.S.C. § 543. Turnover of property by a custodian

(b) A custodian shall—

(1) deliver to the trustee any property of the debtor held by or transferred to such custodian, or proceeds, product, offspring, rents, or profits of such property, that is in such custodian's possession, custody, or control on the date that such custodian acquires knowledge of the commencement of the case; and

(2) file an accounting of any property of the debtor, or proceeds, product, offspring, rents, or profits of such property, that, at any time, came into the possession, custody, or control of such custodian.

(d) After notice and hearing, the bankruptcy court—

(1) may excuse compliance with subsection (a), (b), or (c) of this section, if the interests of creditors and, if the debtor is not insolvent, of equity security holders would be better served by permitting a custodian to continue in possession, custody, or control of such property, and

(2) shall excuse compliance with subsections (a) and (b)(1) of this section if the custodian is an assignee for the benefit of the debtor's creditors that was appointed or took possession more than 120 days before the date of the filing of the petition, unless compliance with such subsections is necessary to prevent fraud or injustice.

would not seem to be implicated in a Section 543 turnover proceeding, at least not on the face of things. But in practice the
difference between turnover by noncustodians under Section 542
and by custodians under Section 543 often may be negligible. Under Section 543(d), the court has discretion to permit a custodian
to retain possession of the property if that is in the best interests of
the creditor body. And under Section 363, if the custodian is representing the interests of a secured creditor, that creditor, or perhaps
the custodian on his behalf, can prevent the trustee's use of any
surrendered property unless adequate protection is furnished.
Thus if both the custodian and the secured creditor resist the trustee's Section 543 turnover effort, the issues are likely to be the
same as in a proceeding under Section 542.

A 1984 amendment adding paragraph (2) to Section 543(d) ordinarily excuses an assignee for the benefit of creditors from the
turnover requirement and permits him to proceed with the administration of the assignment estate, if the general assignment was
made more than 120 days before bankruptcy.

§ 4.03 THE TRUSTEE'S AVOIDING POWERS

One of the fundamental policies of bankruptcy is insuring equality
of distribution among creditors. Although the rights of the parties
are fixed for most purposes as of the date the bankruptcy case is
commenced—that is, the Section 541 estate initially consists of the
debtor's interests in property as of the time of the petition—the fair
distribution principle would be undermined if nothing were done
about actions of the debtor or a creditor before bankruptcy that
have the effect of allowing one creditor to obtain an advantage at
the expense of others. For this reason both present and past bankruptcy laws have granted to the trustee or other representative of
the estate the power to avoid certain transactions or transfers occurring before the commencement of the case. Judicial liens or
other preferences and actual or constructive fraudulent or similar
transfers that would disrupt the intended bankruptcy distributional scheme if allowed to stand are avoidable in bankruptcy if
they occurred within specified prepetition periods.

The various avoiding provisions in the Bankruptcy Code refer

11 U.S.C. § 1107. Rights, powers, and duties of debtor in possession

(a) Subject to any limitations on a trustee serving in a case under this chapter, and to such limitations or conditions as the court prescribes, a debtor in possession shall have all the rights, other than the right to compensation under section 330 of this title, and powers, and shall perform all the functions and duties, except the duties specified in sections 1106(a)(2), (3), and (4) of this title, of a trustee serving in a case under this chapter.

11 U.S.C. § 101. Definitions

In this title—

(50) "transfer" means every mode, direct or indirect, absolute or conditional, voluntary or involuntary, of disposing of or parting with property or with an interest in property, including retention of title as a security interest and foreclosure of the debtor's equity of redemption;

to the trustee's power to invalidate or undo transfers or transactions and do not in terms state that a Chapter 11 debtor in possession has the same power. This drafting technique, however, should be understood in light of Section 1107(a), which provides a debtor in possession with nearly all the trustee's rights and powers. References hereafter to the trustee should be understood to include the debtor in possession.

As would be expected, the term "transfer" appears frequently throughout the avoiding power sections. It is broadly defined in Section 101(50) to cover not only outright dispositions—such as when the debtor conveys Blackacre, transfers the ownership of an automobile, or pays a bill—but also the creation of liens or lesser interests in property—such as when the debtor mortgages his home, pledges stock, or leases or subleases space in a building to a tenant. Moreover, the term includes not only the debtor's voluntary acts but also transfers that are involuntary from the debtor's standpoint, such as when a creditor obtains an attachment or other judicial lien on the debtor's property, a consignor or seller of goods repossesses or reclaims them through self-help, or the debtor's secured creditor causes a foreclosure sale.

Because the avoiding powers are cumulative, it is unnecessary for the trustee to elect a particular one. Sometimes one or more of the provisions will enable the trustee to avoid a transfer; at other times none will work. The discussion that follows focuses on the avoiding power provisions one by one. When a section under consideration is said not to enable the trustee to avoid a given transfer, the reader should nevertheless keep in mind that the transfer in question might well be subject to avoidance under a different avoiding power.

§ 4.03(a) The So-called "Strong-arm Clause": The Trustee as a Judicial Lien Creditor and Bona Fide Purchaser of Real Estate

Section 544(a), sometimes referred to as the "strong-arm clause," provides the trustee with three different hypothetical standings. Probably the most frequently used provision is Section 544(a)(1), which gives the trustee the status and power of a hypothetical judicial lien creditor, one who hypothetically extends credit to the

11 U.S.C. § 544. Trustee as lien creditor and as successor to certain creditors and purchasers

(a) The trustee shall have, as of the commencement of the case, and without regard to any knowledge of the trustee or of any creditor, the rights and powers of, or may avoid any transfer of property of the debtor or any obligation incurred by the debtor that is voidable by—

(1) a creditor that extends credit to the debtor at the time of the commencement of the case, and that obtains, at such time and with respect to such credit, a judicial lien on all property on which a creditor on a simple contract could have obtained such a judicial lien, whether or not such a creditor exists;

(2) a creditor that extends credit to the debtor at the time of the commencement of the case, and obtains, at such time and with respect to such credit, an execution against the debtor that is returned unsatisfied at such time, whether or not such a creditor exists;

U.C.C. § 9-301. Persons Who Take Priority Over Unperfected Security Interests; Rights of "Lien Creditor"

(1) Except as otherwise provided in subsection (2), an unperfected security interest is subordinate to the rights of

(b) a person who becomes a lien creditor before the security interest is perfected;

debtor at the time of the filing of the petition and who, as of the same moment, hypothetically obtains a judicial lien on all property (in which the debtor has any interest) that such a creditor could have reached. The advantage of this standing to the trustee—that is, the substantive content of Section 544(a)(1)—is not found in the Bankruptcy Code. It derives from nonbankruptcy law, usually a state statute, that governs creditors' rights in the context of the transfer in question.[1]

Some examples of nonbankruptcy statutes will help illustrate the application of the strong-arm clause. Under Section 9-301(1)(b) of the Uniform Commercial Code, an Article 9 security interest, though valid as between the debtor and the secured party, is nevertheless junior to the rights of a creditor who obtains a judicial lien on the collateral before the security interest is perfected. Perfection under Article 9 usually occurs by the secured party's filing a financing statement or taking possession of the collateral. If perfection occurs before the judicial lien is obtained, no matter how long perfection was delayed, the secured party prevails over the judicial lien creditor.

With this in mind consider the debtor who borrows money from a bank, giving a security interest in his equipment to secure the loan. The bank fails to perfect before the debtor files bankruptcy. The trustee may invalidate the security interest under Section 544(a)(1), for a creditor who hypothetically extended credit and obtained a judicial lien on the equipment at the time of the petition— the security interest being then unperfected—would defeat the security interest under U.C.C. § 9-301(1)(b). But if the secured party filed a financing statement or otherwise perfected at any time before bankruptcy, even just before, the trustee would lose insofar as Section 544(a)(1) is concerned. On these facts the trustee's hypothetical judicial lien would not prime, or be treated as senior to, the perfected security interest under U.C.C. § 9-301(1)(b).

---

[1]Section 544(a)(2) also gives the trustee, as of the time of the petition, the status of a hypothetical creditor holding an execution returned unsatisfied. In most instances this type of creditor would have no greater rights than a judgment lien or execution lien creditor—rights that the trustee receives as a result of the Section 544(a)(1) ideal judicial lien. However, if in a given context a creditor with an execution returned unsatisfied would have more clout than one with a judicial lien, the trustee could then invoke Section 544(a)(2).

U.C.C. § 6-105. Notice to Creditors

In addition to the requirements of the preceding section, any bulk transfer subject to this Article except one made by auction sale (Section 6-108) is ineffective against any creditor of the transferor unless at least ten days before he takes possession of the goods or pays for them, whichever happens first, the transferee gives notice of the transfer in the manner and to the persons hereafter provided (Section 6-107).

U.C.C. § 6-109. What Creditors Protected; [Credit for Payment to Particular Creditors]

(1) The creditors of the transferor mentioned in this Article are those holding claims based on transactions or events occurring before the bulk transfer, but creditors who become such after notice to creditors is given (Sections 6-105 and 6-107) are not entitled to notice.

Consider another kind of statute, one that gives a creditor powers of avoidance depending upon when he extended credit to the debtor, rather than a U.C.C. Article 9 type of statute that gives a creditor rights depending on the time he obtained a judicial lien. Article 6 of the Uniform Commercial Code requires that certain advance notice be given for bulk transfer transactions within the coverage of that Article. If the notice requirements are not met, the transfer is voidable by any creditor of the transferor who extended credit before the bulk transfer transaction took place. (Those who extend credit to the transferor subsequent to the bulk transfer have no rights under Article 6.) U.C.C. §§ 6-105, 6-109. At any time before the statute of limitations bars suit, a creditor within the protected class may, in the case of a defective bulk transfer, pursue the goods into the hands of the transferee and obtain a judicial lien on them to satisfy his claim. If the transferee disposed of the goods, the creditor may obtain a money judgment against him for their value.

But the trustee cannot use Section 544(a)(1) to avoid a defective bulk transfer. Article 6 gives rights only to creditors who extended credit at a point in time that preceded bankruptcy—that is, before the bulk transfer occurred. Under the strong-arm clause the trustee hypothetically extends credit too late—that is, at bankruptcy. Thus Section 544(a)(1) will work for the trustee in the context of a statute protecting creditors based on the time of their credit extension only in the rare situation when the statute gives rights to subsequent creditors—that is, those who extend credit after the challenged transfer.

So far, the illustrations have involved personal property transfers. Consider now a defective land transaction—for example, the debtor sells Blackacre to a buyer or mortgages it to a lender, and the transferee fails to record the deed or mortgage before bankruptcy occurs. How the trustee fares under Section 544(a)(1) depends upon the applicable recording statute. In some states a judgment lien or some other kind of judicial lien would prevail over an unrecorded land instrument; in those states the trustee could avoid the transfer under Section 544(a)(1). In other states unrecorded land transfers are valid as against subsequent judicial liens; the statutes in these states may protect, for example, bona fide pur-

11 U.S.C. § 544. Trustee as lien creditor and as successor to certain creditors and purchasers

(a) The trustee shall have, as of the commencement of the case, and without regard to any knowledge of the trustee or of any creditor, the rights and powers of, or may avoid any transfer of property of the debtor or any obligation incurred by the debtor that is voidable by—

(3) a bona fide purchaser of real property, other than fixtures, from the debtor, against whom applicable law permits such transfer to be perfected, that obtains the status of a bona fide purchaser and has perfected such transfer at the time of the commencement of the case, whether or not such a purchaser exists.

chasers or encumbrancers for value, but they do not protect or give rights to judicial lienors. In these states Section 544(a)(1) will not work for the trustee.

In an attempt to achieve the same avoidance result in all states when an unrecorded land transfer is involved, the drafters added Section 544(a)(3) to the Code in 1978. It gives the trustee, as of the time of the petition, the status of a hypothetical bona fide purchaser of the debtor's real estate, thus enabling the trustee to invoke the protection of land recording statutes even in states where judicial lienors are not protected. Again, because of the timing principle of the section, if recordation occurs at any point before bankruptcy, Section 544(a)(3) will not operate to avoid the transfer.

Now suppose the relevant land recording statute is a so-called race-notice statute, which requires a purchaser of real estate, in order to prevail over an earlier unrecorded transfer, to be not only bona fide but also the first to record. Section 544(a)(3) enables the trustee to satisfy this type of requirement, for he is, hypothetically, a purchaser who has perfected the debtor's hypothetical transfer to him.

One potential ambiguity in Section 544(a)(3) has been clarified by case law. Suppose that although a real estate transfer made by the debtor has never been recorded, the transferee is in possession of the property. Under state law this circumstance would ordinarily put a potential actual purchaser from the debtor on constructive notice of the possessor's rights. Does either the trustee's hypothetical bona fide purchaser status or the reference in the lead-in clause of Section 544(a) to the immateriality of the trustee's actual knowledge mean that his status under Section 544(a)(3) is free of the constructive or inquiry notice that an actual purchaser would have, thus enabling the trustee to invalidate the unrecorded transfer to a transferee in possession? The courts have ruled against the trustee on this point. The trustee's status under Section 544(a)(3) is construed to be that of a hypothetical purchaser with whatever constructive or inquiry notice state law would impute from the actual facts of the transaction. *E.g., McCannon v. Marston,* 679 F.2d 13 (3d Cir. 1982).

Consider now the application of the strong-arm clause in the context of a statute that permits retroactive perfection—for example, Article 9 of the Uniform Commercial Code as it applies to

U.C.C. § 9-301. Persons Who Take Priority Over Unperfected Security Interests; Rights of "Lien Creditor"

(2) If the secured party files with respect to a purchase money security interest before or within ten days after the debtor receives possession of the collateral, he takes priority over the rights of a transferee in bulk or of a lien creditor which arise between the time the security interest attaches and the time of filing.

11 U.S.C. § 546. Limitations on avoiding powers

(b) The rights and powers of a trustee under sections 544, 545, and 549 of this title are subject to any generally applicable law that permits perfection of an interest in property to be effective against an entity that acquires rights in such property before the date of such perfection. If such law requires seizure of such property or commencement of an action to accomplish such perfection, and such property has not been seized or such action has not been commenced before the date of the filing of the petition, such interest in such property shall be perfected by notice within the time fixed by such law for such seizure or commencement.

purchase-money security interests. Although, as has been noted, a creditor who obtains a judicial lien on collateral before perfection of a security interest in it ordinarily primes the security interest, there is a special rule for a purchase-money security interest. This kind of security interest will prevail over a judicial lien that attaches during the interim between the creation of the security interest and its perfection, if perfection occurs within ten days after the debtor receives possession of the collateral. U.C.C. § 9-301(2). In other words, perfection will relate back so as to defeat the intervening judicial lien as long as perfection is accomplished within the ten-day grace period.

How does Section 544(a) interact with this kind of retroactive perfection? Consider a seller of goods to the debtor who retains a security interest to secure the price. Delivery of the goods occurs two days before bankruptcy, but the financing statement is not filed until five days after the petition. In the interim the trustee becomes a hypothetical judicial lien creditor under Section 544(a)(1). But what rights flow from this status? Conceptually, under U.C.C. § 9-301(2), the trustee's judicial lien will be primed, or defeated, by the subsequent perfection of the purchase-money security interest, as long as that perfection occurs within the ten-day grace period. The possibility of retroactive defeat in these circumstances is built into the nature of the strong-arm clause itself, since, as has been seen, the clause looks to applicable non-bankruptcy law (here U.C.C. § 9-301(2)) for its substantive content. The Code makes the same point a second time, however. Section 546(b) states that the trustee's Section 544 avoiding power (as well as certain other avoiding powers) is limited by the possibility of an effective retroactive perfection under an applicable statute that so permits. An accommodating provision is found in an exception to the automatic stay, Section 362(b)(3), so that without seeking relief from the stay a transferee may perfect a transfer after bankruptcy when perfection will have such retroactive effect.

Finally, it should be emphasized that neither the strong-arm clause nor Section 544(b), discussed next, enables the trustee of a debtor corporation to pierce the corporate veil and to enforce alter ego liability against a corporate principal (or reach his personal assets that never belonged to the debtor) even if creditors of the

11 U.S.C. § 544. Trustee as lien creditor and as successor to certain creditors and purchasers

(b) The trustee may avoid any transfer of an interest of the debtor in property or any obligation incurred by the debtor that is voidable under applicable law by a creditor holding an unsecured claim that is allowable under section 502 of this title or that is not allowable only under section 502(e) of this title.

corporation themselves have such a cause of action. They must bring that lawsuit in their own right. In other words, the strong-arm clause impacts only property in which the debtor has, or at one time had, some interest, not property of a third party who for some reason may be liable to the debtor's creditors (unless that property was transferred by the debtor). *In re Ozark Restaurant Equipment Co., Inc.*, 816 F.2d 1222 (8th Cir. 1987). *But cf. Koch Refining v. Farmers Union Cent. Exchange, Inc.*, 831 F.2d 1339 (7th Cir. 1987); *In re S.I. Acquisition, Inc.*, 817 F.2d 1142 (5th Cir. 1987).

§ 4.03(b) The Trustee as Successor to the Rights of Creditors

Under Section 544(b), the trustee may avoid any transfer that is subject to avoidance by any actual creditor with an allowable unsecured claim. Like the strong-arm clause, Section 544(b) looks to some nonbankruptcy law for its substantive content. But unlike the trustee's status under the strong-arm clause, the trustee's Section 544(b) status is not derived hypothetically. Rather, the trustee must plead and prove the identity and qualifications of an actual creditor holding an allowable unsecured claim who can avoid the transfer in question under nonbankruptcy law.

What does Section 544(b) add to the trustee's arsenal that the hypothetical strong-arm status has not already provided? The answer is that the hypothetical creditor under the strong-arm clause is tied to the date of bankruptcy, whereas an actual unsecured creditor may have greater rights as a result of having extended credit at an earlier date.

Consider again the defective bulk transfer illustration in which the strong-arm clause would not work for the trustee because his hypothetical credit extension came too late. See *supra*, p. 143. Suppose the trustee can find among the claims of the debtor's present unsecured creditors one or more that arose from a credit extension to the debtor before the bulk transfer occurred. A creditor holding such a claim could avoid the bulk transfer under Article 6; accordingly, the trustee can invoke Section 544(b) to the same end.

Section 4 of the Uniform Fraudulent Conveyance Act ("U.F.C.A.") and Section 5(a) of the Uniform Fraudulent Transfer

U.F.C.A. § 4. Conveyances by insolvent

Every conveyance made and every obligation incurred by a person who is or will be thereby rendered insolvent is fraudulent as to creditors without regard to his actual intent if the conveyance is made or the obligation is incurred without a fair consideration.

U.F.T.A. § 5. Transfers Fraudulent as to Present Creditors

(a) A transfer made or obligation incurred by a debtor is fraudulent as to a creditor whose claim arose before the transfer was made or to the obligation was incurred if the debtor made the transfer or incurred the obligation without receiving a reasonably equivalent value in exchange for the transfer or obligation and the debtor was insolvent at that time or the debtor became insolvent as a result of the transfer or obligation.

Act ("U.F.T.A.") provide a similar opportunity. Transfers made by an insolvent debtor for less than fair consideration (U.F.C.A.) or without receipt of reasonably equivalent value (U.F.T.A.) are fraudulent as against, and voidable by, creditors with claims existing at the time of the transfer; creditors who extended credit after the transfer are not similarly protected. If the trustee can find a creditor who falls within the protected class and who still has his allowable unsecured claim at the date of the bankruptcy petition, the Section 544(b) avoiding power is triggered and may enable a reachback of several years to get at transfers too old to be avoided under the trustee's own Section 548 fraudulent transfer avoiding power. See pp. 171–75, *infra*. Section 548 permits avoidance only of fraudulent transfers made within one year before the petition. The sole time limit on the Section 544(b) reachback, however, is the statute of limitations applicable to the claim of the actual creditor relied upon by the trustee to avoid the transfer under Section 4 of the U.F.C.A. or Section 5(a) of the U.F.T.A. Moreover, a trustee who sues under Section 544(b) and state fraudulent transfer law enjoys the benefit of state rules on presumptions, burden of proof, and the like, which may be more favorable than those applicable to a Section 548 cause of action.

The trustee can invoke the avoiding power even though the creditor who could trigger Section 544(b) is uncooperative and refuses to file a proof of claim. The triggering event is the existence of the appropriate claim. All that is required is its allowability (most claims are allowable, *see* § 502); it is not necessary that a proof of claim be actually filed or that the claim be actually allowed. However, the trustee cannot rely on a secured or lien creditor under Section 544(b); only an unsecured claim will do. Thus the trustee cannot invoke Section 544(b) in a U.C.C. Article 9 context if perfection of the security interest under attack occurred before bankruptcy, for only a creditor who obtained a judicial lien before perfection can defeat the security interest. Such a lien creditor, if one actually exists, would be secured, whereas Section 544(b) requires an unsecured claim.

The amount of the trustee's recovery under Section 544(b) can be illustrated by going back to the defective bulk transfer previously discussed. Suppose a debtor within the coverage of Article 6

makes a bulk sale of $100,000 of inventory and the buyer fails to give proper notice. The debtor promptly pays virtually all preexisting creditors, however (perhaps from the sale proceeds), but innocently fails to pay one such creditor holding a $500 claim. When bankruptcy occurs several months later, the creditors then involved had extended their credit subsequent to the bulk transfer, except for the creditor with the still unpaid $500 claim.

Outside of bankruptcy, the transferee would have been exposed only to the extent of the $500, since that is the only claim protected by Article 6. But the Supreme Court, in construing the provision comparable to Section 544(b) in the former Bankruptcy Act, held more than 50 years ago in *Moore v. Bay*, 284 U.S. 4 (1931), that when this avoiding power is triggered by any claim, the trustee may avoid the transfer in its entirety; he is not limited by the amount of the claim on which he relies. In other words, the trustee's judgment in the illustration would be for a return of all the inventory or its $100,000 value. *Moore v. Bay* also held that what the trustee recovers is to be treated like any other asset of the estate, to be distributed pro rata to all creditors under the bankruptcy distributional scheme; the creditor whose claim triggered the recovery receives no special treatment in this regard. Although the opinion of the Court was cryptic, later case law and legal commentary made clear that the case stands for the foregoing propositions. There has been much criticism of *Moore v. Bay* and much debate throughout the legislative process about whether it should be carried forward into the current bankruptcy law. Nevertheless, the legislative history, as well as the similarity between the language in Section 544(b) and in its predecessor section, leaves no room for doubt that the principles of *Moore v. Bay* were incorporated into the 1978 Bankruptcy Code.

§ 4.03(c) Preferences

Perhaps the most important and frequently used avoiding power in the trustee's arsenal is the preference section, Section 547, which is directly designed to achieve the policy of fostering equality of distribution among the creditors of an insolvent debtor—certainly one of bankruptcy's primary goals. The concept of a preference is technical and refined in several respects: the basic definition of a

11 U.S.C. § 547. Preferences

(b) Except as provided in subsection (c) of this section, the trustee may avoid any transfer of an interest of the debtor in property—

(1) to or for the benefit of a creditor;

(2) for or on account of an antecedent debt owed by the debtor before such transfer was made;

(3) made while the debtor was insolvent;

(4) made—

(A) on or within 90 days before the date of the filing of the petition; or

(B) between ninety days and one year before the date of the filing of the petition, if such creditor at the time of such transfer was an insider;

(5) that enables such creditor to receive more than such creditor would receive if—

(A) the case were a case under chapter 7 of this title;

(B) the transfer had not been made; and

(C) such creditor received payment of such debt to the extent provided by the provisions of this title.

(g) For the purposes of this section, the trustee has the burden of proving the avoidability of a transfer under subsection (b) of this section, and the creditor or party in interest against whom recovery or avoidance is sought has the burden of proving the nonavoidability of a transfer under subsection (c) of this section.

11 U.S.C. § 101. Definitions

In this title—

(50) "transfer" means every mode, direct or indirect, absolute or conditional, voluntary or involuntary, of disposing of or parting with property or with an interest in property, including retention of title as a security interest and foreclosure of the debtor's equity of redemption;

preference, § 547(b); the dating of the transfer, § 547(e); and the various exceptions to avoidability, § 547(c).

A preference, as defined by Section 547(b), consists of several elements, all of which must exist: (A) a transfer, (B) of the debtor's property, (C) to or for the benefit of a creditor, (D) for or on account of an antecedent debt, (E) made while the debtor was insolvent, (F) within 90 days before bankruptcy (or within one year before the petition in an "insider" situation), and (G) the effect of which was to give the creditor more than he would have otherwise received in a Chapter 7 distribution. (The trustee has the burden of proof with respect to the Section 547(b) elements. § 547(g)).

Courts and commentators sometimes talk of depletion or diminution of the estate as being an element of a preference. (In this context "estate" refers to the debtor's assets available for distribution.) Technically, however, depletion of the estate is not a statutory requirement. When it is concluded that a transfer is nonpreferential because there was no depletion, the more technically correct reason is that one or more of the specified elements was missing—for example, the property that was transferred did not belong to the debtor, or the transfer was one for present rather than antecedent consideration, or the recipient was fully secured and thus did not receive more than his entitlement under Chapter 7.

§ 4.03(c)(1) Statutory Elements of a Preference

§ 4.03(c)(1)(A) *Transfer.* As noted earlier at p. 139, the definition of "transfer" in Section 101(50) is broad; it covers virtually every means of disposing of property or of an interest in property, voluntarily or involuntarily. Thus, so far as this element is concerned, judicial liens and security interests as well as outright dispositions, such as the payment of money by cash or check, are among the potentially preferential transfers.

§ 4.03(c)(1)(B) *Debtor's Property.* If a third party, even one closely related to the debtor, satisfies an obligation of the debtor, no preference results so long as the debtor's property is not indirectly transferred by reimbursement or the securing of the third party. Similarly, if a corporate debtor issues its own stock to a creditor,

11 U.S.C. § 101. Definitions

In this title—

(9) "creditor" means —

(A) entity that has a claim against the debtor that arose at the time of or before the order for relief concerning the debtor;

(B) entity that has a claim against the estate of a kind specified in section 348(d), 502(f), 502(g), 502(h) or 502(i) of this title; or

(C) entity that has a community claim;

11 U.S.C. § 101. Definitions

In this title—

(31) "insolvent" means—

(A) with reference to an entity other than a partnership, financial condition such that the sum of such entity's debts is greater than all of such entity's property, at a fair valuation, exclusive of—

(i) property transferred, concealed, or removed with intent to hinder, delay, or defraud such entity's creditors; and

(ii) property that may be exempted from property of the estate under section 522 of this title; and

(B) with reference to a partnership, financial condition such that the sum of such partnership's debts is greater than the aggregate of, at a fair valuation—

(i) all of such partnership's property, exclusive of property of the kind specified in subparagraph (A)(i) of this paragraph; and

(ii) the sum of the excess of the value of each general partner's nonpartnership property, exclusive of property of the kind specified in subparagraph (A) of this paragraph, over such partner's nonpartnership debts;

there has been no transfer of the debtor's property and so no preference; the debtor's pool of assets available to satisfy its creditors is not changed or diminished by the issuance or dilution of the outstanding shares. *KDI v. Former Shareholders of Labtron of America*, 536 F.2d 1146 (6th Cir. 1976) (case decided under Bankruptcy Act).

§ 4.03(c)(1)(C) To or for the Benefit of a Creditor. A creditor is someone who holds a prepetition claim against the debtor. § 101(9). (Technically, one who holds a claim arising postpetition but before the order for relief is also defined as a "creditor," but a transfer on account of such a claim cannot be a preference since, as will be seen, the transfer under the preference section must occur prepetition.) The transferee or recipient need not be a creditor, although he usually is. For example, a creditor may direct the debtor to pay the amount owed to someone else, in which event the payment is for the benefit of the creditor although not "to" the creditor. More commonly, a debtor may pay or secure an obligation that has been guaranteed by a third party or upon which there is a co-obligor. In this situation the recipient of the payment or security interest may be a creditor, and the transfer to the recipient may be, or for some reason may not be, a preference. But this transfer is also potentially a preference as to the guarantor or co-obligor: Since the transfer relieves the guarantor or co-obligor of personal liability, it is obviously for that person's benefit; moreover, the guarantor or co-obligor is a "creditor" because he has a contingent claim against the debtor—that is, a claim for reimbursement if he satisfies an obligation for which the debtor is primarily or jointly liable.

§ 4.03(c)(1)(D) Antecedent Debt. Transfers for contemporaneous or future consideration are not preferential because they are not for antecedent debt. "Antecedent" is not a defined term, but it is generally understood to mean that the obligation being paid or secured by the transfer existed prior to the time the transfer was made. Even a short credit extension, however, will satisfy the antecedent debt element. Thus the debtor's repayment of an unsecured loan made to him earlier on the same day is potentially preferential. *National City Bank v. Hotchkiss*, 231 U.S. 50 (1913).

§ 4.03(c)(1)(E) Insolvency. The debtor must be insolvent at the time of the transfer, a financial condition defined in Section

11 U.S.C. § 547. Preferences

(f) For the purposes of this section, the debtor is presumed to have been insolvent on and during the 90 days immediately preceding the date of the filing of the petition.

11 U.S.C. § 101. Definitions

In this title—

(30) "insider" includes—

(A) if the debtor is an individual—

(i) relative of the debtor or of a general partner of the debtor;

(ii) partnership in which the debtor is a general partner;

(iii) general partner of the debtor; or

(iv) corporation of which the debtor is a director, officer, or person in control;

(B) if the debtor is a corporation—

(i) director of the debtor;

(ii) officer of the debtor;

(iii) person in control of the debtor;

(iv) partnership in which the debtor is a general partner;

(v) general partner of the debtor; or

(vi) relative of a general partner, director, officer, or person in control of the debtor;

(C) if the debtor is a partnership—

(i) general partner in the debtor;

(ii) relative of a general partner in, general partner of, or person in control of the debtor;

(iii) partnership in which the debtor is a general partner;

(iv) general partner of the debtor; or

(v) person in control of the debtor;

(D) if the debtor is a municipality, elected official of the debtor or relative of an elected official of the debtor;

(E) affiliate, or insider of an affiliate as if such affiliate were the debtor; and

(F) managing agent of the debtor;

101(31) as involving an excess of liabilities over assets at a fair valuation. The debtor, however, is presumed to be insolvent during the 90-day period preceding bankruptcy. § 547(f). This important presumption means that the burden of going forward with evidence (although not the burden of proof or the risk of nonpersuasion) is shifted to the defendant in the trustee's preference action. *See* FED. R. EVID. 301. If no evidence concerning solvency or insolvency is presented, the trustee will prevail on this element.

§ *4.03(c)(1)(F)* *Within 90 Days Preceding Bankruptcy (or Within One Year in the Case of an "Insider" Preference).* In the ordinary case the transfer must have occurred within 90 days before the petition, but the reachback is one year if the transferee or the creditor who benefited from the transfer was an "insider," a broadly inclusive term under Section 101(30). If an insider transfer occurred more than 90 days before the petition, however, the trustee in an action to avoid it cannot rely on the Section 547(f) presumption of insolvency.

§ *4.03(c)(1)(G)* *The Preferential Effect of the Transfer.* The transfer must have the effect of giving the creditor more than he otherwise would be entitled to in a Chapter 7 liquidation case. If it does not have this effect, the transfer does not violate the policy behind the preference concept of achieving an equitable distribution among all creditors. Thus payment to a fully and validly secured creditor is nonpreferential, for such a creditor would be entitled to full satisfaction out of the proceeds of his collateral in Chapter 7. Similarly, payment to or the securing of a creditor holding a Section 507(a) priority claim is nonpreferential if the estate's assets in Chapter 7 would be sufficient to pay in full other claimants in the same priority class and in all higher classes. But a payment to a partially secured creditor — that is, one whose collateral lacks sufficient value to fully cover the claim — is potentially preferential to the extent that the payment is applied to the unsecured deficiency, as it almost always would be. *Drabkin v. A.I. Credit Corp.,* 800 F.2d 1153 (D.C. Cir. 1986) (payment to partially secured creditor is conclusively presumed to be applied first to unsecured portion of debt). And payment to a "secured" creditor whose security interest is, for some reason, subject to invalidation in bankruptcy is preferential because such a creditor is in reality unsecured in Chapter 7.

Finally, as a matter of arithmetic, a transfer to a general unse-

11 U.S.C. § 547. Preferences

(e)(1) For the purposes of this section —

(A) a transfer of real property other than fixtures, but including the interest of a seller or purchaser under a contract for the sale of real property, is perfected when a bona fide purchaser of such property from the debtor against whom applicable law permits such transfer to be perfected cannot acquire an interest that is superior to the interest of the transferee; and

(B) a transfer of a fixture or property other than real property is perfected when a creditor on a simple contract cannot acquire a judicial lien that is superior to the interest of the transferee.

(2) For the purposes of this section, except as provided in paragraph (3) of this subsection, a transfer is made —

(A) at the time such transfer takes effect between the transferor and the transferee, if such transfer is perfected at, or within 10 days after, such time;

(B) at the time such transfer is perfected, if such transfer is perfected after such 10 days; or

(C) immediately before the date of the filing of the petition, if such transfer is not perfected at the later of—

(i) the commencement of the case; or

(ii) 10 days after such transfer takes effect between the transferor and the transferee.

(3) For the purposes of this section, a transfer is not made until the debtor has acquired rights in the property transferred.

cured creditor ordinarily satisfies the preferential-effect element unless the debtor's estate would turn out to be solvent in Chapter 7 — for even a partial payment to a nonpriority creditor satisfies 100 per cent of that part of his claim. When this payment is added to the creditor's Chapter 7 distributive share on the remaining balance of the claim, the total effect is to give him more than he otherwise would have received absent the partial payment. *See Palmer Clay Prods. Co. v. Brown,* 297 U.S. 227 (1936).

§ 4.03(c)(2) The Timing Rules

Application of the various elements of a Section 547(b) preference is complicated by the need to safeguard against so-called secret transfers, including transfers by way of equitable liens. Otherwise, the creditors might not reasonably learn of an offending transfer before the 90-day or one-year preference period expired, with a resulting frustration of the bankruptcy goal of fair distribution.

For this reason bankruptcy statutes over the years have had certain prophylactic rules providing in one way or another that the transfer for preference purposes is deemed to occur, not necessarily when it took place in fact, but when it became open and notorious — that is, when other creditors were likely to be able to discover it. The drafting technique in recent times has been to relate the dating of the transfer to the concept of "perfection" of the transfer as against third parties.

Thus Section 547(e)(1) begins by stating what is meant by perfection: A transfer of real estate is perfected when a subsequent bona fide purchaser from the debtor can no longer defeat the rights of the transferee. Normally, such perfection occurs at the time the land transfer instrument is recorded. A transfer of personal property or fixtures is perfected when a creditor of the debtor can no longer obtain a judicial lien that primes the transferee's interest. In the context of a transfer by way of an Article 9 security interest, such perfection ordinarily occurs when a financing statement is filed or when the secured party takes possession of the collateral.

Next, Section 547(e)(2) provides that a transfer is deemed to occur at the time it takes place between the debtor and the transferee, so long as the perfection step is taken not later than ten days

11 U.S.C. § 547. Preferences

(e)(1) For the purposes of this section —

(A) a transfer of real property other than fixtures, but including the interest of a seller or purchaser under a contract for the sale of real property, is perfected when a bona fide purchaser of such property from the debtor against whom applicable law permits such transfer to be perfected cannot acquire an interest that is superior to the interest of the transferee; and

(B) a transfer of a fixture or property other than real property is perfected when a creditor on a simple contract cannot acquire a judicial lien that is superior to the interest of the transferee.

(2) For the purposes of this section, except as provided in paragraph (3) of this subsection, a transfer is made —

(A) at the time such transfer takes effect between the transferor and the transferee, if such transfer is perfected at, or within 10 days after, such time;

(B) at the time such transfer is perfected, if such transfer is perfected after such 10 days; or

(C) immediately before the date of the filing of the petition, if such transfer is not perfected at the later of —

(i) the commencement of the case; or

(ii) 10 days after such transfer takes effect between the transferor and the transferee.

(3) For the purposes of this section, a transfer is not made until the debtor has acquired rights in the property transferred.

thereafter. If applicable law requires no perfection step other than making the transfer itself, the transfer occurs when it takes place between the debtor and the transferee. If perfection is delayed beyond the ten-day grace period, the transfer is deemed to occur at perfection; if a transfer remains unperfected at the time of the petition, it dates as of a point immediately before bankruptcy.

Finally, Section 547(e)(3) provides that regardless of non-bankruptcy law, a transfer does not occur for the purpose of the preference section until the debtor has acquired rights in the property transferred. This provision was designed to overrule the rationale of certain decisions under the former Bankruptcy Act that, in an Article 9 security interest context, had dated the transfer — a floating lien on the debtor's receivables — from the time of its perfection step, the filing of a financing statement many months before bankruptcy, although the after-acquired collateral had not come into existence until well within the preference period. *E.g.,* *DuBay v. Williams,* 417 F.2d 1277 (9th Cir. 1969).

The foregoing rules for dating the transfer, and their capacity for converting factually nonpreferential transactions into preferential transfers, may be illustrated by an example. Suppose that two years before bankruptcy a solvent debtor borrowed money from a lender, concurrently granting a security interest in his equipment to secure the loan. The lender through oversight failed to perfect the security interest until shortly before bankruptcy, when a financing statement was filed.

As noted before, the trustee cannot invoke the strong-arm clause to defeat this security interest because it was perfected before the time of the petition. Nor will Section 544(b) invalidate the lien because no actual unsecured creditor exists who could do so. The transfer, however, is an avoidable preference under Section 547, despite the fact that, without the artificial timing rules, three elements of a preference would be lacking: In reality, the security interest was granted for present, not antecedent, consideration; the debtor was not then insolvent; and the transaction occurred outside the preference period. But when the transfer is deemed to occur at the point of perfection (since perfection was delayed beyond the 10-day grace period), it falls within the 90 days preceding bankruptcy. Moreover, at this point the debtor is no doubt insol-

11 U.S.C. § 547. Preferences

(g) For the purposes of this section, the trustee has the burden of proving the avoidability of a transfer under subsection (b) of this section, and the creditor or party in interest against whom recovery or avoidance is sought has the burden of proving the nonavoidability of a transfer under subsection (c) of this section.

11 U.S.C. § 547. Preferences

(c) The trustee may not avoid under this section a transfer—

(1) to the extent that such transfer was—

(A) intended by the debtor and the creditor to or for whose benefit such transfer was made to be a contemporaneous exchange for new value given to the debtor; and

(B) in fact a substantially contemporaneous exchange;

vent, or at least is presumed so by Section 547(f), and the loan obligation incurred two years previously has now become artificially antecedent to the security interest transfer that secures it.

The moral is that belated perfection can make avoidable technical preferences out of transactions that are not factually preferential. It should be further understood that the prophylactic timing rules aimed at smoking out secret transfers can have an impact even when an unperfected transfer is notorious. In the last illustration, widespread knowledge among the debtor's other creditors of the granting of the security interest would not have saved it from avoidance under Section 547.

§ 4.03(c)(3) Exceptions to Preference Avoidance

The scope of the Section 547(b) definition and the effect of the perfection, or timing, rules result in casting the preference net so widely as to bring within its reach a number of transactions that seem "legitimate" — that is, the policy of preference law would not require their invalidation. Thus Section 547(c) immunizes several categories of otherwise avoidable transfers (including at least one, covered by Section 547(c)(2), that very arguably does have the effect of disrupting a fair distributional scheme). If the defendant in a preference action can bring his transfer within one or more of the Section 547(c) provisions, the trustee cannot avoid the preference. The defendant has the burden of proof on these issues. § 547(g).

§ 4.03(c)(3)(A) *The Intended but Not Quite Contemporaneous Transfer.* Section 547(c)(1) excepts from preference avoidance a transfer that is both intended to be one for present value and in fact was substantially contemporaneous with the debtor's receipt of the consideration. For example, the debtor buys and receives goods C.O.D. and pays by his check. Assuming that the transfer is deemed to occur several days later when the drawee bank honors the check and debits the debtor's account (the obligation to pay then being antecedent to the transfer), Section 547(c)(1) nevertheless saves the payment from preference avoidance. Also within this exception is the case in which the debtor borrows and receives the loan proceeds on an intended secured basis, but the parties fail to execute the security documents until a short time later. Section 547(c)(1) does not, however, cover the situation in which an unsecured credit extension

11 U.S.C. § 547. Preferences

(c) The trustee may not avoid under this section a transfer—

(2) to the extent that such transfer was—

(A) in payment of a debt incurred by the debtor in the ordinary course of business or financial affairs of the debtor and the transferee;

(B) made in the ordinary course of business or financial affairs of the debtor and the transferee; and

(C) made according to ordinary business terms;

11 U.S.C. § 547. Preferences

(c) The trustee may not avoid under this section a transfer—

(3) that creates a security interest in property acquired by the debtor—

(A) to the extent such security interest secures new value that was—

(i) given at or after the signing of a security agreement that contains a description of such property as collateral;

(ii) given by or on behalf of the secured party under such agreement;

(iii) given to enable the debtor to acquire such property; and

(iv) in fact used by the debtor to acquire such property; and

(B) that is perfected on or before 10 days after the debtor receives possession of such property;

(albeit a short one) actually was intended—for example, the debtor borrows money in the morning and repays it that afternoon, or the bank makes an unsecured loan to the debtor but changes its mind the next day and obtains collateral for the obligation. In each of these illustrations the transfer is one for substantially contemporaneous consideration, but an original intention that the exchange be one for contemporaneous new value is lacking.

§ *4.03(c)(3)(B) Ordinary Course Payments.* A transfer is immunized from preference avoidance if it is the regular *payment* of a debt incurred in the ordinary course of both the debtor's and the transferee's business and according to ordinary business terms. § 547(c)(2), as amended in 1984. The exception covers only payments, not other kinds of transfers, such as the securing of an obligation. It was intended to prevent the preference section from disrupting routine commercial transactions. Nevertheless, it is a potentially large loophole that could frustrate the competing goal of equitable distribution. For example, the debtor could repay a bank loan or pay one or a few large trade creditors as the claims come due just before bankruptcy, thereby exhausting most of his assets and leaving the remaining creditors with no means of recovery. Whether the amended Section 547(c)(2) actually turns out to be a serious deviation from basic preference policy will depend to a considerable extent on how strictly the courts view the terms "ordinary course" and "ordinary business terms." If, for instance, the last quoted phrase is construed to require the payment to be in very close proximity to the due date of the obligation, the exception in practice may not mean much.

§ *4.03(c)(3)(C) The Enabling Loan.* If a lender makes a loan to the debtor to enable him to buy goods that are to serve as collateral for the loan, the security interest transfer is in reality more like a contemporaneous transaction than like one for antecedent debt. But under the timing rule of Section 547(e)(3), the transfer is deemed not to occur until the debtor obtains rights in the goods, an event that does not take place in an enabling loan context until later, when the loan obligation will be antecedent to the security interest transfer. Section 547(c)(3) is designed to protect the legitimate enabling loan. To come within the exception, the enabling

11 U.S.C. § 547. Preferences

(c) The trustee may not avoid under this section a transfer —

(4) to or for the benefit of a creditor, to the extent that, after such transfer, such creditor gave new value to or for the benefit of the debtor —

(A) not secured by an otherwise unavoidable security interest; and

(B) on account of which new value the debtor did not make an otherwise unavoidable transfer to or for the benefit of such creditor;

11 U.S.C. § 547. Preferences

(c) The trustee may not avoid under this section a transfer —

(5) that creates a perfected security interest in inventory or a receivable or the proceeds of either, except to the extent that the aggregate of all such transfers to the transferee caused a reduction, as of the date of the filing of the petition and to the prejudice of other creditors holding unsecured claims, of any amount by which the debt secured by such security interest exceeded the value of all security interests for such debt on the later of—

(A)(i) with respect to a transfer to which subsection (b)(4)(A) of this section applies, 90 days before the date of the filing of the petition; or

(ii) with respect to a transfer to which subsection (b)(4)(B) of this section applies, one year before the date of the filing of the petition; or

(B) the date on which new value was first given under the security agreement creating such security interest;

lender must promptly perfect and exercise care to police the trans-action, so that he can demonstrate compliance with the specific and technical statutory requirements.

§ *4.03(c)(3)(D) The Subsequent Credit Extension.* A creditor who, after having received an avoidable preference, grants *unsecured* credit to the debtor has in effect restored the previous status quo and is given credit for the restoration by Section 547(c)(4). This section does not, however, embody a "net result" rule; it is not applied by taking the preference period as a whole and offsetting all the unsecured credit extensions against all the preferential transfers. Rather, each credit extension must be matched one by one against a previous preference.

§ *4.03(c)(3)(E) Receivables and Inventory Financing.* The "floating lien" on accounts receivable and on inventory under Article 9 of the Uniform Commercial Code is potentially preferential because the security interest transfer does not occur under Section 547(e)(3) until the accounts and inventory are acquired by the debtor, and the loan obligation may then be antecedent. There-fore, to the extent that accounts are generated from unencumbered inventory or that inventory is purchased within 90 days before the petition, the security interest would be in jeopardy, even though the debtor might have used and disposed of the secured party's collateral that existed before the beginning of the preference pe-riod. Accommodation of legitimate inventory and receivables fi-nancing is the purpose of Section 547(c)(5). Stated in the simplest way, a security interest in inventory and receivables (broadly de-fined in Section 547(a) to include more than accounts receivable) is not subject to preference avoidance except to the extent that the financier's secured position improves during the preference period. The measurement is arbitrarily based on two reference points. Any deficiency between the amount of the debt and the value of the inventory and receivables collateral as of bankruptcy is com-pared with any such deficiency that existed 90 days earlier; the security interest is potentially avoidable only to the extent that the deficiency has decreased during the preference period.

§ *4.03(c)(3)(F) Statutory Liens.* Statutory liens that arise within the preference period are potentially preferential, but Congress intended to deal with them in a specially designed section, Section

11 U.S.C. § 547. Preferences

(c) The trustee may not avoid under this section a transfer —

(6) that is the fixing of a statutory lien that is not avoidable under section 545 of this title;

(7) if, in a case filed by an individual debtor whose debts are primarily consumer debts, the aggregate value of all property that constitutes or is affected by such transfer is less than $600.

11 U.S.C. § 548. Fraudulent transfers and obligations

(a) The trustee may avoid any transfer of an interest of the debtor in property, or any obligation incurred by the debtor, that was made or incurred on or within one year before the date of the filing of the petition, if the debtor voluntarily or involuntarily —

(1) made such transfer or incurred such obligation with actual intent to hinder, delay, or defraud any entity to which the debtor was or became, on or after the date that such transfer was made or such obligation was incurred, indebted; or

(2)(A) received less than a reasonably equivalent value in exchange for such transfer or obligation; and

(B)(i) was insolvent on the date that such transfer was made or such obligation was incurred, or became insolvent as a result of such transfer or obligation;

(ii) was engaged in business or a transaction, or was about to engage in business or a transaction, for which any property remaining with the debtor was an unreasonably small capital; or

(iii) intended to incur, or believed that the debtor would incur, debts that would be beyond the debtor's ability to pay as such debts matured.

545, rather than in the preference section. Thus, as a matter of drafting technique, Section 547(c)(6) excepts from preference avoidance statutory liens that can withstand invalidation under Section 545.

§ 4.03(c)(3)(G) Small Preferences in Consumer Cases. The transaction or litigation costs of recovering relatively small preferences might well outweigh the value to creditors of making the recovery. In response to pressure from the consumer finance industry, the drafters of the 1984 amendments excepted from preference avoidance transfers by an individual consumer debtor to a given creditor of property of a value of less than $600. § 547(c)(7). Although the cost-benefit analysis would appear to be the same for all preferences, the exception applies only to consumer cases, a limitation explainable by the identity of the lobby that sponsored the amendment.

§ 4.03(d) Fraudulent Transfers

Section 548, which embodies the so-called fraudulent transfer avoiding power, is similar in its provisions to the Uniform Fraudulent Conveyance Act and the Uniform Fraudulent Transfer Act. It covers not only certain proscribed transfers but also obligations incurred under specified circumstances. When a debt or obligation is avoided under Section 548, the result is that the claim is not allowed to participate in the case. Furthermore, the section covers transfers and obligations made or incurred not only with an intent to defraud but also with an intent to hinder or delay creditors. A creditor is hindered or delayed when the prompt exercise of his legal rights is interfered with—for example, the debtor might put assets temporarily beyond the reach of legal process, although he may intend to pay the creditor later. Hereafter, the shorthand term "fraudulent transfer" will be used to refer to the broader coverage of this avoiding power.

Section 548 denounces transfers (as broadly defined in Section 101(50), see p. 139, *supra*) made with actual—that is, subjective—intent to defraud existing or future creditors. The section also covers three categories of constructively fraudulent transfers. These categories have a common thread: The debtor must have received less than reasonably equivalent value in exchange for the transfer. If this element exists, then the transfer is constructively fraudulent

11 U.S.C. § 548. Fraudulent transfers and obligations

(a) The trustee may avoid any transfer of an interest of the debtor in property, or any obligation incurred by the debtor, that was made or incurred on or within one year before the date of the filing of the petition, if the debtor voluntarily or involuntarily—

(2)(A) received less than a reasonably equivalent value in exchange for such transfer or obligation; and

(B)(i) was insolvent on the date that such transfer was made or such obligation was incurred, or became insolvent as a result of such transfer or obligation;

(ii) was engaged in business or a transaction, or was about to engage in business or a transaction, for which any property remaining with the debtor was an unreasonably small capital; or

(iii) intended to incur, or believed that the debtor would incur, debts that would be beyond the debtor's ability to pay as such debts matured.

11 U.S.C. § 548. Fraudulent transfers and obligations

(d)(2) In this section—

(A) "value" means property, or satisfaction or securing of a present or antecedent debt of the debtor, but does not include an unperformed promise to furnish support to the debtor or to a relative of the debtor;

11 U.S.C. § 548. Fraudulent transfers and obligations

(d)(1) For the purposes of this section, a transfer is made when such transfer is so perfected that a bona fide purchaser from the debtor against whom applicable law permits such transfer to be perfected cannot acquire an interest in the property transferred that is superior to the interest in such property of the transferee, but if such transfer is not so perfected before the commencement of the case, such transfer is made immediately before the date of the filing of the petition.

if the debtor suffered from at least one of three adverse financial conditions: (1) He was insolvent, as defined in Section 101(31); (2) he was in business, and his capital remaining after the transfer was unreasonably small; or (3) he intended to, or believed he would, incur debts in the future beyond his ability to pay as they matured.

Reasonably equivalent value for Section 548 purposes includes the satisfying or securing of antecedent debt; thus the value received need not be a present consideration. § 548(d)(2)(A). Transfers for antecedent debt are the subject of the preference section, not of the fraudulent transfer section.

But the reasonably equivalent value must have been received by or at least must have benefited the debtor. That the transferee gave such value to a third party might constitute sufficient consideration for the purposes of contract law, but it will not save the transfer from Section 548 avoidance unless the debtor benefited. Thus, for example, a so-called "upstream" transaction, in which a subsidiary corporation mortgages its assets to secure a loan to its parent, is potentially an avoidable fraudulent transfer, provided that the loan funds cannot be shown to benefit the subsidiary and provided that the subsidiary has the requisite financial condition.

A current matter of considerable controversy is whether Section 548 is violated when an insolvent debtor's property is sold at a prepetition foreclosure sale and, as commonly occurs, the lien enforcement sale yields a distressed price, that is, with hindsight the sale brings less than reasonably equivalent value for the property. Courts of appeals have held both that such a foreclosure sale is an avoidable fraudulent transfer, *e.g., Durrett v. Washington National Insurance Co.,* 621 F.2d 201 (5th Cir. 1986), and that it is not. *In re Madrid,* 725 F.2d 1197 (9th Cir. 1984). (*See also In re Verna,* 58 Bankr. 246 (Bankr. C.D. Ca. 1986), discussing the effect of the subsequent statutory amendments of 1984, and holding that the foreclosure did not violate Section 548.)

The reachback of the fraudulent transfer avoiding power is one year; transfers which precede bankruptcy by more than this length of time are not covered. Two points should be mentioned, however, in connection with the reachback. First, a transfer is deemed to occur when it becomes perfected under nonbankruptcy law as against a subsequent bona fide purchaser. § 548(d)(1). Thus a

11 U.S.C. § 548. Fraudulent transfers and obligations

(c) Except to the extent that a transfer or obligation voidable under this section is voidable under section 544, 545, or 547 of this title, a transferee or obligee of such a transfer or obligation that takes for value and in good faith has a lien on or may retain any interest transferred or may enforce any obligation incurred, as the case may be, to the extent that such transferee or obligee gave value to the debtor in exchange for such transfer or obligation.

11 U.S.C. § 101. Definitions

In this title—

(47) "statutory lien" means lien arising solely by force of a statute on specified circumstances or conditions, or lien of distress for rent, whether or not statutory, but does not include security interest or judicial lien, whether or not such interest or lien is provided by or is dependent on a statute and whether or not such interest or lien is made fully effective by statute;

transfer actually older than one year may be reachable if perfection was delayed. Second, as discussed earlier, the trustee may be able to invoke Section 544(b) and state fraudulent transfer law (including, in the states that have enacted it, one of the Uniform Acts, whose provisions are similar to those of Section 548) and so be able to avoid transfers made outside the one-year period. See pp. 149–53, *supra*.

Finally, Section 548(c) has a savings clause provision that gives a measure of protection to transferees who, although involved in a transaction within the coverage of the fraudulent transfer avoiding power, otherwise act in good faith. A transferee who received property in good faith has a lien on it or may retain the interest transferred to the extent of the value given. In other words, the transferee will be no worse off after the transfer than he was before it, although he will not be entitled to keep the benefit of a favorable bargain. This protection under Section 548(c) extends both to an innocent recipient of a transfer made by the debtor with actual fraudulent intent—that is, a recipient who is not privy to the debtor's improper state of mind—and to a transferee who, through hindsight, is found to have given less than reasonably equivalent value.

§ 4.03(e) Statutory Liens and Rights of a Defrauded Seller

For many years now the bankruptcy laws have denied effect in bankruptcy cases to state-created "priority" rights—that is, to state laws that prescribe the order of distribution of insolvent estates. Congress has its own overriding notions concerning what claims should be accorded priority in bankruptcy. *See* § 507. On the other hand, state-created property rights, including lien rights, are generally recognized in bankruptcy unless they run afoul of a specific avoiding power. But a legislature can readily hang a "lien" label on a right to priority, and it is not always easy to draw the line between the two concepts, especially since a statutory lien, if enforced, also has the effect of giving a priority position to the lienor.

The purpose of Section 545 is to leave a statutory lien untouched by bankruptcy if the law creating it, state or federal, intends to make the lien a true property interest. In contrast, if a so-

11 U.S.C. § 545. Statutory liens

The trustee may avoid the fixing of a statutory lien on property of the debtor to the extent that such lien —

(1) first becomes effective against the debtor —

(A) when a case under this title concerning the debtor is commenced;

(B) when an insolvency proceeding other than under this title concerning the debtor is commenced;

(C) when a custodian is appointed or authorized to take or takes possession;

(D) when the debtor becomes insolvent;

(E) when the debtor's financial condition fails to meet a specified standard; or

(F) at the time of an execution against property of the debtor levied at the instance of an entity other than the holder of such statutory lien;

(2) is not perfected or enforceable at the time of the commencement of the case against a bona fide purchaser that purchases such property at the time of the commencement of the case, whether or not such a purchaser exists;

(3) is for rent; or

(4) is a lien of distress for rent.

I.R.C. § 6321. Lien for taxes

If any person liable to pay any tax neglects or refuses to pay the same after demand, the amount (including any interest, additional amount, addition to tax, or assessable penalty, together with any costs that may accrue in addition thereto) shall be a lien in favor of the United States upon all property and rights to property, whether real or personal, belonging to such person.

I.R.C. § 6322. Period of lien

Unless another date is specifically fixed by law, the lien imposed by section 6321 shall arise at the time the assessment is made and shall continue until the liability for the amount so assessed (or a judgment against the taxpayer arising out of such liability) is satisfied or becomes unenforceable by reason of lapse of time.

called statutory lien is merely a priority statute in disguise, the Section 545 avoiding power will strike it down.

"Statutory lien" is defined in Section 101(47) as a lien that is neither dependent upon the parties' agreement to create a charge against property nor obtainable through judicial process by the general run of creditors attempting to enforce their claims against the debtor. Instead it is a lien provided by legislatures for policy reasons, usually for the benefit of governmental units or other identifiable economic groups—for example, tax liens, mechanics' liens, wage liens, landlords' liens, and various types of artisans' liens.

The Section 545 avoiding power does not turn on whether the statutory lien arises within a prescribed period of time before bankruptcy but rather on the character of the lien. If the statutory lien arises only when the debtor becomes insolvent or otherwise experiences financial difficulties, the law creating the so-called lien is functionally similar to a priority statute, and the lien is subject to avoidance. § 545(1). On the other hand, if the lien created by the legislature is too fragile to survive a transfer of the liened property to a bona fide purchaser, then it is not hardy enough to be considered a true property interest and may be avoided. § 545(2). The test is whether the lien is perfected or enforceable against a hypothetical bona fide purchaser as of the time of bankruptcy. Finally, Section 545(3) and (4) make liens for rent generally avoidable.

An example involving the federal tax lien illustrates the operation of Section 545. When a federal tax is assessed, a lien arises on virtually all the taxpayer's property. I.R.C. §§ 6321, 6322. The lien, however, is not valid as against certain third parties—including purchasers from the taxpayer and his judgment lien creditors—until public notice of the lien is appropriately filed. I.R.C. § 6323. Thus if notice of the tax lien has been filed before the taxpayer's bankruptcy, even shortly before, the lien is not avoidable under Section 545, for it is not triggered by one of the specified kinds of deteriorating financial condition; nor would a purchaser who bought property from the taxpayer after the filing

I.R.C. § 6323. Validity and priority against certain persons

(a) Purchasers, holders of security interests, mechanic's lienors, and judgment lien creditors. — The lien imposed by section 6321 shall not be valid as against any purchaser, holder of a security interest, mechanic's lienor, or judgment lien creditor until notice thereof which meets the requirements of subsection (f) has been filed by the Secretary.

11 U.S.C. § 546. Limitations on avoiding powers

(b) The rights and powers of a trustee under sections 544, 545, and 549 of this title are subject to any generally applicable law that permits perfection of an interest in property to be effective against an entity that acquires rights in such property before the date of such perfection. If such law requires seizure of such property or commencement of an action to accomplish such perfection, and such property has not been seized or such action has not been commenced before the date of the filing of the petition, such interest in such property shall be perfected by notice within the time fixed by such law for such seizure or commencement.

U.C.C. § 2-702. Seller's Remedies on Discovery of Buyer's Insolvency

(2) Where the seller discovers that the buyer has received goods on credit while insolvent he may reclaim the goods upon demand made within ten days after the receipt, but if misrepresentation of solvency has been made to the particular seller in writing within three months before delivery the ten day limitation does not apply. Except as provided in this subsection the seller may not base a right to reclaim goods on the buyer's fraudulent or innocent misrepresentation of solvency or of intent to pay.

of the notice be protected against the Government's lien.[2] If bankruptcy occurred before the notice was filed, however, the protection given to purchasers by I.R.C. § 6323 would enable the trustee to invalidate the tax lien under Section 545(2). Moreover, the trustee's status as a judicial lien holder under Section 544(a)(1), together with the protection for judgment lien creditors under I.R.C. § 6323, would enable the trustee also to avoid the unfiled tax lien under the strong-arm clause.[3]

When a statutory lien is subject to retroactive perfection against purchasers under applicable lien law, it may be perfected after bankruptcy in accordance with that law so as to survive avoidance under Section 545(2). For example, mechanic's lien statutes often provide that workers or suppliers may obtain lien rights on real estate to secure claims arising from their work of improvement on that property; they must, however, take steps to perfect or enforce the liens (for example, by filing notice or commencing suit) within specified time periods or the lien rights will be lost. If bankruptcy intervenes before a required subsequent perfection step is taken, Section 545(2) does not automatically enable the trustee to defeat the lien. The mechanic's lienor may effectively complete perfection after the petition, provided he does so in a timely fashion under the mechanic's lien law. If perfection requires seizure of the property or commencement of a suit, the lienor must give notice to the trustee instead. *See* §§ 546(b), 362(b)(3); see also pp. 145–47, *supra.*

A somewhat different but perhaps related problem is presented by the statutory right of a seller of goods to an insolvent debtor to rescind the transaction and reclaim the goods. Section 2-702(2) of the Uniform Commercial Code provides for reclamation if a "defrauded" seller makes a demand within specified times. How does this reclamation right fare against the trustee's avoiding powers if bankruptcy intervenes? Prior to the 1978 Code, trustees argued,

---

[2]With respect to certain kinds of property, the federal tax lien is invalid as against purchasers even though notice has been filed. *See* 26 U.S.C. § 6323(b). To the extent that the estate includes this type of property, therefore, the trustee may invalidate the tax lien under Section 545(2) despite its general perfection before the petition.

[3]It should be noted that even valid or nonavoidable tax liens are subordinated in Chapter 7 liquidation cases to certain unsecured priority claims. § 724(b).

11 U.S.C. § 546. Limitations on avoiding powers

(c) Except as provided in subsection (d) of this section, the rights and powers of a trustee under sections 544(a), 545, 547, and 549 of this title are subject to any statutory or common-law right of a seller of goods that has sold goods to the debtor, in the ordinary course of such seller's business, to reclaim such goods if the debtor has received such goods while insolvent, but —

(1) such a seller may not reclaim any such goods unless such seller demands in writing reclamation of such goods before ten days after receipt of such goods by the debtor; and

(2) the court may deny reclamation to a seller with such a right of reclamation that has made such a demand only if the court —

(A) grants the claim of such a seller priority as a claim of a kind specified in section 503(b) of this title; or

(B) secures such claim by a lien.

inter alia, that the right under U.C.C. § 2-702(2) was tantamount to a statutory lien that, because it was triggered by insolvency, ran afoul of the predecessor statutory lien avoiding power. This argument succeeded in some bankruptcy courts, although at the appellate court level the right of rescission was held not to be an avoidable statutory lien. *E.g., In re PFA Farmers Mkt. Ass'n*, 583 F.2d 992 (8th Cir. 1978). In the 1978 legislation Section 546(c) addressed this issue by providing that a seller with a right to reclaim goods under nonbankruptcy law is not defeated by Section 545 (or by certain other specified avoiding power sections) so long as the seller makes a *written* demand for reclamation not later than ten days after the debtor-buyer received the goods. As construed by most of the courts, any nonbankruptcy rescission or reclamation rights are lost if the terms of Section 546(c) are not strictly complied with, even though the nonbankruptcy requirements for rescission and reclamation may have been met. For example, U.C.C. § 2-702(2) can be complied with even though the reclamation demand is oral. Section 546(c) has also been held by analogy to protect a seller's right to stop goods in transit under U.C.C. §§ 2-702(1) and 2-705(1) as well as his right under Section 2-702(2) to reclaim goods that have been delivered. *In re National Sugar Ref. Co.*, 27 Bankr. 565 (S.D.N.Y. 1983).

§ 4.03(f) Setoff

To the extent that a creditor who has a claim against the debtor and who also is indebted to the debtor is permitted to offset the indebtedness against the claim, that creditor receives better, and arguably preferential, treatment as compared to other creditors who are not in a position to set off. Under the former Bankruptcy Act, however, and now under the Code, the right of setoff has been recognized, at least to some degree, and may be viewed as an exception to the preference avoiding power.

The governing provision is Section 553, which controls over other provisions in the Code (including the preference section) that might be construed to prohibit, limit, or otherwise apply to setoff. Section 553 does not create the right of setoff. But if the right exists under applicable nonbankruptcy law, the section generally validates it without distinguishing between liquidation or reorgani-

11 U.S.C. § 553. Setoff

(a) Except as otherwise provided in this section and in sections 362 and 363 of this title, this title does not affect any right of a creditor to offset a mutual debt owing by such creditor to the debtor that arose before the commencement of the case under this title against a claim of such creditor against the debtor that arose before the commencement of the case, except to the extent that—

(1) the claim of such creditor against the debtor is disallowed other than under section 502(b)(3) of this title;

(2) such claim was transferred, by an entity other than the debtor, to such creditor—

(A) after the commencement of the case; or

(B)(i) after 90 days before the date of the filing of the petition; and

(ii) while the debtor was insolvent; or

(3) the debt owed to the debtor by such creditor was incurred by such creditor—

(A) after 90 days before the date of the filing of the petition;

(B) while the debtor was insolvent; and

(C) for the purpose of obtaining a right of setoff against the debtor.

(b)(1) Except with respect to a setoff of a kind described in section 362(b)(6), 362(b)(7), 365(h)(2), or 365(i)(2) of this title, if a creditor offsets a mutual debt owing to the debtor against a claim against the debtor on or within 90 days before the date of the filing of the petition, then the trustee may recover from such creditor the amount so offset to the extent that any insufficiency on the date of such setoff is less than the insufficiency on the later of—

(A) 90 days before the date of the filing of the petition; and

(B) the first date during the 90 days immediately preceding the date of the filing of the petition on which there is an insufficiency.

(2) In this subsection, "insufficiency" means amount, if any, by which a claim against the debtor exceeds a mutual debt owing to the debtor by the holder of such claim.

(c) For the purposes of this section, the debtor is presumed to have been insolvent on and during the 90 days immediately preceding the date of the filing of the petition.

zation cases, provided that the claims involved are mutual, both arose before the petition, and the creditor's claim is not disallowed under Section 502.

Nevertheless, certain kinds of setoff that have the apparent earmarks of a planned preference are forbidden. Setoffs are prohibited by Section 553(a)(2)(A) for claims against the debtor acquired by the creditor from a third party after commencement of the case and by Section 553(a)(2)(B) for claims acquired from a third party within 90 days of the commencement of the case and while the debtor was insolvent. Setoffs are further prohibited by Section 553(a)(3) for debts owed by the creditor to the debtor (as distinguished from claims against the debtor acquired by the creditor) that were incurred within 90 days of bankruptcy and while the debtor was insolvent, if the debt was incurred for the purpose of obtaining a right of setoff. Whenever insolvency is relevant, Section 553(c) presumes the debtor to have been insolvent during the 90-day period.

Also forbidden are prepetition setoffs during the 90 days before bankruptcy if they work an "improvement of position" over what the creditor could have accomplished by exercising his setoff rights at the beginning of that period. § 553(b). Insolvency is not necessary here. For example, assume a constant bank loan to the debtor of $20,000. Ninety days before bankruptcy the debtor's bank account contains $5,000; it is built up during the next 75 days to $7,500 by ordinary course deposits. At this point the bank sets off the account against the loan. The trustee can recover $2,500 from the bank under Section 553(b): The "insufficiency" at the time of setoff, $12,500, is less by $2,500 than the "insufficiency" of $15,000 that existed 90 days before bankruptcy.

This improvement of position concept applies only to prepetition setoffs. To encourage creditors, particularly banks, not to precipitate bankruptcy filings by exercising their setoff rights, the statute does not limit the amount of permissible setoff if the setoff is authorized after bankruptcy. In the previous illustration the bank may set off the entire $7,500 account when permitted by the court to proceed after the petition.

The holder of the right of setoff gives up something by delaying its exercise until after bankruptcy. The automatic stay of Section

11 U.S.C. § 362. Automatic stay

(a) Except as provided in subsection (b) of this section, a petition filed under section 301, 302, or 303 of this title, or an application filed under section 5(a)(3) of the Securities Investor Protection Act of 1970 (15 U.S.C. 78eee(a)(3)), operates as a stay, applicable to all entities, of—

(7) the setoff of any debt owing to the debtor that arose before the commencement of the case under this title against any claim against the debtor;

11 U.S.C. § 549. Postpetition transactions

(a) Except as provided in subsection (b) or (c) of this section, the trustee may avoid a transfer of property of the estate—

(1) made after the commencement of the case; and

(2)(A) that is authorized only under section 303(f) or 542(c) of this title; or

(B) that is not authorized under this title or by the court.

(b) In an involuntary case, a transfer that occurs after the commencement of such case but before the order for relief to the extent any value, including services, but not including satisfaction or securing of a debt that arose before the commencement of the case, is given after the commencement of the case in exchange for such transfer, notwithstanding any notice or knowledge of the case that the transferee has.

[Continued]

362(a)(7) prohibits setoff without court permission once the petition has been filed. Does this prohibition mean that the trustee or debtor automatically may draw checks on or otherwise use the bank account or that the bank or creditor necessarily must pay over the amount owed to the debtor? The answer is probably no, although the cases to date are conflicting. Whether the debtor or trustee may actually use the account or whether the bank or creditor must actually pay over (or, conversely, whether the bank or creditor will be permitted by the court to exercise setoff rights after bankruptcy) ought to turn on the trustee's or debtor's right to use the "cash collateral" under Section 363, a right that depends on furnishing "adequate protection" to the bank or creditor. See particularly Section 363(a), (c)(2), and (e) and the discussion *infra*, pp. 227–29.

§ 4.03(g) Custodianships

The trustee's ability under Section 543 to supersede a prepetition assignment for the benefit of creditors, receivership, or custodianship and to recover the debtor's property transferred to an assignee, receiver, or custodian may be viewed as an avoiding power. The relevant provisions were discussed earlier at pp. 135–37.

§ 4.03(h) Postpetition Transfers

Although the power to avoid improper postpetition transfers under Section 549 is not technically an avoiding power—since "avoiding power" has been defined as relating to prepetition transfers—it is sufficiently similar to justify its discussion here.

In general, postpetition transfers are avoidable by the trustee under Section 549 if they were not authorized by the court or by some provision of the Code. § 549(a). Transfers by way of sale, lease, exemption, or abandonment, for example, would be authorized and nonavoidable dispositions if the statutory requirements for these transactions were complied with or if court approval was obtained.

Two kinds of unauthorized postpetition transfers are saved from avoidance. First, until constructive notice of the bankruptcy is given by recordation of a copy or notice of the petition in the appropriate land records office, a good faith transferee of real estate who had no

11 U.S.C. § 549. Postpetition transactions

(c) The trustee may not avoid under subsection (a) of this section a transfer of real property to a good faith purchaser without knowledge of the commencement of the case and for present fair equivalent value unless a copy or notice of the petition was filed, where a transfer of such real property may be recorded to perfect such transfer, before such transfer is so perfected that a bona fide purchaser of such property, against whom applicable law permits such transfer to be perfected, could not acquire an interest that is superior to the interest of such good faith purchaser. A good faith purchaser without knowledge of the commencement of the case and for less than present fair equivalent value has a lien on the property transferred to the extent of any present value given, unless a copy or notice of the petition was so filed before such transfer was so perfected.

11 U.S.C. § 542. Turnover of property to the estate

(c) Except as provided in section 362(a)(7) of this title, an entity that has neither actual notice nor actual knowledge of the commencement of the case concerning the debtor may transfer property of the estate, or pay a debt owing to the debtor, in good faith and other than in the manner specified in subsection (d) of this section, to an entity other than the trustee, with the same effect as to the entity making such transfer or payment as if the case under this title concerning the debtor had not been commenced.

11 U.S.C. § 724. Treatment of certain liens

(a) The trustee may avoid a lien that secures a claim of a kind specified in section 726(a)(4) of this title.

11 U.S.C. § 726. Distribution of property of the estate

(a) Except as provided in section 510 of this title, property of the estate shall be distributed—

(4) fourth, in payment of any allowed claim, whether secured or unsecured, for any fine, penalty, or forfeiture, or for multiple, exemplary, or punitive damages, arising before the earlier of the order for relief or the appointment of a trustee, to the extent that such fine, penalty, forfeiture, or damages are not compensation for actual pecuniary loss suffered by the holder of such claim;

knowledge of the pending bankruptcy is protected to the extent he gave present fair equivalent value for the transfer. § 549(c). Second, in the interim between the filing of an involuntary petition and the order for relief, a transferee (regardless of his knowledge of the bankruptcy) is protected in any dealings with the debtor to the extent he gave postpetition value for the transfer. § 549(b).

Finally, under Section 542(c), one who owes money to the debtor or holds property of the estate is not liable to the trustee if, after bankruptcy, that person in good faith and without knowledge of the filing of the case pays the debt or transfers the property to someone other than the trustee. This provision, however, insulates only the payor or transferor; the payment or transfer may be avoided as against the recipient or transferee unless he can find protection in Section 549.

§ 4.03(i) Liens Securing Penalty Claims in Chapter 7 Cases

A lien that secures a penalty, a forfeiture, exemplary damages, or a similar claim that is not for actual pecuniary loss is avoidable by the trustee under Section 724(a). This provision protects unsecured creditors and implements the Chapter 7 distribution scheme prescribed by Section 726, under which penalty claims in general are subordinated to other unsecured claims. See § 726(a)(4). It applies only when the debtor's estate is liquidated under Chapter 7. If the debtor reorganizes under Chapter 11, the lien securing the penalty is unaffected by Section 724(a).

§ 4.03(j) Recovery and Preservation of Avoidable Transfers

The concepts of avoidability and recovery of a given transfer are distinguished in the Code, although an avoidable transfer always is a recoverable one. Apparently, the Code contemplates that the trustee might bring an action to avoid a transfer without seeking to recover it and institute the recovery action later. See § 550(e)(1). It is unlikely, however, that in practice a trustee would bifurcate the actions in this way.

Recovery is dealt with in Section 550. To the extent that a transfer is avoided, the trustee can recover the transferred property or, if the court orders, the value of the property from the initial trans-

11 U.S.C. § 550. Liability of transferee of avoided transfer

(a) Except as otherwise provided in this section, to the extent that a transfer is avoided under section 544, 545, 547, 548, 549, 553(b), or 724(a) of this title, the trustee may recover, for the benefit of the estate, the property transferred, or, if the court so orders, the value of such property, from —

(1) the initial transferee of such transfer or the entity for whose benefit such transfer was made; or

(2) any immediate or mediate transferee of such initial transferee.

(b) The trustee may not recover under section (a)(2) of this section from —

(1) a transferee that takes for value, including satisfaction or securing of a present or antecedent debt, in good faith, and without knowledge of the voidability of the transfer avoided; or

(2) any immediate or mediate good faith transferee of such transferee.

(c) The trustee is entitled to only a single satisfaction under subsection (a) of this section.

(d)(1) A good faith transferee from whom the trustee may recover under subsection (a) of this section has a lien on the property recovered to secure the lesser of—

(A) the cost, to such transferee, of any improvement made after the transfer, less the amount of any profit realized by or accruing to such transferee from such property; and

(B) any increase in the value of such property as a result of such improvement, of the property transferred.

(2) In this subsection, "improvement" includes —

(A) physical additions or changes to the property transferred;

(B) repairs to such property;

(C) payment of any tax on such property;

(D) payment of any debt secured by a lien on such property that is superior or equal to the rights of the trustee; and

(E) preservation of such property.

feree or from the one for whose benefit the transfer was made. § 550(a)(1). The trustee may also pursue subsequent transferees— that is, transferees from the initial transferee—but the chain of subsequent transferees from whom recovery can be made is broken as soon as one takes for value, in good faith, and without knowledge of the avoidability of the initial transfer. § 550(a)(2), (b). In any event, the trustee is entitled to only a single satisfaction. § 550(c).

Good faith transferees of avoidable transfers who have improved the property are given a measure of protection. To the extent of the "improvements," as broadly defined, such transferees will ordinarily have a lien on the property to secure the lesser of the cost of the improvements or the resulting increase in the value of the property. § 550(d).

On occasion the estate would benefit by subrogating to the position of the transferee of an avoidable transfer rather than by invalidating the transfer. An example is the situation in which a junior but indefeasible interest exists in the property that is subject to an avoidable senior interest. Under these circumstances avoidance of the senior interest (as distinguished from subrogation to it) would have the effect of promoting the junior one.

Section 551, which provides that any avoided transfer is automatically "preserved" for the estate, insures that the estate obtains the benefit of the avoiding power. Consider the case of a debtor who grants a security interest in his equipment worth $25,000 to secure a contemporaneous loan of $20,000. The lender delays filing the financing statement for five days. During this interim a trade creditor with a claim for $15,000 obtains an attachment lien on the equipment. Bankruptcy follows within 90 days.

In this example the lender's security interest is not avoidable by the trustee. Perfection of the Article 9 security interest before bankruptcy puts it beyond Section 544, and the contemporaneous nature of the transaction, plus relatively prompt perfection, insulates it from preference attack. But the judicial lien that attached before perfection primes the security interest under U.C.C. § 9-301(1)(b). The judicial lien, in turn, meets all the requirements of an avoidable preference under Section 547. If the trustee merely avoided the judicial lien, the security interest would be promoted to a first lien

11 U.S.C. § 551. Automatic preservation of avoided transfer

Any transfer avoided under section 522, 544, 545, 547, 548, 549, or 724(a) of this title, or any lien void under section 506(d) of this title, is preserved for the benefit of the estate but only with respect to property of the estate.

11 U.S.C. § 546. Limitations on avoiding powers

(a) An action or proceeding under section 544, 545, 547, 548, or 553 of this title may not be commenced after the earlier of—

(1) two years after the appointment of a trustee under section 702, 1104, 1163, 1302, 1202 of this title; or

(2) the time the case is closed or dismissed.

11 U.S.C. § 549. Postpetition transactions

(d) An action or proceeding under this section may not be commenced after the earlier of—

(1) two years after the date of the transfer sought to be avoided; or

(2) the time the case is closed or dismissed.

position, and the lender would be entitled to the first $20,000 of the proceeds of the equipment, the estate receiving the balance of $5,000 rather than the full value of the avoided attachment lien. Section 551, however, automatically preserves the avoided judicial lien for the estate. As a result, the trustee, who now succeeds to this lien's senior position vis-à-vis the security interest, will receive the first $15,000 from the liquidation.

§ 4.03(k) Statute of Limitations on Avoiding Power Actions

An avoiding power action with respect to a prepetition transfer must be brought within two years after the appointment of a trustee or before the case is closed or dismissed, whichever is earlier. § 546(a). A trustee's appointment starts the statute of limitations running regardless of the kind of case or the chapter in which the appointment is made; conversion of the case from one chapter to another does not toll the limitations period once it has started. The time a debtor remains in possession in Chapter 11 does not affect the two-year period if there has been no previous trustee.

The statute of limitations for the institution of an avoiding power suit should not be confused with the length of time before bankruptcy that the trustee can reach back to invalidate transfers under the various avoiding power sections.

Section 549(d) prescribes the statute of limitations for bringing a suit to avoid an unauthorized postpetition transfer. It is two years from the date of the transfer, or the time the case is closed or dismissed, whichever is earlier.

§ 4.04 ABANDONMENT OF PROPERTY OF THE ESTATE

Property that becomes part of the estate ordinarily leaves the estate in one of three ways (not counting the revesting or other transfer of the estate's property that occurs upon or results from confirmation of a plan in a case under one of the rehabilitation chapters): (1) by sale or other disposition under Section 363, discussed at pp. 223-33, *infra;* (2) by the debtor's exempting it under Section 522(b), discussed at pp. 299-305, *infra;* and (3) by an abandonment under Section 554. Abandonment is the process by which the

11 U.S.C. § 554. Abandonment of property of the estate

(a) After notice and a hearing, the trustee may abandon any property of the estate that is burdensome to the estate or that is of inconsequential value and benefit to the estate.

(b) On request of a party in interest and after notice and a hearing, the court may order the trustee to abandon any property of the estate that is burdensome to the estate or that is of inconsequential value and benefit to the estate.

(c) Unless the court orders otherwise, any property scheduled under section 521(1) of this title not otherwise administered at the time of the closing of a case is abandoned to the debtor and administered for purposes of section 350 of this title.

(d) Unless the court orders otherwise, property of the estate that is not abandoned under this section and that is not administered in the case remains property of the estate.

trustee rids the estate of burdensome property (that is, property that is overencumbered or that cannot otherwise be administered or sold for the benefit of the creditors) or property that is not worth administering because of its inconsequential value.[4] The legal effect of abandonment is to revest the debtor with the property interest as of the date of the petition. Technically, the trustee does not abandon property to a secured creditor, although he may physically deliver the collateral to that person. The debtor's revested property interest that results from the abandonment must still be foreclosed by the secured creditor in accordance with applicable law.

A proposed abandonment requires notice and an opportunity for a hearing. § 554(a). Property that has been scheduled but not otherwise disposed of or intentionally abandoned by the time of the closing of the case is deemed abandoned, § 554(c); if unscheduled, however, it remains property of the estate even after the case is closed, unless the court orders otherwise. § 554(d). Finally, the court may order the trustee to abandon property if the trustee fails to act. § 554(b).

---

[4]The power to abandon burdensome assets under Section 554, however, is not unlimited. In a 5-4 decision, the Supreme Court held that the trustee may not abandon environmentally polluted property in violation of state laws that are reasonably designed to protect the public health and safety. Midlantic Nat'l Bank v. New Jersey Dep't of Envtl. Protection, 474 U.S. 494 (1986).

11 U.S.C. § 362. Automatic stay

(a) Except as provided in subsection (b) of this section, a petition filed under section 301, 302, or 303 of this title, or an application filed under section 5(a)(3) of the Securities Investor Protection Act of 1970 (15 U.S.C. 78eee(a)(3)), operates as a stay, applicable to all entities, of—

(1) the commencement or continuation, including the issuance or employment of process, of a judicial, administrative, or other action or proceeding against the debtor that was or could have been commenced before the commencement of the case under this title, or to recover a claim against the debtor that arose before the commencement of the case under this title;

(2) the enforcement, against the debtor or against property of the estate, of a judgment obtained before the commencement of the case under this title;

(3) any act to obtain possession of property of the estate or of property from the estate or to exercise control over property of the estate;

(4) any act to create, perfect, or enforce any lien against property of the estate;

(5) any act to create, perfect, or enforce against property of the debtor any lien to the extent that such lien secures a claim that arose before the commencement of the case under this title;

(6) any act to collect, assess, or recover a claim against the debtor that arose before the commencement of the case under this title;

(7) the setoff of any debt owing to the debtor that arose before the commencement of the case under this title against any claim against the debtor; and

(8) the commencement or continuation of a proceeding before the United States Tax Court concerning the debtor.

5

The Administrative Powers

The "administrative powers" found in Sections 361–366 of the Code are among the most important provisions of the statute, both in terms of making the bankruptcy system work and in affecting the world outside the bankruptcy administration. Although certain of these sections are of special interest in Chapter 11 reorganization cases, the reader should remember that their location in Chapter 3 makes them applicable as well in Chapters 7, 12, and 13. *See* § 103(a). (For the most part they are also applicable in Chapter 9 cases. *See* § 901(a).) The automatic stay of Section 362, in particular, has an almost constant impact in consumer cases as well as in business cases.

§ 5.01 THE AUTOMATIC STAY

One of the principal benefits for the debtor of filing a petition under the Bankruptcy Code is obtaining the protection of the automatic stay provided in Section 362. The filing of a voluntary, joint, or involuntary petition under any chapter automatically operates as a stay against lawsuits and lien enforcement. The purpose of the automatic stay is to give the Chapter 9, 11, 12, or 13 debtor some "breathing time" for rehabilitation, to give the Chapter 7 trustee the protection necessary for administering the assets of the estate, and to relieve the Chapter 7 debtor from the pressure of creditor collection efforts.

§ 5.01(a) Scope of Stay

The scope of the automatic stay is broad. The stay is applicable to all "entities," including governmental units. § 101(14), (26). Sec-

11 U.S.C. § 362. Automatic stay

(a) Except as provided in subsection (b) of this section, a petition filed under section 301, 302, or 303 of this title, or an application filed under section 5(a)(3) of the Securities Investor Protection Act of 1970 (15 U.S.C. 78eee(a)(3)), operates as a stay, applicable to all entities, of—

(1) the commencement or continuation, including the issuance or employment of process, of a judicial, administrative, or other action or proceeding against the debtor that was or could have been commenced before the commencement of the case under this title, or to recover a claim against the debtor that arose before the commencement of the case under this title;

(2) the enforcement, against the debtor or against property of the estate, of a judgment obtained before the commencement of the case under this title;

(3) any act to obtain possession of property of the estate or of property from the estate or to exercise control over property of the estate;

(4) any act to create, perfect, or enforce any lien against property of the estate;

(5) any act to create, perfect, or enforce against property of the debtor any lien to the extent that such lien secures a claim that arose before the commencement of the case under this title;

(6) any act to collect, assess, or recover a claim against the debtor that arose before the commencement of the case under this title;

(7) the setoff of any debt owing to the debtor that arose before the commencement of the case under this title against any claim against the debtor; and

(8) the commencement or continuation of a proceeding before the United States Tax Court concerning the debtor.

tion 106(c) expressly waives sovereign immunity to the extent constitutionally permissible.

The filing of the petition automatically stays the commencement or continuation of most judicial, administrative, or other proceedings against the debtor. The lawsuit or proceeding either must have been commenced before the filing of the petition or must have been eligible to have been commenced under nonbankruptcy law before the filing of the petition. In addition to enjoining pending in personam actions against the debtor, the automatic stay prevents the commencement or continuation of a lawsuit or a proceeding after bankruptcy to recover a claim against the debtor that arose before the filing of the petition.

When a claim arises and whether a proceeding could have been brought before the petition depend on the definition of "claim" in the Bankruptcy Code and on nonbankruptcy federal or state law. "Claim" is defined in Section 101(4) to include contingent and unmatured rights to payment. Therefore, a claim may arise before the petition for the purpose of the automatic stay even though it is contingent or unmatured and thus not ripe for prosecution in a prepetition lawsuit. For example, the right to payment on a five-year note arises when the note is signed and delivered, not when it becomes due; and the right to payment against a guarantor arises upon the giving of the guarantee even though the right to enforce the guarantee may be contingent upon the subsequent nonpayment by the primary obligor. (The nature of a claim is discussed further at pp. 267–71, *infra.*)

The automatic stay does not prevent the commencement of lawsuits to recover claims that arise after the petition, although, as will be seen, the stay does prevent levy on postpetition claims or judgments against property of the estate. § 362(a)(3). To restrain a lawsuit involving a postpetition claim, the representative of the estate must obtain an affirmative injunction under Section 105(a), assuming he is entitled to one on the merits.

In addition to enjoining the commencement or continuation of lawsuits, the stay prevents the enforcement of prepetition judgments against the debtor or against the property of the estate. § 362(a)(2). The creditor's remedy is to file a proof of claim rather than to enforce the judgment; this filing enables the creditor to

11 U.S.C. § 362. Automatic stay

(a) Except as provided in subsection (b) of this section, a petition filed under section 301, 302, or 303 of this title, or an application filed under section 5(a)(3) of the Securities Investor Protection Act of 1970 (15 U.S.C. 78eee(a)(3)), operates as a stay, applicable to all entities, of—

(1) the commencement or continuation, including the issuance or employment of process, of a judicial, administrative, or other action or proceeding against the debtor that was or could have been commenced before the commencement of the case under this title, or to recover a claim against the debtor that arose before the commencement of the case under this title;

(2) the enforcement, against the debtor or against property of the estate, of a judgment obtained before the commencement of the case under this title;

(3) any act to obtain possession of property of the estate or of property from the estate or to exercise control over property of the estate;

(4) any act to create, perfect, or enforce any lien against property of the estate;

(5) any act to create, perfect, or enforce against property of the debtor any lien to the extent that such lien secures a claim that arose before the commencement of the case under this title;

(6) any act to collect, assess, or recover a claim against the debtor that arose before the commencement of the case under this title;

(7) the setoff of any debt owing to the debtor that arose before the commencement of the case under this title against any claim against the debtor; and

(8) the commencement or continuation of a proceeding before the United States Tax Court concerning the debtor.

participate under a plan or in a distribution of the bankruptcy estate. § 501(a). *But see* § 1111(a).

Despite the literal breadth of the statutory language, it is plain that the automatic stay does not prevent a creditor from filing a proof of claim in the bankruptcy case, nor does it prevent actions in the bankruptcy court to have the stay lifted.[1] The filing of a proof of claim is likely to be the unsecured creditor's exclusive remedy, since the stay prevents enforcement of a prepetition judgment against the debtor's as well as the estate's property. § 362(a)(2). This provision protects the debtor's exempt property, property abandoned to the debtor, and property otherwise acquired by the debtor after the date of the filing of the petition from the reach of unsecured creditors. In most cases the automatic stay against enforcement of a prepetition judgment will continue until the debtor receives a discharge, at which time the discharge injunction of Section 524(a)(2), see p. 313, *infra,* will prevent the creditor from enforcing the judgment against the debtor. Of course, if the discharge is denied, the judgment may be enforced.

In addition to its effect on in personam actions, the stay prevents "any act to obtain possession of property of the estate" or to exercise control over that property. § 362(a)(3). (The estate is defined under Section 541 to include, inter alia, all legal and equitable interests of the debtor in property as of the time of the petition.) The stay also forbids any act to obtain possession of property *from* the estate. *Id.* It is possible that the estate will have possession, custody, or control of property that it does not own and in which it has no legal or equitable interest. In this circumstance, despite the fact that the estate has no possessory right, a party who wishes to take possession of the property must nevertheless first obtain relief from the automatic stay. *See* § 362(a)(3). The stay, to the extent it prevents any act to obtain possession of property of or from the estate, is not restricted to acts based on prepetition claims. Thus

---

[1] *See In re* American Spinning Mills, Inc., 43 Bankr. 365, 367 (Bankr. E.D. Pa. 1984): "Although § 362(a) generally bars all debt collection efforts against the debtor or the property of his bankruptcy estate after the filing of the petition, the stay implicitly does not bar a party from commencing an adversary or contested proceeding against the debtor under the caption of the bankruptcy case in the court where the petition is pending."

11 U.S.C. § 362. Automatic stay

(a) Except as provided in subsection (b) of this section, a petition filed under section 301, 302, or 303 of this title, or an application filed under section 5(a)(3) of the Securities Investor Protection Act of 1970 (15 U.S.C. 78eee(a)(3)), operates as a stay, applicable to all entities, of—

(1) the commencement or continuation, including the issuance or employment of process, of a judicial, administrative, or other action or proceeding against the debtor that was or could have been commenced before the commencement of the case under this title, or to recover a claim against the debtor that arose before the commencement of the case under this title;

(2) the enforcement, against the debtor or against property of the estate, of a judgment obtained before the commencement of the case under this title;

(3) any act to obtain possession of property of the estate or of property from the estate or to exercise control over property of the estate;

(4) any act to create, perfect, or enforce any lien against property of the estate;

(5) any act to create, perfect, or enforce against property of the debtor any lien to the extent that such lien secures a claim that arose before the commencement of the case under this title;

(6) any act to collect, assess, or recover a claim against the debtor that arose before the commencement of the case under this title;

(7) the setoff of any debt owing to the debtor that arose before the commencement of the case under this title against any claim against the debtor; and

(8) the commencement or continuation of a proceeding before the United States Tax Court concerning the debtor.

the holder of a postpetition claim or judgment must seek relief from the stay before acting to reach property of the estate or in the estate's possession.

To supplement the foregoing prohibitions, the stay also prohibits any act to create, perfect, or enforce a lien against property of the estate or, if the lien secures a prepetition claim, against property of the debtor. § 362(a)(4), (5). Thus, with respect to such property, lien enforcement is prohibited, even if the collateral is in the possession of a third party; the creation of a lien after bankruptcy is also prohibited, except to the extent that it is authorized by the court or by another provision of the Bankruptcy Code. *E.g.,* §§ 363, 364, 546(c), 549. Although postpetition perfection of a lien is generally prohibited, Section 362(b)(3) contains an exception to permit a postpetition perfection that, under nonbankruptcy law, would have retroactive effect to a date before bankruptcy. See p. 205, *infra.*

Under Section 362(a)(6), the stay prohibits any "act" — for example, self-help or harassing tactics — to collect, assess, or recover a prepetition claim against the debtor. This important provision should prevent creditors from telephoning the debtor at inconvenient times to press for payment of prepetition debts. But it probably does not prevent a creditor from merely soliciting payment or a reaffirmation of a prepetition debt to the extent permitted by Section 524(c), at least so long as the creditor's effort is not coercive or of a harassing nature. *See, e.g., Morgan Guar. Trust Co. v. American Sav. and Loan,* 804 F.2d 1487 (9th Cir. 1986).

The stay forbids the setoff of a prepetition debt owing to the debtor against any claim against the debtor. § 362(a)(7). It does not, however, affect the substantive issue of whether a creditor is entitled to setoff. *See* § 553. One common form of prepetition debt owing by a creditor to the debtor is a deposit account held by the debtor's lender bank. If the debtor owes money to a bank where the debtor has funds on deposit, the account is generally subject to setoff by the bank under applicable nonbankruptcy law. But once the bankruptcy petition is filed, Section 362(a)(7) prohibits the bank from unilaterally setting off the deposit account to satisfy the prepetition debt owed by the debtor. A wholly separate issue is whether the bank may "freeze" the bank account until it obtains

11 U.S.C. § 362. Automatic stay

(b) The filing of a petition under section 301, 302, or 303 of this title, or of an application under section 5(a)(3) of the Securities Investor Protection Act of 1970 (15 U.S.C. 78eee(a)(3)), does not operate as a stay —

(1) under subsection (a) of this section, of the commencement or continuation of a criminal action or proceeding against the debtor;

(2) under subsection (a) of this section, of the collection of alimony, maintenance, or support from property that is not property of the estate;

(3) under subsection (a) of this section, of any act to perfect an interest in property to the extent that the trustee's rights and powers are subject to such perfection under section 546(b) of this title or to the extent that such act is accomplished within the period provided under section 547(e)(2)(A) of this title;

(4) under subsection (a)(1) of this section, of the commencement or continuation of an action or proceeding by a governmental unit to enforce such governmental unit's police or regulatory power;

(5) under subsection (a)(2) of this section, of the enforcement of a judgment, other than a money judgment, obtained in an action or proceeding by a governmental unit to enforce such governmental unit's police or regulatory power;

(6) under subsection (a) of this section, of the setoff by a commodity broker, forward contract merchant, stockbrokers, financial institutions, or securities clearing agency of any mutual debt and claim under or in connection with commodity contracts, as defined in section 761(4) of this title, forward contracts, or securities contracts, as defined in section 741(7) of this title, that constitutes the setoff of a claim against the debtor for a margin payment, as defined in section 741(5) or 761(15) of this title, or settlement payment, as defined in section 741(8) of this title, arising out of commodity contracts, forward contracts, or securities contracts against cash, securities, or other property held by or due from such com-

[Continued]

relief from the stay — an issue on which the decisional law to date has not been uniform.

It is submitted that the "setoff" which is stayed by Section 362(a)(7) is the bookkeeping or record cancellation of the debts against each other; the bank's mere refusal to pay over the funds on demand or to honor checks drawn on the account is a distinguishable concept. *See* § 542(b). Moreover, the bank's holding of a deposit account subject to the right of setoff makes its claim a secured claim under Section 506(a), and the deposit account constitutes cash collateral under Section 363(a). As a result, the bank's interest in the deposit account should be given adequate protection before the debtor in possession or the trustee may use the deposit account over the bank's objection. *See* § 363(c); *e.g., In re Edgins,* 11 B.C.D. 585 (9th Cir. App. Panels 1984) (bank could "freeze" account despite automatic stay). *But cf. United States ex rel. I.R.S. v. Norton,* 717 F.2d 767 (3d Cir. 1983); *United States v. Reynolds,* 764 F.2d 1004 (4th Cir. 1985). This matter is discussed more fully in connection with the use of collateral at p. 227, *infra.*

The scope of the stay is broad but it is not unlimited. For example, the stay does not enjoin honoring a letter of credit issued by a bank in favor of a creditor. *See, e.g., In re Page,* 18 Bankr. 713 (D.D.C. 1982). Moreover, although the cases are split, the trend of authority seems to be that the stay does not stop the running of time so as, for example, to prevent the expiration of an option or the running of a redemption period. *See, e.g., Johnson v. First Nat'l Bank of Montevideo, Minn.,* 719 F.2d 270 (8th Cir. 1983) (stay does not stop the running of state-created statutory redemption periods). *Contra In re Jenkins,* 19 Bankr. 105 (D. Colo. 1982). *See also* § 108(b).

§ 5.01(b) Exceptions to Stay

Several statutory exceptions to the automatic stay appear in Section 362(b). But even if a matter is excepted from the automatic stay or if the stay under Section 362(a) does not apply by its terms, Section 105(a) is nevertheless potentially available to obtain a court-issued injunction, provided the merits of the controversy justify affirmative injunctive relief.

modity broker, forward contract merchant, stockbroker, financial institutions, or securities clearing agency to margin, guarantee, secure, or settle commodity contracts, forward contracts, or securities contracts;

(7) under subsection (a) of this section, of the setoff by a repo participant, of any mutual debt and claim under or in connection with repurchase agreements that constitutes the setoff of a claim against the debtor for a margin payment, as defined in section 741(5) or 761(15) of this title, or settlement payment, as defined in section 741(8) of this title, arising out of repurchase agreements against cash, securities, or other property held by or due from such repo participant to margin, guarantee, secure or settle repurchase agreements;

(8) under subsection (a) of this section, of the commencement of any action by the Secretary of Housing and Urban Development to foreclose a mortgage or deed of trust in any case in which the mortgage or deed of trust held by the Secretary is insured or was formerly insured under the National Housing Act and covers property, or combinations of property, consisting of five or more living units;

(9) under subsection (a) of this section, of the issuance to the debtor by a governmental unit of a notice of tax deficiency; or

(10) under subsection (a) of this section, of any act by a lessor to the debtor under a lease of nonresidential real property that has terminated by the expiration of the stated term of the lease before the commencement of or during a case under this title to obtain possession of such property; or

(11) under subsection (a) of this section, of the presentment of a negotiable instrument and the giving of notice of and protesting dishonor of such an instrument;

(12) under subsection (a) of this section, after the date which is 90 days after the filing of such petition, of the commencement or continuation, and conclusion to the entry of final judgment, of an action which involves a debtor subject to reorganization pursuant to chapter 11 of this title and which was brought by the Secretary of Transportation under the Ship Mortgage Act, 1920 (46

[Continued]

The exceptions to the automatic stay are narrowly drawn. The stay does not apply to criminal proceedings against the debtor, § 362(b)(1), with the possible exception of criminal proceedings that may be characterized as not bona fide—that is, those specifically designed to collect discharged prepetition debts rather than to vindicate the public interest. Nor does the stay prevent the collection of alimony, maintenance, or support from the debtor's exempt or after-acquired property. § 362(b)(2). As previously noted, an exception to the stay permits retroactive perfection of security interests and statutory liens under Section 546(b) or for purposes of the preference section. The perfection must have retroactive effect to a date before the filing of the petition, or the trustee could generally avoid the unperfected lien by using the Section 544(a) strong-arm power; in that event, postpetition perfection would not save the lien. See pp. 139–49, *supra*.

Perhaps the most significant exceptions to the automatic stay permit governmental units to commence or continue actions to enforce their police or regulatory powers and to enforce nonmonetary judgments in pursuit of those powers. § 362(b)(4), (5). The legislative history reveals that these exceptions are to be narrowly construed to permit the states and municipalities to pursue matters affecting public health and safety—such as environmental pollution, consumer fraud, and condemnation of dangerous structures—but are not intended to apply when the state or municipality is pursuing a proprietary interest. *E.g., Missouri v. United States Bankruptcy Court*, 647 F.2d 768 (8th Cir. 1981). *See also In re Corporacion de Servicios Medicos Hosp.*, 805 F.2d 440 (1st Cir. 1986) (exception does not extend to action by governmental agency to enforce contractual rights). Nevertheless, federal, state, and local agencies seem to have interpreted the police or regulatory power more broadly than originally intended, and the courts have often accommodated this position by expanding the application of the Section 362(b)(4) exception.

As previously noted, even if an action pursuant to a police or regulatory power or to enforce an injunction (that is, a nonmonetary judgment) falls within the Section 362(b)(4) or (5) exception to the automatic stay, the court under the authority of Section 105(a) may affirmatively enjoin the governmental entity in an ap-

App. U.S.C. 911 et seq.) (including distribution of any proceeds of sale) to foreclose a preferred ship or fleet mortgage, or a security interest in or relating to a vessel or vessel under construction, held by the Secretary of Transportation under section 207 or title XI of the Merchant Marine Act, 1936 (46 App. U.S.C. 1117 and 1271 et seq., respectively), or under applicable State law; or

(13) under subsection (a) of this section, after the date which is 90 days after the filing of such petition, of the commencement or continuation, and conclusion to the entry of final judgment, of an action which involves a debtor subject to reorganization pursuant to chapter 11 of this title and which was brought by the Secretary of Commerce under the Ship Mortgage Act, 1920 (46 App. U.S.C. 911 et seq.) (including distribution of any proceeds of sale) to foreclose a preferred ship or fleet mortgage in a vessel or a mortgage, deed of trust, or other security interest in or fishing facility held by the Secretary of Commerce under section 207 or title XI of the Merchant Marine Act, 1936 (46 App. U.S.C. 1117 and 1271 et seq., respectively).

propriate case. Although it is clear that the Section 362(b)(5) exception to the stay permits enforcement by a governmental unit of an injunction to prevent the debtor from acting in a particular manner, it is as yet unclear whether the governmental unit can compel the trustee or debtor in possession to spend monies of the estate to remedy a preexisting condition or to remove a continuing condition. (Compare *Ohio v. Kovacs*, 469 U.S. 274 (1985), involving the effect of a bankruptcy discharge in this context, discussed at pp. 267–69, *infra*.)

As modified by the 1984 amendments, the automatic stay does not apply to any act by the debtor's lessor "under a lease of non-residential real property that has terminated by the expiration of the *stated term* of the lease" to obtain possession of the premises. § 362(b)(10) (emphasis added). Apparently, the automatic stay still applies when such lease terminates because of default or for some reason other than expiration of the stated term.

Other exceptions to the automatic stay apply to particular debtors or to particular kinds of collateral. For example, two exceptions permit stockbrokers, commodity brokers, and financial institutions to exercise specified rights of setoff, § 362(b)(6), (7); two other exceptions relate to certain actions by the Secretaries of Transportation and Commerce to foreclose specified ship mortgages. § 362(b)(12), (13). (The latter two exceptions are temporary provisions that apply only to petitions filed before 1990. P.L. 99-509.) And the holder of an interest in aircraft, vessels, or rolling stock is protected in certain Chapter 11 cases and in railroad reorganizations, notwithstanding the automatic stay. *See* §§ 1110, 1168.

§ 5.01(c) Violation of Stay

What are the consequences of violating the automatic stay? Generally, courts have treated violations, if willful, as punishable by contempt. The Bankruptcy Code does not contain a statutory limitation on the contempt power. Thus it has been held that a violator of the automatic stay may be subject to a compensatory civil contempt fine or may be imprisoned until the contempt is purged. Criminal contempt sanctions are also possible. (As to whether bankruptcy judges, as distingushed from the district

11 U.S.C. § 362. Automatic stay

(h) An individual injured by any willful violation of a stay provided by this section shall recover actual damages, including costs and attorneys' fees, and, in appropriate circumstances, may recover punitive damages.

11 U.S.C. § 362. Automatic stay

(c) Except as provided in subsections (d), (e), and (f) of this section —

(1) the stay of an act against property of the estate under subsection (a) of this section continues until such property is no longer property of the estate; and

(2) the stay of any other act under subsection (a) of this section continues until the earliest of—

(A) the time the case is closed;

(B) the time the case is dismissed; or

(C) if the case is a case under chapter 7 of this title concerning an individual or a case under chapter 9, 11, 12, or 13 of this title, the time a discharge is granted or denied.

court, may exercise the contempt power, see pp. 57–61, *supra.*) In addition, actions that violate the stay ordinarily have no legal effect unless the stay is subsequently annulled. *But cf.* § 549(c), discussed *supra*, pp. 185–87; *In re Brooks,* 79 B.R. 479 (9th Cir. App. Panels 1987) (creditor's postpetition perfection of its deed of trust in violation of automatic stay was nevertheless effective where a state was closed without challenge to its encumbrance).

It was originally questioned whether a violation of the automatic stay gave rise to a private right of action for damages, as distinguished from a compensatory civil contempt remedy. Section 362(h), however, added by amendment in 1984, provides that an *individual* injured by any willful violation of the stay is entitled to recover actual damages, including costs and attorney's fees, and, in appropriate circumstances, punitive damages. This private right of action has been extended by court decision to debtors that are partnerships and corporations. *Budget Service Co. v. Better Homes of Virginia, Inc.,* 804 F.2d 289 (4th Cir. 1986).

§ 5.01(d) Duration of Stay

Unless a party subject to the stay moves for and obtains relief from it, the automatic stay of acts other than acts against property of the estate continues in effect until the earliest of (1) "the time the case is closed," (2) "the time the case is dismissed," or (3) "the time a discharge is granted or denied." § 362(c)(2). In a Chapter 11 case, the discharge generally occurs when the plan is confirmed, whereas in the ordinary Chapter 12 or 13 case, the discharge is granted upon completion of the payments required under the plan. (When the automatic stay expires by reason of the granting of the discharge, it is superseded by the injunctive effect of the discharge order. See p. 313, *infra.*)

Unless lifted earlier, the stay of any act against property of the estate terminates when the property ceases to be property of the estate. § 362(c)(1). For example, if the property is sold, abandoned, exempted, or revested on confirmation of a plan, the provisions of the Section 362(a) stay that protect the estate's property terminate so as to permit otherwise lawful acts concerning that property. Of course, if the property leaves the estate and becomes property of the debtor — for example, by exemption or abandonment — the stay pro-

11 U.S.C. § 362. Automatic stay

(f) Upon request of a party in interest, the court, with or without a hearing, shall grant such relief from the stay provided under subsection (a) of this section as is necessary to prevent irreparable damage to the interest of an entity in property, if such interest will suffer such damage before there is an opportunity for notice and a hearing under subsection (d) or (e) of this section.

11 U.S.C. § 362. Automatic stay

(d) On request of a party in interest and after notice and a hearing, the court shall grant relief from the stay provided under subsection (a) of this section, such as by terminating, annulling, modifying, or conditioning such stay —

(1) for cause, including the lack of adequate protection of an interest in property of such party in interest; or

(2) with respect to a stay of an act against property under subsection (a) of this section, if—

(A) the debtor does not have an equity in such property; and

(B) such property is not necessary to an effective reorganization.

visions of Section 362(a) that protect the debtor's property continue
to apply until relief from them is obtained, the case is closed or dismissed, or a discharge is granted or denied.

§ 5.01(e) Relief from Stay

A party in interest may request relief from the stay at any time
during the case by initiating a contested matter under Bankruptcy
Rule 9014. Bankruptcy Rules 4001(a)(1), 9014, and 9013 require
the relief to be requested by noticed motion. Often, local bankruptcy rules are also applicable. In rare circumstances ex parte
relief will be appropriate under Section 362(f) if the movant would
otherwise suffer irreparable injury. For example, the movant might
have a security interest in perishable collateral that the debtor is
not protecting and thus might legitimately need prompt possession. Under such unusual circumstances relief from the stay could
be granted without prior notice to the adverse party, if a verified
motion or declaration clearly shows that the movant will suffer
immediate and irreparable injury, loss, or damage before the adverse party or his attorney can be heard in opposition; in addition,
the movant's attorney must certify to the court in writing any efforts that have been made to give notice and the reasons why
notice should not be required. Bankruptcy Rule 4001(a)(3). Ordinarily, of course, the procedure prescribed by the Bankruptcy
Rules for contested matters, including the provisions for fair notice, will apply.

If relief is indicated, the court can terminate, annul, modify, or
condition the automatic stay. § 362(d). Termination of the stay
simply ends the operation of the stay prospectively. Annulment of
the stay, a rather unusual type of relief, treats the parties as though
the stay had never existed. Thus an annulment retroactively validates an act done in violation of the stay. Modification of the stay
can be used to grant partial relief. For example, a court might
permit a creditor to record a notice of default or take other
preliminary steps toward lien enforcement, to accelerate a debt, or
to commence a lawsuit, but not to take any action to enforce any
judgment or to conduct a lien foreclosure sale of property of the
estate. A common example of modification is a court order that
permits a creditor to bring suit against the debtor to reach the

11 U.S.C. § 362. Automatic stay

(d) On request of a party in interest and after notice and a hearing, the court shall grant relief from the stay provided under subsection (a) of this section, such as by terminating, annulling, modifying, or conditioning such stay—

(1) for cause, including the lack of adequate protection of an interest in property of such party in interest; or

(2) with respect to a stay of an act against property under subsection (a) of this section, if—

(A) the debtor does not have an equity in such property; and

(B) such property is not necessary to an effective reorganization.

debtor's insurance coverage, so long as no steps are taken to enforce the judgment directly against the debtor. A stay can be conditioned in a number of other ways. For example, the court might require the debtor to make specified periodic cash payments to a secured party, in default of which the stay against lien enforcement will automatically terminate.

One ground for relief from the stay of an act against property of either the debtor or the estate requires a showing that (1) the debtor has no equity in the property *and* that (2) the property is not necessary to an effective reorganization. § 362(d)(2). To decide whether the debtor has an equity for this purpose, it is necessary to value the property to determine its worth as compared with the dollar amount of all encumbering liens and charges. The law does not specify the appropriate valuation method or the time when the property is to be valued, and the courts have been inconsistent in resolving these points. The second requirement for relief from the stay under Section 362(d)(2) is that the property is not necessary to an effective reorganization. If the case is a Chapter 7 liquidation case, this element would seem to be satisfied automatically. In a Chapter 9, 11, 12, or 13 case, however, the courts will inquire not only whether the property plays a role in the potential plan but also whether the reorganization or rehabilitation is reasonably likely. *See United Sav. Ass'n of Texas v. Timbers of Inwood Forest Associates, Ltd.,* ____ U.S. ____, 108 S.Ct. 626 (1988). As a practical matter, if the property is important enough for the debtor to defend against the motion for relief from the stay, the court, at least on an interim basis, will usually find the property to be necessary to an effective reorganization and will deny relief insofar as Section 362(d)(2) is concerned.

Section 362(d)(2), just discussed, applies only to relief from the stay of an act against property of the debtor or the estate. In contrast, Section 362(d)(1) provides a more general ground of "cause" for obtaining relief from the stay in any of its aspects, including the stay of an act against property. "Cause" can consist of the lack of adequate protection of the movant's interest in the subject property (of either the debtor or the estate), as explained more fully later. It might also include, among other things, exposure of the property to unreasonable risks because of inadequate insur-

11 U.S.C. § 362. Automatic stay

(d) On request of a party in interest and after notice and a hearing, the court shall grant relief from the stay provided under subsection (a) of this section, such as by terminating, annulling, modifying, or conditioning such stay—

(1) for cause, including the lack of adequate protection of an interest in property of such party in interest; or

(2) with respect to a stay of an act against property under subsection (a) of this section, if—

(A) the debtor does not have an equity in such property; and

(B) such property is not necessary to an effective reorganization.

(e) Thirty days after a request under subsection (d) of this section for relief from the stay of any act against property of the estate under subsection (a) of this section, such stay is terminated with respect to the party in interest making such request, unless the court, after notice and a hearing, orders such stay continued in effect pending the conclusion of, or as a result of, a final hearing and determination under subsection (d) of this section. A hearing under this subsection may be a preliminary hearing, or may be consolidated with the final hearing under subsection (d) of this section. The court shall order such stay continued in effect pending the conclusion of the final hearing under subsection (d) of this section if there is a reasonable likelihood that the party opposing relief from such stay will prevail at the conclusion of such final hearing. If the hearing under this subsection is a preliminary hearing, then such final hearing shall be commenced not later than thirty days after the conclusion of such preliminary hearing.

(g) In any hearing under subsection (d) or (e) of this section concerning relief from the stay of any act under subsection (a) of this section—

(1) the party requesting such relief has the burden of proof on the issue of the debtor's equity in property; and

(2) the party opposing such relief has the burden of proof on all other issues.

ance coverage or unsatisfactory maintenance by the trustee; the movant's desire to liquidate an in personam claim in state court, particularly if complex and unsettled state law questions are involved or if the purpose of the suit is to reach the debtor's insurance carrier; the debtor's unlawful possession of the subject property; the debtor's misconduct; or the bad faith filing of the bankruptcy case itself.

§ 5.01(f) Procedure

Although the motion for relief must allege a ground under Section 362(d), the party opposing relief from the stay has the burden of proof on all issues other than that of equity in the property when this becomes relevant under Section 362(d)(2). *See* § 362(g).

Section 362(e) provides an expedited procedure for obtaining relief from the stay of an act against property of the estate. The provision is intended to put pressure on the court to dispose of this kind of litigation with reasonable dispatch. Thirty days after the filing of a motion for relief, the stay terminates automatically unless the court on the merits enters an order continuing the stay in effect or continuing it in effect pending the conclusion of a final hearing. If the stay is continued in effect at a preliminary hearing pending the conclusion of a final hearing, then the final hearing must commence within 30 days after the preliminary hearing concludes; otherwise, the stay will expire automatically. Bankruptcy Rule 4001(a)(2) further provides for automatic expiration of the stay 30 days following the commencement of the final hearing unless the court before that date denies the requested relief from the stay or orders the stay continued pending conclusion of the final hearing. It must be emphasized again that this expedited procedure applies only with respect to relief from the stay of acts against property of the estate. It will not apply, for example, to a motion for relief from a stay of the commencement or continuation of an in personam lawsuit or from a stay of an act to enforce a lien against property of the debtor.

Courtroom procedure when a motion for relief from the stay is made varies greatly among bankruptcy judges. Some permit attorneys to offer live testimony, whereas others restrict evidence to

written declarations. Some will adjudicate defenses or counter-claims to the motion, whereas others will severely limit defenses and sever counterclaims.

Relief from the automatic stay may also be granted as a result of the parties' agreement. Bankruptcy Rule 4001(d) provides the procedure for obtaining court approval of such an agreement.

§ 5.01(g) Adequate Protection

When a motion is made for relief from the automatic stay of lien enforcement (against either the estate's or the debtor's property), an important issue that often arises is whether the movant's interest in the property is adequately protected. Some methods of providing adequate protection are illustrated in Section 361. (Section 361 does not apply in Chapter 12, which has its own § 1205 dealing with adequate protection.) Before considering the methods, however, it is useful to consider four questions.

First, what is being adequately protected? The creditor is not entitled to protection. Nor is the amount of the creditor's claim. Rather, Sections 361 and 362(d)(1) refer to the interest of the creditor in property as being entitled to the adequate protection.

Second, in what context does the issue of adequate protection arise? Adequate protection is being discussed here in the context of relief from the automatic stay. But the concept is also relevant in the context of the right to use a secured creditor's collateral under Section 363 and in the context of borrowing on already encumbered collateral under Section 364. These other topics are discussed more fully later.

Third, what kinds of interests are entitled to adequate protection? Not all creditors hold interests in property that are so entitled. Unsecured creditors have no specific interest in property and therefore have no interest entitled to adequate protection. It has been held, perhaps questionably, that a landlord's interest in property leased to the debtor is not entitled to adequate protection in the context of relief from the stay but is governed exclusively by Section 365, which covers executory contracts. The Bankruptcy Code itself, however, does not identify the kinds of property rights entitled to adequate protection; it requires only that the right be an

"interest in property." *See, e.g.,* § 363(e). Statistically, adequate protection has most often been accorded to a creditor with either a lien encumbering property of the debtor or the estate or with a right of setoff.

Fourth, what aspect of the property interest requires protection? As noted earlier, the value of the interest in property, not the amount of the debt, is entitled to protection by the literal terms of the Code. Thus when the amount of the debt exceeds the value of the creditor's interest in the collateral, the unsecured portion of the debt is not entitled to adequate protection.

It seems plain that the value of the creditor's interest in property must at least be protected from physical and economic depreciation and insured against unreasonable risk of loss. But there was disagreement among the several courts of appeals that decided the issue as to whether a creditor whose claim was partially unsecured (because the value of his collateral was less than the amount of his claim) was entitled to compensation by way of postpetition interest (as a component of adequate protection) for the delay in foreclosure caused by the automatic stay — that is, for the so-called lost opportunity cost or time value of money, based on the value of the collateral, during the period of delay attributable to the automatic stay.[2] A majority of those courts concluded that adequate protection in this context *did* require such compensation, at least under certain circumstances. The matter was put to rest in *United Sav. Ass'n of Texas v. Timbers of Inwood Forest Associates, Ltd.,* _____ U.S. _____, 108 S.Ct. 626 (1988). The Supreme Court there held that the interest in property that must be adequately protected as a condition of denying relief from the stay under § 362(d)(1) is only the value of the collateral itself, and that a present value analysis is not involved. In other words, such property interest does not include the nonbankruptcy right of an undersecured creditor to take possession of the collateral, enforce the lien, and reinvest the foreclosure proceeds, nor is compensation by way of postpetition interest required for the stay's interference with that right.

---

[2] A fully secured creditor, i.e., one whose claim is less than the value of his security, is entitled by the express provision of Section 506(b) to postpetition interest to the extent the collateral is sufficient to cover it. See p. 277, *infra.*

11 U.S.C. § 361. Adequate protection

When adequate protection is required under section 362, 363, or 364 of this title of an interest of an entity in property, such adequate protection may be provided by—

(1) requiring the trustee to make a cash payment or periodic cash payments to such entity, to the extent that the stay under section 362 of this title, use, sale, or lease under section 363 of this title, or any grant of a lien under section 364 of this title results in a decrease in the value of such entity's interest in such property;

(2) providing to such entity an additional or replacement lien to the extent that such stay, use, sale, lease, or grant results in a decrease in the value of such entity's interest in such property; or

(3) granting such other relief, other than entitling such entity to compensation allowable under section 503(b)(1) of this title as an administrative expense, as will result in the realization by such entity of the indubitable equivalent of such entity's interest in such property.

In Section 361, the Code illustrates three methods of furnishing adequate protection. These methods can be understood by considering their application to a secured creditor. Under Section 361(1), adequate protection can be provided by periodic cash payments to the creditor equal to the decrease in the value of the collateral. Under Section 361(2), adequate protection can be furnished by granting a replacement or additional lien on other property equal to the decrease in the value of the creditor's interest in the collateral. Finally, under Section 361(3), adequate protection may consist of any other relief that will result in the realization of the "indubitable equivalent" of the creditor's interest in the property. Granting the creditor an administrative claim under Section 503(b)(1), however, is specifically excluded as an "indubitable equivalent."

The term "indubitable equivalent" is derived from Judge Learned Hand's use of the words "most indubitable equivalence" in *In re Murel Holding Corp.*, 75 F.2d 941, 942 (2d Cir. 1935). Actually, awarding an "indubitable equivalent" is not a method of adequate protection at all; rather, the "indubitable equivalent" is a standard against which some courts measure proposed forms of adequate protection. It is the only standard mentioned in Section 361 that does not focus merely on a decrease in the creditor's interest in the property. It generally requires that the adequate protection be completely compensatory of the creditor's interest in that property. For example, abandonment of the collateral to the secured party should constitute the "indubitable equivalent" of that creditor's interest, and the legislative history so states. Similarly, sale of the collateral when the secured party has the right to "bid in" the secured claim, with a transfer of the lien to proceeds if the secured creditor is not the purchaser, arguably constitutes the "indubitable equivalent" of the creditor's interest.

The foregoing illustrations are not exclusive. Indeed, statistically the most common way of satisfying the requirement for adequate protection is to demonstrate that the collateral itself has a value that exceeds the amount of the secured claim. Thus if a creditor is oversecured, the amount by which the value of the collateral exceeds the creditor's claim can constitute adequate protection in the form of an "equity cushion." *E.g., In re Mellor*, 734 F.2d 1396 (9th Cir. 1984). Different courts use different standards of

11 U.S.C. § 363. Use, sale, or lease of property

(b)(1) The trustee, after notice and a hearing, may use, sell, or lease, other than in the ordinary course of business, property of the estate.

11 U.S.C. § 102. Rules of construction

In this title—

(1) "after notice and a hearing", or a similar phrase—

(A) means after such notice as is appropriate in the particular circumstances, and such opportunity for a hearing as is appropriate in the particular circumstances; but

(B) authorizes an act without an actual hearing if such notice is given properly and if—

(i) such a hearing is not requested timely by a party in interest; or

(ii) there is insufficient time for a hearing to be commenced before such act must be done, and the court authorizes such act;

valuation to compute the value of collateral in this context. Some use fair market value, whereas others use liquidation value. An equity cushion protects a secured creditor's property interest in present-value terms by permitting postpetition interest to accrue on his claim. § 506(b). Similarly, the holder of a senior lien encumbering property may be adequately protected by a *"value* cushion,"* even though the existence of junior liens leaves the estate with no actual equity in the property. *See In re Mellor, supra.*

The form adequate protection takes in a particular case frequently is determined by the negotiated agreement of the parties. Court approval of this kind of agreement may be obtained through a procedure specified in Bankruptcy Rule 4001(d).

§ 5.02 USE, SALE, AND LEASE OF PROPERTY

The statutory provisions on the use, sale, and lease of property of the estate are found in Section 363. The trustee in a Chapter 7 liquidation case must sell property of the estate so as to reduce it to money for distribution to creditors. To operate the business in a Chapter 11 reorganization case, the trustee or debtor in possession must be able to use, sell, or lease property of the estate even though a third party may have some interest in that property. The legal standards or restrictions governing the use, sale, and lease of property of the estate vary depending on whether the use is in or out of the ordinary course of business and whether the property is "cash collateral" or other property of the estate.

§ 5.02(a) Out of the Ordinary Course of Business

The use, sale, or lease of any property of the estate, other than in the ordinary course of business (or when operation of the business is not authorized) may be accomplished "after notice and a hearing"; that is, advance notice is required, but no court order is necessary unless a timely objection to the proposed transaction is filed. §§ 363(b)(1), 102(1). Bankruptcy Rule 2002(a) generally requires that all creditors receive not less than 20 days' notice by mail of a proposed use, sale, or lease of property other than in the ordinary course of business. Bankruptcy Rule 2002(c)(1) requires

11 U.S.C. § 363. Use, sale, or lease of property

(e) Notwithstanding any other provision of this section, at any time, on request of an entity that has an interest in property used, sold, or leased, or proposed to be used, sold, or leased, by the trustee, the court, with or without a hearing, shall prohibit or condition such use, sale, or lease as is necessary to provide adequate protection of such interest.

the notice to include "the time and place of any public sale, the terms and conditions of any private sale and the time fixed for filing objections." Bankruptcy Rule 6004(b) provides that "an objection to a proposed use, sale, or lease of property shall be filed and served not less than five days before the date set for the proposed action or within the time fixed by the court."

Local bankruptcy rules may impose additional requirements. Moreover, for cause shown, the court may reduce (or enlarge) the time limits specified in the Rules, thus accommodating the occasional need to act swiftly in emergencies. Bankruptcy Rule 9006(b), (c). On the other hand, the debtor should not be able to manufacture an emergency to deprive interested parties of a meaningful opportunity to appear and be heard. *See, e.g., In re Sullivan Ford Sales,* 2 Bankr. 350 (Bankr. D. Me. 1980).

A secured party whose property interest in collateral is not adequately protected may object to a proposed use, sale, or lease of that collateral. § 363(e). The principles discussed earlier in the context of relief from the automatic stay, see pp. 217–23, *supra,* thus can come into play in the context of litigation about the use of collateral.

If a timely objection is made, the court will hold a hearing and will enter an order authorizing or denying the use, sale, or lease of the property in question. If a timely objection is not made, however, the proposed use, sale, or lease may be carried out by the trustee or debtor in possession without a court order, as noted earlier.

Courts ordinarily will not permit a Chapter 11 debtor in possession to use Section 363(b) to sell all or substantially all its assets out of the ordinary course of business before the plan stage of the case, unless an emergency exists or, perhaps, if a clear business necessity for the transaction is articulated. *E.g., In re Lionel Corp.,* 722 F.2d 1063 (2d Cir. 1983). The bulk sale offers a potential way to short-circuit the protection accorded by the plan process, which requires the debtor to distribute a disclosure statement to creditors and to solicit votes on a plan of reorganization. Certainly, when the sale of all the assets involves, in addition to the transfer itself, a significant restructuring of creditors' rights, a court should insist that there be compliance with the statutory protections built into the plan process. *In re Braniff Airways, Inc.,* 700 F.2d 935 (5th Cir. 1983).

11 U.S.C. § 363. Use, sale, or lease of property

(a) In this section, "cash collateral" means cash, negotiable instruments, documents of title, securities, deposit accounts, or other cash equivalents whenever acquired in which the estate and an entity other than the estate have an interest and includes the proceeds, products, offspring, rents, or profits of property subject to a security interest as provided in section 522(b) of this title, whether existing before or after the commencement of a case under this title.

11 U.S.C. § 363. Use, sale, or lease of property

(e) Notwithstanding any other provision of this section, at any time, on request of an entity that has an interest in property used, sold, or leased, or proposed to be used, sold, or leased, by the trustee, the court, with or without a hearing, shall prohibit or condition such use, sale, or lease as is necessary to provide adequate protection of such interest.

11 U.S.C. § 363. Use, sale, or lease of property

(c)(1) If the business of the debtor is authorized to be operated under section 721, 1108, 1304, 1203 or 1204 of this title and unless the court orders otherwise, the trustee may enter into transactions, including the sale or lease of property of the estate, in the ordinary course of business, without notice or a hearing, and may use property of the estate in the ordinary course of business without notice or a hearing.

(2) The trustee may not use, sell, or lease cash collateral under paragraph (1) of this subsection unless—

(A) each entity that has an interest in such cash collateral consents; or

(B) the court, after notice and a hearing, authorizes such use, sale, or lease in accordance with the provisions of this section.

(3) Any hearing under paragraph (2)(B) of this subsection may be a preliminary hearing or may be consolidated with a hearing under subsection (e) of this section, but shall be scheduled in accordance with the needs of the debtor. If the hearing under paragraph (2)(B) of this subsection is a

[Continued]

§ 5.02(b) In the Ordinary Course of Business

If the proposed use, sale, or lease of estate property is in the ordinary course of business, a distinction is made between property that is cash collateral and property that is not. "Cash collateral" means "cash, negotiable instruments, documents of title, securities, deposit accounts, or other cash equivalents in which the estate and an entity other than the estate have an interest." § 363(a). Although inventory and receivables subject to a security interest are not cash collateral under this definition, cash proceeds of inventory and receivables become cash collateral as the cash is collected, either before or after bankruptcy (to the extent that the lien survives under Section 552, see pp. 279–81, *infra*). Unless the court orders otherwise, property of the estate other than cash collateral may be used, sold, or leased in the ordinary course of business without a court order and without advance notice of the intended transaction. A secured party by appropriate motion, however, may insist upon adequate protection as a condition of the trustee's or debtor in possession's continuing to use the noncash collateral. § 363(e).

Cash collateral, on the other hand, may not be used, sold, or leased in the ordinary course of business unless the creditor with an interest in the collateral consents or the court, after notice and a hearing, authorizes the transaction. The court must act promptly to determine whether the creditor's interest in the cash collateral is or will be adequately protected and should schedule the hearing in accordance with the needs of the debtor. § 363(c)(3). Bankruptcy Rule 4001(b) specifies the procedure governing a motion for authorization to use such collateral. Unless the creditor agrees or the court orders otherwise, cash collateral used in the ordinary course of business must be segregated and accounted for. § 363(c)(4).

When adequate protection of any kind of property interest is required by Section 363(e), it may be provided in the manner described earlier. See pp. 217–23, *supra*. Periodic payments are not required when an "equity cushion" exists and constitutes adequate protection. The trustee or debtor in possession has the burden of proof on the issue of adequate protection, whereas the other party

preliminary hearing, the court may authorize such use, sale, or lease only if there is a reasonable likelihood that the trustee will prevail at the final hearing under subsection (e) of this section. The court shall act promptly on any request for authorization under paragraph (2)(B) of this subsection.

(4) Except as provided in paragraph (2) of this subsection, the trustee shall segregate and account for any cash collateral in the trustee's possession, custody, or control.

11 U.S.C. § 363. Use, sale, or lease of property

(*o*) In any hearing under this section —

(1) the trustee has the burden of proof on the issue of adequate protection; and

(2) the entity asserting an interest in property has the burden of proof on the issue of the validity, priority, or extent of such interest.

11 U.S.C. § 363. Use, sale, or lease of property

(d) The trustee may use, sell, or lease property under subsection (b) or (c) of this section only to the extent not inconsistent with any relief granted under section 362(c), 362(d), 362(e), or 362(f) of this title.

11 U.S.C. § 363. Use, sale, or lease of property

(f) The trustee may sell property under subsection (b) or (c) of this section free and clear of any interest in such property of an entity other than the estate, only if —

(1) applicable nonbankruptcy law permits sale of such property free and clear of such interest;

(2) such entity consents;

(3) such interest is a lien and the price at which such property is to be sold is greater than the aggregate value of all liens on such property;

(4) such interest is in bona fide dispute; or

(5) such entity could be compelled, in a legal or equitable proceeding, to accept a money satisfaction of such interest.

(g) Notwithstanding subsection (f) of this section, the trustee may sell property under subsection (b) or (c) of this section free and clear of any vested or contingent right in the nature of dower or curtesy.

asserting an interest in the property has the burden of proof on the issue of the validity, priority, or extent of such interest. § 363(*o*).

Finally, the use, sale, or lease of property under Section 363 may not be inconsistent with relief from the automatic stay granted under Section 362. § 363(d).

§ 5.02(c) Sales of Estate Property Free and Clear of Others' Interests and Sales of Jointly Owned Property

Under certain circumstances set forth in Section 363(f), the trustee or debtor in possession may sell estate property free and clear of the interests of third parties in that property. The various interests then are typically transferred to the proceeds of the sale, without effect on the relative rights; alternatively, adequate protection of the third parties' interests is furnished in some other way. A free-and-clear sale is authorized by Section 363(f) only if one of five conditions is satisfied. First, if applicable nonbankruptcy law permits the sale of property free and clear, this authorization extends to the trustee in a bankruptcy case. Second, a sale free and clear may occur if the entity asserting the interest in the estate property consents. Although express consent after the filing of the bankruptcy case certainly would suffice, it is at least arguable that consent in a prebankruptcy security agreement that is not in default may also be adequate. Third, a sale free and clear may occur if the debtor has an equity in the property—that is, if the interest of the third party "is a lien and the price at which such property is to be sold is greater than the aggregate value of all liens on such property." § 363(f)(3). Fourth, a sale free and clear is permitted if the competing interest is the subject of a bona fide dispute. Fifth, if the entity with the competing interest in the property could be compelled in a legal or equitable proceeding to accept a money satisfaction of the interest, the trustee may sell the property free and clear of that interest.

Under Section 363(g), the trustee may also sell property "free and clear of any vested or contingent right in the nature of dower or curtesy."

Sometimes property only partially owned by the estate may be sold. When the debtor owns an undivided interest in property as a

11 U.S.C. § 363. Use, sale, or lease of property

(h) Notwithstanding subsection (f) of this section, the trustee may sell both the estate's interest, under subsection (b) or (c) of this section, and the interest of any co-owner in property in which the debtor had, at the time of the commencement of the case, an undivided interest as a tenant in common, joint tenant, or tenant by the entirety, only if—

(1) partition in kind of such property among the estate and such co-owners is impracticable;

(2) sale of the estate's undivided interest in such property would realize significantly less for the estate than sale of such property free of the interests of such co-owners;

(3) the benefit to the estate of a sale of such property free of the interests of co-owners outweighs the detriment, if any, to such co-owners; and

(4) such property is not used in the production, transmission, or distribution, for sale, of electric energy or of natural or synthetic gas for heat, light, or power.

(i) Before the consummation of a sale of property to which subsection (g) or (h) of this section applies, or of property of the estate that was community property of the debtor and the debtor's spouse immediately before the commencement of the case, the debtor's spouse, or a co-owner of such property, as the case may be, may purchase such property at the price at which such sale is to be consummated.

(j) After a sale of property to which subsection (g) or (h) of this section applies, the trustee shall distribute to the debtor's spouse or the co-owners of such property, as the case may be, and to the estate, the proceeds of such sale, less the costs and expenses, not including any compensation of the trustee, of such sale, according to the interests of such spouse or co-owners, and of the estate.

(k) At a sale under subsection (b) of this section of property that is subject to a lien that secures an allowed claim, unless the court for cause orders otherwise the holder of such claim may bid at such sale, and, if the holder of such claim purchases such property, such holder may offset such claim against the purchase price of such property.

tenant in common, joint tenant, or tenant by the entirety, the trustee or debtor in possession may sell both the estate's interest and the interest of the co-owner if all of four conditions are met. § 363(h). First, partitioning the property between the estate and the co-owner must be impracticable. Second, the estate's pro rata interest in the proceeds from a sale of the entire property must be significantly greater than the amount that would be realized if only the estate's undivided interest were sold. Third, sale of the entire property must benefit the estate more than it will harm the co-owner. Fourth, the property must not be "used in the production, transmission, or distribution, for sale, of electric energy or of natural or synthetic gas for heat, light, or power."

If the trustee or debtor in possession proposes to sell property free and clear of a vested or contingent right in the nature of dower or curtesy, or to sell community property or the property of a co-owner, either the debtor's spouse or the co-owner of the property, as the case may be, has a right of first refusal to purchase the property at the price at which the sale is to be consummated. § 363(i). If the spouse or co-owner does not purchase the property, the trustee or debtor in possession must distribute the spouse's or co-owner's share of the sale proceeds immediately after the sale. Only the net proceeds will be turned over to the spouse or co-owner, since the costs of the sale (not including the compensation of any trustee) will be deducted from the gross proceeds. § 363(j). Because most community property becomes property of the estate of the first spouse to file—that is, it is not merely the debtor's interest in such property that passes to the estate, *see* § 541(a)(2) and p. 123, *supra*—it is unlikely that any proceeds would be distributed to the nondebtor spouse when community property is sold, even though that spouse has a right of first refusal.

If property subject to a lien is sold out of the ordinary course of business, the secured creditor may, unless the court orders otherwise, credit bid at the sale and offset the amount of his claim against the purchase price of the property. § 363(k).

§ 5.02(d) Procedure

A proceeding to obtain leave to sell "both the interest of the estate and of a co-owner in property" under Section 363(h) or "to

11 U.S.C. § 363. Use, sale, or lease of property

(*l*) Subject to the provisions of section 365, the trustee may use, sell, or lease property under subsection (b) or (c) of this section, or a plan under chapter 11, 12, or 13 of this title may provide for the use, sale, or lease of property, notwithstanding any provision in a contract, a lease, or applicable law that is conditioned on the insolvency or financial condition of the debtor, on the commencement of a case under this title concerning the debtor, or on the appointment of or the taking possession by a trustee in a case under this title or a custodian, and that effects, or gives an option to effect, a forfeiture, modification, or termination of the debtor's interest in such property.

determine the validity, priority, or extent of a lien or other interest in property" is an "adversary proceeding" that must be initiated by a complaint. Bankruptcy Rules 7001(3),(2); 7003. A proceeding to request the use of cash collateral when the secured party does not consent is a "contested matter" that is initiated by motion. Bankruptcy Rule 4001(b). So is a proceeding to sell assets free and clear of liens or other property interests pursuant to § 363(f) or (g). Bankruptcy Rule 6004(c); *see also* Bankruptcy Rule 2002(a)(2) (which requires 20 days' notice to creditors and other parties in interest of such a proposed sale).

On the other hand, as has been noted before, neither a complaint or motion is necessary when the trustee or debtor in possession proposes, in an out of the ordinary course of business transaction, to use or lease property or to conduct a sale that is not free of liens or other property interests. It is sufficient under these circumstances that parties in interest receive 20 days' notice of the proposed use, sale, or lease of the property. Bankruptcy Rules 2002(a)(2), 6004(a). If a timely objection is made in response to such a notice, however, a hearing will be set and the contested matter procedure will govern. Bankruptcy Rule 6004(b), (e).

§ 5.02(e) General Provisions

Subject to the provisions of Section 365 relating to executory contracts, the trustee or debtor in possession may use, sell, or lease property of the estate notwithstanding an ipso facto (or forfeiture) clause in a contract, a lease, or applicable law—that is, a clause giving rights to the nondebtor party conditioned on the insolvency or financial condition of the debtor, on the commencement of a bankruptcy case, or on the appointment of a trustee or a custodian. § 363(*l*). In other words, such a clause is unenforceable in this context. A "due-on-sale" clause, however, appears to be enforceable under the statutory language if property is sold during bankruptcy, provided the clause would otherwise be valid under nonbankruptcy law. *See, e.g., In re Anthony's Restaurant,* 44 Bankr. 542 (Bankr. E.D. Pa. 1984).

Unless a party in interest opposing a sale or lease under Section 363 obtains a stay pending appeal of the order authorizing the transaction, the reversal or modification of the order on appeal

11 U.S.C. § 363. Use, sale, or lease of property

(m) The reversal or modification on appeal of an authorization under subsection (b) or (c) of this section of a sale or lease of property does not affect the validity of a sale or lease under such authorization to an entity that purchased or leased such property in good faith, whether or not such entity knew of the pendency of the appeal, unless such authorization and such sale or lease were stayed pending appeal.

(n) The trustee may avoid a sale under this section if the sale price was controlled by an agreement among potential bidders at such sale, or may recover from a party to such agreement any amount by which the value of the property sold exceeds the price at which such sale was consummated, and may recover any costs, attorneys' fees, or expenses incurred in avoiding such sale or recovering such amount. In addition to any recovery under the preceding sentence, the court may grant judgment for punitive damages in favor of the estate and against any such party that entered into such an agreement in willful disregard of this subsection.

11 U.S.C. § 364. Obtaining credit

(a) If the trustee is authorized to operate the business of the debtor under section 721, 1108, 1304, 1203, or 1204 of this title, unless the court orders otherwise, the trustee may obtain unsecured credit and incur unsecured debt in the ordinary course of business allowable under section 503(b)(1) of this title as an administrative expense.

(b) The court, after notice and a hearing, may authorize the trustee to obtain unsecured credit or to incur unsecured debt other than under subsection (a) of this section, allowable under section 503(b)(1) of this title as an administrative expense.

will not affect the validity of a sale or lease to a good faith purchaser, even if the purchaser knew of the pendency of the appeal. § 363(m); *see* Bankruptcy Rule 8005. Thus the attempted appeal will be dismissed as moot.

The Bankruptcy and Criminal Codes and the Bankruptcy Rules contain several provisions designed to prevent collusive bidding at bankruptcy sales and to prevent real or apparent conflicts of interest on the part of government officials or employees in connection with these sales. *See* § 363(n); 18 U.S.C. § 154; Bankruptcy Rule 6005. The rule just cited also provides that state or local residence or licensing requirements are ineffective to disqualify an appraiser or auctioneer from employment in a bankruptcy case.

§ 5.03 OBTAINING CREDIT

§ 5.03(a) Administrative Priority

Section 364 provides several ways for a trustee or debtor in possession to obtain credit or incur obligations after the commencement of a bankruptcy case. If the business is authorized to operate, as it usually is in a reorganization case, *see* § 1108, the trustee or debtor in possession may obtain unsecured credit or incur unsecured obligations in the ordinary course of business as an administrative expense, § 364(a); unless the court orders otherwise, neither notice, an opportunity for a hearing, nor a court order is necessary. Administrative expenses have first priority status under Section 507(a)(1).

If the business is not authorized to operate or if credit is to be obtained out of the ordinary course of business, a court order is required, after notice and a hearing, to obtain unsecured credit as an administrative expense. § 364(b); *see also* Bankruptcy Rule 4001(c). The creditor is at risk if the obligation is incurred out of the ordinary course of business and without a court order, since the creditor's claim against the estate in such event may be disallowed entirely.

§ 5.03(b) Superpriority or Secured Credit

If a trustee or debtor in possession cannot obtain credit on a

11 U.S.C. § 364. Obtaining credit

(c) If the trustee is unable to obtain unsecured credit allowable under section 503(b)(1) of this title as an administrative expense, the court, after notice and a hearing, may authorize the obtaining of credit or the incurring of debt—

(1) with priority over any or all administrative expenses of the kind specified in section 503(b) or 507(b) of this title;

(2) secured by a lien on property of the estate that is not otherwise subject to a lien; or

(3) secured by a junior lien on property of the estate that is subject to a lien.

11 U.S.C. § 506. Determination of secured status

(c) The trustee may recover from property securing an allowed secured claim the reasonable, necessary costs and expenses of preserving, or disposing of, such property to the extent of any benefit to the holder of such claim.

11 U.S.C. § 364. Obtaining credit

(d)(1) The court, after notice and a hearing, may authorize the obtaining of credit or the incurring of debt secured by a senior or equal lien on property of the estate that is subject to a lien only if—

(A) the trustee is unable to obtain such credit otherwise; and

(B) there is adequate protection of the interest of the holder of the lien on the property of the estate on which such senior or equal lien is proposed to be granted.

(2) In any hearing under this subsection, the trustee has the burden of proof on the issue of adequate protection.

simple administrative expense basis, the court, after notice and a hearing, may authorize a higher status. § 364(c); *see also* Bankruptcy Rule 4001(c). Specifically, the court may authorize the trustee or debtor in possession to obtain credit with special administrative expense priority over any or all other administrative expenses, including those entitled to superpriority under Section 507(b). § 364(c)(1). (It is unclear whether the priority granted under Section 364(c)(1) during a Chapter 11 reorganization case will prime administrative expenses incurred in a superseding Chapter 7 liquidation case. *See* § 726(b).) Instead of or in addition to the foregoing priority, the court may authorize the obtaining of secured credit subject only to preexisting liens. § 364(c)(2), (3).

If, under Section 364(c)(2) or (3), a creditor obtains a lien on property of the estate junior only to existing liens, there might appear to be no need to give that creditor a claim with superpriority over other administrative expenses. Recall, however, that in certain circumstances secured claims are subject to administrative charges under Section 506(c). Also, if a plan is confirmed under Chapter 11, administrative claims must be paid in full on the effective date, whereas it is at least arguable that a secured claim for postpetition credit may be paid in deferred cash payments under the "cram down" provisions discussed later. See pp. 429–33, 409–17, *infra*. *Compare* § 1129(a)(9)(A) *with* § 1129(b)(2)(A).

§ 5.03(c) Borrowing Ahead of Preexisting Liens

Although the foregoing methods should be sufficient for obtaining credit or incurring debt in most circumstances, the Code provides a final, extraordinary method if none of the customary alternatives is adequate: The court, after notice and a hearing, may authorize the trustee or debtor in possession to obtain credit on a "priming lien" basis — that is, the credit will be secured by a lien on estate property senior or equal to preexisting liens. The conditions for this authorization are both that credit not be otherwise obtainable and that the primed, or preexisting, lien interest be "adequately protected." § 364(d); *see also* Bankruptcy Rule 4001(c), (d); pp. 217–23, *supra*. The trustee or debtor in possession has the burden of proof on the issue of adequate protection.

§ 5.03(d) Some Practical Considerations in Obtaining Credit

At the outset of a Chapter 11 reorganization case, the debtor in possession and a secured creditor frequently present to the court an ex parte application requesting authorization for postpetition borrowing. Often the debtor cannot operate its business without fresh funds, for it may not use cash collateral without the secured party's consent or a finding of adequate protection. Because of the advantages under Section 364 of extending postpetition credit, a secured creditor typically prefers to apply collected cash collateral to the payment of its prepetition debt and then to lend fresh money to the debtor in possession, rather than merely to authorize the use of its collateral under Section 363 on an adequate protection basis.

It is not uncommon, moreover, for the secured creditor to try to extract meaningful concessions from the debtor in possession as a condition of making postpetition loans. For example, the secured creditor might require the debtor in possession to stipulate to the validity of the prepetition security interest. He may also require the debtor in possession to seek "cross collateralization" of prepetition and postpetition debt.[3]

Whether the debtor in possession and the secured creditor will succeed in obtaining court approval of the concessions just described will vary from case to case. During the initial stages of a Chapter 11 case, the debtor may have little incentive to resist excessive demands. The debtor needs the credit to survive and if the reorganization fails, it is the unsecured creditors who are likely to suffer the losses from the lender's overreaching. The court is in a

---

[3]"Cross collateralization" is a process by which a lender's prepetition debt is collateralized by both prepetition and postpetition collateral — that is, by collateral existing at the time of the petition as well as by collateral generated after bankruptcy — and the same secured creditor's postpetition loans are collateralized by prepetition and postpetition collateral. To require the postpetition debt to be collateralized by prepetition collateral is not unreasonable. But to require the prepetition debt to be collateralized by postpetition collateral may be objectionable. First, such collateralization of the prepetition debt may result in the collateralization of an undersecured or unsecured prepetition claim. Also, if the secured creditor's prepetition lien is subject to the trustee's avoiding powers, the lien can be set aside or preserved for the benefit of the estate. Through cross collateralization, however, the prepetition debt becomes collateralized by an unassailable security interest in postpetition collateral.

difficult position, for no one may be truly representing the interests of the general creditor body. As a result, bankruptcy judges are usually reluctant to bless prepetition liens in the absence of a true adversarial confrontation or to permit cross collateralization of prepetition and postpetition debt. They often authorize only limited borrowing for a brief period of time and continue the hearing on requests for further borrowing to a date certain. This practice gives the creditors' committee time to obtain counsel and affords such counsel a meaningful opportunity to investigate and perhaps to contest the validity of the secured creditor's prepetition lien and otherwise to represent creditors' interests. In general, however, the necessary, limited borrowings that occur before the continued hearing are unassailable and are afforded the full protection of Section 364. (For a case illustrating the problem at the beginning of a Chapter 11 case of attempting to accommodate the competing interests of the debtor, the lender, and other secured and unsecured creditors, see *In re Center Wholesale, Inc.*, 759 F.2d 1440 (9th Cir. 1985).)

Some courts categorically condemn cross collateralization as "illegal" on the technical basis that Section 364(c) authorizes priority or lien status only for debts incurred *after* court approval. Others apply the doctrine on a case by case basis. Courts seem generally to agree, however, that cross collateralization should not be authorized on an ex parte basis or without adequate advance notice to the creditor body.

§ 5.03(e) Subordination to Liquidation Expenses

As noted earlier, there is some uncertainty about whether the priority accorded by Section 364(c) during a Chapter 11 reorganization case will prevail over expenses of administration in a superseding Chapter 7 liquidation case. To avoid confronting this problem, a court may refuse to authorize borrowing under Section 364(c) or (d) unless the secured creditor is willing by agreement to subordinate whatever position he obtains under Section 364 to all or a specified portion of potential Chapter 7 administrative expenses. Lenders, recognizing the practical problems of bankruptcy administration, ordinarily make the necessary concessions in this regard.

11 U.S.C. § 364. Obtaining credit

(e) The reversal or modification on appeal of an authorization under this section to obtain credit or incur debt, or of a grant under this section of a priority or a lien, does not affect the validity of any debt so incurred, or any priority or lien so granted, to an entity that extended such credit in good faith, whether or not such entity knew of the pendency of the appeal, unless such authorization and the incurring of such debt, or the granting of such priority or lien, were stayed pending appeal.

11 U.S.C. § 365. Executory contracts and unexpired leases

(a) Except as provided in sections 765 and 766 of this title and in subsections (b), (c), and (d) of this section, the trustee, subject to the court's approval, may assume or reject any executory contract or unexpired lease of the debtor.

11 U.S.C. § 365. Executory contracts and unexpired leases

(f)(1) Except as provided in subsection (c) of this section, notwithstanding a provision in an executory contract or unexpired lease of the debtor, or in applicable law, that prohibits, restricts, or conditions the assignment of such contract or lease, the trustee may assign such contract or lease under paragraph (2) of this subsection.

(3) Notwithstanding a provision in an executory contract or unexpired lease of the debtor, or in applicable law that terminates or modifies, or permits a party other than the debtor to terminate or modify, such contract or lease or a right or obligation under such contract or lease on account of an assignment of such contract or lease, such contract, lease, right, or obligation may not be terminated or modified under such provision because of the assumption or assignment of such contract or lease by the trustee.

§ 5.03(f) Effect of Appeal

Occasionally, a party in interest will appeal a court order authorizing the trustee or debtor in possession to obtain credit under Section 364. But unless the appellant obtains a stay pending appeal, the validity of credit extended in "good faith," including any related lien or priority, is not affected by the appeal or by reversal of the authorizing order. § 364(e). (For a controversial case construing the meaning of "good faith" narrowly in this context, see *In re EDC Holding Co.*, 676 F.2d 945 (7th Cir. 1982). A contrary, more liberal reading of "good faith" for the purpose of Section § 364(e) is illustrated by *In re Adams Apple, Inc.*, 829 F.2d 1484 (9th Cir. 1987).)

§ 5.04 EXECUTORY CONTRACTS

Section 365 authorizes the trustee or debtor in possession to reject, assume, or assign executory contracts and unexpired leases. This power is of primary importance in Chapter 11 reorganization cases and in Chapter 9 cases; sometimes it is important as well in Chapters 7, 12, and 13. Although lawyers and courts have had no difficulty in identifying an unexpired lease, they have encountered problems in defining an executory contract.

§ 5.04(a) Definition of "Executory Contract"

"Executory contract" cannot be precisely defined for bankruptcy purposes. Under nonbankruptcy law a contract is executory if any obligation remains to be performed by either party. A narrower definition applies in bankruptcy cases. Most courts to date have accepted, or at least have paid lip service to, the definition advanced by Professor Vern Countryman: An executory contract is one under which the obligations of the debtor and the other party are both so far unperformed that the failure of either to perform "would constitute a material breach excusing the performance of the other." *E.g., In re Select-A-Seat Corp.*, 625 F.2d 290, 292 (9th Cir. 1980). A few courts have taken a functional approach by considering the consequences of applying Section 365 to the contract in terms of benefit to the estate and protection of the nondebtor party.

11 U.S.C. § 365. Executory contracts and unexpired leases

(c) The trustee may not assume or assign any executory contract or unexpired lease of the debtor, whether or not such contract or lease prohibits or restricts assignment of rights or delegation of duties, if—

(1)(A) applicable law excuses a party, other than the debtor, to such contract or lease from accepting performance from or rendering performance to an entity other than the debtor or the debtor in possession or an assignee of such contract or lease, whether or not such contract or lease prohibits or restricts assignment of rights or delegation of duties; and

(B) such party does not consent to such assumption or assignment; or

(2) such contract is a contract to make a loan, or extend other debt financing or financial accommodations, to or for the benefit of the debtor, or to issue a security of the debtor; or

(3) such lease is of nonresidential real property and has been terminated under applicable nonbankruptcy law prior to the order for relief.

11 U.S.C. § 365. Executory contracts and unexpired leases

(e)(1) Notwithstanding a provision in an executory contract or unexpired lease, or in applicable law, an executory contract or unexpired lease of the debtor may not be terminated or modified, and any right or obligation under such contract or lease may not be terminated or modified, at any time after the commencement of the case solely because of a provision in such contract or lease that is conditioned on—

(A) the insolvency or financial condition of the debtor at any time before the closing of the case;

(B) the commencement of a case under this title; or

(C) the appointment of or taking possession by a trustee in a case under this title or a custodian before such commencement.

(2) Paragraph (1) of this subsection does not apply to an executory contract or unexpired lease of the debtor, whether or not such contract or lease prohibits or restricts assignment of rights or delegation of duties, if—

[Continued]

E.g., In re Booth, 19 Bankr. 53 (Bankr. D. Utah 1982); *see also In re Becknell & Crace Coal Co., Inc.,* 761 F.2d 319 (6th Cir. 1985). A court using this approach decides whether a contract is executory by examining the purpose for which the trustee is given the option to assume, assign, or reject the contract under the Bankruptcy Code.

Case law establishes that contracts which have fully terminated before the petition are not executory for the purpose of Section 365. Nor are contracts that create security interests, or financing leases that are construed to be secured transactions.

§ 5.04(b) Forfeiture Clauses

A forfeiture clause is one that provides for the forfeiture of the debtor's interest either in property or under a contract or lease and is triggered by the commencement of a bankruptcy case, by the debtor's financial condition, or by the appointment of a trustee or a receiver. Sometimes forfeiture clauses operate ipso facto, or automatically, either to prevent property from becoming property of the estate or to prevent the trustee from using, selling, or assigning the property. Under other forfeiture clauses there is no automatic forfeiture, but the nondebtor party has the option of effectuating a forfeiture or otherwise modifying the debtor's rights.

The Bankruptcy Code treats the subject of forfeiture clauses in Sections 363(*l*), 365(e) and (f), and 541(c). In general, these provisions render forfeiture clauses unenforceable during bankruptcy cases.

Under certain circumstances, however, forfeiture clauses can have an effect. Bankruptcy law will not revive a property interest, contract, or lease that has been completely terminated under such a clause before the filing of the bankruptcy case. (Of course, despite a forfeiture clause the contract or property right may still have some life left when the petition is filed because of an applicable state antiforfeiture statute. *See In re Waterkist Corp.,* 775 F.2d 1089 (9th Cir. 1985).) Moreover, forfeiture clauses in specified kinds of executory contracts may be effective to prevent assumption of a contract by the trustee or debtor in possession and may actually permit termination of the contract by the nondebtor party after the filing of the bankruptcy petition. *See* § 365(c), (e)(2).

(A)(i) applicable law excuses a party, other than the debtor, to such contract or lease from accepting performance from or rendering performance to the trustee or to an assignee of such contract or lease, whether or not such contract or lease prohibits or restricts assignment of rights or delegation of duties; and

(ii) such party does not consent to such assumption or assignment; or

(B) such contract is a contract to make a loan, or extend other debt financing or financial accommodations, to or for the benefit of the debtor, or to issue a security of the debtor.

These special kinds of contracts include contracts to make a loan, to extend other debt financing or financial accommodations to or for the benefit of the debtor, or to issue a security of the debtor. A forfeiture clause is also enforceable in the context of a so-called "personal contract"—that is, a contract as to which applicable non-bankruptcy law, independently of the contract provisions, excuses the nondebtor party from accepting performance from, or from rendering performance to, someone other than the debtor. By court interpretation this category seems to include, in addition to personal service contracts, any contract that, as a matter of non-bankruptcy law, is nontransferable irrespective of its provisions. *In re Braniff Airways, Inc.,* 700 F.2d 935 (5th Cir. 1983).

§ 5.04(c) Existence of Contract

The trustee or debtor in possession may assume or assign an executory contract or unexpired lease of the debtor only if it is property of the estate. As noted earlier, if the contract was fully terminated before the filing of the bankruptcy case because of the debtor's breach or for some other reason, then nothing is left to become property of the estate. Similarly, according to the majority view, if a noncurable notice of termination was given before the filing of the petition, neither the automatic stay nor Section 365 will prevent the expiration of the contract according to its terms at the end of the notice period. *Moody v. Amoco Oil Co.,* 734 F.2d 1200 (7th Cir. 1984). (Stated another way, it is doubtful that the automatic stay prevents the running of time. Whether the bankruptcy court has authority under Section 105(a) to prevent termination is a separate matter. *Compare Johnson v. First Nat'l Bank of Montevideo, Minn.,* 719 F.2d 270 (8th Cir. 1983), *with In re Thomas J. Grosso Inv., Inc.,* 457 F.2d 168 (9th Cir. 1972).) On the other hand, if the debtor has a right under the contract or under applicable law to cure a prebankruptcy breach and the cure period has not expired when the bankruptcy petition is filed, then the contract will become subject to the general provisions of Section 365. They will control over the more limited time extension of Section 108(b) so as to permit the trustee or debtor in possession, in most instances, to cure a default and assume the executory contract for a consider-

11 U.S.C. § 362. Automatic stay

(a) Except as provided in subsection (b) of this section, a petition filed under section 301, 302, or 303 of this title, or an application filed under section 5(a)(3) of the Securities Investor Protection Act of 1970 (15 U.S.C. 78eee(a)(3)), operates as a stay, applicable to all entities, of—

(3) any act to obtain possession of property of the estate or of property from the estate or to exercise control over property of the estate;

11 U.S.C. § 365. Executory contracts and unexpired leases

(d)(1) In a case under chapter 7 of this title, if the trustee does not assume or reject an executory contract or unexpired lease of residential real property or of personal property of the debtor within 60 days after the order for relief, or within such additional time as the court, for cause, within such 60-day period, fixes, then such contract or lease is deemed rejected.

(4) Notwithstanding paragraphs (1) and (2), in a case under any chapter of this title, if the trustee does not assume or reject an unexpired lease of nonresidential real property under which the debtor is the lessee within 60 days after the date of the order for relief, or within such additional time as the court, for cause, within such 60-day period, fixes, then such lease is deemed rejected, and the trustee shall immediately surrender such nonresidential real property to the lessor.

11 U.S.C. § 365. Executory contracts and unexpired leases

(d)(2) In a case under chapter 9, 11, 12, or 13 of this title, the trustee may assume or reject an executory contract or unexpired lease of residential real property or of personal property of the debtor at any time before the confirmation of a plan but the court, on the request of any party to such contract or lease, may order the trustee to determine within a specified period of time whether to assume or reject such contract or lease.

able period of time, often up until the confirmation of a Chapter 11 plan. *Moody v. Amoco Oil Co., supra.*

Some courts have held that the automatic stay prevents the non-debtor party from acting unilaterally to terminate a contract or lease after the date of the filing of the petition. Section 362(a)(3) is usually relied upon for this conclusion. *See In re Computer Communications, Inc.,* 824 F.2d 725 (9th Cir. 1987).

§ 5.04(d) Time Limits

The Bankruptcy Code itself limits the time within which the trustee or debtor in possession may assume or reject an executory contract or unexpired lease of the debtor. In a Chapter 7 liquidation case and in any kind of case with respect to leases of "nonresidential real property," the trustee or debtor in possession must assume the contract or lease within 60 days after the order for relief, unless this time is extended by the court during the 60-day period. (It is to be expected that courts will liberally grant motions to extend the time to assume or reject leases of nonresidential real property, particularly in Chapter 11 cases.) If no timely assumption occurs, the contract or lease is automatically deemed rejected. § 365(d)(1), (4).

In a case under Chapter 9, 11, 12, or 13, an executory contract or unexpired lease (other than a lease of nonresidential real estate) normally may be assumed at any time before confirmation of the plan. § 365(d)(2). True, the nondebtor party may move the court to compel assumption or rejection by an earlier specified time, *id.,* but despite such a motion courts generally give the trustee or debtor in possession a reasonable, perhaps generous, period in which to make the decision. If no action is taken within the time thus fixed, however, the contract or lease is presumed to be rejected. *Theatre Holding Corp. v. Mauro,* 681 F.2d 102, 104 n.1 (2d Cir. 1982). *But see In re GHR Energy Corp.,* 66 Bankr. 54 (Bankr. S.D. Tex. 1986).

It is not entirely clear what happens in Chapter 9, 11, 12, or 13 if there is neither assumption nor rejection of an ordinary executory contract by the time of the confirmation of a plan. Probably the contract "rides through" in such event — that is, it will be treated as if the bankruptcy had never occurred. *See NLRB v.*

11 U.S.C. § 365. Executory contracts and unexpired leases

(d)(3) The trustee shall timely perform all the obligations of the debtor, except those specified in section 365(b)(2), arising from and after the order for relief under any unexpired lease of nonresidential real property, until such lease is assumed or rejected, notwithstanding section 503(b)(1) of this title. The court may extend, for cause, the time for performance of any such obligation that arises within 60 days after the date of the order for relief, but the time for performance shall not be extended beyond such 60-day period. This subsection shall not be deemed to affect the trustee's obligations under the provisions of subsection (b) or (f) of this section. Acceptance of any such performance does not constitute waiver or relinquishment of the lessor's rights under such lease or under this title.

Bildisco & Bildisco, 465 U.S. 513, 546 n.12 (1984) (concurring and dissenting opinion).

§ 5.04(e) Rights Before Assumption or Rejection

The Code is silent on the rights and obligations of the parties to an executory contract or unexpired lease during the limbo period—that is, the period between the filing of the petition and the time of assumption or rejection. The law appears to be that the nondebtor party must continue to perform if the debtor is not in default. *See* § 365(b)(4); *In re Whitcomb & Keller Mortg. Co., Inc.,* 715 F.2d 375 (7th Cir. 1983). Even if the debtor is in default, that default might be subsequently cured and the contract assumed, as discussed later at pp. 257–59. If an assumption does occur, and the other party has failed to perform, apparently he will be liable for breach of contract. *In re Cochise College Park, Inc.,* 703 F.2d 1339 (9th Cir. 1983). Moreover, in appropriate circumstances the court may order the other party to perform under the executory contract before assumption or rejection. § 105(a). It is unclear whether the nondebtor party can insist on receiving adequate assurance of performance on the part of the trustee or debtor in possession under Section 2-609 of the Uniform Commercial Code. *See* § 365(e).

Neither the debtor nor the trustee need perform under an ordinary contract or lease during the limbo period, although the estate may be liable for breach of contract in the unlikely event that the court subsequently refuses to authorize rejection. *See NLRB v. Bildisco & Bildisco, supra.* In the case of a lease of nonresidential real estate, however, the debtor tenant or his trustee is required to perform in a more or less timely fashion during the period before assumption or rejection. *See* § 365(d)(3).

§ 5.04(f) Rejection

The trustee or debtor in possession uses Section 365 to assume, assign, or reject an executory contract or unexpired lease. What is the purpose or effect of a rejection? It constitutes a breach—but the trustee or debtor in possession could breach by refusing to perform without needing the aid of the Code. The effect of rejection under Section 365(a) is that the breach ordinarily will be

11 U.S.C. § 365. Executory contracts and unexpired leases

(g) Except as provided in subsections (h)(2) and (i)(2) of this section, the rejection of an executory contract or unexpired lease of the debtor constitutes a breach of such contract or lease —

(1) if such contract or lease has not been assumed under this section or under a plan confirmed under chapter 9, 11, 12, or 13 of this title, immediately before the date of the filing of the petition;

11 U.S.C. § 502. Allowance of claims or interests

(g) A claim arising from the rejection, under section 365 of this title or under a plan under chapter 9, 11, 12, or 13 of this title, of an executory contract or unexpired lease of the debtor that has not been assumed shall be determined, and shall be allowed under subsection (a), (b), or (c) of this section or disallowed under subsection (d) or (e) of this section, the same as if such claim had arisen before the date of the filing of the petition.

11 U.S.C. § 365. Executory contracts and unexpired leases

(g) Except as provided in subsections (h)(2) and (i)(2) of this section, the rejection of an executory contract or unexpired lease of the debtor constitutes a breach of such contract or lease —

(2) if such contract or lease has been assumed under this section or under a plan confirmed under chapter 9, 11, 12, or 13 of this title —

(A) if before such rejection the case has not been converted under section 1112, 1307, or 1308 of this title, at the time of such rejection; or

(B) if before such rejection the case has been converted under section 1112 or 1307 of this title —

(i) immediately before the date of such conversion, if such contract or lease was assumed before such conversion; or

(ii) at the time of such rejection, if such contract or lease was assumed after such conversion.

treated as a prepetition breach rather than as a breach after bankruptcy, when it occurs in fact. §§ 365(g), 502(g). Thus the claim resulting from the breach is a general claim and not an administrative expense claim. In addition, rejection excuses the trustee or debtor in possession from future performance under the contract or lease. This result is of particular importance when the obligation would be subject to the remedy of specific performance outside bankruptcy: Through rejection under Section 365(a), the estate may nevertheless substitute a damage claim for an otherwise undesirable performance obligation.

Rejection, like assumption, is subject to court approval. § 365(a). For the most part, the developing case law on rejection applies a business-judgment standard. That is, courts ordinarily defer to the trustee's or debtor in possession's business judgment concerning whether the contract should be rejected. *E.g., Lubrizol Enterprises v. Richmond Metal Finishers,* 756 F.2d 1043 (4th Cir. 1985). (Earlier cases under the former Bankruptcy Act sometimes used a "burdensomeness" rather than a business-judgment standard; that is, a contract could not be rejected unless its performance would cause an actual loss to the estate, as distinguished from performance being merely less profitable than nonperformance.) In unusual situations, however, such as when rejection would benefit the estate only slightly and harm the nondebtor party substantially, the court might refuse to permit it. At least one decision indicates that the bankruptcy court has discretion to prevent a solvent estate from rejecting an executory contract or unexpired lease if rejection would benefit only the debtor and not creditors. *In re Chi-Feng Huang,* 23 Bankr. 798 (9th Cir. App. Panels 1982).

As noted, rejection ordinarily gives the nondebtor party a prepetition claim against the estate for damages. If the trustee or debtor in possession has assumed a contract during the bankruptcy case, however, a subsequent rejection creates a claim with the status of a priority administrative expense of the case in which the assumption occurred. § 365(g)(2). Generally, the measure of damages is determined by applicable nonbankruptcy law; the Code itself, however, limits the allowability of the nonpriority claim of a lessor under a rejected or breached lease of real estate and that of an

11 U.S.C. § 1113. Rejection of collective bargaining agreements

(c) The court shall approve an application for rejection of a collective bargaining agreement only if the court finds that—

(1) the trustee has, prior to the hearing, made a proposal that fulfills the requirements of subsection (b)(1);

(2) the authorized representative of the employees has refused to accept such proposal without good cause; and

(3) the balance of the equities clearly favors rejection of such agreement.

(e) . . . [I]f essential to the continuation of the debtor's business, or in order to avoid irreparable damage to the estate, the court, after notice and a hearing, may authorize the trustee to implement interim changes in the terms . . . provided by a collective bargaining agreement. . . .

(f) No provision of this title shall be construed to permit a trustee to unilaterally terminate or alter any provisions of a collective bargaining agreement prior to compliance with the provisions of this section.

employee under a terminated employment contract. § 502(b)(6), (7); see p. 275, *infra.*

A claim for damages that arises from the rejection of a contract or lease involving someone else's property must be distinguished from the separate administrative obligation of the estate to pay for the postpetition use of that property before the estate returns it. For example, suppose the trustee uses or occupies leased property for a period of time before rejecting the lease. He has incurred an independent administrative expense liability in addition to the nonpriority claim resulting from the rejection, but the measure of the administrative expense is not entirely clear. Some courts have required the estate to pay fair market value for the use; others, seeing the issue as one of preventing unjust enrichment, base the allowance on the value of the use to the estate, which may be less than an objective fair valuation. In any event, the 1984 amendments governing leases of nonresidential real estate require the trustee to pay at the lease rental rate for the use and occupancy of the property after the date of the order for relief. § 365(d)(3).

§ 5.04(g) Rejection of Labor Contracts

Collective bargaining agreements are executory contracts that are potentially subject to rejection under Section 365. But because of the competing federal policy embodied in the National Labor Relations Act, the Supreme Court held in *NLRB v. Bildisco & Bildisco, supra,* that court authorization to reject labor contracts should be based on criteria more stringent than the business-judgment standard; that is, a labor contract may be rejected only if it is burdensome *and* if the balance of the equities favors rejection. A majority in *Bildisco* decided, however, that pending court approval of a proposed rejection, the debtor could unilaterally refuse to comply with its obligations under the agreement.

Labor's dissatisfaction with the *Bildisco* result was an important force behind the 1984 amendments. Section 1113 in particular, applicable only in Chapter 11 cases, raised the *Bildisco* standard for rejection even higher by virtually eliminating the debtor's power to abrogate or modify the contract unilaterally without court permission during the limbo period.

11 U.S.C. § 365. Executory contracts and unexpired leases

(a) Except as provided in sections 765 and 766 of this title and in subsections (b), (c), and (d) of this section, the trustee, subject to the court's approval, may assume or reject any executory contract or unexpired lease of the debtor.

(b)(1) If there has been a default in an executory contract or unexpired lease of the debtor, the trustee may not assume such contract or lease unless, at the time of assumption of such contract or lease, the trustee —

(A) cures, or provides adequate assurance that the trustee will promptly cure, such default;

(B) compensates, or provides adequate assurance that the trustee will promptly compensate, a party other than the debtor to such contract or lease, for any actual pecuniary loss to such party resulting from such default; and

(C) provides adequate assurance of future performance under such contract or lease.

(2) Paragraph (1) of this subsection does not apply to a default that is a breach of a provision relating to —

(A) the insolvency or financial condition of the debtor at any time before the closing of the case;

(B) the commencement of a case under this title; or

(C) the appointment of or taking possession by a trustee in a case under this title or a custodian before such commencement.

(3) For the purposes of paragraph (1) of this subsection and paragraph (2)(B) of subsection (f), adequate assurance of future performance of a lease of real property in a shopping center includes adequate assurance —

(A) of the source of rent and other consideration due under such lease, and in the case of an assignment, that the financial condition and operating performance of the proposed assignee and its guarantors, if any, shall be similar to the financial condition and operating performance of the debtor and its guarantors, if any, as of the time the debtor became the lessee under the lease;

(B) that any percentage rent due under such lease will not decline substantially;

[Continued]

§ 5.04(h) Assumption

In certain circumstances an executory contract or unexpired lease may be potentially beneficial, and the estate may wish to assume it so as to bind the other party. Most executory contracts are subject to assumption. Those that are not are the so-called "personal contracts" and the others specified in Section 365(c), which were mentioned earlier at pp. 245–47 in connection with the enforceability of forfeiture clauses.

To be effective, an assumption requires court approval; the 1978 Code was intended to overrule the former doctrine that there could be an "implied assumption" through the trustee's conduct. § 365(a).

An assumption makes the debtor's executory contract the estate's contract, just as if the estate had originally entered into it after bankruptcy. Thus, as noted earlier, a breach by the estate of a contract that has been assumed creates an administrative expense for the damages. § 365(g)(2).

If the debtor is not in default under the executory contract or unexpired lease, only court approval is required in order to assume it. § 365(a). Moreover, if the only default is the breach of a provision concerning the insolvency or financial condition of the debtor, the commencement of the bankruptcy case, or the appointment of or taking possession by a trustee or a custodian, the contract may be assumed without curing that default. § 365(b)(2).

Otherwise, to assume the executory contract or unexpired lease, the trustee or debtor in possession must obtain court approval and, at the time of assumption, must cure any defaults, other than those concerning financial condition, or provide adequate assurance of a prompt cure. § 365(b)(1)(A), (b)(2). In addition, the estate either must compensate the nondebtor party for any actual pecuniary loss caused by the default or must assure prompt compensation. § 365(b)(1)(B). This "cure" or "compensation" may require paying attorney's fees to the nondebtor party if the fees were incurred as a result of the default and in reasonable reliance on it. Finally, the trustee or debtor in possession must provide the nondebtor party with adequate assurance of future performance under the contract or lease. § 365(b)(1)(C). The

(C) that assumption or assignment of such lease is subject to all the provisions thereof, including (but not limited to) provisions such as a radius, location, use, or exclusivity provision, and will not breach any such provision contained in any other lease, financing agreement, or master agreement relating to such shopping center; and

(D) that assumption or assignment of such lease will not disrupt any tenant mix or balance in such shopping center.

(4) Notwithstanding any other provision of this section, if there has been a default in an unexpired lease of the debtor, other than a default of a kind specified in paragraph (2) of this subsection, the trustee may not require a lessor to provide services or supplies incidental to such lease before assumption of such lease unless the lessor is compensated under the terms of such lease for any services and supplies provided under such lease before assumption of such lease.

11 U.S.C. § 365. Executory contracts and unexpired leases

(f)(1) Except as provided in subsection (c) of this section, notwithstanding a provision in an executory contract or unexpired lease of the debtor, or in applicable law, that prohibits, restricts, or conditions the assignment of such contract or lease, the trustee may assign such contract or lease under paragraph (2) of this subsection.

(2) The trustee may assign an executory contract or unexpired lease of the debtor only if—

(A) the trustee assumes such contract or lease in accordance with the provisions of this section; and

(B) adequate assurance of future performance by the assignee of such contract or lease is provided, whether or not there has been a default in such contract or lease.

(3) Notwithstanding a provision in an executory contract or unexpired lease of the debtor, or in applicable law that terminates or modifies, or permits a party other than the debtor to terminate or modify, such contract or lease or a right or obligation under such contract or lease on account of an assignment of such contract or lease, such contract, lease, right, or obligation may not be terminated or modified under such provision because of the assumption or assignment of such contract or lease by the trustee.

term "adequate assurance" derives from § 2-609(1) of the Uniform Commercial Code; it is not a term of art but is to be given a practical, pragmatic construction. *Richmond Leasing Co. v. Capital Bank, N.A.,* 762 F.2d 1303 (5th Cir. 1985).

Special provisions govern adequate assurance in the context of the assumption of a lease of real property in a shopping center. Section 365(b)(3) requires assurance of many elements, including tenant mix, percentage rents, and source of rents. The Code does not define "shopping center"; its meaning must evolve as case law develops.

§ 5.04(i) Assignment

The Code gives the trustee or debtor in possession the power to assign an executory contract or unexpired lease, notwithstanding a prohibition on assignability in the contract or under applicable nonbankruptcy law. § 365(f)(1). That is, any provision that prohibits, restricts, or conditions the assignment of the contract or lease, or that is perceived by a court to be intended to burden an attempted assignment, is overridden by the bankruptcy law and is unenforceable. *See* § 365(f)(3). It is likely that a lease provision requiring increased rent in the event of an assignment will be ineffective as against the assignee, for it is a device designed to prohibit or condition assignment. Moreover, a cross-default provision — that is, a provision in related but separate leases that assignment of one lease constitutes a default under the other lease — is unlikely to be enforced. In addition, a use restriction in a lease, at least a restriction designed to discourage assignment rather than to protect legitimate interests of the lessor, probably will not be enforced (except in the context of a shopping center lease).

Before an executory contract or unexpired lease may be assigned, it must be assumed. § 365(f)(2)(A). Certain kinds of contracts, however, may not be assumed without the other party's consent, as discussed earlier, *see* § 365(c) and *supra,* pp. 257, 245–47, and thus cannot be assigned over his objection.

In addition to meeting the requirements for assumption, the trustee or debtor in possession must provide the nondebtor party with adequate assurance of future performance by the assignee, whether or not there has been a default in the contract or lease.

11 U.S.C. § 365. Executory contracts and unexpired leases

(*l*) If an unexpired lease under which the debtor is the lessee is assigned pursuant to this section, the lessor of the property may require a deposit or other security for the performance of the debtor's obligations under the lease substantially the same as would have been required by the landlord upon the initial leasing to a similar tenant.

11 U.S.C. § 365. Executory contracts and unexpired leases

(k) Assignment by the trustee to an entity of a contract or lease assumed under this section relieves the trustee and the estate from any liability for any breach of such contract or lease occurring after such assignment.

11 U.S.C. § 365. Executory contracts and unexpired leases

(h)(1) If the trustee rejects an unexpired lease of real property of the debtor under which the debtor is the lessor, or a timeshare interest under a timeshare plan under which the debtor is the timeshare interest seller, the lessee or timeshare interest purchaser under such lease or timeshare plan may treat such lease or timeshare plan as terminated by such rejection, where the disaffirmance by the trustee amounts to such a breach as would entitle the lessee or timeshare interest purchaser to treat such lease or timeshare plan as terminated by virtue of its own terms, applicable nonbankruptcy law, or other agreements the lessee or timeshare interest purchaser has made with other parties; or, in the alternative, the lessee or timeshare interest purchaser may remain in possession of the leasehold or timeshare interest under any lease or timeshare plan the term of which has commenced for the balance of such term and for any renewal or extension of such term that is enforceable by such lessee or timeshare interest purchaser under applicable nonbankruptcy law.

(2) If such lessee or timeshare interest purchaser remains in possession as provided in paragraph (1) of this subsection, such lessee or timeshare interest purchaser may offset against the rent reserved under such lease or moneys due for such timeshare interest for the balance of the term after the date of the rejection of such lease or timeshare interest,

[Continued]

§ 365(f)(2)(B). Whether such adequate assurance has been given is a factual matter that the court must resolve if there is opposition to a proposed assignment. Section 365(*l*) authorizes a landlord to require a deposit or other security for performance under an assigned lease to the same extent he would require it from a similar lessee on an initial leasing. Of course, this deposit or other security might constitute the adequate assurance of future performance required as a condition of assignment under Section 365(f)(2)(B).

After an assignment of the contract or lease, the estate is not liable for postassignment defaults. § 365(k). This result is different from that which would obtain under nonbankruptcy law.

§ 5.04(j) The Debtor as Landlord or as Contract Vendor of Real Estate; Timeshare Contracts

For the most part, Section 365 is designed to benefit the estate, but several of its provisions protect the nondebtor party under a lease or executory contract involving real estate.

If the trustee or debtor in possession rejects an unexpired lease of real property under which the debtor is the lessor, the lessee may treat the lease as terminated by the rejection and file a claim for damages or may elect to remain in possession of the leasehold for the remainder of the term and for any renewal or extension period. § 365(h)(1). A lessee who remains in possession may, as the exclusive remedy for the breach, offset damages caused by the debtor's nonperformance against rent coming due after the rejection. § 365(h)(2). Under the 1984 amendments a timeshare interest purchaser from a debtor-seller is given the same options as a lessee of real estate from a debtor.

Similarly, a buyer in possession under an executory contract for the sale of real estate from a debtor-vendor is protected by options given in Section 365(i). The 1984 amendments specifically made this provision applicable also to timeshare contracts. If the trustee or debtor in possession rejects, the buyer may treat the contract as terminated and assert a claim for damages or may, as the exclusive remedy for the breach, elect to remain in possession with the right to offset his damages against payments coming due under the contract. When the contract payments are completed or satisfied, the

and any such renewal or extension thereof, any damages occurring after such date caused by the nonperformance of any obligation of the debtor under such lease or timeshare plan after such date, but such lessee or timeshare interest purchaser does not have any rights against the estate on account of any damages arising after such date from such rejection, other than such offset.

(i)(1) If the trustee rejects an executory contract of the debtor for the sale of real property or for the sale of a time-share interest under a timeshare plan, under which the purchaser is in possession, such purchaser may treat such contract as terminated, or, in the alternative, may remain in possession of such real property or timeshare interest.

(2) If such purchaser remains in possession—

(A) such purchaser shall continue to make all payments due under such contract, but may, offset against such payments any damages occurring after the date of the rejection of such contract caused by the nonperformance of any obligation of the debtor after such date, but such purchaser does not have any rights against the estate on account of any damages arising after such date from such rejection, other than such offset; and

(B) the trustee shall deliver title to such purchaser in accordance with the provisions of such contract, but is relieved of all other obligations to perform under such contract.

(j) A purchaser that treats an executory contract as terminated under subsection (i) of this section, or a party whose executory contract to purchase real property from the debtor is rejected and under which such party is not in possession, has a lien on the interest of the debtor in such property for the recovery of any portion of the purchase price that such purchaser or party has paid.

11 U.S.C. § 366. Utility service

(a) Except as provided in subsection (b) of this section, a utility may not alter, refuse, or discontinue service to, or discriminate against, the trustee or the debtor solely on the basis of the commencement of a case under this title or that a debt owed by the debtor to such utility for service rendered before the order for relief was not paid when due.

land purchaser is entitled to delivery of title. § 365(i)(2)(B). A land contract buyer who is not in possession or who chooses to treat the rejection as a termination of the contract is given a lien on the property to secure the return of whatever part of the purchase price he has paid. § 365(j).

§ 5.05 UTILITY SERVICE

Section 366 of the Code contains two special provisions concerning utilities. A utility is prohibited from altering or discriminating in future service to the debtor or the trustee solely because of an unpaid debt for services rendered before the order for relief. Nor is the commencement of a bankruptcy case a valid basis for a utility to alter, refuse, or discontinue service to the debtor or the estate. § 366(a). Significantly, both the estate and the debtor receive the protection of Section 366(a). This protection is of particular importance when the debtor is an individual.

The Code does not define "utility." The term may be broad enough to cover a condominium association or any other public or private monopoly provider of electric energy, natural or synthetic gas, water, telephone service, or other similar services. It is also possible that the definition will be expanded to apply to new forms of transmitted energy, such as satellite communication or cable television service.

Unless, within 20 days after the order for relief, the trustee or the debtor furnishes the utility with "adequate assurance of payment, in the form of a deposit or other security" for future service, the utility is permitted to alter, refuse, or discontinue service. § 366(b). It is unclear whether the utility may unilaterally terminate service if such adequate assurance of payment is proffered but the utility contests its sufficiency. In any event, the utility may request a hearing at which the court will determine the issues. *Id.* In this context "adequate assurance" under Section 366 apparently is not equivalent to "adequate protection" under Section 361. Some courts have determined that granting the utility a claim for an administrative expense is sufficient adequate assurance when the debtor's operations are profitable after the date of the filing of the petition. Although the statute does not allocate the burden of proof

11 U.S.C. § 366. Utility service

(b) Such utility may alter, refuse, or discontinue service if neither the trustee nor the debtor, within 20 days after the date of the order for relief, furnishes adequate assurance of payment, in the form of a deposit or other security, for service after such date. On request of a party in interest and after notice and a hearing, the court may order reasonable modification of the amount of the deposit or other security necessary to provide adequate assurance of payment.

11 U.S.C. § 525. Protection against discriminatory treatment

(a) Except as provided in the Perishable Agricultural Commodities Act, 1930 (7 U.S.C. 499a–499s), the Packers and Stockyards Act, 1921 (7 U.S.C. 181–229), and section 1 of the Act entitled "An Act making appropriations for the Department of Agriculture for the fiscal year ending June 30, 1944, and for other purposes," approved July 12, 1943 (57 Stat. 422; 7 U.S.C. 204), a governmental unit may not deny, revoke, suspend, or refuse to renew a license, permit, charter, franchise, or other similar grant to, condition such a grant to, discriminate with respect to such a grant against, deny employment to, terminate the employment of, or discriminate with respect to employment against, a person that is or has been a debtor under this title or a bankrupt or a debtor under the Bankruptcy Act, or another person with whom such bankrupt or debtor has been associated, solely because such bankrupt or debtor is or has been a debtor under this title or a bankrupt or debtor under the Bankruptcy Act, has been insolvent before the commencement of the case under this title, or during the case but before the debtor is granted or denied a discharge, or has not paid a debt that is dischargeable in the case under this title or that was discharged under the Bankruptcy Act.

on the issue of adequate assurance, that burden apparently should fall on the trustee or the debtor.

If the debtor is current on the utility bill, some courts have found that the utility is not entitled to receive adequate assurance of payment under Section 366(b). Stated another way, if the utility is not entitled to alter, refuse, or discontinue service as a matter of nonbankruptcy law, neither Section 366(b) nor the filing of the bankruptcy petition adds to its rights.

Other sections of the Code may also prevent the utility from altering, refusing, or discontinuing service. For example, when the debtor's relationship with the utility can be classified as a property interest, the automatic stay of Section 362 might prevent the utility from acting against that property interest—for example, by attempting to change the debtor's telephone number. In addition, the utility might be a "governmental unit" as defined in Section 101(26) and thus be subject to the provisions of Section 525(a), which protect the debtor against certain kinds of discriminatory treatment.

11 U.S.C. § 101. Definitions

In this title—

(4) "claim" means—

(A) right to payment, whether or not such right is reduced to judgment, liquidated, unliquidated, fixed, contingent, matured, unmatured, disputed, undisputed, legal, equitable, secured, or unsecured; or

(B) right to an equitable remedy for breach of performance if such breach gives rise to a right to payment, whether or not such right to an equitable remedy is reduced to judgment, fixed, contingent, matured, unmatured, disputed, undisputed, secured, or unsecured;

6

Distribution of the Estate

§ 6.01 WHAT IS A CLAIM?

Only those who hold "claims" against the debtor or the estate can share in the distribution of the estate as creditors. (Of course, holders of ownership interests in a debtor may share in that capacity in the distribution under a Chapter 11 plan.) The concept of a claim is of fundamental importance also because only claims can be discharged under the Code. "Claim" is defined in Section 101(4) as any right to payment, plus any right to an equitable remedy for breach of performance if that breach also gives rise to a right to payment. For example, a right against the debtor for specific performance of a contract to sell real estate is a claim, since money damages, at least in some amount, are an alternative remedy to specific performance. Probably the definition means that if the right against the debtor can be quantified as a dollar amount, or is in effect a monetary right against the debtor, the right is a claim for Code purposes. In this view, most of the rights one can enforce against the debtor are claims.

Ohio v. Kovacs, 469 U.S. 274 (1985), illustrates the breadth of the definition. The case involved a mandatory injunction, obtained under the state environmental protection laws, requiring the debtor to clean up certain pollution he had caused. The issue was whether the state's right against the debtor was a claim. The Supreme Court ruled that it was, with the result that the bankruptcy discharge barred further efforts to force compliance with the injunction. In the Court's view, the state in effect was seeking to make the debtor pay money, since that was the only way he could comply. (The opinion specifically left open the question whether the state could subject the debtor to criminal prosecution or crimi-

267

11 U.S.C. § 102. Rules of construction

In this title—

(2) "claim against the debtor" includes claim against property of the debtor;

nal contempt sanctions for noncompliance with the environmental laws.)

In contrast, the Supreme Court has indicated "serious doubts" as to whether Congress intended to include within the definition of claim a state court criminal judgment ordering restitution as a condition of the debtor's probation. *Kelly v. Robinson,* _____ U.S. _____, 107 S. Ct. 353 (1986).

The phrase "claim against the debtor" includes a "claim against property of the debtor." § 102(2). Thus, for example, a creditor holding a nonrecourse note secured by a mortgage on the debtor's home or a secured creditor who, under applicable law, is prohibited from obtaining an in personam deficiency judgment, nevertheless has a claim against the debtor within the meaning of the Code. The extent to which such creditors can share in the distribution of the estate, beyond being able to look to their collateral, depends on the allowability of the claim, §§ 502(b)(1), 1111(b), a matter discussed later.

The Code definition of a claim is not affected by whether the right to payment is liquidated or unliquidated, contingent or noncontingent, disputed or admitted, matured or not due, or secured or unsecured. § 101(4).

The point in time at which a right or potential right becomes a claim is an important and sometimes difficult question. The answer may affect the creditor's participation in the distribution and the effect of the discharge upon the right. One might suppose that there is no claim until all the conditions have occurred that are necessary for the debtor's legal liability. But this cannot be so in every case because the Code recognizes contingent claims as "claims," and by definition such claims involve a condition precedent to liability that has not yet occurred. No doubt claims based on contract arise when the contract becomes binding, whether or not the debtor's obligation is conditional. Tort claims ordinarily would arise when all the elements of the tort have occurred, although there certainly may be exceptions to this proposition. The problem is illustrated by the controversial case of *In re M. Frenville Co., Inc.,* 744 F.2d 332 (3d Cir. 1984). Certain banks sued the debtor's accountants after bankruptcy for their prepetition negligence in preparing financial statements. The accountants then

11 U.S.C. § 501. Filing of proofs of claims or interests

(a) A creditor or an indenture trustee may file a proof of claim. An equity security holder may file a proof of interest.

(b) If a creditor does not timely file a proof of such creditor's claim, an entity that is liable to such creditor with the debtor, or that has secured such creditor, may file a proof of such claim.

(c) If a creditor does not timely file a proof of such creditor's claim, the debtor or the trustee may file a proof of such claim.

11 U.S.C. § 1111. Claims and interests

(a) A proof of claim or interest is deemed filed under section 501 of this title for any claim or interest that appears in the schedules filed under section 521(1) or 1106(a)(2) of this title, except a claim or interest that is scheduled as disputed, contingent, or unliquidated.

11 U.S.C. § 502. Allowance of claims or interests

(a) A claim or interest, proof of which is filed under section 501 of this title, is deemed allowed, unless a party in interest, including a creditor of a general partner in a partnership that is a debtor in a case under chapter 7 of this title, objects.

(b) . . . if such objection to a claim is made, the court, after notice and a hearing, shall determine the amount of such claim. . . .

cross complained against the debtor for indemnity and contribution based on the debtor's conduct, which also had occurred before the petition. The court held that the cross complaint involved a postpetition claim (so that it was not subject to the automatic stay) because, under applicable state law, the accountants' indemnity claim did not arise until the accountants were sued after bankruptcy. The court said that the result would have been different if the indemnity claim had been based on a prepetition contract therefor. In any event, the *Frenville* decision has been criticized and some other courts already have declined to follow it. *E.g., Grady v. A.H. Robins Co., Inc. (In re A.H. Robins Co., Inc.),* 839 F.2d 198 (4th Cir. 1988); *In re Johns-Manville Corp.,* 57 Bankr. 680 (Bankr. S.D.N.Y. 1986); *In re Baldwin-United Corp.,* 48 Bankr. 901 (Bankr. S.D. Ohio 1985); *see also In re Baldwin-United Corp. Litigation,* 765 F.2d 343, 348 n.4 (2d Cir. 1985) (questioning *Frenville* but not deciding whether the court would follow it).

Additional complications stem from the possibility that a claim may exist — that is, in the sense that a creditor has a present right to payment as against the debtor — but the creditor is unaware of this fact. For example, the debtor may have embezzled money but his employer has not yet discovered the loss, or perhaps an asbestos tort victim has an irreversible disease but no symptoms have yet become manifest. It remains to be seen whether the creditor's lack of awareness of the claim will affect the determination of when it is deemed to arise for bankruptcy purposes.

§ 6.02 ALLOWANCE OF CLAIMS

Having a claim does not of itself entitle a creditor to share in the distribution of the assets of the bankruptcy estate; the claim also must be *allowed*. Except for certain secured claims held by creditors who wish to look only to the value of their collateral for payment, discussed more fully later, every claim must go through the allowance process before its holder is entitled to a distribution on account of the claim.

The first step in the allowance process is filing a proof of claim. Bankruptcy Rules 3002(a), 3003(c). In Chapter 11 cases, certain claims listed on the debtor's schedules are *deemed* filed, a status that

11 U.S.C. § 502. Allowance of claims or interests

(b) Except as provided in subsections (e)(2), (f), (g), (h) and (i) of this section, if such objection to a claim is made, the court, after notice and a hearing, shall determine the amount of such claim in lawful currency of the United States as of the date of the filing of the petition, and shall allow such claim in such amount except to the extent that —

(1) such claim is unenforceable against the debtor and property of the debtor, under any agreement or applicable law for a reason other than because such claim is contingent or unmatured;

11 U.S.C. § 502. Allowance of claims or interests

(c) There shall be estimated for purpose of allowance under this section —

(1) any contingent or unliquidated claim, the fixing or liquidation of which, as the case may be, would unduly delay the administration of the case; or

(2) any right to payment arising from a right to an equitable remedy for breach of performance.

meets the filing requirement. § 1111(a); Bankruptcy Rule 3003(b). Official Forms promulgated by the Supreme Court, which can be found in the appendix to Title 11, prescribe the contents of proofs of claim. *See* Official Forms Nos. 19–21.

The time for filing claims (when there is no deemed filing) is prescribed by the Bankruptcy Rules. An untimely filing generally results either in subordination of the claim to timely filed ones in Chapter 7, *see* § 726(a)(2), (3), or in what is tantamount to disallowance of the claim in Chapters 11 and 13. Bankruptcy Rules 3002(a), 3003(c)(2). In Chapters 7 and 13, the claims filing period ordinarily expires 90 days after the date of the Section 341(a) creditors' meeting. Bankruptcy Rule 3002(c). In Chapter 11, the court in each case sets a specific date after which the filing of claims is barred. Bankruptcy Rule 3003(c)(3).

Once a proof of claim is filed or deemed filed, it is automatically considered allowed, unless a party in interest objects to allowance on one of the statutory grounds. § 502(a). Usually, the party with standing to object is the representative of the estate — that is, the trustee or the Chapter 11 debtor in possession. If an objection is filed, Bankruptcy Rule 3007 requires 30 days' notice of a hearing on it.

Section 502(b) enumerates eight grounds for disallowance. The most important and most frequently stated ground is that the "claim is unenforceable . . . for a reason other than because such claim is contingent or unmatured." § 502(b)(1). In other words, any defense that the debtor may have had to the enforceability of the claim outside of bankruptcy is a good defense to the allowance of the claim against the estate, with the two specified exceptions. Examples of such defenses are failure of consideration, the statute of limitations, the statute of frauds, usury, defective merchandise, accord and satisfaction, violation of a federal or state consumer protection law, and payment of the debt. Section 558 further specifies that the debtor may not effectively waive any defense after the commencement of the case. That a claim is speculative or contingent or that its amount is difficult to ascertain does not constitute a basis for disallowance. In these circumstances the Code requires the court to do the best it can in estimating the allowable amount. § 502(c).

It is clear that under Section 502(b)(1), a nonrecourse secured claim is *allowable* as against the property that constitutes the collat-

11 U.S.C. § 502. Allowance of claims or interests

(b) . . . if such objection to a claim is made, the court . . . shall . . . allow such claim in such amount except to the extent that —

(2) such claim is for unmatured interest;

(3) if such claim is for a tax assessed against property of the estate, such claim exceeds the value of the interest of the estate in such property;

(4) if such claim is for services of an insider or attorney of the debtor, such claim exceeds the reasonable value of such services;

(5) such claim is for a debt that is unmatured on the date of the filing of the petition and that is excepted from discharge under section 523(a)(5) of this title;

(6) if such claim is the claim of a lessor for damages resulting from the termination of a lease of real property, such claim exceeds —

(A) the rent reserved by such lease, without acceleration, for the greater of one year, or 15 percent, not to exceed three years, of the remaining term of such lease, following the earlier of —

(i) the date of the filing of the petition; and

(ii) the date on which such lessor repossessed or the lessee surrendered, the leased property; plus

(B) any unpaid rent due under such lease, without acceleration, on the earlier of such dates;

(7) if such claim is the claim of an employee for damages resulting from the termination of an employment contract, such claim exceeds —

(A) the compensation provided by such contract, without acceleration, for one year following the earlier of —

(i) the date of the filing of the petition; or

(ii) the date on which the employer directed the employee to terminate, or such employee terminated, performance under such contract; plus

(B) any unpaid compensation due under such contract, without acceleration, on the earlier of such dates; or

(8) such claim results from a reduction, due to late payment, in the amount of an otherwise applicable credit available to the debtor in connection with an employment tax on wages, salaries, or commissions earned from the debtor.

eral, even though the nonrecourse obligation is not enforceable against the debtor personally and thus is not allowable as against the estate in general.

Section 502(b)(2) disallows claims for unmatured interest, such as an original issue discount. This provision, together with the lead-in clause of Section 502(b), requiring the court to allow claims "as of the date of the filing of the petition," establish the general rule that interest on claims ceases to accrue at the date of bankruptcy. In other words, postpetition interest is generally not allowable.

Section 502(b)(3) disallows property tax claims that exceed the value of the debtor's equity in the property. Section 502(b)(4) disallows claims of insiders or the debtor's attorneys to the extent that the claim exceeds the reasonable value of their services, and Section 502(b)(5) prevents a former spouse from sharing in the distribution of the estate to the extent of any unmatured portion of an alimony or support claim. However, since alimony and support claims, whether they are allowable or not, are ordinarily excepted from discharge, the former spouse is free to pursue his or her rights against the debtor outside of bankruptcy.

The allowability of a landlord's claim for damages under a terminated lease of real property is limited under Section 502(b)(6) by a sliding scale formula. The limitation is the actual damages for the termination (as measured under nonbankruptcy law), not to exceed 1 year's rent; or if 15 per cent of the remaining term of the lease exceeds 1 year (that is, if the unexpired term exceeds 6 2/3 years), then the limitation is the rent reserved by the lease for 15 per cent of the remaining term, not to exceed 3 years. In addition, the landlord's damage claim may include any unpaid accrued rent and any actual damage to the premises.

Section 502(b)(7) similarly limits the claim of an employee for damages resulting from the termination of an employment contract. The maximum damage claim is the amount to which the employee was entitled for the one year following termination of the contract, plus unpaid prepetition or pretermination salary and expenses.

Section 502(b)(8) disallows certain tax penalty claims assessed under the Federal Unemployment Tax Act.

In addition to the Section 502(b) grounds for disallowance, Section

11 U.S.C. § 502. Allowance of claims or interests

(d) Notwithstanding subsections (a) and (b) of this section, the court shall disallow any claim of any entity from which property is recoverable under section 542, 543, 550, or 553 of this title or that is a transferee of a transfer avoidable under section 522(f), 522(h), 544, 545, 547, 548, 549, or 724(a) of this title, unless such entity or transferee has paid the amount, or turned over any such property, for which such entity or transferee is liable under section 522(i), 542, 543, 550, or 553 of this title.

(e)(1) . . . the court shall disallow any claim for reimbursement or contribution of an entity that is liable with the debtor on or has secured the claim of a creditor, to the extent that—

(A) such creditor's claim against the estate is disallowed;

(B) such claim for reimbursement or contribution is contingent as of the time of allowance or disallowance of such claim for reimbursement or contribution; or

(C) such entity asserts a right of subrogation to the rights of such creditor under section 509 of this title.

11 U.S.C. § 506. Determination of secured status

(a) An allowed claim of a creditor secured by a lien on property in which the estate has an interest, or that is subject to setoff under section 553 of this title, is a secured claim to the extent of the value of such creditor's interest in the estate's interest in such property, or to the extent of the amount subject to setoff, as the case may be, and is an unsecured claim to the extent that the value of such creditor's interest or the amount so subject to setoff is less than the amount of such allowed claim. Such value shall be determined in light of the purpose of the valuation and of the proposed disposition or use of such property, and in conjunction with any hearing on such disposition or use or on a plan affecting such creditor's interest.

(b) To the extent that an allowed secured claim is secured by property the value of which, after any recovery under subsection (c) of this section, is greater than the amount of such claim, there shall be allowed to the holder of such claim, interest on such claim, and any reasonable fees, costs, or charges provided for under the agreement under which such claim arose.

502(e) sets forth independent grounds for disallowance of a guarantor's or surety's claim for reimbursement or contribution. Finally, Section 502(d) provides for disallowance of a claim held by a creditor who has received or is liable for an avoidable transfer unless he surrenders the transferred property or its value. *See also* Bankruptcy Rule 3002(c)(3).

§ 6.03 SECURED CLAIMS

Once a claim has been allowed, Section 506(a) and (b) determine whether it is to be treated as a secured claim, and if so, to what extent. If the creditor has collateral of greater value than the amount of the claim, the claim is fully secured. Moreover, to the extent that the collateral is sufficient, the allowable amount of the secured claim includes postpetition interest to the date of payment, plus reasonable costs and attorney's fees as provided for in the contract, despite the general rule applicable to unsecured claims that interest ceases to be allowable as of the date of bankruptcy. On the other hand, if the value of the collateral is less than the amount owing to the creditor, the claim is bifurcated for bankruptcy purposes: It is a secured claim to the extent of the value of the collateral and an unsecured claim for the balance — that is, the deficiency.

Nonbankruptcy law, usually state law, plays an important role here. Whether the creditor "has collateral" or a lien to secure the claim depends initially on his having a valid lien outside of bankruptcy. This principle is subject to the qualification that liens which are valid outside of bankruptcy nevertheless may be invalidated by one of the trustee's or debtor's avoiding powers. See pp. 137–91, *supra;* 305–09, *infra.* Moreover, whether the creditor will have an unsecured claim for any deficiency turns on his having in personam recourse rights against the debtor under nonbankruptcy law. *But see* § 1111(b). The Code itself provides that a right of setoff is treated the same as collateral for the purpose of Section 506(a) and (b) and for determining a creditor's secured status.

The value of the collateral is to be determined in the light of the purpose of the valuation. § 506(a). For example, if the secured creditor is permitted to liquidate the collateral and the issue is the extent to which the creditor's claim should be treated as an unse-

11 U.S.C. § 506. Determination of secured status

(d) To the extent that a lien secures a claim against the debtor that is not an allowed secured claim, such lien is void, unless —

(1) such claim was disallowed only under section 502(b)(5) or 502(e) of this title; or

(2) such claim is not an allowed secured claim due only to the failure of an entity to file a proof of such claim under section 501 of this title.

11 U.S.C. § 506. Determination of secured status

(c) The trustee may recover from property securing an allowed secured claim the reasonable, necessary costs and expenses of preserving, or disposing of, such property to the extent of any benefit to the holder of such claim.

11 U.S.C. § 552. Postpetition effect of security interest

(a) Except as provided in subsection (b) of this section, property acquired by the estate or by the debtor after the commencement of the case is not subject to any lien resulting from any security agreement entered into by the debtor before the commencement of the case.

(b) Except as provided in sections 363, 506(c), 522, 544, 545, 547, and 548 of this title, if the debtor and an entity entered into a security agreement before the commencement of the case and if the security interest created by such security agreement extends to property of the debtor acquired before the commencement of the case and to proceeds, product, offspring, rents, or profits of such property, then such security interest extends to such proceeds, product, offspring, rents, or profits acquired by the estate after the commencement of the case to the extent provided by such security agreement and by applicable nonbankruptcy law, except to any extent that the court, after notice and a hearing and based on the equities of the case, orders otherwise.

cured one, then most likely the court would look to the liquidation value of the collateral to determine the deficiency.

A secured creditor who desires to look only to the value of the collateral without asserting an unsecured deficiency claim against the estate need not file a proof of claim, § 506(d)(2), although he may choose to do so. Failure to file does not affect the validity of the lien. *Cf. In re Tarnow,* 749 F.2d 464 (7th Cir. 1984). Ordinarily, the secured creditor moves for relief from the automatic stay so that he may proceed with lien enforcement in accordance with nonbankruptcy law. He is entitled to relief from the stay unless given "adequate protection." § 362(d), (f); see pp. 211–23, *supra.* Alternatively, he may wait until the automatic stay self-destructs under the statute and then proceed to enforce his lien. § 362(c)(1); see p. 209, *supra.* Moreover, he may demand "adequate protection" to the extent that the trustee or debtor in possession proposes to use, sell, or lease the collateral. § 363(e); see pp. 223–29, *supra.* Sometimes circumstances may motivate the secured creditor to wait until the trustee liquidates the collateral and pays him from the proceeds. *See* § 725; H.R. REP. No. 595, 95th Cong., 1st Sess. 382–83 (1977) [hereinafter cited in this chapter as "House Report"]. Other times, he may be satisfied to wait to see what the Chapter 11 or 13 plan proposes for his secured claim. *See* §§ 1124, 1129(a)(8), 1325(a)(5); pp. 383–85, 401–23; 339–41, 343–45, *infra.*

These observations about a secured claim and a secured creditor assume that the lien or security interest is enforceable under applicable nonbankruptcy law and that it is not invalidated or subordinated by a specific provision of the Bankruptcy Code. The potential impact of the trustee's and the debtor's avoiding powers on otherwise valid liens is discussed at pp. 137–91, *supra,* and pp. 305–09, *infra.* Two other provisions of the Code should be noted here. First, the trustee may surcharge a secured party's collateral to recover reasonable and necessary expenses incurred by the estate in connection with preserving or disposing of the property, to the extent that these expenditures benefited the secured creditor. § 506(c). Second, after-acquired property clauses in security agreements, although ordinarily enforceable under applicable nonbankruptcy law, may be overridden by Section 552. In general,

11 U.S.C. § 507. Priorities

(a) The following expenses and claims have priority in the following order:

(1) First, administrative expenses allowed under section 503(b) of this title, and any fees and charges assessed against the estate under chapter 123 of title 28.

(2) Second, unsecured claims allowed under section 502(f) of this title.

(3) Third, allowed unsecured claims for wages, salaries, or commissions, including vacation, severance, and sick leave pay—

(A) earned by an individual within 90 days before the date of the filing of the petition or the date of the cessation of the debtor's business, whichever occurs first; but only

(B) to the extent of $2,000 for each such individual.

(4) Fourth, allowed unsecured claims for contributions to an employee benefit plan—

(A) arising from services rendered within 180 days before the date of the filing of the petition or the date of the cessation of the debtor's business, whichever occurs first; but only

(B) for each such plan, to the extent of—

(i) the number of employees covered by each such plan multiplied by $2,000; less

(ii) the aggregate amount paid to such employees under paragraph (3) of this subsection, plus the aggregate amount paid by the estate on behalf of such employees to any other employee benefit plan.

[Continued]

the section provides that property acquired after bankruptcy is not subject to any lien created by a prepetition security agreement, except to the extent that the postpetition property represents the proceeds, rents, products, or the like of collateral acquired before the petition.

§ 6.04 PRIORITY CLAIMS

In a bankruptcy case certain allowed unsecured claims are entitled to priority in distribution over other unsecured claims. Section 507(a) of the Bankruptcy Code establishes the following priority system:

1. The first priority, § 507(a)(1), is for administrative expenses, which are determined and allowed under Section 503(b) of the Code. They include the costs and expenses of preserving the estate or operating the business after the petition, and all professional fees and charges that are allowed, such as trustees', attorneys', or accountants' fees. Postpetition rent or other storage charges, costs of sale or liquidation of property, and related expenses are all allowable as administrative expenses and are entitled to first priority in the distribution of the unencumbered assets of the estate. So are liabilities stemming from torts committed by the trustee, the debtor in possession, or their agents during the course of operation of the business or administration of the estate. *See Reading Co. v. Brown,* 391 U.S. 471 (1968) (case decided under the former Bankruptcy Act).

2. Claims (including tax claims) arising in the ordinary course of the debtor's business after the filing of an involuntary petition and before the entry of the order for relief (or the appointment of the trustee) are entitled to second priority under Section 507(a)(2).

3. Wage, salary, or commission claims, including vacation, severance, and sick leave pay, are entitled to third priority to the extent of $2,000 per individual, if earned "within 90 days before the date of the filing of the petition or the date of the cessation of the debtor's business," if that occurred before bankruptcy. § 507(a)(3).

11 U.S.C. § 507. Priorities

(5) Fifth, allowed unsecured claims of persons —

(A) engaged in the production or raising of grain, as defined in section 557(b)(1) of this title, against a debtor who owns or operates a grain storage facility, as defined in section 557(b)(2) of this title, for grain or the proceeds of grain, or

(B) engaged as a United States fisherman against a debtor who has acquired fish or fish produce from a fisherman through a sale or conversion, and who is engaged in operating a fish produce storage or processing facility —

but only to the extent of $2,000 for each such individual.

(6) Sixth, allowed unsecured claims of individuals, to the extent of $900 for each such individual, arising from the deposit, before the commencement of the case, of money in connection with the purchase, lease, or rental of property, or the purchase of services, for the personal, family, or household use of such individuals, that were not delivered or provided.

(7) Seventh, allowed unsecured claims of governmental units, only to the extent that such claims are for —

(A) a tax on or measured by income or gross receipts —

(i) for a taxable year ending on or before the date of the filing of the petition for which a return, if required, is last due, including extensions, after three years before the date of the filing of the petition;

(ii) assessed within 240 days, plus any time plus 30 days during which an offer in compromise with respect to such tax that was made within 240 days after such assessment was pending, before the date of the filing of the petition; or

(iii) other than a tax of a kind specified in section 523(a)(1)(B) or 523(a)(1)(C) of this title, not assessed before, but assessable, under applicable law or by agreement, after, the commencement of the case;

(B) a property tax assessed before the commencement of the case and last payable without penalty after one year before the date of the filing of the petition;

[Continued]

4. The fourth priority is for contributions to employee benefit plans, such as health and life insurance plans, pension plans, and the like. The contributions must be related to employee services rendered within 180 days before bankruptcy or the cessation of the business, if that occurred earlier. Instead of including employee benefit contributions in the general wage priority provision, the Code sets them out separately in this fourth category so as not to diminish the direct third priority recovery of the employees. The combined amount of the claims in the third and fourth priority classes may not exceed $2,000 per employee.

5. The fifth priority is for farmers who have sold to a "grain storage facility" and for United States fishermen who have sold their fish or fish produce to a debtor that operates a "fish produce storage or processing facility." § 507(a)(5)(A), (B). This priority, like the wage priority, is limited to $2,000 per individual and therefore is not likely to have a significant ameliorating effect on the plight of even those farmers and fishermen to whom it applies.

6. The sixth priority is for claims of up to $900 held by *individuals* who have made deposits with the debtor "in connection with the purchase, lease, or rental of property, or the purchase of services" for *consumer* use and who have not received the goods or services. § 507(a)(6). This priority includes layaway deposits for consumer goods, security deposits with landlords for apartment rent, prepayment of health club memberships, and the like; it does not include warranty claims, however.

7. The seventh priority, § 507(a)(7), is for *unsecured* tax claims. Tax claims that are supported by liens are secured claims, provided the liens withstand the bankruptcy avoiding powers. As such, they do not fall within the seventh priority class, which includes only unsecured taxes. In Chapter 7, a tax lien claim, although subordinated to some extent in the distribution of the estate, nevertheless ranks ahead of the seventh priority taxes. *See* § 724(b).

Income taxes will generally be granted a priority if the tax return was required to be filed within the three years preced-

(C) a tax required to be collected or withheld and for which the debtor is liable in whatever capacity;

(D) an employment tax on a wage, salary, or commission of a kind specified in paragraph (3) of this subsection earned from the debtor before the date of the filing of the petition, whether or not actually paid before such date, for which a return is last due, under applicable law or under any extension, after three years before the date of the filing of the petition;

(E) an excise tax on—

(i) a transaction occurring before the date of the filing of the petition for which a return, if required, is last due, under applicable law or under any extension, after three years before the date of the filing of the petition; or

(ii) if a return is not required, a transaction occurring during the three years immediately preceding the date of the filing of the petition;

(F) a customs duty arising out of the importation of merchandise—

(i) entered for consumption within one year before the date of the filing of the petition;

(ii) covered by an entry liquidated or reliquidated within one year before the date of the filing of the petition; or

(iii) entered for consumption within four years before the date of the filing of the petition but unliquidated on such date, if the Secretary of the Treasury certifies that failure to liquidate such entry was due to an investigation pending on such date into assessment of antidumping or countervailing duties or fraud, or if information needed for the proper appraisement or classification of such merchandise was not available to the appropriate customs officer before such date; or

(G) a penalty related to a claim of a kind specified in this paragraph and in compensation for actual pecuniary loss.

ing bankruptcy or after bankruptcy, so long as the tax year ended before bankruptcy. In addition, income taxes that were assessed within 240 days before bankruptcy or that are still assessable at the time of bankruptcy are granted priority.

Taxes withheld or collected from others, such as the amount withheld from employees' wages for income taxes or social security, are granted priority, no matter how long before bankruptcy the debtor-employer's liability to the taxing agency arose and regardless of whether the debtor is liable for the withholding to the taxing agency directly or as a "responsible person." According to the majority view, this provision also grants unlimited priority to sales or excise taxes when the tax is imposed on a buyer but is collected by the debtor-seller. *E.g., DeChiaro v. New York State Tax Comm'n,* 760 F.2d 432 (2d Cir. 1985). An excise tax that the debtor is liable to pay directly in its own capacity is entitled to seventh priority only if the transaction giving rise to the excise tax occurred within three years before bankruptcy or, if a return is required, if the return is due within three years before bankruptcy.

Seventh priority status is also given to the employer's own liability for employment taxes on third priority wages (as distinguished from the employees' portion of these taxes that was withheld from their wages) and to employment taxes on wages paid before the petition, if the applicable return was required to be filed within three years before bankruptcy. § 507(a)(7)(D).

Property taxes and customs duties generally are entitled to priority only if assessed within one year before bankruptcy or related to a transaction that occurred during that time.

A claim arising from an erroneous tax refund has the same priority as the underlying tax. § 507(c). It is not treated as a tax that arises when the government discovers the improvident refund.

No priority is given to claims of federal, state, or other governmental entities unless their claims fall within the tax or other priority categories just described. In particular, the general priority statute in favor of the United States, 31 U.S.C. § 3713, does not apply in cases under the Code.

11 U.S.C. § 507. Priorities

(d) An entity that is subrogated to the rights of a holder of a claim of a kind specified in subsection (a)(3), (a)(4), (a)(5), or (a)(6) of this section is not subrogated to the right of the holder of such claim to priority under such subsection.

11 U.S.C. § 726. Distribution of property of the estate

(a) Except as provided in section 510 of this title, property of the estate shall be distributed—

(1) first, in payment of claims of the kind specified in, and in the order specified in, section 507 of this title;

(b) Payment on claims of a kind specified in paragraph (1), (2), (3), (4), (5), (6), or (7) of section 507(a) of this title, or in paragraph (2), (3), (4), or (5) of subsection (a) of this section, shall be made pro rata among claims of the kind specified in each such particular paragraph, except that in a case that has been converted to this chapter . . . a claim allowed under section 503(b) of this title incurred under this chapter after such conversion has priority over a claim allowed under section 503(b) of this title incurred under any other chapter of this title or under this chapter before such conversion and over any expenses of a custodian superseded under section 543 of this title.

11 U.S.C. § 507. Priorities

(b) If the trustee, under section 362, 363, or 364 of this title, provides adequate protection of the interest of a holder of a claim secured by a lien . . . and if, notwithstanding such protection, such creditor has a claim allowable under subsection (a)(1) of this section arising from the stay . . . under section 362 . . . from the use, sale, or lease of such property under section 363 . . . or from the granting of a lien under section 364(d) . . . then such creditor's claim under such subsection shall have priority over every other claim allowable under such subsection.

11 U.S.C. § 364. Obtaining credit

(c) If the trustee is unable to obtain unsecured credit allowable under section 503(b)(1) of this title as an administrative expense, the court, after notice and a hearing, may authorize the obtaining of credit or the incurring of debt—

(1) with priority over any or all administrative expenses of the kind specified in section 503(b) or 507(b) of this title;

Whether someone who succeeds to the rights of the original holder of a priority claim also succeeds to the priority status is not entirely clear. Section 507(d) provides that a subrogee of the original holder does not subrogate to the priority. But cases such as *In re Missionary Baptist Found. of America*, 667 F.2d 1244 (5th Cir. 1982), hold that an assignee, as distinguished from a subrogee, does succeed to the priority status.

In a Chapter 7 liquidation case, the various priority classes are paid in the order in which they are listed in Section 507(a)(1)–(7). § 726(a)(1). Within a given priority level the claims generally share pro rata when there are insufficient assets to fully satisfy that class. § 726(b). However, some exceptions to this general rule apply to the first priority category of administrative expenses. If a Chapter 11, 12, or 13 case is superseded by a Chapter 7 liquidation case, the Chapter 7 administrative expenses have a superpriority over the administrative expenses of the superseded case. § 726(b). In addition, when adequate protection is provided to a secured creditor and hindsight reveals it to have been inadequate, the resulting unsecured claim of the secured party is accorded superpriority over the other administrative expenses of that case. § 507(b). Finally, in connection with borrowing orders under Section 364(c)(1), discussed earlier at pp. 235–37, the court may grant the lender an administrative expense priority that is senior to the other administrative expenses.

In Chapters 11, 12, and 13, the plan must provide for full cash payment of all priority claims, although the payment of claims within certain priority classes may be stretched out over a period of time. See pp. 431–33, 339, *infra*.

§ 6.05 THE DISTRIBUTION SCHEME IN CHAPTER 7

§ 6.05(a) In General

Distribution in Chapters 11 and 13, which will be discussed later, and in Chapter 12 is governed mainly by the terms of the plan, although, as just noted, the Code itself mandates that certain

11 U.S.C. § 725. Disposition of certain property

After the commencement of a case under this chapter, but before final distribution of property of the estate under section 726 of this title, the trustee, after notice and a hearing, shall dispose of any property in which an entity other than the estate has an interest, such as a lien, and that has not been disposed of under another section of this title.

11 U.S.C. § 726. Distribution of property of the estate

(a) Except as provided in section 510 of this title, property of the estate shall be distributed —

(1) first, in payment of claims of the kind specified in, and in the order specified in, section 507 of this title;

(2) second, in payment of any allowed unsecured claim, other than a claim of a kind specified in paragraph (1), (3), or (4) of this subsection, proof of which is —

(A) timely filed under section 501(a) of this title;

(B) timely filed under section 501(b) or 501(c) of this title; or

(C) tardily filed under section 501(a) of this title, if —

(i) the creditor that holds such claim did not have notice or actual knowledge of the case in time for timely filing of a proof of such claim under section 501(a) of this title; and

(ii) proof of such claim is filed in time to permit payment of such claim;

(3) third, in payment of any allowed unsecured claim proof of which is tardily filed under section 501(a) of this title, other than a claim of the kind specified in paragraph (2)(C) of this subsection;

(4) fourth, in payment of any allowed claim, whether secured or unsecured, for any fine, penalty, or forfeiture, or for multiple, exemplary, or punitive damages, arising before the earlier of the order for relief or the appointment of a trustee, to the extent that such fine, penalty, forfeiture, or damages are not compensation for actual pecuniary loss suffered by the holder of such claim;

(5) fifth, in payment of interest at the legal rate from the date of the filing of the petition, on any claim paid under paragraph (1), (2), (3), or (4) of this subsection; and

(6) sixth, to the debtor.

provisions be made for specified priority claims. In Chapter 7, on the other hand, the scheme of distribution is statutorily prescribed.

A secured claim by its very nature is entitled to be paid in full out of the proceeds of the collateral that secures it (subject to proper preservation or disposition charges under Section 506(c), referred to earlier) before any of those proceeds may be used to pay unsecured claims. This principle is recognized in Section 725. The liquidation proceeds that are available for unsecured creditors (including both the proceeds of collateral remaining after the satisfaction of valid liens and the proceeds of free assets of the estate) are then distributed in accordance with Section 726, as follows:

First, the Section 507(a) priority claims are paid, in the order of their priority. § 726(a)(1).

Second, under Section 726(a)(2), allowed unsecured nonpriority claims are paid, provided that they were either timely filed under Section 501 and Bankruptcy Rule 3002(c) *or* tardily filed under circumstances that excuse late filing (lack of notice or knowledge of the case) and in time to permit distribution on the claim. Moreover, if a claim is for a fine, a penalty, punitive damages, or the like, it is paid under Section 726(a)(2) only to the extent that it is for actual pecuniary loss suffered by the holder of the claim.

Third in line are allowed unsecured claims that are tardily filed, when the tardiness is not excusable. § 726(a)(3).

Fourth paid are allowed penalty-type claims, secured or unsecured, that are not compensation for actual pecuniary loss suffered by the holder of the claim. § 726(a)(4). (The lien securing a penalty claim is subject to avoidance under Section 724(a).) Penalty claims are not disallowed; they are only subordinated to the claims of other unsecured creditors. In practice, however, this treatment generally has the same effect as disallowance.

If at any of the foregoing levels of distribution there are insufficient funds to fully pay the claims at that level, the available proceeds are prorated. § 726(b).

Fifth, if any property of the estate remains, Section 726(a)(5) requires the payment of postpetition interest on all unsecured claims. Interest is paid at the legal rate (the rate on judgments) and is prorated among all unsecured claims, including the Section

11 U.S.C. § 726. Distribution of property of the estate

(c) Notwithstanding subsections (a) and (b) of this section, if there is property of the kind specified in section 541(a)(2) of this title, or proceeds of such property, in the estate, such property or proceeds shall be segregated from other property of the estate, and such property or proceeds and other property of the estate shall be distributed as follows:

(1) Claims allowed under section 503 of this title shall be paid either from property of the kind specified in section 541(a)(2) of this title, or from other property of the estate, as the interest of justice requires.

(2) Allowed claims, other than claims allowed under section 503 of this title, shall be paid in the order specified in subsection (a) of this section, and, with respect to claims of a kind specified in a particular paragraph of section 507 of this title or subsection (a) of this section, in the following order and manner:

(A) First, community claims against the debtor or the debtor's spouse shall be paid from property of the kind specified in section 541(a)(2) of this title, except to the extent that such property is solely liable for debts of the debtor.

(B) Second, to the extent that community claims against the debtor are not paid under subparagraph (A) of this paragraph, such community claims shall be paid from property of the kind specified in section 541(a)(2) of this title that is solely liable for debts of the debtor.

(C) Third, to the extent that all claims against the debtor including community claims against the debtor are not paid under subparagraph (A) or (B) of this paragraph such claims shall be paid from property of the estate other than property of the kind specified in section 541(a)(2) of this title.

(D) Fourth, to the extent that community claims against the debtor or the debtor's spouse are not paid under subparagraph (A), (B), or (C) of this paragraph, such claims shall be paid from all remaining property of the estate.

507(a) priorities, without regard to the priority or level of distribution of the claim and without regard to whether the claim would otherwise bear interest outside of bankruptcy. Thus postpetition interest on a penalty claim under this provision is of the same rank as postpetition interest on a priority wage or tax claim.

Finally, in the unlikely event that any surplus remains after the payment of all claims and postpetition interest, it is returned to the debtor under Section 726(a)(6).

§ 6.05(b) Community Property Complications

Recall that in community property states the debtor's estate created by Section 541 includes both the debtor's and the spouse's interests in most of the community property. Fair treatment of those community or spouse's creditors who, outside of bankruptcy, could reach that community property requires that they, like the debtor's creditors, be permitted to share in the distribution. Section 101(6), (9)(C), and (11) contain the definitions necessary to achieve this end, and Section 726(c) prescribes the distributive scheme.

The House Report at 383–84 explains the details of the distribution of community property. In general, Section 726(c) provides for the segregation of community property from the debtor's separate property and for the allocation of administrative expenses between both kinds. Then community claims are paid from community property. Next, unpaid community claims and noncommunity claims are paid from the debtor's separate property.

§ 6.06 SUBORDINATION OF CLAIMS

Cutting across what has been said about the priority or distribution level of secured and unsecured claims, and about the proration of funds at any given level, is the possibility that a particular claim might be subject to subordination for one reason or another and thus be taken out of its normal place in the pecking order. Section 510 contains certain provisions relating to subordination. Under Section 510(a), the court is required to enforce contractual subordination agreements among creditors according to their terms.

The inherent power of the bankruptcy court to subordinate claims

11 U.S.C. § 510. Subordination

(a) A subordination agreement is enforceable in a case under this title to the same extent that such agreement is enforceable under applicable nonbankruptcy law.

(b) For the purpose of distribution under this title, a claim arising from rescission of a purchase or sale of a security of the debtor or of an affiliate of the debtor, for damages arising from the purchase or sale of such a security, or for reimbursement or contribution allowed under section 502 on account of such a claim, shall be subordinated to all claims or interests that are senior to or equal the claim or interest represented by such security, except that if such security is common stock, such claim has the same priority as common stock.

(c) Notwithstanding subsections (a) and (b) of this section, after notice and a hearing, the court may—

(1) under principles of equitable subordination, subordinate for purposes of distribution all or part of an allowed claim to all or part of another allowed claim or all or part of an allowed interest to all or part of another allowed interest; or

(2) order that any lien securing such a subordinated claim be transferred to the estate.

on equitable or fairness grounds, as established in cases such as *Pepper v. Litton,* 308 U.S. 295 (1939), is codified in Section 510(c).

Finally, under Section 510(b), claims for rescission or damages arising from the purchase or sale of a security (or for reimbursement or contribution allowed on account of such claims) are subordinated in distribution to a level immediately below the level of the security in question; if, however, the security is common stock, the claim is treated on the distribution level of the common stock. This provision adopts the view of Professors Slain and Kripke that subordination of such claims is a matter of rewarding expectations. Slain & Kripke, *The Interface Between Securities Regulation and Bankruptcy — Allocating the Risks of Illegal Securities Issuance Between Securityholders and the Issuer's Creditors,* 48 N.Y.U. L. Rev. 261 (1973). The position to which these claims are subordinated under Section 510(b) discourages the assertion of securities rescission claims instead of the claim or interest represented by the security itself. A more complete analysis of Section 510(b) appears in the House Report at 194–96.

11 U.S.C. § 521. Debtor's duties

The debtor shall —

(1) file a list of creditors, and unless the court orders otherwise, a schedule of assets and liabilities, a schedule of current income and current expenditures, and a statement of the debtor's financial affairs;

(2) if an individual debtor's schedule of assets and liabilities includes consumer debts which are secured by property of the estate —

(A) within thirty days after the date of the filing of a petition under chapter 7 of this title or on or before the date of the meeting of creditors, whichever is earlier . . ., the debtor shall file with the clerk a statement of his intention with respect to the retention or surrender of such property . . .;

(B) within forty-five days after the filing of a notice of intent under this section . . . the debtor shall perform his intention with respect to such property . . .; and

(C) nothing in subparagraphs (A) and (B) of this paragraph shall alter the debtor's or the trustee's rights with regard to such property under this title;

(3) if a trustee is serving in the case, cooperate with the trustee as necessary to enable the trustee to perform the trustee's duties under this title;

(4) if a trustee is serving in the case, surrender to the trustee all property of the estate and any recorded information, including books, documents, records, and papers, relating to property of the estate, whether or not immunity is granted under section 344 of this title; and

(5) appear at the hearing required under section 524(d) of this title.

11 U.S.C. § 343. Examination of the debtor

The debtor shall appear and submit to examination under oath at the meeting of creditors under section 341(a) of this title. Creditors, any indenture trustee, any trustee or examiner in the case, or the United States trustee may examine the debtor. The United States trustee may administer the oath required under this section.

7

The Individual Debtor and His Fresh Start

The discussion in this chapter focuses on statutory provisions that have their most important or frequent application in cases involving individual debtors, ordinarily in Chapter 7 or Chapter 13. The reader should remember, however, that many of the sections are potentially applicable to debtors who are partnerships or corporations and to Chapter 11 and Chapter 12 cases as well.

§ 7.01 THE DEBTOR'S DUTIES; IMMUNITY

The debtor's prescribed duties are found for the most part in Section 521. *See also* Bankruptcy Rule 4002. The debtor must, unless the court orders otherwise, file certain required documents, including a schedule of assets and liabilities, a statement of financial affairs, and a schedule of current income and expenses. § 521(1). The form and content of these papers are set forth in the Official Forms promulgated by the Supreme Court. Moreover, the debtor must in general turn over to the trustee all property and records relating to the estate and cooperate in the administration of the estate. § 521(4), (3). Section 343 mandates his attendance at the Section 341(a) meeting of creditors. There the debtor is subject to examination by the trustee, the United States trustee, and creditors. Further examination on other occasions as well may be ordered by the court pursuant to Bankruptcy Rule 2004. The debtor is also required to attend the Section 524(d) discharge hearing if one is held in the case. § 521(5); see p. 331, *infra*.

In addition, a debtor with secured consumer debts must promptly file a statement of his intentions concerning them — that is, a state-

11 U.S.C. § 727. Discharge

(a) The court shall grant the debtor a discharge, unless—

(6) the debtor has refused, in the case—

(A) to obey any lawful order of the court, other than an order to respond to a material question or to testify;

(B) on the ground of privilege against self-incrimination, to respond to a material question approved by the court or to testify, after the debtor has been granted immunity with respect to the matter concerning which such privilege was invoked; or

(C) on a ground other than the properly invoked privilege against self-incrimination, to respond to a material question approved by the court or to testify;

ment setting forth whether he intends to keep, surrender, or redeem the collateral and whether he intends to reaffirm the secured indebtedness. According to the statute, moreover, the debtor must perform these stated intentions within 45 days after declaring them. § 521(2); *see also* Bankruptcy Rule 1007(b)(3).

Failure to comply with the statutory duties can have serious consequences for the debtor. The United States trustee may move to dismiss a voluntary petition (or to convert a Chapter 11 or Chapter 13 case to Chapter 7) if the debtor fails to file on time the schedules, lists, or other information required by Section 521(1). §§ 707(a)(3), 1112(e), 1307(c)(9). Contempt or criminal sanctions for violation of a statutory duty are also possible, depending on the nature of the dereliction and the debtor's related mental state. *See* 18 U.S.C. § 152. Moreover, the violation may well give rise to a ground for objection to discharge in a Chapter 7 case. *See* § 727.

The statutory duties sometimes collide with, and therefore may have to give way to, the debtor's Fifth Amendment privilege against self-incrimination. Unless immunity is granted, testimony cannot be compelled when the constitutional privilege is validly asserted. (In this connection, see Section 727(a)(6), which, as a statutory matter, protects the debtor against denial of discharge for a valid assertion of the privilege.) Whether the privilege against self-incrimination extends to protecting the contents of the records or papers of an individual debtor, especially when the documents relate to property of the estate, is far from clear. In recent times the courts have seemed to narrow the scope of the privilege in this context, holding that the contents of papers are not testimonial in nature and therefore are not protected. But even if the contents of records are not testimonial, the act of producing them may itself be testimonial under certain circumstances, in which event production cannot constitutionally be compelled. For a discussion of the difficult line-drawing that must be done when the statutory duty to produce records in bankruptcy is resisted on constitutional grounds, see, e.g., *Butcher v. Bailey,* 753 F.2d 465 (6th Cir. 1985).

A constitutional privilege against self-incrimination that otherwise exists is vitiated if the witness is granted appropriate use and derivative use immunity. *E.g., Kastigar v. United States,* 406 U.S. 441 (1972). The Criminal Code, Title 18 U.S.C., Part V, provides

11 U.S.C. § 522. Exemptions

(b) Notwithstanding section 541 of this title, an individual debtor may exempt from property of the estate the property listed in either paragraph (1) or, in the alternative, paragraph (2) of this subsection. In joint cases filed under section 302 of this title and individual cases filed under section 301 or 303 of this title by or against debtors who are husband and wife, and whose estates are ordered to be jointly administered under Rule 1015(b) of the Bankruptcy Rules, one debtor may not elect to exempt property listed in paragraph (1) and the other debtor elect to exempt property listed in paragraph (2) of this subsection. If the parties cannot agree on the alternative to be elected, they shall be deemed to elect paragraph (1), where such election is permitted under the law of the jurisdiction where the case is filed. Such property is—

(1) property that is specified under subsection (d) of this section, unless the State law that is applicable to the debtor under paragraph (2)(A) of this subsection specifically does not so authorize; or, in the alternative,

(2)(A) any property that is exempt under Federal law, other than subsection (d) of this section, or State or local law that is applicable on the date of the filing of the petition at the place in which the debtor's domicile has been located for the 180 days immediately preceding the date of the filing of the petition, or for a longer portion of such 180-day period than in any other place; and

(B) any interest in property in which the debtor had, immediately before the commencement of the case, an interest as a tenant by the entirety or joint tenant to the extent that such interest as a tenant by the entirety or joint tenant is exempt from process under applicable nonbankruptcy law.

(c) Unless the case is dismissed, property exempted under this section is not liable during or after the case for any debt of the debtor that arose, or that is determined under section 502 of this title as if such debt had arisen, before the commencement of the case, except—

(1) a debt of a kind specified in section 523(a)(1) or 523(a)(5) of this title; or

[Continued]

the mechanism for conferring this kind of immunity, and Section 344 incorporates this procedure for cases under the Bankruptcy Code. In practice, a debtor does not often receive immunity, but in the rare case when it is granted, he must testify; a debtor who then refuses to do so may be punished by contempt sanctions or by the denial of discharge. *See* § 727(a)(6)(B).

§ 7.02 EXEMPTIONS

One way the Bankruptcy Code works to give the debtor a fresh start is through the exemption provisions. Section 522(b) authorizes an *individual* debtor to exempt—that is, to take out of the estate and keep—certain property interests. What is thus exempted cannot thereafter be reached by prepetition unsecured creditors (other than taxing agencies holding nondischargeable claims and claimants for spousal or child support). § 522(c). Nor is exempted property ordinarily liable for any part of the administrative expenses in the case. § 522(k). Liens on the exempted property may be enforced, however, unless they are avoided under some other provision of the Code. § 522(c).

The former Bankruptcy Act looked to the law of the state of the debtor's domicile to determine what property could be exempted in bankruptcy. The resulting lack of uniformity in bankruptcy throughout the nation was criticized by some, and the Commission on the Bankruptcy Laws of the United States proposed a uniform federal bankruptcy exemption system. But political realities forced a compromise, or rather two compromises, to be incorporated in the 1978 legislation. First, the debtor was to have the choice between a specified federal list of exemptions and the exemption provisions of his own state law, which might be more or less favorable for him. Second, each state was granted the power to "opt out" of the federal exemption alternative, § 522(b)(1), and thus limit its domiciliaries to state-created exemptions in their bankruptcies. To date, nearly three-fourths of the states have enacted opt-out legislation, so that the federal exemption alternative is presently available only in a relatively few states. Appellate courts have upheld the constitutionality of Congress's permitting the states to opt out against arguments that this authorization vio-

(2) a debt secured by a lien that is—

(A)(i) not avoided under subsection (f) or (g) of this section or under section 544, 545, 547, 548, 549, or 724(a) of this title; and

(ii) not void under section 506(d) of this title; or

(B) a tax lien, notice of which is properly filed.

11 U.S.C. § 522. Exemptions

(k) Property that the debtor exempts under this section is not liable for payment of any administrative expense except—

(1) the aliquot share of the costs and expenses of avoiding a transfer of property that the debtor exempts under subsection (g) of this section . . . and

(2) any costs and expenses of avoiding a transfer under subsection (f) or (h) of this section, or of recovery of property under subsection (i)(1) of this section, that the debtor has not paid.

11 U.S.C. § 522. Exemptions

(d) The following property may be exempted under subsection (b)(1) of this section:

(1) The debtor's aggregate interest, not to exceed $7,500 in value, in real property or personal property that the debtor or a dependent of the debtor uses as a residence . . . or in a burial plot. . . .

(2) The debtor's interest, not to exceed $1,200 in value, in one motor vehicle.

(3) The debtor's interest, not to exceed $200 in value in any particular item or $4,000 in aggregate value, in household furnishings, household goods, wearing apparel, appliances, books, animals, crops, or musical instruments, that are held primarily for . . . personal, family, or household use. . . .

(4) The debtor's aggregate interest, not to exceed $500 in value, in jewelry. . . .

(5) The debtor's aggregate interest in any property, not to exceed in value $400 plus up to $3,750 of any

[Continued]

lates the requirement that bankruptcy laws be uniform and that the opt-out provision amounts to an impermissible delegation of congressional power to the states. *E.g., Rhodes v. Stewart,* 705 F.2d 159 (6th Cir. 1983).

Where the choice between state and federal exemptions still exists, the debtor must elect one or the other and may not mix the two. Since the 1984 amendments, spouses who are joint debtors under the Code or whose cases are jointly administered must both make the same choice. § 522(b).

It is not always clear whether a given state law is an exemption statute. The general understanding, however, is that a state exemption statute is one which makes certain property unreachable by execution and other judicial process for the purpose of insuring that the debtor retains the minimum means necessary to survive. Under this definition a statute that makes property unreachable by creditors through judicial process for some other reason is not an exemption law; for example, a liquor license granted by the state may be made nonleviable, not for the debtor's benefit, but rather to enable the state to better control its ownership.

Under Section 522, a debtor who relies on state exemption law is entitled also to claim as exempt any interest in joint tenancy or tenancy by the entirety property that is not reachable by process under the state law and any property that is exempt under nonbankruptcy federal law. § 522(b)(2). Examples of the latter are the federal statutes that exempt veterans' benefits, federal civil service retirement payments, social security benefits, and the like. However, ERISA pension plans containing nonassignability and nonleviability provisions are *not* considered by the appellate courts to be the subject of a federal exemption statute for this purpose, nor, according to the majority view, are such plans excludable from the estate as spendthrift trusts under Section 541(c)(2). *See, e.g., In re Goff,* 706 F.2d 574 (5th Cir. 1983); pp. 129–31, *supra.*

The federal bankruptcy exemption alternative, § 522(d), in those states where it is still in effect, is a fairly liberal set of provisions as compared with typical state exemption laws. The reader should note, for example, the $7,500 homestead exemption provided by Section 522(d)(1), together with the so-called "wildcard" or "spillover" provision in Section 522(d)(5): A debtor who has not claimed

unused amount of the exemption provided under paragraph (1) of this subsection.

(6) The debtor's aggregate interest, not to exceed $750 in value, in any implements, professional books, or tools, of the trade. . . .

(7) Any unmatured life insurance contract owned by the debtor, other than a credit life insurance contract.

(8) The debtor's aggregate interest, not to exceed in value $4,000 . . . in any . . . interest under, or loan value of, any unmatured life insurance contract owned by the debtor under which the insured is the debtor or an individual of whom the debtor is a dependent.

(9) Professionally prescribed health aids for the debtor or a dependent of the debtor.

(10) The debtor's right to receive —

(A) a social security benefit, unemployment compensation, or a local public assistance benefit;

(B) a veterans' benefit;

(C) a disability, illness, or unemployment benefit;

(D) alimony, support, or separate maintenance, to the extent reasonably necessary for the support of the debtor and any dependent of the debtor;

(E) a payment under a stock bonus, pension, profit-sharing, annuity, or similar plan or contract on account of illness, disability, death, age, or length of service, to the extent reasonably necessary for the support of the debtor and any dependent. . . .

(11) The debtor's right to receive, or property that is traceable to —

(A) an award under a crime victim's reparation law;

(B) a payment on account of the wrongful death of an individual of whom the debtor was a dependent, to the extent reasonably necessary for the support of the debtor and any dependent of the debtor;

(C) a payment under a life insurance contract that insured the life of an individual of whom the debtor was a dependent . . . to the extent reasonably necessary for . . . support . . . .

[Continued]

the full homestead exemption may, to the extent of the unused amount, exempt any kind of property up to a value of $3,750 (plus $400). If both spouses are debtors, they can together exempt up to $7,500 (plus $800) under the "wildcard" provision. *See* § 522(m).

As noted previously, pp. 129–31, *supra,* Section 541(c)(2) excludes from the estate the debtor's interest in a spendthrift trust, to the extent that it is not reachable by creditors under applicable state law. Although this section is not technically an exemption provision, it has the similar effect of permitting the debtor to keep the property interest.

When applicable law specifies what is exempt by reference to the kind of property involved, the debtor may try to maximize his benefits through prepetition exemption planning. That is, the debtor might convert assets of a nonexempt type into property of an exempt nature. This conversion might be accomplished, for example, by selling one item and buying another. Or the debtor could borrow on the security of nonexempt collateral, thereby reducing the equity that can pass to the estate, and use the loan proceeds either to purchase an exempt item or to pay down another loan secured by property of an already exempt type. Some appellate decisions have held that this practice is both unobjectionable and effective, provided that the property claimed as exempt was not itself acquired through fraud. *E.g., Wudrick v. Clements,* 451 F.2d 988 (9th Cir. 1971). The legislative history of Section 522 also suggests that exemption planning is permissible. *See* H.R. REP. No. 595, 95th Cong., 1st Sess. 361 (1977) [hereinafter cited in this chapter as "House Report"]. Other courts, however, have frowned on the practice and have penalized in one way or another the debtor who engages in it. The problem is discussed in Resnick, *Prudent Planning or Fraudulent Transfer? The Use of Nonexempt Assets To Purchase or Improve Exempt Property on the Eve of Bankruptcy,* 31 RUTGERS L. REV. 615 (1978).

Any waiver of exemptions (as distinguished from the granting of a lien on exempt property) given by the debtor to an unsecured creditor is unenforceable as a matter of overriding federal policy, even though the waiver might be effective in some states. § 522(e).

The procedure for obtaining exemptions is governed by Section 522(*l*), which is implemented by the Bankruptcy Rules. Normally the debtor's schedules or Chapter 13 statement must specify the

(D) a payment, not to exceed $7,500, on account of personal bodily injury, not including pain and suffering or compensation for actual pecuniary loss, of the debtor or an individual of whom the debtor is a dependent; or

(E) a payment in compensation of loss of future earnings of the debtor or an individual of whom the debtor is or was a dependent, to the extent reasonably necessary for . . . support. . . .

11 U.S.C. § 522. Exemptions

(m) Subject to the limitations in subsection (b), this section shall apply separately with respect to each debtor in a joint case.

11 U.S.C. § 522. Exemptions

(e) A waiver of an exemption executed in favor of a creditor that holds an unsecured claim against the debtor is unenforceable . . . . A waiver by the debtor of a power under subsection (f) or (h) . . . , under subsection (g) or (i) . . . , or under subsection (i) . . . is unenforceable. . . .

11 U.S.C. § 522. Exemptions

(*l*) The debtor shall file a list of property that the debtor claims as exempt under subsection (b) of this section. If the debtor does not file such a list, a dependent of the debtor may file such a list, or may claim property as exempt from property of the estate on behalf of the debtor. Unless a party in interest objects, the property claimed as exempt on such list is exempt.

11 U.S.C. § 522. Exemptions

(f) Notwithstanding any waiver of exemptions, the debtor may avoid the fixing of a lien on an interest of the debtor in property to the extent that such lien impairs an exemption to which the debtor would have been entitled under subsection (b) of this section, if such lien is—

(1) a judicial lien; or

[Continued]

items claimed as exempt. *See* Bankruptcy Rules 1007, 4003; Official Forms Nos. 6, 10. A dependent, however, can make the claim if the debtor fails to do so. The weight of authority is that amendments should be liberally permitted to correct or supplement the original claim if it was somehow deficient. *E.g., Tignor v. Parkinson,* 729 F.2d 977 (4th Cir. 1984). The trustee or creditors must file timely objections to the exemptions, ordinarily within 30 days after the Section 341(a) meeting (or within 30 days after the filing of an amendment). *See* Bankruptcy Rule 4003(b). Otherwise, the debtor's claimed exemptions are automatically allowed. § 522(*l*). The court resolves the issues if timely objections are made.

§ 7.03 THE DEBTOR'S AVOIDING POWERS

The debtor's power to avoid transfers of or liens upon exempt property and to claim exemptions out of transfers recovered by the trustee enhance the value of his exemption rights. Several provisions of Section 522 work to this end, the most important of which is Section 522(f). To the extent that a judicial lien impairs an exemption — that is, makes the exempt property less valuable to the debtor than it would be in the absence of the judicial lien — he may avoid the lien under Section 522(f)(1) regardless of how long before bankruptcy it arose. This avoiding power and the one provided by Section 522(f)(2), discussed next, do not enable avoidance to the extent that the lien reaches value in property beyond what the debtor may exempt.

Under Section 522(f)(2), a provision that had no counterpart in pre-Code bankruptcy law, a debtor may avoid, to the extent it impairs his exemptions, a nonpossessory, nonpurchase-money security interest in tools of the trade and similar items, health aids, and virtually every kind of consumer goods other than an automobile. Congress was convinced that lenders did not take this type of security interest in exempt goods of relatively small liquidation value as true collateral. Rather, in practice a lien on the necessaries of life was a leverage device to force reaffirmation of otherwise dischargeable debts. Hence avoidance was called for by the fresh-start principle. The courts have divided on the issue of whether the debtor may use Section 522(f)(2) to invalidate liens on

(2) a nonpossessory, nonpurchase-money security interest in any—

(A) household furnishings, household goods, wearing apparel, appliances, books, animals, crops, musical instruments, or jewelry that are held primarily for the personal, family, or household use of the debtor or a dependent of the debtor;

(B) implements, professional books, or tools, of the trade . . . ; or

(C) professionally prescribed health aids . . . .

11 U.S.C. § 522. Exemptions

(g) . . . the debtor may exempt under subsection (b) of this section property that the trustee recovers . . . to the extent that the debtor could have exempted such property under subsection (b) of this section if such property had not been transferred, if—

(1)(A) such transfer was not a voluntary transfer . . . ; and

(B) the debtor did not conceal such property; or

(2) the debtor could have avoided such transfer under subsection (f)(2) of this section.

(h) The debtor may avoid a transfer . . . or recover a setoff to the extent that the debtor could have exempted such property under subsection (g)(1) of this section if the trustee had avoided such transfer, if—

(1) such transfer is avoidable by the trustee . . . and

(2) the trustee does not attempt to avoid such transfer.

(i)(1) If the debtor avoids a transfer or recovers a setoff under subsection (f) or (h) of this section, the debtor may . . . exempt any property so recovered under subsection (b) of this section.

(2) . . . a transfer avoided . . . may be preserved for the benefit of the debtor to the extent that the debtor may exempt such property under subsection (g) of this section or paragraph (1) of this subsection.

exempt property of considerable per unit value when the literal terms of the statute seem to make the avoiding power applicable. *Compare Augustine v. United States,* 675 F.2d 582 (3d Cir. 1982), *with In re Thompson,* 750 F.2d 628 (8th Cir. 1984). *But cf. In re La Fond,* 791 F.2d 623 (8th Cir. 1986) (limiting *Thompson* to its facts, i.e., an action to avoid a lien under § 522(f)(2)(A), and following *Augustine* with respect to lien avoidance under § 522(f)(2)(B)).

Although, in permitting states to opt out of the federal exemption alternative, Congress did not intend to delegate the authority to override other provisions of Section 522, a few state legislatures have attempted nevertheless to vitiate the debtor's Section 522(f)(2) avoiding power. Any such direct effort no doubt would violate the supremacy clause of the Constitution. But the attempt has been indirect, first through the opt out by restricting the debtor to state law exemptions and then either by defining what is exempt in terms of only the debtor's equity in encumbered property, so that the potentially avoidable security interest does not technically impair any exemption, or by completely denying exempt status to encumbered property. To date, these efforts at end runs around Section 522(f)(2) have had mixed success. *E.g., compare In re Maddox,* 713 F.2d 1526 (11th Cir. 1983) *and In re Taylor,* 73 Bankr. 149 (9th Cir. App. Panels 1987) (state law cannot deprive debtor of Section 522(f)(2) avoiding power), *with In re McManus,* 681 F.2d 353 (5th Cir. 1982), *and In re Pine,* 717 F.2d 281 (6th Cir. 1983) (state law was effective to prevent use of Section 522(f)(2)).

Under Section 522(g), exemptions may be claimed out of property recovered by the trustee pursuant to one of his avoiding powers, if the debtor had not voluntarily made the transfer or if it would have been subject to Section 522(f)(2) avoidance. And, if the trustee fails to pursue an action to avoid an involuntary transfer of potentially exempt property (or a transfer subject to Section 522(f)(2) avoidance), the debtor may do so and claim an exemption out of the recovery. § 522(h), (i).

The debtor's avoiding powers under Section 522 may not be effectively waived. § 522(e).

Finally, the potential avoiding power effect of Section 506(a) and (d) should not be overlooked. A debtor who wants to keep exempt property that is overencumbered arguably is entitled to have any

11 U.S.C. § 506. Determination of secured status

(a) An allowed claim of a creditor secured by a lien . . . or . . . setoff . . . is a secured claim to the extent of the value of . . . such property, or to the extent of the amount subject to setoff, as the case may be, and is an unsecured claim to the extent that the value . . . is less than the amount of such allowed claim. . . .

(d) To the extent that a lien secures a claim against the debtor that is not an allowed secured claim, such lien is void, unless—

(1) such claim was disallowed only under section 502(b)(5) or 502(e) of this title; or

(2) such claim is not an allowed secured claim due only to the failure of any entity to file a proof of such claim under section 501 of this title.

11 U.S.C. § 722. Redemption

An individual debtor may, whether or not the debtor has waived the right to redeem under this section, redeem tangible personal property intended primarily for personal, family, or household use, from a lien securing a dischargeable consumer debt, if such property is exempted under section 522 of this title or has been abandoned under section 554 of this title, by paying the holder of such lien the amount of the allowed secured claim of such holder that is secured by such lien.

lien declared invalid under these provisions to the extent that the amount owed to the secured creditor exceeds the value of the collateral at the time of bankruptcy. Then, if the debtor's equity should subsequently increase, either through appreciation of the property's value or the reduction of senior encumbrances, the debtor will receive the benefit of the increase. The decisions to date, however, reach divergent conclusions with respect to the debtor's ability to use Section 506(d) in this manner. *E.g., compare In re Worrell,* 67 Bankr. 16 (C.D. Ill. 1986) *and In re Whitener,* 63 Bankr. 701 (Bankr. E.D. Pa. 1986) (debtor may avoid lien under § 506(d)) *with In re Maitland,* 61 Bankr. 130 (Bankr. E.D. Va. 1986) (debtor cannot use § 506(d) in this context) *and Matter of Lindsey,* 823 F.2d 189 (7th Cir. 1987) (debtor may "strip down" a partially secured claim to the value of the collateral under § 506(a) and (d), but if the debt is in default, the creditor is entitled to foreclose the lien for the stripped down amount).

§ 7.04 REDEMPTION

Rounding out the series of provisions designed to enhance the value of the debtor's exemption rights is the power to redeem exempt (or abandoned) consumer goods from an otherwise non-avoidable lien. Section 722 applies in Chapter 7 cases to liens securing dischargeable consumer debts. The provision is likely to have its most important use in connection with purchase-money security interests and security interests in automobiles, since the debtor ordinarily cannot invalidate these types of liens with his Section 522(f)(2) avoiding power. Redemption is accomplished by paying the lienholder the amount of the allowed secured claim; pursuant to Section 506(a), this amount equals the value of the collateral. Redemption thus provides a valuable benefit because outside of bankruptcy the debtor would have to pay the full obligation owed to the creditor to satisfy the lien, even though such amount might well exceed the collateral's value, particularly in the context of a security interest in consumer goods. Unless the secured party agrees otherwise, the redemption amount under Section 722 must be tendered by way of a lump sum cash payment. *In re Bell,* 700 F.2d 1053 (6th Cir. 1983).

11 U.S.C. § 521. Debtor's duties

The debtor shall —

(2) if an individual debtor's schedule of assets and liabilities includes consumer debts which are secured by property of the estate —

(A) within thirty days after the date of the filing of a petition under chapter 7 of this title or on or before the date of the meeting of creditors, whichever is earlier, or within such additional time as the court, for cause within such period fixes, the debtor shall file with the clerk a statement of his intention with respect to the retention or surrender of such property and, if applicable, specifying that such property is claimed as exempt, that the debtor intends to redeem such property, or that the debtor intends to reaffirm debts secured by such property;

(B) within forty-five days after the filing of a notice of intent under this section, or within such additional time as the court, for cause, within such forty-five day period fixes, the debtor shall perform his intention with respect to such property, as specified by subparagraph (A) of this paragraph; and

(C) nothing in subparagraphs (A) and (B) of this paragraph shall alter the debtor's or the trustee's rights with regard to such property under this title;

11 U.S.C. § 727. Discharge

(a) The court shall grant the debtor a discharge, unless—

(1) the debtor is not an individual;

(b) Except as provided in section 523 of this title, a discharge under subsection (a) of this section discharges the debtor from all debts that arose before the date of the order for relief . . . whether or not a proof of claim . . . is filed . . . or . . . allowed. . . .

The debtor must file a statement of an intention to redeem within 30 days after filing the Chapter 7 petition, or before the Section 341(a) meeting if that occurs earlier, and should perform the stated intention within 45 days thereafter or within whatever further time the court allows. § 521(2). The penalty for noncompliance with these statutory requirements, however, is unclear. *See* § 521(2)(C).

Although the power to redeem under Section 722 is a Chapter 7 provision, the debtor can obtain a similar and perhaps even more beneficial redemption result through a Chapter 13 plan. As will be seen later, pp. 343–45, *infra,* the plan may provide for the satisfaction of a secured claim by periodic payments equal to the value of the collateral, together with an interest factor to compensate for the time value of the deferred installments.

§ 7.05   THE DISCHARGE AND ITS EFFECT

Although any "person" (an individual, a partnership, or a corporation) is eligible for Chapter 7 relief, only an "individual" debtor is granted a discharge in a liquidation case. § 727(a)(1). The same is obviously true in Chapter 13 because the relief it offers is available only to individuals. In Chapter 11, however, an order of confirmation ordinarily has a discharge effect for all debtors, regardless of their organizational form, *see* § 1141(d); the same is true of a discharge granted in Chapter 12. § 1228.

In essence the discharge is an order that bars the debtor's in personam liability on "claims" within its scope. § 524(a). The scope, however, varies somewhat depending on the kind of case in which the discharge is granted. In Chapter 7, claims (other than claims nondischargeable under Section 523(a)) that arose before the order for relief are discharged. § 727(b). In voluntary cases the result is that prepetition claims are discharged and those that arose after the petition are not. The Chapter 11 discharge extends to claims that arose before the order of confirmation. § 1141(d)(1). Under Chapters 12 and 13, the discharge covers claims provided for in the plan. §§ 1228, 1328. What a claim is — and the problem of determining when a claim arises — was discussed earlier at pp. 267–71. *See,* especially, *Ohio v. Kovacs,* 469 U.S. 274 (1985).

11 U.S.C. § 1141. Effect of confirmation

(d)(1) Except as otherwise provided in this subsection, in the plan, or in the order confirming the plan, the confirmation of a plan—

(A) discharges the debtor from any debt that arose before the date of such confirmation . . .

(d)(2) The confirmation of a plan does not discharge an individual debtor from any debt excepted from discharge under section 523 of this title.

11 U.S.C. § 1328. Discharge

(a) As soon as practicable after completion by the debtor of all payments under the plan . . . the court shall grant the debtor a discharge of all debts provided for by the plan or disallowed under section 502 of this title, except any debt—

(1) provided for under section 1322(b)(5) of this title; or

(2) of the kind specified in section 523(a)(5) of this title.

11 U.S.C. § 524. Effect of discharge

(a) A discharge in a case under this title—

(1) voids any judgment at any time obtained, to the extent that such judgment is a determination of the personal liability of the debtor with respect to any debt discharged under section 727, 944, 1141, 1228, or 1328 of this title, whether or not discharge of such debt is waived;

(2) operates as an injunction against the commencement or continuation of an action, the employment of process, or an act, to collect, recover or offset any such debt as a personal liability of the debtor, whether or not discharge of such debt is waived; and

(3) operates as an injunction against the commencement or continuation of an action, the employment of process, or an act, to collect or recover from, or offset against, property of the debtor of the kind specified in section 541(a)(2) of this title that is acquired after the commencement of the case, on account of any allowable community claim, except a community claim that is excepted from discharge . . . whether or not discharge of the debt based on such community claim is waived.

A lien on the debtor's or the estate's property, if not set aside under one of the avoiding powers, is not affected by a discharge of the underlying obligation that it secures, although any unsecured deficiency would be barred.[1] *E.g., Chandler Bank of Lyons v. Ray,* 804 F.2d 577 (10th Cir. 1986).

As will be seen, certain kinds of claims are nondischargeable even though the debtor is granted a discharge, and these may vary depending upon the chapter under which relief is sought. See pp. 319–27, 347, 435–39, *infra.* But if a claim is subject to discharge in a given case, it is barred whether or not the claim is allowed or allowable and whether or not a proof of claim is filed. *E.g.,* §§ 727(b), 1141(d), 1228, 1328. Moreover, as a general proposition the debtor may not waive the effect of the discharge. § 524(a). After bankruptcy, however, and subject to court approval, the debtor may waive the discharge entirely, §§ 727(a)(10), 1141(d)(4), 1228(a), 1328(a), although such a waiver rarely occurs.

The discharge not only bars or voids in personam judgments on dischargeable-type claims but also acts as a permanent injunction, superseding the automatic stay, against judicial proceedings or nonjudicial collection efforts (for example, self-help remedies) with respect to such claims. § 524(a)(1), (2). It also enjoins to a specified extent actions against community property acquired after bankruptcy by a debtor and spouse, § 524(a)(3), (b), whether or not the spouse is a debtor.

The discharge, however, does not affect the liability of anyone else who is a co-obligor with the debtor on a discharged obligation or who is secondarily liable for the debtor's discharged debt. § 524(e). See p. 359, *infra.*

Finally, although the debtor may not waive a discharge in advance, and although restrictions are placed on his ability to make binding reaffirmation agreements, nothing prevents the debtor from voluntarily paying a discharged debt, either in whole or in

---

[1]In Chapter 11, an order of confirmation includes a discharge order, but its effect is broader. Among other things, the provisions of a confirmed Chapter 11 plan bind not only creditors but also property dealt with by the plan; thus the confirmation order arguably may affect both lien enforcement and in personam liability. *See* § 1141; pp. 435–37, *infra. See also* §§ 1227, 1327. *But cf. In re* Simmons, 765 F.2d 547 (5th Cir. 1985) (Chapter 13).

11 U.S.C. § 524. Effect of discharge

(e) Except as provided in subsection (a)(3) of this section, discharge of a debt of the debtor does not affect the liability of any other entity on, or the property of any other entity for, such debt.

(f) Nothing contained in subsection (c) or (d) of this section prevents a debtor from voluntarily repaying any debt.

11 U.S.C. § 525. Protection against discriminatory treatment

(a) . . . a governmental unit may not deny, revoke, suspend, or refuse to renew a license, permit, charter, franchise, or other similar grant to, condition such a grant to, discriminate with respect to such a grant against, deny employment to, terminate the employment of, or discriminate with respect to employment against, a person that is or has been a debtor under this title . . . solely because such bankrupt or debtor is or has been a debtor under this title . . . , has been insolvent before the commencement of the case under this title, or during the case but before the debtor is granted or denied a discharge, or has not paid a debt that is dischargeable. . . .

(b) No private employer may terminate the employment of, or discriminate with respect to employment against, an individual who is or has been a debtor under this title, . . . solely because such debtor . . . —

(1) is or has been a debtor under this title . . . ;

(2) has been insolvent before the commencement of a case under this title or during the case but before the grant or denial of a discharge; or

(3) has not paid a debt that is dischargeable. . . .

part; and he may pay one debt or a few without becoming obligated to pay others. *See* § 524(f).

§ 7.06 PROTECTION AGAINST DISCRIMINATORY TREATMENT

Section 525(a), which was enacted in 1978, prohibits governmental units from discriminating against a debtor in employment, in licensing, or in making similar grants "solely because" he has been in bankruptcy, has failed to pay a discharged debt, or was insolvent before being granted a discharge. The legislative history makes clear that this section is not preemptive. Courts may expand the antidiscrimination policy beyond the statutory language to help the debtor make a fresh start. For example, according to the House Report at 367, a court may prohibit a union from ousting a member who has failed to pay a debt to the union's credit union if union membership is a prerequisite to employment in the industry in which the debtor works. *But cf. In re Goldrich,* 771 F.2d 28 (2d Cir. 1985) (Section 525 does not prohibit state from denying student loan to a debtor who discharged an earlier student loan). The legislative history also makes clear that Section 525(a) does not prohibit discrimination on bases other than those listed. For example, the debtor's postbankruptcy financial condition or managerial ability can be a basis for discrimination. In other words, if any ground for discrimination exists besides bankruptcy, predischarge insolvency, or failure to pay a discharged debt, the action of a governmental unit is not controlled by Section 525(a). Since the 1984 amendments adding Section 525(b), a private party is similarly prohibited from discriminating against a debtor with respect to employment on bankruptcy-related grounds.

Finally, any form of pressure exerted against a debtor, including the withholding of privileges either by a governmental unit or by a private party, in an attempt to collect a discharged debt would violate the automatic stay and the discharge injunction. §§ 362(a)(6), 524(a)(2).

11 U.S.C. § 727. Discharge

(a) The court shall grant the debtor a discharge, unless —

(1) the debtor is not an individual;

(2) the debtor, with intent to hinder, delay, or defraud a creditor . . . has transferred, removed, destroyed, mutilated, or concealed . . . —

(A) property of the debtor, within one year before the date of the filing of the petition; or

(B) property of the estate, after the date of the filing of the petition;

(3) the debtor has concealed, destroyed, mutilated, falsified, or failed to keep or preserve any recorded information, including books, documents, records, and papers, from which the debtor's financial condition or business transactions might be ascertained, unless such act or failure to act was justified under all of the circumstances of the case;

(4) the debtor knowingly and fraudulently, in or in connection with the case —

(A) made a false oath or account;

(B) presented or used a false claim;

(C) gave, offered, received, or attempted to obtain money, property, or advantage, or a promise of money, property, or advantage, for acting or forbearing to act; or

(D) withheld from an officer of the estate entitled to possession under this title, any recorded information . . . ;

(5) the debtor has failed to explain satisfactorily, before determination of denial of discharge under this paragraph, any loss of assets or deficiency of assets to meet the debtor's liabilities;

(6) the debtor has refused, in the case —

(A) to obey any lawful order of the court, other than an order to respond to a material question or to testify;

(B) on the ground of privilege against self-incrimination, to respond to a material question . . . after the debtor has been granted immunity . . . ; or

(C) on a ground other than the properly invoked

[Continued]

§ 7.07 OBJECTIONS TO THE DEBTOR'S DISCHARGE; REVOCATION OF DISCHARGE

As noted previously, p. 311, *supra,* only debtors who are individuals are eligible for discharge in Chapter 7. An individual debtor who is shown to have engaged in certain prohibited conduct, however, may be denied a discharge as to all debts; the grounds for denying the discharge apply only in a Chapter 7 liquidation case or in a Chapter 11 case that amounts substantially to a liquidation. §§ 727(a), 1141(d)(3). In any event, these grounds are not relevant in Chapters 12 and 13. *See* §§ 1228, 1225, 1328, 1325.

The grounds for denial of discharge to an individual debtor in a Chapter 7 case, § 727(a), include that: (1) the debtor, within one year before bankruptcy, fraudulently transferred or concealed property "with intent to hinder, delay, or defraud a creditor"; (2) the debtor failed to keep adequate financial records; (3) the debtor engaged in certain specified criminal misconduct during the bankruptcy case or refused to obey a lawful court order or to testify (but invoking the Fifth Amendment privilege against self-incrimination is not a ground for denial of discharge unless the debtor has been granted immunity); (4) the debtor failed to explain satisfactorily any losses or deficiency of assets, apparently whether or not the failure to explain resulted from the invocation of the Fifth Amendment privilege; and (5) the debtor obtained a discharge in a previous liquidation, reorganization, or Chapter 13 case filed less than six years before the commencement of the pending case; however, if in a previous Chapter 13 case the debtor paid at least 70 per cent of his debts and used his best efforts, then the six-year discharge bar does not apply in the Chapter 7 case.

Even though one or more of the grounds for denial of discharge might in fact exist, the order granting the discharge is routinely entered by the court unless a creditor, the trustee, or the United States trustee has timely filed a complaint objecting to the discharge. §§ 727(c)(1); Bankruptcy Rule 4004. "Timely" ordinarily means within 60 days after the Section 341(a) meeting, Bankruptcy Rule 4004(a); creditors are informed of this date in the notice sent to them shortly after the beginning of the case. In the great majority of bankruptcies, at least in recent years, no one

privilege against self-incrimination, to respond to a material question approved by the court or to testify;

(7) the debtor has committed any act specified in paragraph (2), (3), (4), (5), or (6) of this subsection, on or within one year before the date of the filing of the petition, or during the case, in connection with another case, under this title or under the Bankruptcy Act, concerning an insider;

(8) the debtor has been granted a discharge . . . in a case commenced within six years before the date of the filing of the petition;

(9) the debtor has been granted a discharge under section 1228 or 1328 . . . in a case commenced within six years before the date of the filing of the petition, unless payments under the plan in such case totaled at least—

(A) 100 percent of the allowed unsecured claims in such case; or

(B)(i) 70 percent of such claims; and

(ii) the plan was proposed by the debtor in good faith, and was the debtor's best effort; or

(10) the court approves a written waiver of discharge executed by the debtor after the order for relief under this chapter.

11 U.S.C. § 523. Exceptions to discharge

(a) A discharge under section 727, 1141, 1228(a), 1228(b), or 1328(b) of this title does not discharge an individual debtor from any debt—

(1) for a tax or a customs duty—

(A) of the kind and for the periods specified in section 507(a)(2) or 507(a)(7) of this title, whether or not a claim for such tax was filed or allowed;

(B) with respect to which a return, if required—

(i) was not filed; or

(ii) was filed after the date on which such return was last due, under applicable law or under any extension, and after two years before the date of the filing of the petition; or

(C) with respect to which the debtor made a fraudulent return or willfully attempted in any manner to evade or defeat such tax;

[Continued]

bothers to press objections, and the debtor receives the discharge when the prescribed period expires. If a complaint is filed, however, it begins an adversary proceeding that leads to a trial and judgment determining whether the debtor is entitled to a discharge. Bankruptcy Rule 7001(4). The burden of proof here is on the objector. Bankruptcy Rule 4005.

A discharge, once granted, may be revoked on specified grounds, including the debtor's having obtained it fraudulently or his commission of certain kinds of misconduct after the discharge order was entered. § 727(d). Normally the statute of limitations on revocation expires one year after the discharge is granted. *See* § 727(e).

§ 7.08 NONDISCHARGEABLE DEBTS

Despite the granting of the discharge, certain debts are nevertheless nondischargeable in Chapter 7. (The same debts are nondischargeable in Chapter 12. § 1228(a), (c).) (Nondischargeable debts in Chapters 11 and 13 will be referred to later. See pp. 435–39, 347, *infra*.) Unlike the Section 727 grounds for denying the debtor's discharge, which are infrequently litigated, the grounds for nondischargeability are the subject of constant litigation in the bankruptcy courts. They are specified in Section 523(a) and are discussed in the following paragraphs.

§ 7.08(a) Certain Taxes

Taxes entitled to priority under Section 507(a), see pp. 283–85, 281, *supra,* are excepted from discharge. In general, these are the relatively recent taxes and the so-called trust fund taxes, regardless of age. In addition, whether or not they have priority status, taxes as to which a fraudulent return or no return was filed, or as to which there was a late filing within two years before bankruptcy, are nondischargeable. § 523(a)(1)(B), (C).

§ 7.08(b) Fraudulently Incurred Obligations

This category, found in Section 523(a)(2), covers liabilities incurred by fraud, false representations, and the like. A rebuttable presumption of fraud—that is, of nondischargeability—arises from

(2) for money, property, services, or an extension, renewal, or refinancing of credit, to the extent obtained by—

(A) false pretenses, a false representation, or actual fraud, other than a statement respecting the debtor's or an insider's financial condition;

(B) use of a statement in writing—

(i) that is materially false;

(ii) respecting the debtor's or an insider's financial condition;

(iii) on which the creditor to whom the debtor is liable for such money, property, services, or credit reasonably relied; and

(iv) that the debtor caused to be made or published with intent to deceive; or

(C) for purposes of subparagraph (A) of this paragraph, consumer debts owed to a single creditor and aggregating more than $500 for "luxury goods or services" incurred by an individual debtor on or within forty days before the order for relief under this title, or cash advances aggregating more than $1,000 that are extensions of consumer credit under an open end credit plan obtained by an individual debtor on or within twenty days before the order for relief under this title, are presumed to be nondischargeable . . . ;

(3) neither listed nor scheduled under section 521(1) of this title, with the name, if known to the debtor, of the creditor to whom such debt is owed, in time to permit—

(A) if such debt is not of a kind specified in paragraph (2), (4), or (6) of this subsection, timely filing of a proof of claim, unless such creditor had notice or actual knowledge of the case in time for such timely filing; or

(B) if such debt is of a kind specified in paragraph (2), (4), or (6) of this subsection, timely filing of a proof of claim and timely request for a determination of dischargeability of such debt under one of such paragraphs, unless such creditor had notice or actual knowledge of the case in time for such timely filing and request;

(4) for fraud or defalcation while acting in a fiduciary capacity, embezzlement, or larceny;

the debtor's incurring certain debts for luxuries or obtaining certain consumer loans shortly before filing his petition. When the fraud or false representation involves a statement of the debtor's (or of an insider's) financial condition, the statement must have been in writing and the creditor must have reasonably relied upon it in extending the credit.

Because there had been a considerable history of creditors' attempting to use the fraud ground of nondischargeability in an unfair and improper manner, Section 523(d) provides that a debtor who prevails in litigation involving the dischargeability of a consumer debt under Section 523(a)(2) is ordinarily entitled to an award of his attorney's fees and costs.

§ 7.08(c) Debts Not Timely Scheduled

Under Section 523(a)(3), a debt that is not scheduled in time for the creditor to file a proof of claim or a complaint alleging nondischargeability under Section 523(c) is nondischargeable unless the creditor obtained actual knowledge of the bankruptcy in time to file the claim or complaint. The existence of this ground of nondischargeability highlights the importance to the debtor of properly preparing the bankruptcy schedules.

§ 7.08(d) Fiduciary Fraud, Larceny, and Embezzlement

Section 523(a)(4) excepts from discharge liabilities for larceny, embezzlement, or fraud or defalcation while acting in a fiduciary capacity. For the latter, it is established that only the breach of a technical trust or fiduciary relationship is material; the breach of a trust imposed for remedial purposes is not sufficient.

§ 7.08(e) Spousal and Child Support

Obligations for alimony, maintenance, or support of the debtor's spouse or child are nondischargeable under Section 523(a)(5); on the other hand, debts representing a property settlement are subject to discharge. Both the legislative history and case law establish that the characterization of an obligation for this purpose is a matter of federal law, *see, e.g., In re Calhoun,* 715 F.2d 1103 (6th Cir. 1983); *cf. Forsdick v. Turgeon,* 812 F.2d 801 (2d Cir. 1987); but in

11 U.S.C. § 523. Exceptions to discharge

    (a) A discharge under section 727, 1141, 1228(a), 1228(b), or 1328(b) of this title does not discharge an individual debtor from any debt—

    (5) to a spouse, former spouse, or child of the debtor, for alimony to, maintenance for, or support of such spouse or child, in connection with a separation agreement, divorce decree, or other order of a court of record, or property settlement agreement, but not to the extent that—

    (A) such debt is assigned to another entity, voluntarily, by operation of law, or otherwise (other than debts . . . assigned to the Federal Government or to a State or any political subdivision of such State); or

    (B) such debt includes a liability designated as alimony, maintenance, or support, unless such liability is actually in the nature of alimony, maintenance, or support;

    (6) for willful and malicious injury by the debtor to another entity or to the property of another entity;

    (7) to the extent such debt is for a fine, penalty, or forfeiture payable to and for the benefit of a governmental unit, and is not compensation for actual pecuniary loss, other than a tax penalty—

    (A) relating to a tax of a kind not specified in paragraph (1) of this subsection; or

    (B) imposed with respect to a transaction or event that occurred before three years before the date of the filing of the petition;

actuality the courts have had to look, at least to some extent, to state law for guidance.

Although the statutory language indicates that a nondischargeable support obligation must be owed "to" the spouse or child, the decisions for the most part have held that liabilities for such support are within the Section 523(a)(5) exception even when they run in favor of a third party. *E.g., In re Calhoun, supra.*

Assignment of the alimony or support obligation to someone other than a governmental unit will destroy the nondischargeable character of the debt. § 523(a)(5)(A).

§ 7.08(f) Willful and Malicious Injuries

Under Section 523(a)(6), liabilities based on intentional torts that injure the person or property of another are nondischargeable. According to the majority view of the courts that have construed the provision, negligence or recklessness, even when it is gross, is not enough for this purpose.[2] Actual hatred or ill will probably need not be shown, but there is a divergence of views concerning whether intent to cause injury, as distinguished from intent to do the act, is a requirement of Section 523(a)(6). Damages resulting from the debtor's intentional (as distinguished from technical) conversion of a secured party's collateral often are held nondischargeable under this section. *See, e.g., In re Cecchini,* 780 F.2d 1440 (9th Cir. 1986). *But cf. In re Long,* 774 F.2d 875 (8th Cir. 1985).

§ 7.08(g) Governmental Fines, Penalties, and Noncompensatory Debts

Section 523(a)(7) makes governmental fines and penalties nondischargeable to the extent that they are not "compensation for actual pecuniary loss." Interpreting the quoted phrase, the Supreme Court has held that a restitution obligation imposed on the debtor as a condition of probation in a state criminal case is nondischargeable under the section even though the restitution

---

[2] A liability stemming from driving while intoxicated may be an exception to this statement. *See, e.g., In re* Adams, 761 F.2d 1422 (9th Cir. 1985). *Contra In re* Compos, 768 F.2d 1155 (10th Cir. 1985). *See also* § 523(a)(9), discussed at pp. 325–27, *infra.*

11 U.S.C. § 523. Exceptions to discharge

(a) A discharge under section 727, 1141, 1228(a), 1228(b), or 1328(b) of this title does not discharge an individual debtor from any debt—

(8) for an educational loan made, insured, or guaranteed by a governmental unit, or made under any program funded in whole or in part by a governmental unit or a nonprofit institution, unless—

(A) such loan first became due before five years (exclusive of any applicable suspension of the repayment period) before the date of the filing of the petition; or

(B) excepting such debt from discharge under this paragraph will impose an undue hardship on the debtor and the debtor's dependents;

(9) to any entity, to the extent that such debt arises from a judgment or consent decree . . . against the debtor wherein liability was incurred . . . as a result of the debtor's operation of a motor vehicle while legally intoxicated . . . ;

amount represents the loss caused by the criminal conduct. *Kelly v. Robinson,* __ U.S. __, 107 S. Ct. 353 (1986). Not included within the Section 523(a)(7) category of debts, however, are tax penalties related to dischargeable taxes or to a transaction or event that occurred more than three years before the date of the filing of the bankruptcy petition — such debts are dischargeable. Private penalties and the like do not fall within the Section 523(a)(7) exception and are potentially dischargeable.

§ 7.08(h) Educational Loans

Debts arising from educational loans made, insured, or guaranteed by a governmental unit or funded by a nonprofit institution are nondischargeable under Section 523(a)(8), provided that the first payment on the loan did not become due more than five years before bankruptcy. When the due date of the first installment falls outside the five-year period, the entire debt (not merely the older installments) becomes dischargeable. *In re Nunn,* 788 F.2d 617 (9th Cir. 1986). Even though an educational loan might meet the time requirement for nondischargeability, the court nevertheless has discretion under Section 523(a)(8)(B) to discharge the obligation if undue hardship to the debtor and his dependents would otherwise occur. The reported decisions to date, however, indicate that bankruptcy judges in general have strictly applied the undue hardship provision and have permitted only debtors with the bleakest of financial prospects to invoke it. Moreover, a 1981 amendment to 42 U.S.C. § 294f(g) seems to supersede the "undue hardship" provision and to apply a stricter dischargeability standard to loans made for health education purposes under that statute. This amendment permits dischargeability only if the court finds, inter alia, that nondischarge would be "unconscionable."

§ 7.08(i) Drunk Driving Judgments

Added in 1984 as a nondischargeable type of debt is a judgment or consent decree for damages based on a debtor's driving a motor vehicle while legally intoxicated. § 523(a)(9). According to the majority view, this type of judgment need not have been entered before the bankruptcy case was filed but may be obtained postpetition

11 U.S.C. § 523. Exceptions to discharge

(a) A discharge under section 727, 1141, 1228(a), 1228(b), or 1328(b) of this title does not discharge an individual debtor from any debt—

(10) that was or could have been listed or scheduled by the debtor in a prior case concerning the debtor . . . in which the debtor waived discharge, or was denied a discharge under section 727(a)(2), (3), (4), (5), (6), or (7) of this title. . . .

11 U.S.C. § 523. Exceptions to discharge

(b) Notwithstanding subsection (a) of this section, a debt that was excepted from discharge under subsection (a)(1), (a)(3), or (a)(8) of this section . . . in a prior case concerning the debtor . . . is dischargeable in a case under this title unless, by the terms of subsection (a) of this section, such debt is not dischargeable in the case under this title.

after the automatic stay is lifted. *See, e.g., Leach v. Reckley,* 63 Bankr. 724 (S.D. Ind. 1986). *Contra In re Hudson,* 73 Bankr. 649 (9th Cir. App. Panels 1987) (for Section 523(a)(9) to apply, judgment must have been entered prior to the order for relief). Even without a judgment, a drunk driving liability may fall within the willful and malicious injury ground for nondischargeability under Section 523(a)(6). *See, e.g., In re Adams, supra* note 2. *Contra In re Compos, supra* note 2.

§ 7.08(j) Debts Involved in a Prior Bankruptcy Case

It has long been the law that failure to obtain a discharge in a bankruptcy case has a res judicata effect, so that all debts that could have been discharged in that case are rendered nondischargeable for all time. This principle is carried forward into the Bankruptcy Code as the final category of nondischargeable debts—debts that were or could have been scheduled in an earlier bankruptcy case in which the debtor waived discharge or was denied a discharge on any ground other than that provided by Section 727(a)(8) or (9) (prior discharge within six years). § 523(a)(10). The denial of a discharge solely because the debtor had been discharged in a previous case within six years does not have a res judicata effect; in a subsequent bankruptcy after the six-year period has expired, the debtor can discharge the debts involved in the earlier case. (Dismissal of a bankruptcy case does not have a res judicata effect unless the court for cause orders otherwise. *See* § 349(a).)

The foregoing discussion has no application to a debtor who received a discharge in an earlier case but failed to discharge a particular debt either because it was not timely scheduled under Section 523(a)(3) or because it was a tax claim or an educational loan of too recent vintage to be eligible for discharge under Section 523(a)(1) or (8). The res judicata principle is not implicated in this context; such claims that survived the first bankruptcy can be discharged in a later case so long as they are not then nondischargeable on some other ground. § 523(b).

§ 7.08(k) Procedure for Determining Dischargeability

Litigation about whether a particular claim is dischargeable is

11 U.S.C. § 523. Exceptions to discharge

(c) Except as provided in subsection (a)(3)(B) of this section, the debtor shall be discharged from a debt of a kind specified in paragraph (2), (4), or (6) of subsection (a) of this section, unless, on request of the creditor to whom such debt is owed, and after notice and a hearing, the court determines such debt to be excepted from discharge under paragraph (2), (4), or (6), as the case may be, of subsection (a) of this section.

ordinarily brought before the bankruptcy judge. State courts occasionally exercise jurisdiction over dischargeability issues, except in proceedings involving the so-called 2-4-6 debts (see the discussion that follows). In the bankruptcy court an action to determine dischargeability is classified as an adversary proceeding, Bankruptcy Rule 7001(6); the procedure is governed by Part VII of the Bankruptcy Rules together with the specific provisions of Rule 4007.

Either the debtor or the creditor can institute the action by filing a dischargeability complaint. There is no time limit on bringing the suit unless the claim is alleged to be nondischargeable under paragraphs (2), (4), or (6) of Section 523(a) — the so-called 2-4-6 debts — which are the fraud, fiduciary breach, and willful and malicious injury categories. Congress singled out these kinds of potentially nondischargeable debts for special procedural treatment because of a history of abusive practices by creditors under the sections of the former Bankruptcy Act that corresponded to the Code's 2-4-6 provisions. The goal is to smoke out any potential reliance by a creditor on one of these grounds early in the bankruptcy case, when the debtor is more likely to have access to his lawyer, and to require that the litigation proceed before a bankruptcy judge, who, it is perceived, is not so likely as some state courts to be hostile to discharged bankrupts. Thus Section 523(c) and the implementing rule, Bankruptcy Rule 4007(c), require a creditor who contends that his claim is nondischargeable under Section 523(a)(2), (4), or (6) to file the complaint within 60 days after the first date set for the Section 341(a) meeting or within any extended time that the court for cause may order. All creditors are informed of this date in the notice sent to them early in the case. Missing the deadline means that the debt is discharged, even though it might actually fall within one of the 2-4-6 categories, unless the creditor can invoke some other basis for nondischargeability.

The policy behind the grant of exclusive, or at least paramount, jurisdiction over dischargeability matters to the bankruptcy court is so strong that ordinary res judicata principles are relaxed somewhat to implement the policy. Thus it is established that res judicata does not preclude looking behind a state court judgment and even taking additional evidence to determine whether the original

11 U.S.C. § 524. Effect of discharge

(d) In a case concerning an individual, when the court has determined whether to grant or not to grant a discharge under section 727, 1141, 1228, or 1328 of this title, the court may hold a hearing at which the debtor shall appear in person. At any such hearing, the court may inform the debtor that a discharge has been granted or the reason why a discharge has not been granted. If a discharge has been granted and if the debtor desires to make an agreement of the kind specified in subsection (c) of this section, then the court shall hold a hearing at which the debtor shall appear in person and at such hearing the court shall—

(1) inform the debtor—

(A) that such an agreement is not required under this title, under nonbankruptcy law, or under any agreement not made in accordance with the provisions of subsection (c) of this section; and

(B) of the legal effect and consequences of—

(i) an agreement of the kind specified in subsection (c) of this section; and

(ii) a default under such an agreement;

(2) determine whether the agreement that the debtor desires to make complies with the requirements of subsection (c)(6) of this section, if the consideration for such agreement is based in whole or in part on a consumer debt that is not secured by real property of the debtor.

underlying claim embodied in the judgment is dischargeable or nondischargeable. *Brown v. Felsen,* 442 U.S. 127 (1979). There may still be some room for the application of collateral estoppel to facts actually litigated and determined in an earlier state court lawsuit, *see Brown v. Felsen, supra,* at 139 n.10, but even this doctrine has sometimes been applied in a relaxed fashion. *E.g., In re Daley,* 776 F.2d 834 (9th Cir. 1985).

§ 7.09 REAFFIRMATION AND THE DISCHARGE HEARING

Unlike the predecessor Bankruptcy Act, the Bankruptcy Code imposes both procedural and substantive restrictions on the debtor's ability to make a binding reaffirmation agreement, that is, an agreement to repay an otherwise dischargeable obligation.

Under Section 524(d), an individual debtor who desires to reaffirm such a debt must appear at a so-called discharge hearing. *See also* Bankruptcy Rule 4008. The intended purpose of the hearing is threefold. First, it is supposed to impress upon the individual debtor the judicial nature and seriousness of the bankruptcy remedy. Second, it provides the debtor with an explanation by the court of the discharge and a warning about the reaffirmation of discharged debts. Third, if the debtor wishes to reaffirm any debt, the hearing gives the court an opportunity to determine whether the reaffirmation agreement meets the requirements of Section 524(c), discussed next, for making a reaffirmation enforceable. In a case in which no reaffirmation is intended, the court may, but need not, order the debtor's attendance at a Section 524(d) hearing. Not surprisingly, however, few bankruptcy judges hold discharge hearings when the statute does not mandate one. (For a critical view of the utility of the Section 524(d) hearing, see *In re Rennels,* 37 Bankr. 81 (Bankr. W.D. Ky. 1984).)

The procedural and substantive provisions concerning reaffirmation agreements were enacted by Congress in 1978 to correct a perceived deficiency in practice under pre-Code bankruptcy law. Congress found that when the ability to reaffirm was not restricted, debtors too often were induced by pressure, cajolery, or feelings of guilt to promise to pay their debts after bankruptcy; by thus reinstating their discharged obligations, these debtors lost the fresh-start

11 U.S.C. § 524. Effect of discharge

(c) An agreement between a holder of a claim and the debtor, the consideration for which, in whole or in part, is based on a debt that is dischargeable in a case under this title is enforceable . . . only if—

(1) such agreement was made before the granting of the discharge under section 727, 1141, 1228, or 1328 of this title;

(2) such agreement contains a clear and conspicuous statement which advises the debtor that the agreement may be rescinded at any time prior to discharge or within sixty days after such agreement is filed with the court, whichever occurs later, by giving notice of rescission . . . ;

(3) such agreement has been filed with the court and, if applicable, accompanied by a declaration or an affidavit of the attorney that represented the debtor during the course of negotiating an agreement under this subsection, which states that such agreement—

(A) represents a fully informed and voluntary agreement by the debtor; and

(B) does not impose an undue hardship on the debtor or a dependent of the debtor;

(4) the debtor has not rescinded such agreement at any time prior to discharge or within sixty days after such agreement is filed with the court, whichever occurs later . . . ;

(5) the provisions of subsection (d) of this section have been complied with; and

(6)(A) in a case concerning an individual who was not represented by an attorney during the course of negotiating an agreement under this subsection, the court approves such agreement as—

(i) not imposing an undue hardship . . . ; and

(ii) in the best interest of the debtor.

(B) Subparagraph (A) shall not apply to the extent that such debt is a consumer debt secured by real property.

benefits that bankruptcy law contemplated. No one seriously contended that debtors who were willing and able to pay discharged obligations should not be permitted to do so. But during the legislative process leading to the 1978 Code, some reformers did urge that all agreements or promises to pay such debts should be legally unenforceable.

Congress did not accept these proposals in full but did provide some protection for the debtor against himself. Under Section 524(c), as presently in force, a reaffirmation agreement must meet the following requirements to be effective: First, it must be entered into by the debtor and creditor before the discharge is granted; consequently, the creditor cannot wait too long to induce the debtor to reaffirm. Second, the debtor has the right to rescind the agreement at any time before discharge or within 60 days after the agreement was filed with the court, whichever is later; the agreement must contain a statement informing the debtor of this "cooling off" period. Third, as discussed previously, the discharge hearing procedure must be complied with and the warnings about reaffirmation given by the court. Finally, if a lawyer negotiated the agreement for the debtor, he must certify among other things that performance will not impose an undue hardship; if there was no such lawyer involvement, then the court must approve the agreement as being in the debtor's best interests and not imposing an undue hardship. Court approval is not needed, however, for reaffirmation of a consumer debt secured by real estate.

§ 7.10 THE CHAPTER 13 ALTERNATIVE

In general, Chapter 13 provides for the debtor's rehabilitation through a court-confirmed plan under which creditors are paid in whole or in part, usually under the supervision of a Chapter 13 trustee and usually out of earnings or other monies received by the debtor after the filing of the petition.

§ 7.10(a) Eligibility

Only "an individual with regular income" who has fixed unsecured debts of under $100,000 and fixed secured debts of under

11 U.S.C. § 109. Who may be a debtor

(e) Only an individual with regular income that owes, on the date of the filing of the petition, noncontingent, liquidated, unsecured debts of less than $100,000 and noncontingent, liquidated, secured debts of less than $350,000, or an individual with regular income and such individual's spouse, except a stockbroker or a commodity broker, that owe, on the date of the filing of the petition, noncontingent, liquidated, unsecured debts that aggregate less than $100,000 and noncontingent, liquidated, secured debts of less than $350,000 may be a debtor under chapter 13 of this title.

11 U.S.C. § 101. Definitions

In this title —

(29) "individual with regular income" means individual whose income is sufficiently stable and regular to enable such individual to make payments under a plan under chapter 13 of this title, other than a stockbroker or a commodity broker;

11 U.S.C. § 1301. Stay of action against codebtor

(a) Except as provided in subsections (b) and (c) of this section, after the order for relief under this chapter, a creditor may not act, or commence or continue any civil action, to collect all or any part of a consumer debt of the debtor from any individual that is liable on such debt with the debtor, or that secured such debt, unless —

(1) such individual became liable on or secured such debt in the ordinary course of such individual's business; or

(2) the case is closed, dismissed, or converted to a case under chapter 7 or 11 of this title.

(b) A creditor may present a negotiable instrument, and may give notice of dishonor of such an instrument.

$350,000 is eligible for Chapter 13 relief; the monetary limits remain the same if both the debtor and a spouse file. § 109(e). The quoted phrase is defined by Section 101(29) to mean an individual whose source of income is sufficiently stable to enable performance under the plan. But the legislative history indicates, and the case law has held, that the income need not be the debtor's future earnings in the usual sense; disability or social security benefits, for example, may qualify as income for this purpose. Nor is Chapter 13 available only to debtors who are employees of others. Debtors who operate their own small businesses as proprietorships may invoke Chapter 13, provided that their debts do not exceed the monetary limits.

§ 7.10(b) Voluntariness

A Chapter 13 case may be commenced only by a debtor's voluntary petition, *see* §§ 301, 303(a), and only a debtor may propose a Chapter 13 plan, § 1321, or modify it before confirmation. § 1323. Moreover, the weight of authority is that the debtor has the absolute right to dismiss a Chapter 13 case under Section 1307(b) even though the interests of creditors might be better served by conversion to Chapter 7 under Section 1307(c). Although an amendment to Section 1329(a) in 1984 apparently permits modification of a plan after confirmation without the debtor's consent, Chapter 13 remains essentially voluntary in nature.

§ 7.10(c) The Codebtor Automatic Stay

The general automatic stay of Section 362, discussed more fully at pp. 195–223 *supra,* applies in Chapter 13 to halt, among other things, lawsuits against the debtor and lien enforcement against his and the estate's property. In addition, the commencement of a case under Chapter 13 also operates as a stay of civil collection actions against certain codebtors of the debtor. § 1301. Section 1301 is carefully drawn, but the protection it affords is significant. Without court permission, creditors are barred from attempting to collect a consumer debt from a nonprofessional codebtor. § 1301(a). (Thus a surety company in the business of guaranteeing loans is not protected by the codebtor stay. *See* § 1301(a)(1).) A "consumer debt" is

11 U.S.C. § 1301. Stay of action against codebtor

(c) On request of a party in interest and after notice and a hearing, the court shall grant relief from the stay provided by subsection (a) of this section with respect to a creditor, to the extent that—

(1) as between the debtor and the individual protected under subsection (a) of this section, such individual received the consideration for the claim held by such creditor;

(2) the plan filed by the debtor proposes not to pay such claim; or

(3) such creditor's interest would be irreparably harmed by continuation of such stay.

(d) Twenty days after the filing of a request under subsection (c)(2) of this section for relief from the stay provided by subsection (a) of this section, such stay is terminated with respect to the party in interest making such request, unless the debtor or any individual that is liable on such debt with the debtor files and serves upon such party in interest a written objection to the taking of the proposed action.

11 U.S.C. § 1306. Property of the estate

(a) Property of the estate includes, in addition to the property specified in section 541 of this title—

(1) all property of the kind specified in such section that the debtor acquires after the commencement of the case but before the case is closed, dismissed, or converted . . . ; and

(2) earnings from services performed by the debtor after the commencement of the case but before the case is closed, dismissed, or converted. . . .

(b) Except as provided in a confirmed plan or order confirming a plan, the debtor shall remain in possession of all property of the estate.

defined in Section 101(7) as a "debt incurred by an individual primarily for a personal, family, or household purpose."

A creditor may obtain relief from the codebtor stay in three situations, which are listed in Section 1301(c). First, if the debtor was not really the primary obligor (or, tracking the language of Section 1301(c)(1), as between the debtor and the codebtor the latter received the consideration for the claim held by the creditor), the stay will be lifted as to the codebtor. This provision, among other things, covers the case in which the debtor is an accommodation endorser. Second, relief may be obtained under Section 1301(c)(2) to the extent that the plan filed by the debtor does not propose to satisfy the creditor's claim. The 1984 amendment adding Section 1301(d) gives a procedural advantage to a creditor who seeks relief on this ground. Third, relief may be obtained under Section 1301(c)(3) if the creditor would suffer irreparable injury by continuation of the stay as to the codebtor. Relief from the stay imposed by Section 1301 is automatic when the case is closed, dismissed, or converted to Chapter 7 or 11. § 1301(a)(2).

The creditor's substantive rights against the codebtor are not affected by the stay. Only the time and manner in which payment may be collected are affected. Section 108(c) extends the statute of limitations on actions to collect against a codebtor, granting a stayed creditor a minimum of 30 days to proceed against the codebtor after the stay terminates or expires. On the other hand, the Section 1301 stay prevents a creditor with psychological security— that is, the leverage on the debtor resulting from the ability to pressure the debtor's friend, relative, or employer—from exerting undue influence to extract preferential treatment under a plan. *See generally* House Report at 121–23.

§ 7.10(d) Property of the Estate

The Chapter 13 estate includes not only the property interests specified in Section 541, see pp. 123–33, *supra,* but also property acquired by the debtor after the commencement of the case together with the debtor's earnings from services performed after the petition. § 1306(a). However, normally the debtor rather than the trustee is entitled to the possession of the estate property,

11 U.S.C. § 1327. Effect of confirmation

(b) Except as otherwise provided in the plan or the order confirming the plan, the confirmation of a plan vests all of the property of the estate in the debtor.

11 U.S.C. § 1322. Contents of plan

(a) The plan shall—

(1) provide for the submission of all or such portion of future earnings or other future income of the debtor to the supervision and control of the trustee as is necessary for the execution of the plan;

(2) provide for the full payment, in deferred cash payments, of all claims entitled to priority under section 507 of this title, unless the holder of a particular claim agrees to a different treatment of such claim; and

(3) if the plan classifies claims, provide the same treatment for each claim within a particular class.

(b) Subject to subsections (a) and (c) of this section, the plan may—

(1) designate a class or classes of unsecured claims, as provided in section 1122 of this title, but may not discriminate unfairly against any class so designated; however, such plan may treat claims for a consumer debt of the debtor if an individual is liable on such consumer debt with the debtor differently than other unsecured claims;

(2) modify the rights of holders of secured claims, other than a claim secured only by a security interest in real property that is the debtor's principal residence, or of holders of unsecured claims, or leave unaffected the rights of holders of any class of claims;

(3) provide for the curing or waiving of any default;

(4) provide for payments on any unsecured claim to be made concurrently with payments on any secured claim or any other unsecured claim;

(5) notwithstanding paragraph (2) of this subsection, provide for the curing of any default within a reasonable time and maintenance of payments while the case is pending on any unsecured claim or secured claim on which the last payment is due after the date on which the final payment under the plan is due;

§ 1306(b), and the confirmation of a plan ordinarily revests that property in the debtor. § 1327(b).

§ 7.10(e) The Plan

Section 1322 governs what a Chapter 13 plan *must* provide and what it *may* provide. The debtor's plan typically classifies creditors according to their legal rights and specifies the treatment each class is to receive. (The discussion of classification in Chapter 11 plans, pp. 385–93, *infra*, is relevant to classification in Chapter 13.) The plan may, subject to certain standards of fairness that protect the classes, modify the rights of any class of unsecured claims or leave the class unaffected. It may also modify the rights of secured creditors, other than one whose sole collateral is a mortgage or other security interest on the debtor's home, or leave any secured claim unaffected. Moreover, a Chapter 13 plan can affect even a defaulted home mortgage in one important way: If foreclosure was not completed before the petition (and perhaps even if it was), the defaults may be cured over a reasonable period of time, the debt brought current and reinstated, and repayment then made according to the original terms of the mortgage indebtedness, even though under state law there might have been a nonreversible acceleration of the entire obligation. *See, e.g., In re Taddeo,* 685 F.2d 24 (2d Cir. 1982) (construing Section 1322(b)(2), (3), and (5)); *In re Glass,* 760 F.2d 1428 (6th Cir. 1985).

As noted earlier, the Chapter 13 debtor usually commits a portion of his anticipated future earnings or revenues to making payments under the plan. But the Code apparently is flexible enough to permit him to fund the plan in whole or in part out of any other property he presently has or might acquire in the future, including any existing exempt property. *See* § 1322(b)(8). Section 1322(a)(1) mandates only that the debtor submit to the supervision and control of the trustee whatever future income is necessary to execute the plan.

The plan must provide for the full cash payment of priority claims (not including postpetition interest) in installments over a period of time. § 1322(a)(2).

Finally, neither an original nor a modified plan may provide for

11 U.S.C. § 1322. Contents of plan

(b) Subject to subsections (a) and (c) of this section, the plan may—

(6) provide for the payment of all or any part of any claim allowed under section 1305 of this title;

(7) subject to section 365 of this title, provide for the assumption, rejection, or assignment of any executory contract or unexpired lease of the debtor not previously rejected under such section;

(8) provide for the payment of all or part of a claim against the debtor from property of the estate or property of the debtor;

(9) provide for the vesting of property of the estate, on confirmation of the plan or at a later time, in the debtor or in any other entity; and

(10) include any other appropriate provision not inconsistent with this title.

(c) The plan may not provide for payments over a period that is longer than three years, unless the court, for cause, approves a longer period, but the court may not approve a period that is longer than five years.

11 U.S.C. § 1325. Confirmation of plan

(a) Except as provided in subsection (b), the court shall confirm a plan if—

(1) the plan complies with the provisions of this chapter and with the other applicable provisions of this title;

(2) any fee, charge, or amount required under chapter 123 of title 28, or by the plan, to be paid before confirmation, has been paid;

(3) the plan has been proposed in good faith and not by any means forbidden by law;

(4) the value, as of the effective date of the plan, of property to be distributed under the plan on account of each allowed unsecured claim is not less than the amount that would be paid on such claim if the estate of the debtor were liquidated under chapter 7 of this title on such date;

[Continued]

payments over a period exceeding three years unless the court approves a longer period, not to exceed five years. §§ 1322(c), 1329(c).

§ 7.10(f) Confirmation Standards

Section 1325 prescribes the standards for court confirmation of a proposed Chapter 13 plan. Notably absent is any requirement that unsecured creditors vote on the plan or accept it. And, as will be seen, confirmation can also be "crammed down" on most objecting secured creditors.

The plan itself, of course, must comply with the requirements of Section 1322, discussed under the preceding heading.

Section 1325(a)(4) affords unsecured creditors a minimum standard of financial protection: In essence they cannot be given less than they would receive in a Chapter 7 case. Since debtors in most Chapter 13 cases have virtually no nonexempt assets, their unsecured creditors typically would receive no distribution in Chapter 7 — thus the requirement of Section 1325(a)(4) ordinarily poses little difficulty for debtors. (Although a creditor holding a claim that would be nondischargeable in Chapter 7 could reach property acquired by the debtor after bankruptcy, such potential recovery does not affect the application of Section 1325(a)(4). The comparison for the purpose of this provision is between what the Chapter 13 plan offers and what the creditor would receive from the distribution of a hypothetical Chapter 7 *estate. In re Rimgale,* 669 F.2d 426 (7th Cir. 1982).)

From the inception of the 1978 Act, many bankruptcy judges viewed Section 1325(a)(4) as providing only illusory protection for unsecured creditors and considered this to be a flaw in the statute. They were also troubled by the perception that a number of debtors were taking advantage of Chapter 13 relief (which sometimes is considerably greater than that available in Chapter 7) by proposing plans calling for payments well below their ability to pay. As a result, some judges read an additional financial standard for confirmation into the otherwise boilerplate language of Section 1325(a)(3) that "the plan has been proposed in good faith." For example, some judges required the debtor to make "meaningful" payments (as distinguished from nominal payments or no pay-

11 U.S.C. § 1325. Confirmation of plan

(a) Except as provided in subsection (b), the court shall confirm a plan if—

(5) with respect to each allowed secured claim provided for by the plan—

(A) the holder of such claim has accepted the plan;

(B)(i) the plan provides that the holder of such claim retain the lien securing such claim; and

(ii) the value, as of the effective date of the plan, of property to be distributed under the plan on account of such claim is not less than the allowed amount of such claim; or

(C) the debtor surrenders the property securing such claim to such holder; and

(6) the debtor will be able to make all payments under the plan and to comply with the plan.

(b)(1) If the trustee or the holder of an allowed unsecured claim objects to the confirmation of the plan, then the court may not approve the plan unless, as of the effective date of the plan—

(A) the value of the property to be distributed under the plan on account of such claim is not less than the amount of such claim; or

(B) the plan provides that all of the debtor's projected disposable income to be received in the three-year period beginning on the date that the first payment is due under the plan will be applied to make payments under the plan.

(2) For purposes of this subsection, "disposable income" means income which is received by the debtor and which is not reasonably necessary to be expended—

(A) for the maintenance or support of the debtor or a dependent of the debtor; or

(B) if the debtor is engaged in business, for the payment of expenditures necessary for the continuation, preservation, and operation of such business.

11 U.S.C. § 1329. Modification of plan after confirmation

(a) At any time after confirmation of the plan but before the completion of payments under such plan, the plan may be modified, upon request of the debtor, the trustee, or the holder of an allowed unsecured claim, to—

[Continued]

ments at all) to unsecured creditors under the plan. Others required the plan to represent the debtor's "best efforts," regardless of the size of the payments or the percentage recovery for creditors. In contrast, some bankruptcy judges held that the "good faith" requirement contained no financial component at all. At the appellate court level, although the decisions construing "good faith" were not entirely consistent, the usual tendency was to deemphasize the fixed financial standard in favor of deciding on a case by case basis whether a particular debtor had abused the spirit of Chapter 13. *See, e.g., Flygare v. Boulden,* 709 F.2d 1344 (10th Cir. 1983) (listing various factors to be considered in determining whether a plan is proposed in "good faith," including the amount of the proposed payments and the debtor's ability to pay, the accuracy of the debtor in reporting financial data and whether he has attempted to mislead, the extent of proposed modification of secured debt, whether the debts to be modified would be dischargeable in Chapter 7, and the frequency with which the debtor has sought relief under the Code).

Section 1325(b), one of the 1984 amendments, was intended to resolve this judicial controversy by providing an additional statutory financial standard going beyond Section 1325(a)(4) for the protection of unsecured creditors. The new section provides that a plan may not be confirmed over the objections of the trustee or of an unsecured creditor unless it provides for the payment in full of the objecting creditor or represents a commitment of all the debtor's "disposable income" over a period of three years. Generally, "disposable income" means income not reasonably needed for the support of the debtor or his dependents. As thus defined, this commitment seems to be the equivalent of the plan's representing the best efforts of the debtor. It is important to remember that if the debtor's ability to perform improves or worsens after confirmation but before completion of payments under the plan, the trustee or an unsecured creditor, as well as the debtor, may seek modification of the payments so as to reflect the revised best efforts of the debtor. *See* § 1329(a).

The confirmation requirement for a secured claim can be met in one of three ways. First, the plan may be confirmed with the secured creditor's consent or vote. *See* § 1325(a)(5)(A). Second, it may be confirmed despite the creditor's rejection if the debtor abandons the collateral. *See* § 1325(a)(5)(C). Third, and of greatest signifi-

(1) increase or reduce the amount of payments on claims of a particular class provided for by the plan;

(2) extend or reduce the time for such payments; or

(3) alter the amount of the distribution to a creditor whose claim is provided for by the plan to the extent necessary to take account of any payment of such claim other than under the plan.

(c) A plan modified under this section may not provide for payments over a period that expires after three years after the time that the first payment under the original confirmed plan was due, unless the court, for cause, approves a longer period, but the court may not approve a period that expires after five years after such time.

cance, the Chapter 13 plan may be "crammed down." That is, the plan may be confirmed without the consent of a secured creditor (other than the holder of a home mortgage) if, under the plan, the creditor is to retain his lien and is to receive property or payments with a present value (as of the effective date of the plan) of not less than the value of the collateral. In other words, cram down entails payments to the secured creditor, on a present value basis, of not less than the allowed amount of the secured claim. *See* § 1325(a)(5)(B). Thus the debtor through a Chapter 13 plan can, in effect, redeem property from a secured claim by installment payments, whereas such redemption under Section 722 in a Chapter 7 case would require a lump sum cash payment unless the creditor otherwise consented. See p. 309, *supra*.

The present value concept, of course, requires a determination of the appropriate interest rate to be applied in discounting the future installments to the time of the plan's effective date. Bankruptcy courts have varied greatly in their approaches to selecting the interest rate; many have balked at using a rate that they consider too burdensome to the debtor. Conceptually at least, the fair market rate of interest must be used in order to calculate the true present value, whether or not this rate is burdensome; thus the rate should take into account not only the risk-free cost of the use of money but also the creditworthiness of the particular debtor. *See, e.g., United States v. Neal Pharmacal Co.*, 789 F.2d 1283 (8th Cir. 1986); *In re Southern States Motor Inns, Inc.*, 709 F.2d 647 (11th Cir. 1983).

Finally, confirmation requires a finding of feasibility — that is, that the debtor predictably can perform on his promises under the plan. § 1325(a)(6).

It is not relevant in Chapter 13 that the debtor may have been guilty of conduct specified in Section 727(a) that constitutes a ground for objection to discharge. In other words, inability to obtain a Chapter 7 discharge does not affect confirmation. In particular, the six-year ground for objection to discharge under Section 727(a)(8) and (9) does not apply. Thus effective Chapter 13 relief is available even to those debtors who recently benefited from other bankruptcy relief.

11 U.S.C. § 1328. Discharge

(a) As soon as practicable after completion by the debtor of all payments under the plan, . . . the court shall grant the debtor a discharge of all debts provided for by the plan or disallowed under section 502 of this title, except any debt —

    (1) provided for under section 1322(b)(5) of this title; or

    (2) of the kind specified in section 523(a)(5) of this title.

11 U.S.C. § 1328. Discharge

(b) At any time after the confirmation of the plan and after notice and a hearing, the court may grant a discharge to a debtor that has not completed payments under the plan only if —

    (1) the debtor's failure to complete such payments is due to circumstances for which the debtor should not justly be held accountable;

    (2) the value . . . of property actually distributed under the plan on account of each allowed unsecured claim is not less than the amount that would have been paid on such claim if the estate of the debtor had been liquidated under chapter 7 . . . ; and

    (3) modification of the plan under section 1329 of this title is not practicable.

(c) A discharge granted under subsection (b) of this section discharges the debtor from all unsecured debts provided for by the plan or disallowed under section 502 of this title, except any debt —

    (1) provided for under section 1322(b)(5) of this title; or

    (2) of a kind specified in section 523(a) of this title.

§ 7.10(g) Discharge and Its Effect

Unlike the Chapter 11 confirmation order, the confirmation order in Chapter 13 does not act as a discharge. The regular Chapter 13 discharge is granted at the time payments under the plan are completed. § 1328(a). But its legal effect is much greater than in Chapter 7, which leaves the debtor with the various nondischargeable debts listed in Section 523(a). All claims are normally discharged in Chapter 13, with two exceptions: any extended long-term debts provided for in the plan, § 1328(a)(1), and nondischargeable alimony or support obligations. § 1328(a)(2).[3] Thus relief from fraud and intentional tort liabilities, among others, is potentially available in Chapter 13.

Even though the debtor fails to complete his payments under the plan, a so-called hardship discharge may be granted if modification is not practicable, the default is beyond the debtor's power to control, and creditors have already been paid under the plan at least as much as they would have received from liquidation under Chapter 7. § 1328(b). Unlike the regular discharge under Section 1328(a), however, a hardship discharge does not discharge any of the Section 523(a) nondischargeable debts. § 1328(c)(2).

---

[3]A third exception is found in 42 U.S.C. § 294f(g), which apparently leaves loans for health education covered by that provision nondischargeable even in Chapter 13, unless the strict standards of the section are met.

11 U.S.C. § 101. Definitions

In this title—

(35) "person" includes individual, partnership, and corporation, but does not include governmental unit, *Provided, however,* That any governmental unit that acquires an asset from a person as a result of operation of a loan guarantee agreement, or as receiver or liquidating agent of a person, will be considered a person for purposes of section 1102 of this title.

11 U.S.C. § 303. Involuntary cases

(b) An involuntary case against a person is commenced by the filing with the bankruptcy court of a petition under chapter 7 or 11 of this title—

(3) if such person is a partnership—

(A) by fewer than all of the general partners in such partnership; or

(B) if relief has been ordered under this title with respect to all of the general partners in such partnership, by a general partner in such partnership, the trustee of such a general partner, or a holder of a claim against such partnership;

8

Partnerships

As is true in most other areas of law, general rules of bankruptcy law yield to exceptions when partnerships are involved. In more or less the chronological order of a bankruptcy case, the following discussion considers the special principles that apply in the context of partnership bankruptcy.

§ 8.01 COMMENCEMENT OF THE CASE

A partnership is included within the definition of "person" in Section 101(35) and is conceptually distinct from the partners who compose it. Both general partnerships and limited partnerships are eligible to be debtors under the Code, whether or not the partners are also in bankruptcy. A voluntary case is commenced when the partnership files a petition with the clerk of the court under Chapter 7, 11 or 12. § 301. Bankruptcy Rule 1002. Partnerships are not eligible to be debtors in cases under Chapter 9 or 13.

It would appear that a partnership, by agreement, could authorize in advance fewer than all its general partners to file a voluntary bankruptcy petition on the firm's behalf. Bankruptcy Rule 1004(a), however, requires that *all* general partners consent to a voluntary petition, although all need not actually execute the document. The requisite consent apparently must be specific consent. *In re Channel 64 Joint Venture,* 61 Bankr. 255 (Bankr. S.D. Ohio 1986) (partners may give advance consent to voluntary petition by provision in partnership agreement).

There are also special rules for involuntary cases against a partnership. If a petition is filed on behalf of the firm without the consent of all general partners, it is considered "involuntary" under Section 303(b)(3)(A); thus an allegation of a Section 303(h) ground

11 U.S.C. § 303. Involuntary cases

(d) The debtor, or a general partner in a partnership debtor that did not join in the petition, may file an answer to a petition under this section.

for relief is required, either that the debtor is generally not paying its debts as they become due, or that a general assignment for the benefit of creditors was made or a general receiver was appointed within the preceding 120 days. As with any other involuntary petition, there may be liability for damages if the petition is not well founded. § 303(i).

A partnership may also be the subject of an involuntary petition if orders for relief under Title 11 (that is, any chapter of the Code) have been made with respect to all the general partners. In that event, any general partner in the partnership, his trustee, or a creditor of the partnership has standing to file the involuntary petition. § 303(b)(3)(B).[1] As is true for any involuntary petition, a Section 303(h) ground for relief must be alleged.

Of course, creditors may commence an involuntary case against the partnership in the ordinary way by filing a petition under Section 303(b)(1) or (2). Creditors who have claims against individual partners but not against the partnership, however, would not qualify as petitioning creditors against the firm, nor would they be entitled to participate otherwise in the partnership case.

Any general partner who does not join in the petition has standing to file an answer and to contest an involuntary petition. § 303(d).

Although a number of special rules apply to partnerships, only a few special principles govern the bankruptcy of an individual or corporate debtor who happens to be a partner. All or some of the partners may individually file voluntarily or may be the subject of an involuntary petition, whether or not the partnership is a debtor in a bankruptcy case. It is important to recognize, however, that a creditor of a partnership normally has a claim against the general partners as well, as a matter of nonbankruptcy law; thus a partnership creditor would be a qualified petitioning creditor against any general partner, although his right to participate in a Chapter 7 distribution of the partner's estate is affected by Section 723(c), discussed at pp. 353–55, *infra*.

---

[1] The rules contain special provisions for issuance of summons and service when the petition is filed under Section 303(b)(3)(A) or (B). Bankruptcy Rule 1004(b).

11 U.S.C. § 723. Rights of partnership trustee against general partners

(a) If there is a deficiency of property of the estate to pay in full all claims which are allowed in a case under this chapter concerning a partnership and with respect to which a general partner of the partnership is personally liable, the trustee shall have a claim against such general partner for the full amount of the deficiency.

(b) To the extent practicable, the trustee shall first seek recovery of such deficiency from any general partner in such partnership that is not a debtor in a case under this title. Pending determination of such deficiency, the court may order any such partner to provide the estate with indemnity for, or assurance of payment of, any deficiency recoverable from such partner, or not to dispose of property.

(c) Notwithstanding section 728(c) of this title, the trustee has a claim against the estate of each general partner in such partnership that is a debtor in a case under this title for the full amount of all claims of creditors allowed in the case concerning such partnership. Notwithstanding section 502 of this title, there shall not be allowed in such partner's case a claim against such partner on which both such partner and such partnership are liable, except to any extent that such claim is secured only by property of such partner and not by property of such partnership. The claim of the trustee under this subsection is entitled to distribution in such partner's case under section 726(a) of this title the same as any other claim of a kind specified in such section.

(d) If the aggregate that the trustee recovers from the estates of general partners under subsection (c) of this section is greater than any deficiency not recovered under subsection (b) of this section, the court, after notice and a hearing, shall determine an equitable distribution of the surplus so recovered, and the trustee shall distribute such surplus to the estates of the general partners in such partnership according to such determination.

§ 8.02 ADMINISTRATION OF THE CASE

Nothing in the statute prohibits the same person from serving as trustee for the estates of both a debtor partner and a debtor partnership. If the court orders a joint administration of the estates of a general partner and the partnership, then the trustee of the partnership will serve as the trustee in the partner's case unless the court, for cause, orders separate trustees. Bankruptcy Rule 2009(e). The appointment of separate trustees would be appropriate if the interests of the different estates are seriously in conflict.

§ 8.03 RIGHTS OF CHAPTER 7 PARTNERSHIP TRUSTEE AGAINST PARTNERS AND THEIR ESTATES

Section 723 gives rights to a partnership trustee in a Chapter 7 case whether or not the general partners are debtors in cases under the Code. Under Section 723(a), he has a claim against *each* general partner for the full amount of any deficiency in the partnership estate — that is, the amount by which that estate is insufficient to pay the partnership creditors. An exception is made if the partnership is liable on a debt but the general partner is not personally liable, such as in the situation of "nonrecourse" financing at the partnership level. To the extent practicable, the trustee is required first to seek recovery of the deficiency from any partner who is not in bankruptcy; the court may issue appropriate orders (for example, an order requiring indemnity or restraining disposition of the partner's property) to ensure that the deficiency, as ultimately determined, will be collectible. § 723(b).

The Chapter 7 partnership trustee is given a claim against the estate of each general partner who is a debtor under Chapter 7, 11, 12, or 13; the claim encompasses the full amount of all "claims of creditors" allowed in the partnership case.[2] § 723(c). Ordinarily this claim of the trustee preempts the right of a partnership credi-

---

[2]This amount does not include administrative expenses of the partnership case, since "creditor" is defined in Section 101(9) as the holder of a prepetition claim.

11 U.S.C. § 101. Definitions

In this title —

(31) "insolvent" means —

(B) with reference to a partnership, financial condition such that the sum of such partnership's debts is greater than the aggregate of, at a fair valuation —

(i) all of such partnership's property, exclusive of property of the kind specified in subparagraph (A)(i) of this paragraph; and

(ii) the sum of the excess of the value of each general partner's nonpartnership property, exclusive of property of the kind specified in subparagraph (A) of this paragraph, over such partner's nonpartnership debts;

tor to have a claim allowed in the partner's case.[3] In the unlikely event that recovery from the estates of the general partners creates a surplus in the partnership estate, the bankruptcy court will order an equitable refund of the excess funds. § 723(d).

Although Section 723, because of its location in the Bankruptcy Code, applies directly only when the partnership is a debtor in a liquidation case under Chapter 7, it may have indirect application to a partnership in a case under Chapter 11 or 12, since confirmation of a reorganization or family farmer plan ordinarily requires, inter alia, a comparison of what the plan offers with what creditors would receive in a hypothetical Chapter 7 liquidation. *See* § 1129(a)(7); pp. 399–401, *infra;* § 1225(a)(4).

§ 8.04 AVOIDING POWERS

Owing to the so-called entity theory of partnership, which distinguishes the firm from the partners who compose it, the avoiding powers of a partnership trustee apply to transfers of partnership property but not to transfers of property of an individual general partner. *Liberty Nat'l Bank v. Bear,* 276 U.S. 215 (1928).

Insolvency is sometimes a relevant element of an avoiding power cause of action. When the debtor is a partnership, the combined net worths of the general partners is part of the calculation. That is, the firm is insolvent under Section 101(31)(B) when the partnership's debts exceed both the value of its assets and the amount by which each general partner's personal nonexempt property exceeds his individual debts.[4] Thus a partnership with one highly solvent general partner may be considered solvent even though the partnership is insolvent on its own balance sheet and the other general partners are hopelessly insolvent.

---

[3]A partnership creditor also has a claim against nondebtor partners that is not preempted by the partnership trustee's Section 723(c) claim against debtor partners. However, to the extent the creditor receives a payment from a nondebtor partner, Section 508(b) provides for a suspension of distribution to the creditor in cases under the Code so as to equalize his overall distribution with that of other partnership creditors who did not receive outside payments.

[4]Property fraudulently transferred by the partnership or by the general partners is not counted as an asset.

11 U.S.C. § 548. Fraudulent transfers and obligations

(b) The trustee of a partnership debtor may avoid any transfer of an interest of the debtor in property, or any obligation incurred by the debtor, that was made or incurred on or within one year before the date of the filing of the petition, to a general partner in the debtor, if the debtor was insolvent on the date such transfer was made or such obligation was incurred, or became insolvent as a result of such transfer or obligation.

11 U.S.C. § 502. Allowance of claims or interests

(a) A claim or interest, proof of which is filed under section 501 of this title, is deemed allowed, unless a party in interest, including a creditor of a general partner in a partnership that is a debtor in a case under chapter 7 of this title, objects.

Section 548(b), which relates to fraudulent transfers, gives the trustee of a bankrupt partnership an avoiding power beyond those discussed earlier. See pp. 171–75, *supra*. In particular, such trustee may avoid the transfer of partnership property or the incurring of an obligation to a general partner in the debtor if the transaction occurred within one year before the petition and if the partnership was then insolvent or became insolvent as a result of the transaction. Thus it is unnecessary under this provision to prove actual fraudulent intent or that the debtor failed to receive reasonably equivalent value for the transfer or obligation.

§ 8.05 THE PARTNER'S CASE

Property of the partner's estate includes his interest in the partnership but not the assets of the firm. The partner's trustee, therefore, has the right to participate in the distribution of the property of the partnership only after the partnership's creditors have been satisfied. As previously discussed, the trustee of the partnership, if the firm is a debtor under Chapter 7, may assert a claim in the partner's case that preempts the claims of partnership creditors against the partner's estate.

§ 8.06 DISTRIBUTION

A creditor of a general partner has special standing to object to claims filed against the estate of a partnership debtor. § 502(a). Consequently, such creditor can protect the partner's "equity" interest in the partnership. Of course, the general partner himself (and a limited partner as well) has an ownership interest and should be considered a party in interest for the purpose of objecting to claims if the partnership is potentially solvent.

When the firm is a limited partnership, the interest of a limited partner is an ownership interest, not a creditor interest. §§ 101-(15)(B), 101(16).

11 U.S.C. § 727. Discharge

(a) The court shall grant the debtor a discharge, unless—

(1) the debtor is not an individual;

11 U.S.C. § 1141. Effect of confirmation

(d)(1) Except as otherwise provided in this subsection, in the plan, or in the order confirming the plan, the confirmation of a plan—

(A) discharges the debtor from any debt that arose before the date of such confirmation, and any debt of a kind specified in section 502(g), 502(h), or 502(i) of this title, whether or not—

(i) a proof of the claim based on such debt is filed or deemed filed under section 501 of this title;

(ii) such claim is allowed under section 502 of this title; or

(iii) the holder of such claim has accepted the plan; and

(B) terminates all rights and interests of equity security holders and general partners provided for by the plan.

(3) The confirmation of a plan does not discharge a debtor if—

(A) the plan provides for the liquidation of all or substantially all of the property of the estate;

(B) the debtor does not engage in business after consummation of the plan; and

(C) the debtor would be denied a discharge under section 727(a) of this title if the case were a case under chapter 7 of this title.

11 U.S.C. § 524. Effect of discharge

(e) Except as provided in subsection (a)(3) of this section, discharge of a debt of the debtor does not affect the liability of any other entity on, or the property of any other entity for, such debt.

§ 8.07 DISCHARGE

Partnerships do not receive discharges in Chapter 7. § 727(a)(1). A partnership in a Chapter 11 case will be discharged upon confirmation of a reorganization plan unless the plan provides for the liquidation of all or substantially all the property of the estate and the partnership does not engage in business after consummation of the plan. § 1141(d). In a partnership Chapter 12 case, the discharge is ordinarily granted upon completion of payments under the plan. § 1228.

An individual debtor who is a partner is eligible for a discharge in his own case under Chapter 7, 11, 12, or 13 and may discharge both personal debts and personal liability for firm debts. A partnership or corporate debtor that is a partner in a partnership is eligible for a discharge under Chapter 11 or 12 but not under Chapter 7.

Ordinarily a discharge granted to a partnership (available only in Chapter 11 or 12) will not discharge the general partners from personal liability, either for the firm's debts or for their own. § 524(e). It is not unusual, however, for a partnership plan under Chapter 11 to contain provisions that attempt to discharge the liability of nondebtor partners for partnership obligations. At least when an objection to this kind of provision is timely made, the courts generally do not permit the effort to succeed. (Indeed, one court has gone so far as to hold that even a creditor's actual acceptance of a plan containing a similar provision — one that released a nondebtor guarantor of the debtor's obligation — did not bar that creditor from pursuing the guarantor. *See, e.g., Union Carbide Corp. v. Newboles,* 686 F.2d 593 (7th Cir. 1982) (case decided under the former Bankruptcy Act); *see also Underhill v. Royal,* 769 F.2d 1426 (9th Cir. 1985); *Contra Republic Supply Co. v. Shoaf,* 815 F.2d 1046 (5th Cir. 1987); *Levy v. Cohen,* 19 Cal. 3d 165, 561 P.2d 252, 137 Cal. Rptr. 162 (1977); *cf. Stoll v. Gottleib,* 305 U.S. 165, 170–71 (1938).)

9

Chapter 11 Reorganizations

§ 9.01 INTRODUCTION

Chapter 11 reorganization, an alternative to liquidation bankruptcy, is available to any form of business enterprise that is eligible for bankruptcy relief.[1] Armed with the administrative powers to reject executory contracts, including collective bargaining agreements, and to use a secured party's collateral and borrow money, and protected by the automatic stay against lien enforcement and in personam actions, a Chapter 11 debtor is given breathing room and powerful tools to rescale its operations and, in time, to modify both the debt and equity portions of its capital structure. Reorganization can be effected by the consent of each class of creditors and ownership interests, or by court decree under the "cram down" power. Generally, the debtor itself is in charge of the reorganization process, but creditors, shareholders, and other parties in interest have a voice and may seek the appointment of a reorganization trustee. Once appointed, the trustee takes over the operation of the business and the management of the plan process.

The Code has a built-in bias favoring reorganization over liquidation. Thus, as the Supreme Court has said, "[t]he fundamental purpose of reorganization is to prevent a debtor from going into liquidation, with an attendant loss of jobs and possible misuse of economic resources." *NLRB v. Bildisco & Bildisco,* 465 U.S. 513, 528 (1984). "By permitting reorganization, Congress anticipated

---

[1] Actually, Chapter 11 appears to be available to any eligible "person," whether or not the debtor is engaged in a business in the ordinary sense, and a passive investor might find Chapter 11 useful. On the other hand, the courts of appeals have disagreed concerning whether a debtor not engaged in business is eligible. *See, e.g., In re* Moog, 774 F.2d 1073 (11th Cir. 1985) (nonbusiness debtor is eligible); *contra* Wamsgans v. Boatmen's Bank of De Sota, 804 F.2d 503 (8th Cir. 1986). But in any event, most Chapter 11 cases involve some kind of business.

11 U.S.C. § 103. Applicability of chapters

(a) Except as provided in section 1161 of this title, chapters 1, 3, and 5 of this title apply in a case under chapter 7, 11, 12, or 13 of this title.

that the business would continue to provide jobs, to satisfy creditors' claims, and to produce a return for its owners. . . . Congress presumed that the assets of the debtor would be more valuable if used in a rehabilitated business than if 'sold for scrap.' " *United States v. Whiting Pools, Inc.,* 462 U.S. 198, 203 (1983); *see* H.R. Rep. No. 595, 95th Cong., 1st Sess. 220 (1977) [hereinafter cited in this chapter as "House Report"].[2]

§ 9.01(a) Applicability of Other Chapters

Chapter 11 itself does not contain all the important provisions on business reorganization. The generally applicable sections found in Chapters 1, 3, and 5 of the Code apply in Chapter 11 cases, see p. 19, *supra;* as a result, understanding business reorganization law requires a knowledge of the Code in general. And, of course, the court system is governed by provisions in Title 28 of the United States Code.

§ 9.01(b) Eligibility for Relief

Reorganization cases under Chapter 11 may be commenced voluntarily by, or involuntarily against, any eligible debtor. See pp. 107–19, *supra.* Consequently, individuals, partnerships, and corporations, with the exception of certain financial institutions and stock and commodity brokers, generally are qualified. See pp. 103–07, *supra.* Voluntary petitions need not allege either that the debtor is insolvent or that it is unable to pay its debts as they mature.

---

[2]Despite the Code's bias in favor of reorganization, the courts have no license to use their equity powers to override specific provisions of the statute for the purpose of protecting the debtor's business operations or its chances for successful reorganization. Section 105(a) is not intended to give bankruptcy courts such unfettered discretion. "[A]bsent a specific grant of authority from Congress or exceptional circumstances, a bankruptcy court may not exercise its equitable powers to create substantive rights which do not exist under state law." Johnson v. First Nat'l Bank of Montevideo, Minn., 719 F.2d 270, 274 (8th Cir. 1983).

11 U.S.C. § 1101. Definitions for this chapter

In this chapter—

(1) "debtor in possession" means debtor except when a person that has qualified under section 322 of this title is serving as trustee in the case;

11 U.S.C. § 1107. Rights, powers, and duties of debtor in possession

(a) Subject to any limitations on a trustee serving in a case under this chapter, and to such limitations or conditions as the court prescribes, a debtor in possession shall have all the rights, other than the right to compensation under section 330 of this title, and powers, and shall perform all the functions and duties, except the duties specified in sections 1106(a)(2), (3), and (4) of this title, of a trustee serving in a case under this chapter.

11 U.S.C. § 1112. Conversion or dismissal

(a) The debtor may convert a case under this chapter to a case under chapter 7 of this title unless—

(1) the debtor is not a debtor in possession;

(2) the case originally was commenced as an involuntary case under this chapter; or

(3) the case was converted to a case under this chapter other than on the debtor's request.

(b) Except as provided in subsection (c) of this section, on request of a party in interest or the United States trustee, and after notice and a hearing, the court may convert a case under this chapter to a case under chapter 7 of this title or may dismiss a case under this chapter, whichever is in the best interest of creditors and the estate, for cause, including—

(1) continuing loss to or diminution of the estate and absence of a reasonable likelihood of rehabilitation;

(2) inability to effectuate a plan;

(3) unreasonable delay by the debtor that is prejudicial to creditors;

(4) failure to propose a plan under section 1121 of this title within any time fixed by the court;

[Continued]

§ 9.02 PREPLAN MATTERS

§ 9.02(a) The Concept of Debtor in Possession

The Code in general is drafted in terms of the powers and duties of the trustee as the representative of the estate. In Chapter 11, however, a trustee is appointed only when one is needed. See pp. 375–77, *infra*. Normally the debtor in its capacity as "debtor in possession" remains as the estate's representative, in which event it has the powers and duties conferred by the various Code provisions on a trustee. § 1107(a). By definition, a "debtor in possession" is the debtor when no trustee is serving in the Chapter 11 case. § 1101(1).

§ 9.02(b) Conversion to Chapter 7 Liquidation Bankruptcy or Dismissal

A Chapter 11 debtor may convert the Chapter 11 case to Chapter 7 liquidation bankruptcy at any time, unless a Chapter 11 trustee has been appointed, the Chapter 11 petition was filed by creditors and was thus involuntary, or the case was converted to Chapter 11 at the request of someone other than the debtor. § 1112(a). (Dismissal of the petition at the instance of the debtor is subject to the provisions of Section 1112(b), discussed next.)

Parties in interest other than the debtor may also seek conversion or dismissal of Chapter 11 cases if there are statutory grounds for doing so.[3] Section 1112(b) provides a nonexclusive list of grounds for conversion or dismissal: continuing losses in the operation of the business without a reasonable prospect for rehabilitation, inability to effectuate a plan or failure to propose a plan within the time fixed by the court, failure to confirm or effectuate a plan that is filed, revocation of confirmation or default under a confirmed plan, failure to pay certain specified fees and charges, or any "unreasonable delay by the debtor that is prejudicial to creditors." Under Section 1112(e), the United States trustee may move in a voluntary case for dismissal or conversion to Chapter 7

---

[3]Involuntary conversion to Chapter 7 is not permitted if the debtor is a farmer or if a corporate debtor is not a moneyed, business, or commercial corporation. § 1112(c).

(5) denial of confirmation of every proposed plan and denial of a request made for additional time for filing another plan or a modification of a plan;

(6) revocation of an order of confirmation under section 1144 of this title, and denial of confirmation of another plan or a modified plan under section 1129 of this title;

(7) inability to effectuate consummation of a confirmed plan;

(8) material default by the debtor with respect to a confirmed plan;

(9) termination of a plan by reason of the occurrence of a condition specified in the plan; or

(10) nonpayment of any fees or charges required under chapter 12 of title 28.

(c) The court may not convert a case under this chapter to a case under chapter 7 of this title if the debtor is a farmer or a corporation that is not a moneyed, business, or commercial corporation, unless the debtor requests such conversion.

(d) The court may convert a case under this chapter to a case under chapter 13 of this title only if—

(1) the debtor requests such conversion; and

(2) the debtor has not been discharged under section 1141(d) of this title; and

(3) if the debtor requests conversion to chapter 12 of this title, such conversion is equitable.

(e) Except as provided in subsections (c) and (f), the court, on request of the United States trustee, may convert a case under this chapter to a case under chapter 7 of this title or may dismiss a case under this chapter, whichever is in the best interest of creditors and the estate if the debtor in a voluntary case fails to file, within fifteen days after the filing of the petition commencing such case or such additional time as the court may allow, the information required by paragraph (1) of section 521. . . .

(f) Notwithstanding any other provision of this section, a case may not be converted to a case under another chapter of this title unless the debtor may be a debtor under such chapter.

on the ground of the debtor's failure to file on time the requisite lists of creditors, schedules, and other information referred to in Section 521(1). Case law has added an additional ground: If the filing was for an improper purpose and imposes upon the jurisdiction of the court — that is, if the filing was in "bad faith" — the case may be dismissed. See pp. 109–11, *supra*.

The Code and its legislative history seem clearly to indicate that a court may not convert or dismiss a case upon its own motion but may act only upon a request by a party in interest or the United States trustee. *In re Gusam Restaurant Corp.*, 737 F.2d 274 (2d Cir. 1984). Nevertheless, some courts have issued orders of conversion or dismissal sua sponte, *e.g.*, *In re Cricker*, 46 Bankr. 229 (N.D. Ind. 1985), and the 1986 amendment to Section 105(a) conceivably lends some support to their doing so. With the extension of the U.S. trustee system nationwide, however, a court should rarely act on its own in matters of this kind.

§ 9.02(c) Claims

Unlike Chapter 7, Chapter 11 permits creditors or owners whose claims or interests are scheduled by the debtor or trustee as admittedly owing or valid to participate in the case without filing proofs of claim or interest; that is, filing is unnecessary unless the schedules fail to list the claim or interest or list it as "disputed, contingent, or unliquidated." § 1111(a). If a creditor's claim or an owner's interest is listed as disputed, contingent, or unliquidated, if it is not listed at all, or if a creditor is not satisfied to rely on the scheduled amount of his claim, then a proof of claim or interest must be filed. §§ 1111(a), 501(a). Once filed (or deemed filed), the claim or interest is deemed allowed unless contested. § 502(a).

Secured creditors may, but need not, file claims in order to receive the benefit of their collateral; they must file (unless the claims are scheduled as admittedly owing) if they wish to participate as unsecured creditors for any deficiency. §§ 501(a), 502(a), 1111(a). The failure of a secured party to file a claim does not affect the validity of his lien. *In re Tarnow*, 749 F.2d 464 (7th Cir. 1984). Once a secured claim has been filed, the court, on application of the debtor, trustee, or secured party, will determine how much of the claim is secured and how much is unsecured.

11 U.S.C. § 1111. Claims and interests

(a) A proof of claim or interest is deemed filed under section 501 of this title for any claim or interest that appears in the schedules filed under section 521(1) or 1106(a)(2) of this title, except a claim or interest that is scheduled as disputed, contingent, or unliquidated.

11 U.S.C. § 501. Filing of proofs of claims or interests

(a) A creditor or an indenture trustee may file a proof of claim. An equity security holder may file a proof of interest.

11 U.S.C. § 502. Allowance of claims or interests

(a) A claim or interest, proof of which is filed under section 501 of this title, is deemed allowed, unless a party in interest, including a creditor of a general partner in a partnership that is a debtor in a case under chapter 7 of this title, objects.

11 U.S.C. § 341. Meetings of creditors and equity security holders

(a) Within a reasonable time after the order for relief in a case under this title, the United States trustee shall convene and preside at a meeting of creditors.

(b) The United States trustee may convene a meeting of any equity security holders.

(c) The court may not preside at, and may not attend, any meeting under this section including any final meeting of creditors.

11 U.S.C. § 1102. Creditors' and equity security holders' committees

(a)(1) As soon as practicable after the order for relief under chapter 11 of this title, the United States trustee shall appoint a committee of creditors holding unsecured claims and may appoint additional committees of creditors or of equity holders as the United States trustee deems appropriate.

[Continued]

§ 506(a); *see also* § 1111(b), discussed *infra,* pp. 419–23. See generally pp. 277–81, *supra.*

§ 9.02(d) Meetings of Creditors and Equity Security Holders

The United States trustee must convene and preside at a meeting of creditors in a Chapter 11 case, § 341(a); he may call a meeting of equity security holders but rarely does so. § 341(b). In practice, the meeting of creditors in Chapter 11 is of little practical significance; creditors usually conduct their important business through the vehicle of the creditors' committee appointed under the Code. *See* §§ 1102, 1103.

§ 9.02(e) Committees of Creditors and Equity Security Holders; Their Appointment, Powers, and Duties

The committee of creditors holding unsecured claims, § 1102-(a)(1), (b), is intended by the statute to play a key role in Chapter 11 practice. Because the debtor normally remains in possession of its assets and manages its affairs and because the court has been relieved of most administrative matters, the responsibility for monitoring the operations of the debtor and its compliance with appropriate bankruptcy procedures has been given to the creditors' committee (under the general supervision of the United States trustee). The statute presumes that the committee is eager to serve and is adequately staffed. This presumption seems to be borne out in the larger cases, since the stakes are high and creditors are truly interested in the outcome; the system apparently works well in these cases. In more routine cases, however, creditors are often apathetic, and as a result, supervision of Chapter 11 administration falls entirely on the shoulders of the United States trustee.

The statute provides that at the earliest practicable time after the order for relief, the United States trustee shall appoint an unsecured creditors' committee, § 1102(a)(1), which ordinarily is to consist of the seven creditors with the largest claims who are willing to serve. § 1102(b)(1). If the creditors themselves chose a committee before the commencement of the case, and if it was selected fairly and is in fact representative, then this prefiling committee may serve as the committee of unsecured creditors in the Chapter 11

(2) On request of a party in interest, the court may order the appointment of additional committees of creditors or of equity security holders if necessary to assure adequate representation of creditors or of equity security holders. The court United States trustee shall appoint any such committee.

(b)(1) A committee of creditors appointed under subsection (a) of this section shall ordinarily consist of the persons, willing to serve, that hold the seven largest claims against the debtor of the kinds represented on such committee, or of the members of a committee organized by creditors before the commencement of the case under this chapter, if such committee was fairly chosen and is representative of the different kinds of claims to be represented.

(2) A committee of equity security holders appointed under subsection (a)(2) of this section shall ordinarily consist of the persons, willing to serve, that hold the seven largest amounts of equity securities of the debtor of the kinds represented on such committee.

11 U.S.C. § 1103. Powers and duties of committees

(a) At a scheduled meeting of a committee appointed under section 1102 of this title, at which a majority of the members of such committee are present, and with the court's approval, such committee may select and authorize the employment by such committee of one or more attorneys, accountants, or other agents, to represent or perform services for such committee.

(b) An attorney or accountant employed to represent a committee appointed under section 1102 of this title may not, while employed by such committee, represent any other entity having an adverse interest in connection with the case. Representation of one or more creditors of the same class as represented by the committee shall not per se constitute the representation of an adverse interest.

11 U.S.C. § 1109. Right to be heard

(b) A party in interest, including the debtor, the trustee, a creditors' committee, an equity security holders' committee, a creditor, an equity security holder, or any indenture trustee, may raise and may appear and be heard on any issue in a case under this chapter.

case. *Id.* The Bankruptcy Rules impose additional and sometimes burdensome requirements for the recognition of prefiling committees. *See* Bankruptcy Rules 2007, 2019.

Additional committees of secured creditors, unsecured creditors, or stockholders may be authorized by the court as needed, in which event the appointments are made by the United States trustee. § 1102(a)(2). Subject to court approval, the committee may select lawyers, accountants, and other agents at a scheduled meeting attended by a majority of the committee members. § 1103(a). An attorney or accountant thus chosen may not represent any other entity with an interest adverse to the estate, but continued representation of one or more creditors of the same class as the committee represents does not per se constitute the representation of an adverse interest. § 1103(b).

As the primary counterweight to the various powers of the debtor in possession, creditors' and equity security holders' committees are granted broad powers to participate in all aspects of the Chapter 11 case. The committees are specifically entitled to the status of a "party in interest" and have the right to be heard on any issue. § 1109(b). According to one view they are entitled, as a matter of right under Section 1109(b), to intervene in litigation affecting the estate. *In re Marin Motor Oil, Inc.,* 689 F.2d 445 (3d Cir. 1982), *cert. denied,* 495 U.S. 1207 (1983). *Contra Fuel Oil Supply & Terminaling v. Gulf Oil Corp.,* 762 F.2d 1283 (5th Cir. 1985) (pursuant to Bankruptcy Rule 7024, creditors' committee may not intervene in pending adversary proceeding unless it has grounds for doing so under Federal Rule of Civil Procedure 24(a)(2) or (b)). If the debtor in possession refuses to bring actions against third parties, some courts have held that the creditors' committee itself can be the party plaintiff. The better practice, however, would seem to be for the court, under appropriate circumstances, to authorize the committee to sue in the name of the debtor in possession.

In addition to the generic powers stemming from the committee's "standing" under Section 1109(b), the Code authorizes the committee to perform a number of specific functions. For example, it may determine whether to oppose the continued operation of the business, may determine whether the court should be asked to appoint a trustee or an examiner to investigate the financial affairs of the debtor, and may

11 U.S.C. § 1103. Powers and duties of committees

(c) A committee appointed under section 1102 of this title may—

(1) consult with the trustee or debtor in possession concerning the administration of the case;

(2) investigate the acts, conduct, assets, liabilities, and financial condition of the debtor, the operation of the debtor's business and the desirability of the continuance of such business, and any other matter relevant to the case or to the formulation of a plan;

(3) participate in the formulation of a plan, advise those represented by such committee of such committee's determinations as to any plan formulated, and collect and file with the court acceptances or rejections of a plan;

(4) request the appointment of a trustee or examiner under section 1104 of this title; and

(5) perform such other services as are in the interest of those represented.

11 U.S.C. § 1108. Authorization to operate business

Unless the court, on request of a party in interest and after notice and a hearing, orders otherwise, the trustee may operate the debtor's business.

generally consult with the debtor or trustee about the administration of the case. § 1103(c). In a typical case the committee at the appropriate time performs a most important function, namely, the negotiation and consideration of the kind of plan it will recommend for the satisfaction of creditors' claims. § 1103(c)(3).

§ 9.02(f) Keeping the Ship Afloat: Operating the Business, Achieving Stability, and Protecting the Estate

One of the most important issues in the early days of a Chapter 11 case is whether the business should continue to operate. Operation of the business by the debtor in possession or the trustee does not require an affirmative court order; rather, operation is authorized unless the court orders otherwise. § 1108. Upon the request of a party in interest (but not sua sponte) and after notice and a hearing, the court may order termination of the business operation, *id.*, or, as discussed earlier, convert the case to liquidation bankruptcy or dismiss it. § 1112. The statute provides no standards for ordering the termination of operations. Obvious reasons might include continuing losses with little prospect for recovery, the possibility of the estate's being unable to pay its own postpetition obligations, and the violation of applicable nonbankruptcy law, such as the business's noncompliance with environmental regulations. When a business that is basically sound is being operated by the debtor in possession in violation of bankruptcy procedures and requirements, the appointment of a trustee or examiner under Section 1104 is a more likely result than the termination of business operations under Section 1108.

During the period between the filing of the case and the formulation of the reorganization plan, steps must be taken to stem operational losses and to place the business enterprise on a sound economic footing. This turnaround period may involve months or even years of operation under the Chapter 11 court umbrella, for until an economically viable venture has been assured or is at least predictable, no feasible reorganization plan (other than a liquidation plan) can be formulated or effected. The efforts made and the steps taken during this time are sometimes referred to colloquially as "keeping the ship afloat."

The statutory administrative powers, §§ 361–366, which en-

11 U.S.C. § 1104. Appointment of trustee or examiner

(a) At any time after the commencement of the case but before confirmation of a plan, on request of a party in interest or the United States trustee, and after notice and a hearing, the court shall order the appointment of a trustee—

(1) for cause, including fraud, dishonesty, incompetence, or gross mismanagement of the debtor by current management, either before or after the commencement of the case, or similar cause, but not including the number of holders of securities of the debtor or the amount of assets or liabilities of the debtor; or

(2) if such appointment is in the interests of creditors, any equity security holders, and other interests of the estate, without regard to the number of holders of securities of the debtor or the amount of assets or liabilities of the debtor.

hance the ability of the business to survive at the preplan stage, were discussed earlier. Although these sections apply in any kind of case under the Code, they are of special importance in Chapter 11 cases. In particular, the ability to dispose of unprofitable assets, to use a secured party's collateral, to borrow or finance the operation, and to reject undesirable executory contracts or cure defaults and assume beneficial ones, and the general breathing room afforded by the automatic stay, are crucial to the ultimate success of the reorganization.[4] Litigation about the attempted use of these powers occurs frequently at the beginning of or during the Chapter 11 case unless the competing interests can be accommodated by negotiated solutions.

§ 9.02(g) Appointment of a Trustee or Examiner

Probably the most important decision the creditors or their committee face in the early stages of a Chapter 11 case is whether to attempt to replace the debtor in possession by seeking the appointment of a trustee. Congress explicitly rejected the notion that an independent and disinterested trustee should be routinely appointed in Chapter 11. In particular, it rejected the argument of the Securities and Exchange Commission that a trustee should be appointed in every public case of significant size.

Section 1104(a) provides that a trustee may be appointed "for cause" or in the interests of creditors, stockholders, and other interests of the estate; the magnitude of the case or its public nature is expressly made irrelevant for this purpose. Illustrations of cause include "fraud, dishonesty, incompetence, or gross mismanagement . . . by *current* management . . . before or after the commencement of the case." § 1104(a)(1) (emphasis added). The court may not order the appointment of a trustee on its own initiative. It

---

[4]Lessors of, and secured creditors with purchase-money security interests in, certain aircraft and vessels are given special protection in Chapter 11 insofar as the automatic stay and the estate's ability to use their collateral are concerned. § 1110. A similar provision applies in railroad reorganizations. § 1168. There are also two exceptions to the automatic stay authorizing foreclosure actions by the Secretaries of Transportation and Commerce with respect to certain ship mortgages. § 362(b)(12), (13). These provisions should be consulted whenever a problem arises involving these kinds of special collateral.

11 U.S.C. § 1109. Right to be heard

(a) The Securities and Exchange Commission may raise and may appear and be heard on any issue in a case under this chapter, but the Securities and Exchange Commission may not appeal from any judgment, order, or decree entered in the case.

11 U.S.C. § 1106. Duties of trustee and examiner

(a) A trustee shall—

(1) perform the duties of a trustee specified in sections 704(2), 704(5), 704(7), 704(8), and 704(9) of this title;

(2) if the debtor has not done so, file the list, schedule, and statement required under section 521(1) of this title;

(3) except to the extent that the court orders otherwise, investigate the acts, conduct, assets, liabilities, and financial condition of the debtor, the operation of the debtor's business and the desirability of the continuance of such business, and any other matter relevant to the case or to the formulation of a plan;

(4) as soon as practicable—

(A) file a statement of any investigation conducted under paragraph (3) of this subsection . . . ; and

(B) transmit a copy or a summary of any such statement to any committee . . . , to any indenture trustee, and to such other entity as the court designates;

(5) as soon as practicable, file a plan under section 1121 of this title, file a report of why the trustee will not file a plan, or recommend conversion of the case to a case under chapter 7, 12, or 13 of this title or dismissal of the case;

(6) for any year for which the debtor has not filed a tax return required by law, furnish, without personal liability, such information as may be required by the governmental unit with which such tax return was to be filed, in light of the condition of the debtor's books and records and the availability of such information; and

(7) after confirmation of a plan, file such reports as are necessary or as the court orders.

may do so, after notice and a hearing, only on request by the United States trustee or by a party in interest, including the debtor, a creditors' or equity security holders' committee, a creditor, a stockholder, or an indenture trustee. §§ 1104(a), 1109(b). In addition, the Securities and Exchange Commission has standing to be heard on the issue of the appointment of a trustee, although it does not have the right of appeal. § 1109(a). The United States trustee after consultation with the parties in interest and subject to court approval appoints the trustee once the court has determined that one is needed. §§ 1104(c). "At any time before confirmation . . . , on request of a party in interest or the United States trustee, and after notice and a hearing, the court may terminate the trustee's appointment and restore the debtor to possession. . . . " § 1105.

If appointed, the trustee becomes the central and dominant figure in the reorganization process. "Congress contemplated that when a trustee is appointed, he assumes control of the business, and the debtor's directors are 'completely ousted.' " *Commodity Futures Trading Comm'n v. Weintraub,* 471 U.S. 343, 352–53 (1985) (citing and quoting House Report at 220–21). His specific duties, listed in Sections 1106 and 704, include assuming the general responsibility for conducting the business operation and performing the related reporting requirements, filing the schedules and statement of affairs, and investigating the conduct of prior management. Of central importance is his duty to evaluate the desirability of continued operations and, if the trustee can, to develop a feasible plan. Although the debtor's exclusivity period for filing a reorganization plan is automatically terminated upon the appointment of a trustee, § 1121(c)(1); see p. 381, *infra,* so that it is then legally permissible for any party in interest to propose a plan, creditors tend to defer initially to the trustee in connection with the formulation, proposal, and confirmation of a plan.

The Code also contains provisions for the appointment of an examiner when there is no trustee. §§ 1104(b), 1106(b). These provisions give the court a less drastic alternative than the complete ouster of the debtor. *See* 5 COLLIER ON BANKRUPTCY ¶ 1104.03 (15th ed. 1985). If the court orders that an examiner should be appointed, the United States trustee makes the appointment. § 1104(c). The examiner's role, unless expanded by the court, is to conduct an

11 U.S.C. § 704. Duties of trustee

The trustee shall—

(2) be accountable for all property received;

(5) if a purpose would be served, examine proofs of claims and object to the allowance of any claim that is improper;

(7) unless the court orders otherwise, furnish such information concerning the estate and the estate's administration as is requested by a party in interest;

(8) if the business of the debtor is authorized to be operated, file . . . periodic reports . . . of the operation of such business . . . ; and

(9) make a final report and file a final account of the administration of the estate with the court and with the United States trustee.

11 U.S.C. § 1104. Appointment of trustee or examiner

(b) If the court does not order the appointment of a trustee under this section, then at any time before the confirmation of a plan, on request of a party in interest or the United States trustee, and after notice and a hearing, the court shall order the appointment of an examiner to conduct such an investigation of the debtor as is appropriate, including an investigation of any allegations of fraud, dishonesty, incompetence, misconduct, mismanagement, or irregularity in the management of the affairs of the debtor of or by current or former management of the debtor, if—

(1) such appointment is in the interests of creditors, any equity security holders, and other interests of the estate; or

(2) the debtor's fixed, liquidated, unsecured debts, other than debts for goods, services, or taxes, or owing to an insider, exceed $5,000,000.

11 U.S.C. § 1106. Duties of trustee and examiner

(b) An examiner appointed under section 1104(c) of this title shall perform the duties specified in paragraphs (3) and (4) of subsection (a) of this section, and, except to the extent that the court orders otherwise, any other duties of the trustee that the court orders the debtor in possession not to perform.

appropriate investigation of the debtor and its prior and current management, § 1104(b), and to report his findings. § 1106(a)(4). Upon the request of a party in interest or the United States trustee, the appointment of an examiner is mandatory in cases in which borrowed money debt exceeds $5 million; it is discretionary with the court in all other cases. § 1104(b). The appointment of an examiner does not displace the debtor in possession; despite such an appointment, the debtor in possession continues to exercise its regular powers and is required to perform its regular duties except to the extent the court orders otherwise. § 1106(b).

§ 9.03 THE CHAPTER 11 PLAN

The heart of Chapter 11 is found in Sections 1121 through 1129, which deal with the formulation and confirmation of Chapter 11 plans. These provisions create a flexible framework that permits debtors, large or small, public or private, to scale down or restructure debt with the consent of the requisite majorities of their creditors. In addition, the possibility exists for ownership interests to be retained, in whole or in part, even in the case of an insolvent debtor. By way of counterbalance, a number of built-in protections assure adequate disclosure in connection with the proposed plan and minimum financial guarantees for claimants and interest holders who decline to accept it.

Moreover, Chapter 11 provides a procedure that accommodates prefiling reorganization or workout attempts for both public and private corporations. Recognizing that considerable negotiations often precede the filing of the Chapter 11 petition, the plan provisions of Chapter 11 permit the parties to negotiate a plan and effectively obtain its acceptance before the actual filing of the case. When prepetition reorganization is feasible, usually in the smaller cases, it is possible under the statute to file a Chapter 11 case and to actually confirm a plan within only a few weeks.

§ 9.03(a) Who May File a Plan; Plan Exclusivity

Although either the debtor, creditors, or any other "party in interest" may file a plan, the debtor generally has an exclusive

11 U.S.C. § 1121. Who may file a plan

(a) The debtor may file a plan with a petition commencing a voluntary case, or at any time in a voluntary case or an involuntary case.

(b) Except as otherwise provided in this section, only the debtor may file a plan until after 120 days after the date of the order for relief under this chapter.

(c) Any party in interest, including the debtor, the trustee, a creditors' committee, an equity security holders' committee, a creditor, an equity security holder, or any indenture trustee, may file a plan if and only if—

(1) a trustee has been appointed under this chapter;

(2) the debtor has not filed a plan before 120 days after the date of the order for relief under this chapter; or

(3) the debtor has not filed a plan that has been accepted, before 180 days after the date of the order for relief under this chapter, by each class of claims or interests that is impaired under the plan.

(d) On request of a party in interest made within the respective periods specified in subsections (b) and (c) of this section and after notice and a hearing, the court may for cause reduce or increase the 120-day period or the 180-day period referred to in this section.

period of several months at the beginning of the case in which to negotiate, file, and seek acceptances of its plan. More particularly, the debtor may file a plan at the commencement of the case or at any time during the course of the proceeding. § 1121(a). If no trustee is appointed, generally *only* the debtor may file a plan during the first 120 days after the order for relief. § 1121(b). Upon application made within this exclusivity period, the court may extend or reduce the period "for cause." § 1121(d). The court must exercise its independent judgment as to whether cause exists, and requests for extensions of the exclusivity period are not to be routinely granted. *In re Lake in the Woods,* 10 Bankr. 338 (E.D. Mich. 1981). *See also In re Timbers of Inwood Forest Associates, Ltd.,* 808 F.2d 363 (5th Cir. 1987) (*en banc*), *aff'd sub nom. United Sav. Ass'n of Texas v. Timbers of Inwood Forest Associates, Ltd.,* _____ U.S. _____, 108 S.Ct. 626 (1988). If a plan is filed during the exclusivity period, the debtor is given an additional exclusivity period — up until 180 days after the order for relief — in which to obtain the necessary acceptances. § 1121(c)(3). This additional period is also subject to extension or reduction for cause before it expires. § 1121(d).

Creditors or other parties in interest have two ways to reduce the debtor's exclusivity period and thereby become able to file their own plan. *See* § 1121(c). The most direct route, but one that is not likely to succeed, is to apply to the court for reduction of the 120- or 180-day period. § 1121(d). Grounds for such reduction are not itemized beyond the requirement that the reduction be for "cause." A second route is to obtain the appointment of a trustee, for the debtor's plan exclusivity then terminates automatically. From that time forward any party in interest, including the trustee, a creditors' committee, an equity security holders' committee, a creditor, or an equity security holder — as well as the debtor itself — may file a plan. § 1121(c)(1).

The creditors' potential ability to file a plan balances the debtor's control of the Chapter 11 process and tends to make the debtor more responsive to the desires of the creditors. Although Chapter 11 particularly the "fair and equitable" rule, discussed *infra,* pp. 409–19, protects legitimate ownership interests against unfair imposition, the ability of creditors or others to effect, through a plan, a sale of the

11 U.S.C. § 1123. Contents of plan

(a) Notwithstanding any otherwise applicable non-bankruptcy law, a plan shall—

(1) designate, subject to section 1122 of this title, classes of claims, other than claims of a kind specified in section 507(a)(1), 507(a)(2), or 507(a)(7) of this title, and classes of interests;

(2) specify any class of claims or interests that is not impaired under the plan;

(3) specify the treatment of any class of claims or interests that is impaired under the plan;

(4) provide the same treatment for each claim or interest of a particular class, unless the holder of a particular claim or interest agrees to a less favorable treatment of such particular claim or interest;

(5) provide adequate means for the plan's implementation, such as—

(A) retention by the debtor of all or any part of the property of the estate;

(B) transfer of all or any part of the property of the estate to one or more entities, whether organized before or after the confirmation of such plan;

(C) merger or consolidation of the debtor with one or more persons;

(D) sale of all or any part of the property of the estate, either subject to or free of any lien, or the distribution of all or any part of the property of the estate among those having an interest in such property of the estate;

(E) satisfaction or modification of any lien;

(F) cancellation or modification of any indenture or similar instrument;

(G) curing or waiving of any default;

(H) extension of a maturity date or a change in an interest rate or other term of outstanding securities;

(I) amendment of the debtor's charter; or

(J) issuance of securities of the debtor, or of any entity referred to in subparagraph (B) or (C) of this paragraph, for cash, for property, for existing securities, or in exchange for claims or interests, or for any other appropriate purpose;

business as a going concern, rather than to have a liquidation forced upon them unless they accept the debtor's plan, tends to motivate the debtor to be more flexible during the negotiation process.

§ 9.03(b) Contents of a Plan

Reorganization plans are essentially like contracts between the debtor and its creditors. In general, Chapter 11 is flexible enough to accommodate whatever deal the parties with creditor or ownership interests in the debtor can work out among themselves. Virtually any kind of consideration can be distributed as part of the plan.

The Code makes a few plan provisions mandatory. § 1123(a). Every plan must divide the creditors' claims and the ownership interests into classes, except for certain priority claims that are not classified, § 1123(a)(1); must state which classes are "not impaired" under the plan, § 1123(a)(2); and must specify how the plan is to satisfy the "impaired" classes, § 1123(a)(3). Impairment, or more accurately, nonimpairment, is the subject of Section 1124, discussed *infra,* at pp. 401–09.

An important provision, Section 1123(a)(4), requires that the plan must treat every claim or interest in a given class in the same way unless the holders individually agree to accept less favorable treatment. A plan provision that gives holders of claims or interests of a single class an election between alternative treatments — for example, allowing a choice between either an immediate cash settlement of 50 per cent or 75 per cent payable over two years — complies with Section 1123(a)(4) as long as everyone within the class may make the election.

The plan must also set forth adequate means for its implementation. Section 1123(a)(5) illustrates what might constitute such adequate means and at the same time empowers the reorganized debtor to take the steps listed in that section regardless of otherwise applicable and conflicting nonbankruptcy law. *See* §§ 1123(a), 1142. The means of plan implementation referred to in Section 1123(a)(5) include selling assets, modifying contracts, issuing securities, merging or consolidating with another company, and amending the corporate charter, all without compliance with any requirement of the general corporation law for the vote of shareholders.

11 U.S.C. § 1123. Contents of plan

(a) Notwithstanding any otherwise applicable non-bankruptcy law, a plan shall—

(6) provide for the inclusion in the charter of the debtor, if the debtor is a corporation, or of any corporation referred to in paragraph (5)(B) or (5)(C) of this subsection, of a provision prohibiting the issuance of nonvoting equity securities, and providing, as to the several classes of securities possessing voting power, an appropriate distribution of such power among such classes, including, in the case of any class of equity securities having a preference over another class of equity securities with respect to dividends, adequate provisions for the election of directors representing such preferred class in the event of default in the payment of such dividends; and

(7) contain only provisions that are consistent with the interests of creditors and equity security holders and with public policy with respect to the manner of selection of any officer, director, or trustee under the plan and any successor to such officer, director, or trustee.

11 U.S.C. § 1123. Contents of plan

(b) Subject to subsection (a) of this section, a plan may—

(1) impair or leave unimpaired any class of claims, secured or unsecured, or of interests;

(2) subject to section 365 of this title, provide for the assumption, rejection, or assignment of any executory contract or unexpired lease of the debtor not previously rejected under such section;

(3) provide for—

(A) the settlement or adjustment of any claim or interest belonging to the debtor or to the estate; or

(B) the retention and enforcement by the debtor, by the trustee, or by a representative of the estate appointed for such purpose, of any such claim or interest;

(4) provide for the sale of all or substantially all of the property of the estate, and the distribution of the proceeds of such sale among holders of claims or interests; and

(5) include any other appropriate provision not inconsistent with the applicable provisions of this title.

The provisions on the treatment of priority claims that appear in the confirmation section, Section 1129(a)(9), may also be regarded as mandatory provisions of a plan. These are discussed at pp. 431–33, *infra*.

Finally, the plan must contain certain provisions on the voting rights of securities of the reorganized debtor and must not violate any public policy concerning the manner of selecting officers and directors. § 1123(a)(6), (7).

Virtually any other proposal that creative minds can formulate is permitted in a plan. Section 1123(b) suggests the possible scope. Not all classes of claims or ownership interests have to be affected by the plan. That is, any or all classes may be impaired or left unimpaired, § 1123(b)(1), and the treatment of an impaired class may consist of anything that does not violate an express provision of the Bankruptcy Code. *See* § 1123(b)(5). Executory contracts may be rejected or assumed as part of the plan as well as during the preplan stage of the case. § 1123(b)(2). Liquidation plans are permissible. § 1123(b)(4). Causes of action held by the estate may be settled as part of the plan, or lawsuits may be retained and prosecuted by the plan proponent or the representative of the estate. § 1123(b)(3). The catchall provision states that the plan may contain any other appropriate provision that is not in conflict with the Code. § 1123(b)(5). It has been held, however, that a plan may not appropriately provide for invalidating liens under one of the avoiding powers. That is, lien avoidance must be accomplished through an adversary proceeding under Part VII of the Bankruptcy Rules. *In re Commercial Western Fin. Corp.*, 761 F.2d 1329 (9th Cir. 1985).

§ 9.03(c) Classification of Claims and Interests

Classification is a key concept of the reorganization plan and process. Voting by classes is the mechanism by which a plan is accepted; alternatively, specified minimum protections for the classes may substitute for their acceptance. As previously stated, except for certain priority claims referred to in Section 1123(a)(1), the reorganization plan must place all claims and ownership interests in established classes, § 1123(a)(1), and provide the same treatment for each claim or interest within the class, unless the holder

11 U.S.C. § 1122. Classification of claims or interests

(a) Except as provided in subsection (b) of this section, a plan may place a claim or an interest in a particular class only if such claim or interest is substantially similar to the other claims or interests of such class.

(b) A plan may designate a separate class of claims consisting only of every unsecured claim that is less than or reduced to an amount that the court approves as reasonable and necessary for administrative convenience.

individually agrees to less favorable treatment. § 1123(a)(4). Since the vote of the requisite majority of a class determines whether the class has accepted a plan, and since acceptance by each impaired class is necessary to confirm a plan on a consensual basis, the manner in which claims and interests are placed into the classes can be of profound importance in achieving confirmation. Similarly, the ability to take advantage of the often beneficial provisions of the nonimpairment section, Section 1124, including the possibility of reversing acceleration, see pp. 401–09, *infra*, may turn on whether a proposed classification is appropriate.

Section 1122 is the sole statutory basis for classifying claims or interests in Chapter 11. It authorizes, for administrative convenience, a separate class of unsecured claims, which usually consists of all claims of less than a relatively small amount and of claims that are reduced to that amount voluntarily by the claim holders. *See* § 1122(b). Typically, the plan will provide for this class to be paid in cash in full at confirmation, a provision that eliminates the need to solicit large numbers of acceptances from a creditor class whose total claims are relatively insignificant in amount. Apart from the administrative convenience provision, the classification section states only that "a plan may place a claim or an interest in a particular class only if such claim or interest is substantially similar to other claims or interests of such class." § 1122(a). Note that it does not provide, certainly not expressly, that all similar claims or interests must be placed in the same class. In other words, there are two distinct questions here: *May* a group of claims or interests be placed in the same class, and *must* they be?

"Similarity," which is not a defined term, apparently has to do with the quality or priority of the legal rights of the claim or interest holder against the debtor or the debtor's property, arguably in a liquidation context. Thus an unsecured claim based on contract is similar to one based on tort; a claim based on an unsecured note bearing a high interest rate is similar to an open account debt that bears no interest; a contingent or unmatured claim seems similar to a matured, liquidated one if both are unsecured—for in an ordinary liquidation case, all these unsecured claims would participate at the same level of distribution. Accordingly, it would seem that all of them *could be* classified together in a Chapter 11 plan.

Claims or interests with different legal priorities on liquidation would seem clearly to be dissimilar and to belong in different classes.[5] Thus claims entitled to priority in distribution under Section 507(a)(3)–(6) should be classified according to their priority rank and should be separated from unsecured claims not entitled to priority. (Claims entitled to priority under Section 507(a)(1), (2), and (7) are not classified at all. *See* § 1123(a)(1).) Generally, each secured claim belongs in its own separate class, either because its collateral is different—for example, a first mortgage on Blackacre is different from a first mortgage on Whiteacre—or because claims secured by the same collateral have different priority rankings—for example, a first mortgage on Blackacre is different from a second mortgage on Blackacre. *See, e.g., In re Commercial Western Fin. Corp., supra.* If, however, multiple obligations are secured by the same collateral and have the same priority, such as a bond issue secured by one mortgage or, perhaps, a series of mechanic's lien claims arising out of the same work of improvement, then the several secured claims are similar and may be placed in one class because each of the secured creditors has the same legal rights on liquidation of the collateral—a pro rata share of the liquidation proceeds. At the equity level preferred stock interests are different from, and should not be classified with, common stock interests.

Whether unsecured claims having the same rights on liquidation, which could properly be classified together, may nevertheless be placed in separate classes in the plan is not yet entirely clear. For example, may trade debt and unsecured bank debt be separately classified and therefore be treated differently under the plan, even though their rights on liquidation are identical? If both types of claims are placed in the same class, Section 1123(a)(4) would ordinarily require that they all receive the same treatment under the plan. Or may one unsecured loan with a favorable interest rate be separately classified and left unimpaired—that is, treated according

---

[5]There is a complication when a claim has a different priority in Chapter 7 than it does in Chapter 11, as occasionally occurs. For example, a penalty is subordinated in distribution by Section 726(a)(4), but there is no comparable provision applicable in Chapter 11. How this situation affects proper classification is not clear. *But see* Granada Wines v. New England Teamsters and Trucking Indus. Pension Fund, 748 F.2d 42 (1st Cir. 1984).

11 U.S.C. § 1129. Confirmation of plan

(a) The court shall confirm a plan only if all of the following requirements are met:

(1) The plan complies with the applicable provisions of this title.

to its contract terms—while the class of other unsecured debt is treated differently?

Whether the classification is legally permissible can be a crucial issue for the court's determination, since if it is not permissible, the plan does not comply with the requirements of Chapter 11 for proper classification and thus cannot be confirmed. § 1129(a)(1). Even a dissenting member of an accepting class has standing to object to the plan's proposed classification on the ground that it violates the standards of Section 1122.

The legislative history indicates that Section 1122 was intended to codify the case law under the former Bankruptcy Act regarding the classification of claims and equity interests. House Report at 406; S. REP. No. 989, 95th Cong., 2d Sess. 118 (1978). The difficulty is that the classification provisions in Chapters X, XI, and XII of that Act differed among themselves, and none were phrased like Section 1122(a). If one looks to Section 357(1) of former Chapter XI (former 11 U.S.C. § 757(1)) as representing the pre-Code law intended to be codified by Section 1122(a), it can be forcefully argued that there is a permissible flexibility in classifying similar claims either together or in separate classes. Section 357(1) permitted the plan to include "provisions for treatment of unsecured debts on a parity one with the other, or for the division of such debts into classes and the treatment thereof in different ways." And the ancient legislative history of the predecessor of that section was even clearer, one statement being that the section contemplated the possibility of "payment in full of small claims or a settlement with a bank on terms different from the settlement with merchandise creditors" subject to the "inherent restriction that the classification must be upon a reasonable basis." *Analysis of H.R. 12889*, 74th Cong., 2d Sess. 42 n.3. (1936).

The history is not conclusive, however, and the courts to date are divided in their interpretation of the degree of flexibility built into Section 1122(a). One line of authority holds that all claims of equal legal priority must be placed in the same class (subject to the administrative convenience exception of Section 1122(b)). *E.g., Granada Wines v. New England Teamsters and Trucking Indus. Pension Fund, supra* note 5. Another, more flexible, position, exemplified by the majority of cases such as *In re AOV Industries, Inc.*, 792 F.2d

1140 (D.C. Cir. 1986), *Matter of Jersey City Medical Center,* 817 F.2d 1055 (3d Cir. 1987) (Chapter 9), and *In re U.S. Truck Co., Inc.,* 800 F.2d 581 (6th Cir. 1986), is that Section 1122(a) does not establish a rigid standard to be applied. Rather, similar types of claims may be separately classified, at least when there is a legitimate reason for doing so. According to this view, separate classification of similar claims is especially justifiable when the disparity between the proposed treatment accorded the different classes is reasonable and not unfairly discriminatory, the separate classification is necessary as a practical matter to carry out the terms of the plan, and there is no attempt to use the separate classification to improperly manipulate the voting process.

§ 9.04 CONFIRMATION OF THE CHAPTER 11 PLAN

§ 9.04(a) In General

Chapter 11 is designed to accommodate the confirmation of both consensual plans and those that are not accepted by all the classes (cram down plans). The theory of the drafters of Chapter 11 was that the norm would be the consensual plan — the plan that is accepted by the requisite majority of every impaired class. The various checks and balances built into the system provide ample incentive for the parties to negotiate a generally agreeable settlement. Section 1129(a) provides for confirmation of the consensual plan. It permits junior classes to receive value in the reorganized debtor even though senior classes are not fully compensated, so long as the senior classes are given value of not less than what they would receive in a liquidation. If one or more impaired classes do not consent, however, confirmation must meet the cram down requirements of Section 1129(b): No reorganization value may be given to a junior class under the plan unless the senior, nonaccepting class has been compensated in full. The time-consuming difficulties and complicated valuation problems that cram down involves are themselves a major factor in stimulating the parties to work out a consensual arrangement. *See* Broude, *Cramdown and Chapter 11 of the Bankruptcy Code: The Settlement Imperative,* 39 Bus. Law. 441 (1984).

The Code's requirements for plan confirmation and the relation-

11 U.S.C. § 1126. Acceptance of plan

(c) A class of claims has accepted a plan if such plan has been accepted by creditors, other than any entity designated under subsection (e) of this section, that hold at least two-thirds in amount and more than one-half in number of the allowed claims of such class held by creditors, other than any entity designated under subsection (e) of this section, that have accepted or rejected such plan.

(d) A class of interests has accepted a plan if such plan has been accepted by holders of such interests, other than any entity designated under subsection (e) of this section, that hold at least two-thirds in amount of the allowed interests of such class held by holders of such interests, other than any entity designated under subsection (e) of this section, that have accepted or rejected such plan.

(e) On request of a party in interest, and after notice and a hearing, the court may designate any entity whose acceptance or rejection of such plan was not in good faith, or was not solicited or procured in good faith or in accordance with the provisions of this title.

ship of the various relevant sections to each other may be better understood by considering three questions: First, what is the vote needed for a class to accept a plan, and what is the process by which that vote is obtained? Second, what financial protection is given to the nonaccepting members of an accepting class? Third, when is confirmation possible without the actual acceptance of all classes? The answers to these questions are found not only in Section 1129 but also in several other sections on which it depends.

§ 9.04(b) The Concept of Acceptance by a Class; How Acceptances Are Obtained

One of the most important concepts of Chapter 11 is that members of a class by majority vote can bind the entire class to accept the plan. If the requisite majority of a creditor class, for example, is willing to accept a partial payment, an extension of the maturities of their claims, or stock — either as partial payment or payment in full — the settlement binds the nonaccepting creditors as well as those who affirmatively vote for it. Under the Code a class of claims has accepted a plan when the holders of a majority in number *and* two-thirds in amount of the claims in the class approve the plan; only the claims of creditors who actually vote are counted for this purpose. § 1126(c). A class of "interests" (that is, owners, usually stockholders) has accepted the plan when the holders of two-thirds in amount of the interests voted (that is, two-thirds of the shares voted) have accepted it. § 1126(d). Since, as just noted, only members of the class who actually vote are counted, a debtor who proposes a plan with the support of the creditors' committee ordinarily has little difficulty in obtaining the necessary majority acceptances by the various classes. When there is creditor apathy, the votes of a small minority of the outstanding claims can result in acceptance. (Any acceptance or rejection that was not in good faith or that was not obtained in good faith or in compliance with the Code may be excluded from the computations. § 1126(e).)

Because of the importance of the voting process, Congress has insisted that there be disclosure of adequate information, particularly of financial data, in connection with the solicitation of acceptances or rejections of a plan. Thus disclosure is central to the Chapter 11 plan confirmation process. House Report at 226. In

11 U.S.C. § 1125. Postpetition disclosure and solicitation

(b) An acceptance or rejection of a plan may not be solicited after the commencement of the case under this title from a holder of a claim or interest with respect to such claim or interest, unless, at the time of or before such solicitation, there is transmitted to such holder the plan or a summary of the plan, and a written disclosure statement approved, after notice and a hearing, by the court as containing adequate information. The court may approve a disclosure statement without a valuation of the debtor or an appraisal of the debtor's assets.

11 U.S.C. § 1126. Acceptance of plan

(b) For the purposes of subsections (c) and (d) of this section, a holder of a claim or interest that has accepted or rejected the plan before the commencement of the case under this title is deemed to have accepted or rejected such plan, as the case may be, if—

(1) the solicitation of such acceptance or rejection was in compliance with any applicable nonbankruptcy law, rule, or regulation governing the adequacy of disclosure in connection with such solicitation; or

(2) if there is not any such law, rule, or regulation, such acceptance or rejection was solicited after disclosure to such holder of adequate information, as defined in section 1125(a) of this title.

11 U.S.C. § 1125. Postpetition disclosure and solicitation

(a) In this section—

(1) "adequate information" means information of a kind, and in sufficient detail, as far as is reasonably practicable in light of the nature and history of the debtor and the condition of the debtor's books and records, that would enable a hypothetical reasonable investor typical of holders of claims or interests of the relevant class to make an informed judgment about the plan, but adequate information need not include such information about any other possible or proposed plan;

any Chapter 11 case, large or small, public or private, there may be no solicitation of votes *after* the filing of the case "unless, at the time of or before such solicitation, there is transmitted [to creditors and owners] the plan or a summary of the plan, and a written disclosure statement approved . . . by the court as containing adequate information." § 1125(b). (The distinction between negotiating with creditors over the terms of a proposed plan, which is permissible without a disclosure satement, and the solicitation of votes, which is subject to Section 1125(b), is discussed in *In re Synder*, 51 Bankr. 432 (Bankr. D. Utah 1985).) If acceptances of a plan were obtained *before* the filing of the Chapter 11 case, they may be counted, provided there was no violation of any applicable nonbankruptcy law or regulation concerning the adequacy of disclosure in connection with the solicitation. § 1126(b)(1). If no such law applied, the acceptances are valid if the court finds that the prepetition solicitation was accompanied by adequate disclosure. § 1126(b)(2). Bankruptcy Rule 3018(b), which deals with prepetition solicitation, further requires that the plan itself was transmitted to substantially all impaired creditors and stockholders and that they had a reasonable time to consider it.

The bankruptcy court plays an important role in monitoring the adequacy of disclosure, particularly in the typical case involving postpetition solicitation of acceptances. A proponent must file a proposed disclosure statement, Bankruptcy Rule 3016(c); the court then considers and rules on its adequacy at an important hearing. § 1125(b); Bankruptcy Rule 3017. In this effort the court will have, or should have, the assistance of the debtor or trustee and the creditors' committee and the input of the United States trustee, one of whose statutory responsibilities is the monitoring of disclosure statements. 28 U.S.C. § 586(a)(3)(B). The relevant issue at the hearing is whether the proposed statement contains "adequate information" to enable a class to make an informed judgment about the plan. § 1125(a)(1). "Adequate information" should be construed flexibly. For example, large cases require a different type of disclosure than small cases. An amendment in 1984 specifically provides that adequate information need not include information about other possible or competing plans. § 1125(a)(1).

Consistent with the legislative intent to streamline the reorgani-

11 U.S.C. § 1125. Postpetition disclosure and solicitation

(c) The same disclosure statement shall be transmitted to each holder of a claim or interest of a particular class, but there may be transmitted different disclosure statements, differing in amount, detail, or kind of information, as between classes.

(d) Whether a disclosure statement required under subsection (b) of this section contains adequate information is not governed by any otherwise applicable nonbankruptcy law, rule, or regulation, but an agency or official whose duty is to administer or enforce such a law, rule, or regulation may be heard on the issue of whether a disclosure statement contains adequate information. Such an agency or official may not appeal from, or otherwise seek review of, an order approving a disclosure statement.

(e) A person that solicits acceptance or rejection of a plan, in good faith and in compliance with the applicable provisions of this title, or that participates, in good faith and in compliance with the applicable provisions of this title, in the offer, issuance, sale, or purchase of a security, offered or sold under the plan, of the debtor, of an affiliate participating in a joint plan with the debtor, or of a newly organized successor to the debtor under the plan, is not liable, on account of such solicitation or participation, for violation of any applicable law, rule, or regulation governing solicitation of acceptance or rejection of a plan or the offer, issuance, sale, or purchase of securities.

11 U.S.C. § 1129. Confirmation of plan

(a) The court shall confirm a plan only if all of the following requirements are met:

(7) With respect to each impaired class of claims or interests—

(A) each holder of a claim or interest of such class—

(i) has accepted the plan; or

(ii) will receive or retain under the plan on account of such claim or interest property of a value, as of the effective date of the plan, that is not less than the amount that such holder would so receive or retain if the debtor were liquidated under chapter 7 of this title on such date;

zation process, the court may approve the disclosure statement without a full valuation hearing or an appraisal of the debtor's assets, § 1125(b), even though some kind of valuation evidence ordinarily is necessary at confirmation. Congress clearly intended that a going concern valuation at the disclosure hearing stage should not be required as a routine matter but only when valuation on this basis is necessary to provide adequate information. *See id.;* House Report at 227.

The Code contains a "safe harbor" provision for attorneys, accountants, and creditors' committees that must prepare disclosure information from the often inadequate records of a financially disorganized debtor. Honest mistakes in disclosure will not result in liability under nonbankruptcy law for soliciting acceptances or rejections of a plan or for offering securities under it. In the language of Section 1125(e), once the court has approved the disclosure statement, parties who solicit acceptances or rejections of a plan or who participate in the offer of securities under the plan "in good faith" are "not liable, on account of such solicitation or participation, for violation of any applicable law, rule, or regulation governing solicitation of acceptance or rejection of a plan or the offer, issuance, sale, or purchase of securities."

§ 9.04(c) The Financial Protection for Dissenting Members of an Accepting Class: The "Best Interests" Test

Whether or not a class of claims or interests accepts a plan by the requisite majorities, the dissenting members of the class are protected against unfair or unreasonable imposition by the requirement that all nonaccepting members of the class, whether they vote or not, must receive at least as much as they would realize in a Chapter 7 liquidation of the debtor. This guaranteed floor, found in Section 1129(a)(7)(A)(ii), is often referred to as the "best interests" test.[6] It requires that each nonaccepting member of the class must "receive or retain under the plan on account of such claim or interest property of a value, as of the effective date of the

---

[6]Chapter XI of the former Bankruptcy Act required for confirmation of an arrangement that "it is for the best interests of the creditors." § 366(2). This phrase was judicially construed to mean that the arrangement could not give the creditors less than what they would receive in a liquidation of the debtor.

11 U.S.C. § 1124. Impairment of claims or interests

(3) provides that, on the effective date of the plan, the holder of such claim or interest receives, on account of such claim or interest, cash equal to—

(A) with respect to a claim, the allowed amount of such claim; or

plan, that is not less than the amount that such holder would so receive or retain if the debtor were liquidated under chapter 7 of this title on such date." The best interests test does not come into play when all members of the class affirmatively vote to accept the plan. § 1129(a)(7)(A)(i). Nor does it apply to unimpaired classes, with respect to which all members are deemed to accept. §§ 1126(f), 1129(a)(7); see discussion 401–09, *infra*.

§ 9.04(d) When Is Confirmation Possible Without the Actual Acceptance of All Classes?

If the affirmative vote of all classes of creditors and ownership interests were required for confirmation of a plan, successful reorganizations could be held hostage to the wishes of small groups of creditors or owners. Chapter 11 contemplates the possibility of plans proposed by creditors. If they are to have an effective right to file a plan, which may well provide for a change of ownership of the debtor or a transfer of the business as a going concern, there must be some way of confirming that plan despite objections by the current ownership interests. Chapter 11 is also likely to be ineffective unless the unreasonable opposition of a creditor class or classes can be overridden under appropriate circumstances.

The classes of claims or interests that must affirmatively accept a plan, and the circumstances that sometimes substitute for actual acceptance, are governed by the interaction of two sections of Chapter 11, the confirmation section, Section 1129, and the non-impairment section, Section 1124. A requirement for confirmation is that as to each class of claims and interests either (1) it has accepted the plan (that is, the requisite majority vote has been obtained), § 1129(a)(8)(A); (2) it is "not impaired" by the plan, §§ 1129(a)(8)(B), 1124; or (3) the plan "does not discriminate unfairly" and complies with the "fair and equitable" rule. § 1129(b).

§ 9.04(d)(1) Nonimpairment — Section 1124

As just stated, one substitute for actual acceptance is nonimpairment, a concept dealt with in Section 1124. (In the language of Section 1126(f), a class that is not impaired and all its members are "conclusively presumed to have accepted the plan.") Generally,

11 U.S.C. § 1124. Impairment of claims or interests

Except as provided in section 1123(a)(4) of this title, a class of claims or interests is impaired under a plan unless, with respect to each claim or interest of such class, the plan—

(1) leaves unaltered the legal, equitable, and contractual rights to which such claim or interest entitles the holder of such claim or interest;

if the plan simply "leaves unaltered the legal, equitable, and contractual rights" of a class of creditors or owners, § 1124(1), or merely cures a default that led to acceleration of the debt and reinstates the obligation, § 1124(2), or fully pays the class of creditors or owners in cash at the time the plan becomes effective, § 1124(3), then the class so treated by the plan is not impaired. When the class's rights are otherwise affected by a plan, there is an impairment even if the change is beneficial. The consequence of impairment is to entitle a nonaccepting class to the protection of the fair and equitable rule of Section 1129(b).

As noted, there are three kinds of nonimpairment:

§ 9.04(d)(1)(A) Unaltered Classes—Section 1124(1). The following examples illustrate the concept of a class that is not impaired because the plan "leaves unaltered the legal, equitable, and contractual rights" of its members. § 1124(1).

1. A note secured by a mortgage on Blackacre is not in default and the plan proposes to pay it exactly according to its original terms. The class consisting of the secured mortgage claim is not impaired and its affirmative acceptance of the plan is not necessary. But if the plan proposed to increase the interest rate of the note (and not otherwise to alter its terms), the change, though beneficial to the claimant, would constitute an impairment.

2. An insolvent corporation has $6 million in senior unsecured debt, $2 million in public subordinated debt, and 100 common stockholders. Under the reorganization plan the senior creditor class is to receive $3 million cash in settlement; subordinated debt and shareholder interests are to remain as if no bankruptcy had ever been filed. Only the class of senior unsecured creditors has been impaired, and only the vote of those creditors is necessary. The two classes consisting of the subordinated debt and the stockholders' interests are left "unaltered," and thus their acceptance of the plan is unnecessary.

3. Under the plan the business assets are transferred to a new entity and the former ownership interest is eliminated, or, without a transfer of assets, the entire equity in the reorganized debtor is issued to the former creditors or to new investors. The class consisting of the former stockholders' interests is obviously

11 U.S.C. § 1124. Impairment of claims or interests

Except as provided in section 1123(a)(4) of this title, a class of claims or interests is impaired under a plan unless, with respect to each claim or interest of such class, the plan—

(3) provides that, on the effective date of the plan, the holder of such claim or interest receives, on account of such claim or interest, cash equal to—

(A) with respect to a claim, the allowed amount of such claim; or

(B) with respect to an interest, if applicable, the greater of—

(i) any fixed liquidation preference to which the terms of any security representing such interest entitle the holder of such interest; or

(ii) any fixed price at which the debtor, under the terms of such security, may redeem such security from such holder.

not left "unaltered"; therefore it is impaired. But consider the case of an insolvent debtor in which the stock interest is valueless. The plan provides for satisfying claims by issuing a specified amount of new stock to the creditors and further provides that the former stockholders are to retain their original shares. As a result, the debtor becomes solvent and the original stock, previously valueless, now has a positive value. There nevertheless is an impairment of the class of former stockholders. They originally owned 100 per cent of the debtor; under the plan they will own less. Thus their relationship to the debtor, or their rights with respect to the debtor, are altered, and the class is thus "impaired"—even though the value of those rights may have been enhanced. Indeed, a class of shareholders is probably impaired whenever shares of the type held by those shareholders are issued to others under a plan. This does *not* mean that the plan cannot be confirmed, for the class might accept the plan or it might be crammed down without class acceptance.

§ *9.04(d)(1)(B) Cash Out—Section 1124(3).* Closely akin to the concept of rights being left "unaltered" is Section 1124(3), which provides that full cash payment on the effective date of the plan will leave a class of claims or of preferred stock unimpaired.[7] The cash payment to a creditor class, however, need cover only the allowed amount of the claims. (As discussed previously, see p. 275, *supra,* postpetition interest generally is not allowable on unsecured claims, and other parts of a claim may also be disallowed under Section 502(b).) The claim of a partially secured creditor is allowed as secured to the extent of the value of the collateral and

---

[7]The effective date, although not defined in the statute, is a time specified in the plan that usually should be established as a date relatively soon after the order of confirmation. Former Chapter XI did not have this concept but mandated that certain claims, including administration expenses, be paid, and that other steps be taken, *at confirmation.* But typically the amounts required to be paid, particularly the administration expenses, could not be determined so quickly, and as a result it was often impossible to avoid falling into technical default under the confirmed plan. The device of the effective date introduces the necessary flexibility in Chapter 11 under the Code. By setting the date in the reasonable future following confirmation, the plan proponent is given the opportunity to mechanically comply with the Chapter 11 requirements. *See generally In re* Wonder Corp. of America, 70 Bankr. 1018 (Bankr. D. Conn. 1987).

11 U.S.C. § 1124. Impairment of claims or interests

Except as provided in section 1123(a)(4) of this title, a class of claims or interests is impaired under a plan unless, with respect to each claim or interest of such class, the plan —

(2) notwithstanding any contractual provision or applicable law that entitles the holder of such claim or interest to demand or receive accelerated payment of such claim or interest after the occurrence of a default —

(A) cures any such default that occurred before or after the commencement of the case under this title, other than a default of a kind specified in section 365(b)(2) of this title;

(B) reinstates the maturity of such claim or interest as such maturity existed before such default;

(C) compensates the holder of such claim or interest for any damages incurred as a result of any reasonable reliance by such holder on such contractual provision or such applicable law; and

(D) does not otherwise alter the legal, equitable, or contractual rights to which such claim or interest entitles the holder of such claim or interest;

ordinarily is allowed as unsecured to the extent of the deficiency. § 506(a), see p. 277, *supra.* If the effect of the Section 1111(b)(2) election, discussed *infra,* pp. 419–23, is disregarded for the moment, the class consisting of the bifurcated secured claim would be left unimpaired if the plan offered cash to the creditor in an amount equal to the value of the collateral. The balance of the claim would be part of the unsecured creditors' class.

§ 9.04(d)(1)(C) *Reversing Acceleration — Section 1124(2).* Assuredly the most important feature of Section 1124 is the power it gives the plan proponent to reverse the acceleration of an obligation so as to be able to take advantage of the original favorable terms of a given indebtedness. In Section 1124(2), Congress has provided for a limited authority to cure certain prepetition and postpetition economic defaults that trigger acceleration, even though there is no right to cure under otherwise applicable law. The plan must cure any default, compensate the creditor for damages resulting from action taken in reliance on the default, and otherwise leave the claim unaltered. If these requirements are met, the creditor's claim is deemed unimpaired under Section 1124(2), and the claimant's acceptance of the plan is not required. A default that consists of a breach of a provision relating to the debtor's financial condition, such as an insolvency or bankruptcy clause, need not be cured in order to leave the class unimpaired.

An example may help illustrate the application and usefulness of the Section 1124(2) provision: Suppose the debtor had a term loan agreement calling for payments of $100,000 a year over a ten-year period with an interest rate substantially below the current market rate. When the debtor defaulted on one installment, the creditor declared a default and accelerated the entire balance due pursuant to the contract. Although this acceleration may be irreversible under applicable nonbankruptcy law, Section 1124(2) permits a plan to provide for curing the default — by paying $100,000 (plus any reliance damages suffered by the creditor as a result of the default) — and for reinstating the original maturity and the other terms of the loan. The class would be unimpaired, and the creditor, even though dissatisfied with the plan, would be deemed to accept it. If, however, the plan proposed to change the interest rate, to extend the maturity date of future installments under the

11 U.S.C. § 1129. Confirmation of plan

(a) The court shall confirm a plan only if all of the following requirements are met:

(8) With respect to each class of claims or interests—

(A) such class has accepted the plan; or

(B) such class is not impaired under the plan.

11 U.S.C. § 1129. Confirmation of plan

(b)(1) Notwithstanding section 510(a) of this title, if all of the applicable requirements of subsection (a) of this section other than paragraph (8) are met with respect to a plan, the court, on request of the proponent of the plan, shall confirm the plan notwithstanding the requirements of such paragraph if the plan does not discriminate unfairly, and is fair and equitable, with respect to each class of claims or interests that is impaired under, and has not accepted, the plan.

loan agreement, or otherwise to affect the claim in any way, there would be an impairment.

How does the fact that a default on a secured debt may have resulted in the commencement of a prepetition foreclosure proceeding affect the power to cure and reinstate the obligation under Section 1124(2)? The authorities to date are not entirely consistent, but the majority of decisions interpreting the section (and the analogous provisions in Chapter 13, Section 1322(b)(3) and (5)) view it broadly so as to implement the congressional policy favoring rehabilitation over liquidation. Thus the reinstatement probably can be accomplished even after a foreclosure judgment and probably at least up until the time an actual foreclosure sale occurs. *See, e.g., In re Madison Hotel Assocs.,* 749 F.2d 410 (7th Cir. 1984); *In re Glenn,* 760 F.2d 1428 (6th Cir. 1985) (Chapter 13).

Although Section 1124(2)(A) and (C), which cover curing the default and compensating the claimant for reliance damages, do not specify when such payment must be made, the law apparently requires the plan to provide for payment in cash not later than the effective date of the plan. *See, e.g., In re Jones,* 32 Bankr. 951 (Bankr. D. Utah 1983). To date, the courts have differed as to whether the amounts required to cure defaults under Section 1124(2)(A) must include interest, *In re Carr,* 32 Bankr. 343 (Bankr. N.D. Ga. 1983); *In re Forest Hills Assocs.,* 40 Bankr. 410 (Bankr. S.D.N.Y. 1984) (interest not required); *In re Manville Forest Products Corp.,* 60 Bankr. 403 (S.D.N.Y. 1986) (interest must be paid on arrearages of both principal and interest that came due prior to the cure). The argument that compensation under Section 1124(2)(C) must provide for the payment of the difference between the present value of the accelerated loan and the value of the loan as reinstated has been rejected. *In re Rainbow Forest Apartments,* 33 Bankr. 576 (Bankr. N.D. Ga. 1983).

§ 9.04(d)(2) Cram Down — Section 1129(b)

Section 1129(a)(8) nominally requires for confirmation that every impaired class must accept the plan. Nevertheless, Section 1129(b) permits confirmation over the objection of an impaired class or classes, provided the plan "does not discriminate unfairly" and is "fair and equitable" as to those classes. This statutory

scheme recognizes an important principle of reorganization law: that a plan proponent must have the power, under certain protective conditions, to "cram down" a plan on dissenting classes of impaired creditors and owners. *See generally* Klee, *All You Ever Wanted to Know About Cram Down Under the New Bankruptcy Code,* 53 AM. BANKR. L.J. 133 (1979).

§ 9.04(d)(2)(A) Some Background History and Explanation of the "Fair and Equitable" (or "Absolute Priority") Rule. In corporate reorganization under Chapter X of the former Bankruptcy Act, as in equity receivership reorganization practice that preceded it, a plan was required to be "fair and equitable." This phrase was interpreted by the Supreme Court to embody the so-called "absolute priority" principle — that is, that the plan must fully compensate classes with senior rights in the debtor before junior classes can be given any value in the reorganized company. Stated another way, classes with legal or contractual seniority over other classes must be fully compensated in the order of their seniority. For example, general unsecured creditors must be fully compensated before stockholders may participate; preferred stockholders with a liquidation preference must be fully compensated before the common stockholders may receive value. The absolute priority principle was inflexibly applied, even when the classes were willing to waive it by their majority votes. As a result, a plan that offered creditors less than 100 per cent compensation was nonconfirmable in Chapter X unless stockholders' interests were eliminated.

Full compensation to senior classes in this context does not mean that cash payment is necessary. Ordinarily the consideration or compensation distributed under a plan consists primarily of securities of the reorganized debtor, perhaps equity securities, or notes or other debt securities, or a combination of both. The value of these securities, which determines the amount of compensation to the class, depends in turn on the valuation of the reorganized debtor that the securities represent.

It is well established that the valuation of the debtor for this purpose is not a liquidation value, unless the debtor is worth more on this basis than as a "going concern." Rather, it ordinarily involves a "going concern" or "reorganization" valuation. Typically this entails, roughly, predicting the reorganized debtor's average

annual future net income and then capitalizing that amount at an appropriate capitalization rate — or more accurately, discounting the debtor's projected future net income stream to present value at an appropriate rate.

Merely to state the absolute priority rule and what it entails even in this simplistic way makes clear that it involves a high degree of crystal-ball gazing. Predicting future net income is certainly inexact; choosing the appropriate discount or capitalization rate for the particular debtor is a matter about which the financial experts often disagree widely.

Because of the inflexible and limiting demands of the absolute priority rule and the unpredictability involved in any attempt to make the necessary calculations to apply it, Congress (over the strenuous objection of the Securities and Exchange Commission) chose not to make "fair and equitable" a routine requirement for confirmation. Thus, under the Code, if all impaired classes accept the plan, the senior classes in effect waive their right to insist upon full compensation before junior classes may share. (As seen earlier, pp. 399–401, *supra,* the standard of financial protection for the dissenters within accepting classes is only the "not less than liquidation" floor of Section 1129(a)(7)(A)(ii).) However, if an impaired class refuses to accept the plan, the "fair and equitable" requirement becomes applicable through Section 1129(b) to protect that class and in effect all classes junior to it.

The foregoing observations reemphasize the potential importance of the Section 1124 nonimpairment concept. When a class is left unimpaired, its affirmative vote is not needed; yet the proponent need not confront the difficulties and obstacles of the absolute priority rule. On the other hand, the lurking presence of the absolute priority rule influences the negotiating process with respect to a plan. Seniors are willing to give up reorganization values to juniors to achieve a consensual plan so as to avoid the time, expense, and risks that are involved in testing the rule. Juniors are motivated to make only reasonable demands because application of the absolute priority rule may result in their receiving nothing under the reorganization plan.

§ 9.04(d)(2)(B) "Fair and Equitable" Under Section 1129(b). A considerable body of case law has built up over the years construing

11 U.S.C. § 1129. Confirmation of plan

(b)(1) Notwithstanding section 510(a) of this title, if all of the applicable requirements of subsection (a) of this section other than paragraph (8) are met with respect to a plan, the court, on request of the proponent of the plan, shall confirm the plan notwithstanding the requirements of such paragraph if the plan does not discriminate unfairly, and is fair and equitable, with respect to each class of claims or interests that is impaired under, and has not accepted, the plan.

11 U.S.C. § 1129. Confirmation of plan

(b)(2) For the purpose of this subsection, the condition that a plan be fair and equitable with respect to a class includes the following requirements:

(B) With respect to a class of unsecured claims —

(i) the plan provides that each holder of a claim of such class receive or retain on account of such claim property of a value, as of the effective date of the plan, equal to the allowed amount of such claim; or

(ii) the holder of any claim or interest that is junior to the claims of such class will not receive or retain under the plan on account of such junior claim or interest any property.

(C) With respect to a class of interests —

(i) the plan provides that each holder of an interest of such class receive or retain on account of such interest property of a value, as of the effective date of the plan, equal to the greatest of the allowed amount of any fixed liquidation preference to which such holder is entitled, any fixed redemption price to which such holder is entitled, or the value of such interest; or

(ii) the holder of any interest that is junior to the interests of such class will not receive or retain under the plan on account of such junior interest any property.

and refining the meaning of the fair and equitable rule. For one thing, it has been established that not only must a senior class be fully compensated but also that it cannot be overcompensated, for overcompensation would give the senior class reorganization values that in fairness belonged to juniors. By way of illustration: In the case of a debtor whose reorganization value made it solvent, creditors could not be given all the stock in the reorganized company over the objection of stockholders who had some equity.

The use of the term "fair and equitable" in Section 1129(b)(1) was intended to incorporate this judicial gloss into the Code (although to some extent Section 1129(b) does in fact relax the application of the absolute priority rule). In addition, Section 1129(b)(2) particularizes some nonexclusive requirements of the rule as applied to different kinds of classes. In some ways these illustrative requirements are merely a statement in different words of what the absolute priority rule means.

Under Section 1129(b)(2)(B), a plan is fair and equitable as to a class of unsecured claims (so that it may be confirmed despite the class's opposition) if it provides the members of the class with consideration having a present value, as of the plan's effective date, of not less than the full allowed amounts of the claims in the class. Thus if the class is to be compensated by the issuance of the debtor's notes in the principal amount of the allowed claims in the class, the notes must bear a market rate of interest so as to meet the present value requirement. Alternatively, if the class is not to be fully compensated under the plan, no junior class may receive anything. § 1129(b)(2)(B)(ii). This is merely another way of stating the traditional absolute priority rule. That is, the reorganization value of the debtor as it was being distributed in the order of the seniority of the classes ran out before the unsecured creditor class could be fully compensated.

The fair and equitable rule applies similarly to ownership interests. Holders of senior stock interests—for example, the preferred stockholders—must be given on a present value basis consideration equal to their full preference rights; otherwise, the holders of common, or junior, stock interests may not receive or retain any value under the reorganization plan. § 1129(b)(2)(C). It was held under the former Bankruptcy Act, however, that to the extent

11 U.S.C. § 1129. Confirmation of plan

(b)(2) For the purpose of this subsection, the condition that a plan be fair and equitable with respect to a class includes the following requirements:

(A) With respect to a class of secured claims, the plan provides —

(i)(I) that the holders of such claims retain the liens securing such claims, whether the property subject to such liens is retained by the debtor or transferred to another entity, to the extent of the allowed amount of such claims; and

(II) that each holder of a claim of such class receive on account of such claim deferred cash payments totaling at least the allowed amount of such claim, of a value, as of the effective date of the plan, of at least the value of such holder's interest in the estate's interest in such property;

(ii) for the sale, subject to section 363(k) of this title, of any property that is subject to the liens securing such claims, free and clear of such liens, with such liens to attach to the proceeds of such sale, and the treatment of such liens on proceeds under clause (i) or (iii) of this subparagraph; or

(iii) for the realization by such holders of the indubitable equivalent of such claims.

stockholders or others with an interest in the debtor contributed new capital to the reorganized debtor, they could be given interests in the debtor in recognition of their new contributions. *See, e.g., Case v. Los Angeles Lumber Products Co.,* 308 U.S. 106 (1939). Apparently this new contribution exception to the absolute priority rule was carried over into the Bankruptcy Code, *see, e.g., In re U.S. Truck Co., Inc.,* 800 F.2d 581 (6th Cir. 1986); in other words, the "fair and equitable" requirement, when it applies, limits the participation of junior classes only "on account of" their preexisting claims or interests. *See* §1129(b)(2)(B)(ii), 1129(b)(2)(C)(ii). *(But see Norwest Bank Worthington v. Ahlers,* ____ U.S. ____, ____ n.3, 108 S.Ct. 963, 967 n.3 (1988) (questioning but declining to decide whether there *is* any new contribution exception under the 1978 Code, but holding that in any event, if the exception indeed now exists, it may not be satisfied by a contribution of intangibles such as future labor, experience, or expertise, that only a new contribution of tangible capital could suffice).)

The fair and equitable principle is stated differently for a secured creditor class. Generally, its requirements are complied with if the creditor retains his lien on the collateral, or on the proceeds of sale if the collateral is sold, and receives under the plan deferred cash payments[8] that have a present value as of the plan's effective date at least equal to the value of the collateral (or at least equal to the allowed amount of the claim if that is less). § 1129(b)(2)(A)(i), (ii). (Recall that the allowed amount of a secured claim when the collateral's value is less than the debt ordinarily is the value of the collateral.) Meeting this requirement typically entails paying a market rate of interest on the deferred installments. The practical effect of the provision is to permit the restructuring of the payment period of a secured debt or any of its other terms, as long as the present value of the stream of future payments is assured by the appropriate interest rate. An alternative section, Section 1129(b)(2)(A)(iii), intended as a reservoir of judicial power to permit other fair and equitable treatment of secured creditor classes, enables the cram down of any plan provision that assures the real-

---

[8]If the secured claim were paid in full in cash as of the plan's effective date, its class would be unimpaired under Section 1124(3) and the requirements of Section 1129(b) would not be reached.

ization by the secured creditor of the "indubitable equivalent" of his claim.

§ 9.04(d)(3) Nonimpairment and Cram Down Revisited: The Partially Secured Creditor and Section 1111(b)

A fuller understanding of nonimpairment and cram down requires consideration of how these concepts apply to a partially secured or undersecured creditor class (that is, to a class consisting of one or more creditors whose claims exceed the value of their collateral) in light of the provisions of Section 1111(b). A bit of history may help explain the purpose of this section.

Under Chapter XII of the former Bankruptcy Act, which dealt with real property arrangements (as well as in Chapter X), it was possible to cram down a plan provision on a secured creditor if it called for full payment of the value of his interest in the collateral. Thus, by refinancing or otherwise, the property could be freed from the lien. Particularly during a real estate depression, this treatment was disadvantageous to a holder of a defaulted mortgage whose claim exceeded the collateral's depressed value. Through a cash out, he could be deprived of his legal right to cause foreclosure, credit bid up to the full contractual amount of the claim, and upon becoming the purchaser, hold the property for its appreciation in better times. The mortgage holder's plight, moreover, was exacerbated if his claim, as was common in real estate financing, was a nonrecourse obligation (that is, an obligation as to which the debtor had no in personam liability beyond the collateral). In such event the mortgage holder not only had to accept a low current market value for the collateral but also had no right under nonbankruptcy law to recover the unsecured deficiency, and thus had no allowable claim in the Chapter XII case.

But for Section 1111(b), the same possibilities would exist under the Code. As seen previously, a partially secured obligation is bifurcated into a secured claim, equal to the value of the collateral, and an unsecured claim for the deficiency. § 506(a). If the original obligation is a nonrecourse one, either because of contract or ap-

11 U.S.C. § 1111. Claims and interests

(b)(1)(A) A claim secured by a lien on property of the estate shall be allowed or disallowed under section 502 of this title the same as if the holder of such claim had recourse against the debtor on account of such claim, whether or not such holder has such recourse, unless—

(i) the class of which such claim is a part elects, by at least two-thirds in amount and more than half in number of allowed claims of such class, application of paragraph (2) of this subsection; or

(ii) such holder does not have such recourse and such property is sold under section 363 of this title or is to be sold under the plan.

(B) A class of claims may not elect application of paragraph (2) of this subsection if—

(i) the interest on account of such claims of the holders of such claims in such property is of inconsequential value; or

(ii) the holder of a claim of such class has recourse against the debtor on account of such claim and such property is sold under section 363 of this title or is to be sold under the plan.

(2) If such an election is made, then notwithstanding section 506(a) of this title, such claim is a secured claim to the extent that such claim is allowed.

plicable law,[9] then there is no enforceable unsecured claim against the debtor for the deficiency, and it is disallowed by Section 502(b)(1). The secured claim, however, could be left unimpaired under Section 1124(3) through a cash out for only the value of the collateral and could be crammed down under Section 1129(b) as long as the present value of the deferred payments under the plan was not less than the value of the collateral.

Although the statutory language is rather convoluted, Section 1111(b) is designed to give a measure of relief to partially secured creditors, but only when the collateral is not sold during the case or under the plan.[10] It begins by giving the creditor, for the purpose of allowing his claim in the Chapter 11 case, an unsecured claim for his deficiency, whether or not he has a recourse claim outside of bankruptcy. The section does not create personal liability on a nonrecourse claim for any purpose other than to prescribe the treatment of the claim under the plan. Alternatively (unless the creditor's interest in the collateral is of inconsequential value), the creditor may elect under Section 1111(b)(2) to have his claim allowed as a secured claim for its full contractual amount rather than in a lower amount equal to the collateral's value, as Section 506(a) generally mandates. The election may be made before the conclusion of the hearing on the disclosure statement or at a later date fixed by the court. Bankruptcy Rule 3014. The price of making the election is the waiver of any unsecured claim for the deficiency, even if the creditor holds a recourse obligation.

---

[9]For example, in some states no deficiency judgment is permitted on a purchase-money security interest in real estate.

[10]The thought is that if the property is sold, the partially secured creditor will have the opportunity to credit bid at the sale up to the full contract amount of his claim, see § 363(k), and thus will not be deprived of any bargained-for rights. Section 1111(b) may be deficient, however, in not expressly requiring that the kind of sale which precludes its applicability must be one at which the creditor has an opportunity to bid. *But see In re* Woodridge North Apts., Ltd., 71 Bankr. 189 (Bankr. N.D. Cal. 1987) (nonrecourse creditor entitled to Section 1111(b) deficiency claim unless he is given opportunity to credit bid at sale). It is also unclear whether Section 1111(b) applies if the collateral is abandoned, surrendered to the secured party, or, in the case of an individual debtor, exempted. *But see* Matter of DRW Property Co. 82, 57 Bankr. 987 (Bankr. N.D. Tex. 1986) (Section 1111(b) does not apply if collateral is abandoned or foreclosed upon following lifting of automatic stay).

11 U.S.C. § 1124. Impairment of claims or interests

(3) provides that, on the effective date of the plan, the holder of such claim or interest receives, on account of such claim or interest, cash equal to—

(A) with respect to a claim, the allowed amount of such claim;

11 U.S.C. § 1129. Confirmation of plan

(b)(2) For the purpose of this subsection, the condition that a plan be fair and equitable with respect to a class includes the following requirements:

(A) With respect to a class of secured claims, the plan provides—

(i)(I) that the holders of such claims retain the liens securing such claims, whether the property subject to such liens is retained by the debtor or transferred to another entity, to the extent of the allowed amount of such claims; and

(II) that each holder of a claim of such class receive on account of such claim deferred cash payments totaling at least the allowed amount of such claim, of a value, as of the effective date of the plan, of at least the value of such holder's interest in the estate's interest in such property;

(ii) for the sale, subject to section 363(k) of this title, of any property that is subject to the liens securing such claims, free and clear of such liens, with such liens to attach to the proceeds of such sale, and the treatment of such liens on proceeds under clause (i) or (iii) of this subparagraph; or

(iii) for the realization by such holders of the indubitable equivalent of such claims.

How do the concepts of nonimpairment and cram down interact with Section 1111(b)? A partially secured creditor who makes the Section 1111(b)(2) election has an allowed secured claim equal to the total contractual amount owing to him; therefore the plan cannot leave the claim unimpaired under Section 1124(3) without providing for payment of that full amount in cash. Thus, without the creditor's consent, the claim must either be fully paid or dealt with by way of cram down under Section 1129(b). But at the cram down stage the protection given to a partially secured creditor is far from complete. If the election is made, the total of the stream of payments must *nominally* equal at least the full contractual amount of the claim, but the present value of those deferred payments need only be equal to the value of the collateral. § 1129(b)(2)(A)(i)(II). One way to meet the cram down requirement in this context is to give the creditor a note with a nominal face value equal to the amount of the claim but with an interest rate sufficiently lower than the market rate so as to make the note on a discounted basis worth the value of the collateral.

Of course, the lien remains on the property or on its proceeds, but economically the creditor is no better off by making the election — on a present value basis he receives only the value of the collateral whether he elects or not. Yet by electing, the creditor gives up the potentially valuable right to participate in the unsecured creditor class for the deficiency. Perhaps, if the unsecured deficiency claim is large enough, the partially secured creditor's negative vote could defeat the acceptance of the plan by the unsecured class. Most of the time, therefore, the partially secured creditor class is well advised not to elect. On the other hand, if the election is made and the debtor subsequently defaults after confirmation, the creditor has an enforceable lien securing his full claim rather than a lien securing a lesser amount. And some financial institutions for their own accounting reasons may prefer to carry a secured claim at its full nominal face value rather than to write it down, even though, as crammed down, it has an economic value considerably lower than face value.

§ 9.04(e) Application of Some of the Foregoing Principles to a Hypothetical Confirmation Problem

Some simple illustrations of the application of the nonimpairment

and cram down principles to a concrete fact situation may be helpful: The debtor corporation owes $5 million secured by all the company's assets; its unsecured indebtedness consists only of senior bank loans of $6 million and contractually subordinated debt of $2 million. If completely liquidated, the assets would sell for $7 million net; however, the projected future earnings of the business are such that, when they are capitalized at the appropriate rate, the debtor would have a reorganization, or going concern, value of $11 million. (Administrative expenses will be ignored for the purpose of this example, and there are no other priority claims.) The excess of the total liabilities ($13 million) over the assets valued on a going concern basis ($11 million) indicates a negative net worth of $2 million. The prereorganization balance sheet thus looks like this:

Before Reorganization

(in 000s)

Assets (at going concern value)	$11,000	Secured debt	$ 5,000
		Senior unsecured debt	6,000
(Net liquidation value $7,000)		Subordinated debt	2,000
		Shareholder equity (deficit)	(2,000)
	$11,000		$11,000

The simple reorganization plan calls for treating the secured creditor exactly according to the terms of its contract. (If there are any existing defaults, they will be promptly cured.) The class of senior unsecured creditors is to receive notes in the principal amount of 80 per cent of their claims, payable in installments over five years and bearing a market rate of interest; on account of the balance of these claims, the class is to be issued 100 per cent of the new common stock of the corporation. The class of subordinated unsecured creditors is to be paid $1 million cash, in full settlement, to be raised from the sale of $1 million worth of surplus inventory. The original stockholders' interest in the debtor is to be eliminated. Giving effect to the reorganization plan would produce the following financial structure:

After Reorganization

(in 000s)

Assets (at going concern value, after appropriate adjustment to reflect the disposition of $1 million worth of surplus inventory)	$10,000	Secured debt	$ 5,000
		Notes payable to (senior) unsecured debt	4,800
		Subordinated debt	-0-
		Shareholder equity (now held by the former senior debt creditors)	200
	$10,000		$10,000

First, can this plan be confirmed with respect to classes that accept it? In other words, does it satisfy the "not less than liquidation" or "best interests" protection accorded by Section 1129(a)(7)(A)(ii) for dissenting members within an accepting class? The answer is yes. In a hypothetical Chapter 7 case, the $7 million of net liquidation proceeds would be distributed as follows: first, $5 million to the secured class; then the remaining $2 million to the senior debt holders. Nothing would be left for the subordinated debt holders and the stockholders. The plan proposes treatment at least as favorable as this for each of the classes. (Technically, since the secured class is unimpaired, Section 1129(a)(7) is inapplicable as to it.)

Next, note that the rights of the classes other than the secured creditor class are altered by the plan—they are impaired. *See* § 1124. Acceptance by the requisite majority vote of each of these three classes is thus necessary unless the plan can be crammed down on one or more of them under Section 1129(b).[11] The conclusion will be that cram down is possible with respect to the subordinated debt and the shareholders but not with respect to the senior unsecured debt; acceptance of the plan by the latter class is required for confirmation.

As to the class of subordinated debt, the plan is "fair and equitable." Although the payment of $1 million to the members of the class does not equal their allowed claims of $2 million, there is no proposed distribution to any junior class (that is, to the sharehold-

---

[11]Since the original stockholders are given nothing under the plan, their class is deemed to reject the plan, § 1126(g), even if in fact they desired or actually voted to accept it.

11 U.S.C. § 1129. Confirmation of plan

(a) The court shall confirm a plan only if all of the following requirements are met:

(1) The plan complies with the applicable provisions of this title.

(2) The proponent of the plan complies with the applicable provisions of this title.

(3) The plan has been proposed in good faith and not by any means forbidden by law.

(4) Any payment made or to be made by the proponent, by the debtor, or by a person issuing securities or acquiring property under the plan, for services or for costs and expenses in or in connection with the case, or in connection with the plan and incident to the case, has been approved by, or is subject to the approval of, the court as reasonable;

(5)(A)(i) The proponent of the plan has disclosed the identity and affiliations of any individual proposed to serve, after confirmation of the plan, as a director, officer, or voting trustee of the debtor, an affiliate of the debtor participating in a joint plan with the debtor, or a successor to the debtor under the plan; and

(ii) the appointment to, or continuance in, such office of such individual, is consistent with the interests of creditors and equity security holders and with public policy; and

(B) the proponent of the plan has disclosed the identity of any insider that will be employed or retained by the reorganized debtor, and the nature of any compensation for such insider.

(6) Any governmental regulatory commission with jurisdiction, after confirmation of the plan, over the rates of the debtor has approved any rate change provided for in the plan, or such rate change is expressly conditioned on such approval.

(12) All fees payable under section 1930, as determined by the court at the hearing on confirmation of the plan, have been paid or the plan provides for the payment of all such fees on the effective date of the plan.

ers); thus, as to the subordinated debt class, the plan meets the requirement of Section 1129(b)(2)(B)(ii). If, however, the plan proposed to give or leave any interest in the reorganized debtor to the stockholders on account of their shares, this requirement would not have been met and the plan then could not be crammed down on the subordinated debt.

The analysis is similar for the shareholder class. No class above it is being overcompensated by the plan, and the reorganization value ran out before the shareholders could be reached in an absolute priority distribution of that value. As can be seen, the lowest class is always subject to cram down unless there is overcompensation of some senior class.

The "fair and equitable" requirement of Section 1129(b)(2)(B) is not satisfied, however, in the case of the class of senior unsecured debt. It is not being given the full $6 million allowed amount of its claims. The plan proposes only $5 million of reorganization value for this class, consisting of notes worth $4.8 million plus new equity worth $0.2 million. Thus, since the plan gives some value to a junior class—$1 million to the subordinated debt—the cram down requirements are not met as to the senior unsecured debt. Only by its voluntary acceptance—that is, by the requisite majority vote—can the class of senior unsecured claims be bound.

§ 9.04(f) Other Requirements for Confirmation

§ 9.04(f)(1) The Boilerplate

The first half-dozen requirements for confirmation in Section 1129(a)(1)–(6) are of a routine nature, having been taken over by and large from the confirmation provisions in the former Chapter X statute. Not surprisingly, Section 1129(a)(1) and (2) require the plan and its proponent to comply with applicable Title 11 law. If, for example, the classification of claims and interests is found to be improper or if the prescribed disclosure process was violated, Section 1129(a)(1) or (2) would supply the basis for denying confirmation. Similarly, the plan must be proposed "in good faith and not by any means forbidden by law." § 1129(a)(3). There are also requirements for disclosure and for court approval of certain payments of

11 U.S.C. § 1129. Confirmation of plan

(a) The court shall confirm a plan only if all of the following requirements are met:

(9) Except to the extent that the holder of a particular claim has agreed to a different treatment of such claim, the plan provides that—

(A) with respect to a claim of a kind specified in section 507(a)(1) or 507(a)(2) of this title, on the effective date of the plan, the holder of such claim will receive on account of such claim cash equal to the allowed amount of such claim;

(B) with respect to a class of claims of a kind specified in section 507(a)(3), 507(a)(4), or 507(a)(5) or 507(a)(6) of this title, each holder of a claim of such class will receive—

(i) if such class has accepted the plan, deferred cash payments of a value, as of the effective date of the plan, equal to the allowed amount of such claim; or

(ii) if such class has not accepted the plan, cash on the effective date of the plan equal to the allowed amount of such claim; and

(C) with respect to a claim of a kind specified in section 507(a)(7) of this title, the holder of such claim will receive on account of such claim deferred cash payments, over a period not exceeding six years after the date of assessment of such claim, of a value, as of the effective date of the plan, equal to the allowed amount of such claim.

costs and fees made or to be made in connection with the plan or with the case and additional disclosure requirements concerning the identities of officers, directors, and other insiders who are to be connected with the reorganized debtor. § 1129(a)(4), (5). These requirements are often satisfied by the inclusion of the necessary information in the disclosure statement. If the debtor is a utility or is otherwise subject to rate regulation, the blessing of the appropriate regulatory commission must be obtained with respect to the reorganized company's proposed rate schedule. § 1129(a)(6). Finally, Section 1129(a)(12) provides that all filing fees and charges against the Chapter 11 estate require by 28 U.S.C. Section 1930 must be paid not later than the plan's effective date.

§ 9.04(f)(2) Provisions With Respect To Priority Claims

To be confirmed, a plan must contain certain prescribed provisions for the payment of claims entitled to priority under Section 507(a). Thus, under Section 1129(a)(9)(A), first priority administrative expenses and certain other postpetition claims — that is, those entitled to second priority under Section 507(a)(2) — must be paid in full in cash on the plan's effective date, unless the requirement is waived individually by a particular claimant. This requirement explains why there is no need to classify the first two priority categories. *See* § 1123(a)(1). Their treatment is mandated, they do not vote as a class, and they cannot bind each other. Priority tax claims may be paid over a period of six years, measured from the date of the assessment of the tax, provided that the present value of the deferred installments as of the plan's effective date is equal to the allowed amounts of the claims. § 1129(a)(9)(C). Although, like other unsecured claims, priority taxes ordinarily are not entitled to postpetition interest as a matter of the allowability of the claims, the present value requirement of Section 1129(a)(9)(C) entails the inclusion of an appropriate interest factor from the plan's effective date forward, as long as the taxes are to be paid on a deferred basis. *See In re Southern States Motor Inns, Inc.*, 709 F.2d 647 (11th Cir. 1983); *United States v. Neal Pharmacal Co.*, 789 F.2d 1283 (8th Cir. 1986) (appropriate interest rate is prevailing market rate for a loan of the term of the payout period to a borrower of the debtor's

11 U.S.C. § 1129. Confirmation of plan

(a) The court shall confirm a plan only if all of the following requirements are met:

(10) If a class of claims is impaired under the plan, at least one class of claims that is impaired under the plan has accepted the plan, determined without including any acceptance of the plan by any insider.

creditworthiness). The consent of the taxing agency to the extended payment schedule is not needed.

Finally, the remaining priority classes — for employee and employee benefit plan claims, farmers and fishermen, and consumer deposit creditors — must be paid in full in cash on the effective date of the plan unless, by the requisite majority vote, the class binds itself to an extension arrangement for its claims. If the latter course is accepted, the present value of the deferred cash installments, as of the plan's effective date, must equal the full allowed amount of the claims. § 1129(a)(9)(B).

§ 9.04(f)(3) Acceptance by at Least One Impaired Class of Claims

If all classes are left unimpaired by the plan, confirmation is theoretically possible without the affirmative acceptance of any class, but confirmation without the affirmative acceptance of at least one class is not possible if the plan creates an impaired creditor class. Thus a plan is not confirmable if it contemplates cram down of all impaired creditor classes (such as might occur in a pure liquidation plan for an insolvent debtor or perhaps in the case of a debtor that proposes to extend the maturity of all debt over the creditors' dissent). Section 1129(a)(10) provides that if there is an impaired class of claims, at least one such impaired class must accept the plan; in this context the vote of any member of the class who is an insider is not counted.

§ 9.04(f)(4) Feasibility

For policy reasons a plan should not be confirmed unless there is a reasonable likelihood not only that the plan's promises will be fulfilled — for example, that the payments will be made as provided — but also that the reorganized business will survive as an economically viable entity. *See, e.g., In re Acequia, Inc.,* 787 F.2d 1352 (9th Cir. 1986) (proponent must show plan has reasonable probability of success); *In re Pizza of Hawaii, Inc.,* 761 F.2d 1374 (9th Cir. 1985) (to confirm court must estimate or take into account large disputed claim that could impair performance under plan). This so-called feasibility concept is designed to prevent the adverse economic and social conse-

11 U.S.C. § 1129. Confirmation of plan

(a) The court shall confirm a plan only if all of the following requirements are met:

(11) Confirmation of the plan is not likely to be followed by the liquidation, or the need for further financial reorganization, of the debtor or any successor to the debtor under the plan, unless such liquidation or reorganization is proposed in the plan.

11 U.S.C. § 1127. Modification of plan

(a) The proponent of a plan may modify such plan at any time before confirmation, but may not modify such plan so that such plan as modified fails to meet the requirements of sections 1122 and 1123 of this title. After the proponent of a plan files a modification of such plan with the court, the plan as modified becomes the plan.

(b) The proponent of a plan or the reorganized debtor may modify such plan at any time after confirmation of such plan and before substantial consummation of such plan, but may not modify such plan so that such plan as modified fails to meet the requirements of sections 1122 and 1123 of this title. Such plan as modified under this subsection becomes the plan only if circumstances warrant such modification and the court, after notice and a hearing, confirms such plan as modified, under section 1129 of this title.

(c) The proponent of a modification shall comply with section 1125 of this title with respect to the plan as modified.

(d) Any holder of a claim or interest that has accepted or rejected a plan is deemed to have accepted or rejected, as the case may be, such plan as modified, unless, within the time fixed by the court, such holder changes such holder's previous acceptance or rejection.

11 U.S.C. § 1141. Effect of confirmation

(a) Except as provided in subsections (d)(2) and (d)(3) of this section, the provisions of a confirmed plan bind the debtor, any entity issuing securities under the plan, any entity acquiring property under the plan, and any creditor, equity security holder, or general partner in the debtor, whether or not the claim or interest of such creditor, equity security holder, or general partner is impaired under the plan and whether or not such creditor, equity security holder, or general partner has accepted the plan.

quences of another business failure and to protect against deception those who will have future dealings with the enterprise that emerges from the Chapter 11 case.

The Code's statement of the feasibility requirement, which appears in Section 1129(a)(11), is that "[c]onfirmation . . . is not likely to be followed by . . . liquidation, or the need for further financial reorganization" unless the plan itself is a liquidation plan or contemplates a merger or the like. The issues here are whether the reorganized debtor can reasonably be expected to have future net earnings and cash flow sufficient to meet its restructured interest and dividend requirements, as well as to amortize the principal of the restructured debts; whether the proposed new capital structure, including the relationship of debt to equity in the reorganized company, is excessive or sound; and perhaps whether any new securities to be issued are of a misleading nature.

§ 9.05 MODIFICATION OF A PLAN

Modification of a plan is dealt with in Section 1127. A proponent of a plan may modify it at any time before confirmation, provided that the plan as modified complies with the Code requirements for an original plan—that is, complies with Sections 1122 and 1123—and with the disclosure requirements of Section 1125. The modified plan then becomes the plan. An acceptance of the original plan is counted as an acceptance of the modified plan, provided that it is not revoked within a time fixed by the court. § 1127(d). Minor modifications that do not adversely change the treatment of the creditors or interest holders need not be resubmitted to them. *See* Bankruptcy Rule 3019.

After confirmation and before substantial consummation, *see* § 1101(2), a modification complying with the other provisions of Chapter 11 may be proposed. However, the modified plan replaces the original plan only if "circumstances warrant" and the court chooses to confirm the modified plan. § 1127(b).

§ 9.06 EFFECT OF CONFIRMATION; POSTCONFIRMATION MATTERS

Congress in Chapter 11 intended that the confirmed plan would work a pervasive reorganization by, among other things, discharg-

11 U.S.C. § 1141. Effect of confirmation

(b) Except as otherwise provided in the plan or the order confirming the plan, the confirmation of a plan vests all of the property of the estate in the debtor.

(c) Except as provided in subsections (d)(2) and (d)(3) of this section and except as otherwise provided in the plan or in the order confirming the plan, after confirmation of a plan, the property dealt with by the plan is free and clear of all claims and interests of creditors, equity security holders, and of general partners in the debtor.

(d)(1) Except as otherwise provided in this subsection, in the plan, or in the order confirming the plan, the confirmation of a plan—

(A) discharges the debtor from any debt that arose before the date of such confirmation, and any debt of a kind specified in section 502(g), 502(h), or 502(i) of this title, whether or not—

(i) a proof of the claim based on such debt is filed or deemed filed under section 501 of this title;

(ii) such claim is allowed under section 502 of this title; or

(iii) the holder of such claim has accepted the plan; and

(B) terminates all rights and interests of equity security holders and general partners provided for by the plan.

(2) The confirmation of a plan does not discharge an individual debtor from any debt excepted from discharge under section 523 of this title.

(3) The confirmation of a plan does not discharge a debtor if—

(A) the plan provides for the liquidation of all or substantially all of the property of the estate;

(B) the debtor does not engage in business after consummation of the plan; and

(C) the debtor would be denied a discharge under section 727(a) of this title if the case were a case under chapter 7 of this title.

(4) The court may approve a written waiver of discharge executed by the debtor after the order for relief under this chapter.

ing all obligations to creditors, whether or not the creditors partici-
pated in the reorganization process. The provisions of a plan bind
creditors whether or not their claims are impaired and whether or
not they have accepted the plan. § 1141(a). Unless otherwise provided in the plan, the debtor, on confirmation, is vested with all
the property of the estate, § 1141(b), "free and clear of all claims
and interests of creditors, equity security holders, and of general
partners." § 1141(c). The Code provides that in cases involving
corporate or partnership debtors, confirmation acts as a discharge
of any debt that arose before confirmation, whether or not a proof
of claim was filed or allowed and whether or not the creditor has
accepted the plan. § 1141(d)(1)(A). Confirmation also terminates
all the rights and interests of stockholders and general partners
provided for by the plan. § 1141(d)(1)(B).

Whether, despite the broad statutory language, confirmation
can constitutionally discharge the claim of a creditor who lacks
timely notice or knowledge of the pendency of the case is not clear.
Probably the Fifth Amendment would override the literal statutory
language if the creditor received no notice at all. But one court
held in a questionable opinion that the due process clause prevented discharging a claim when the creditor, who was generally
aware of the Chapter 11 case, failed to receive notice of the hearing on confirmation. *Reliable Elec. Co., Inc. v. Olson Constr. Co.,* 726
F.2d 620 (10th Cir. 1984); *see also Broomall Industries v. Data Design
Logic Systems,* 786 F.2d 401 (Fed. Cir. 1986). Other courts seem-
ingly would conclude that general notice or knowledge of the pendency of the case is sufficient. *See, e.g., In re Gregory,* 705 F.2d 1118
(9th Cir. 1983) (chapter 13); *cf. In re Penn. Cent. Transp. Co.,* 771
F.2d 762 (3d Cir. 1985) (Bankruptcy Act case) (due process does
not preclude discharge of existing claim of which creditor is unaware, where creditor had notice of claims filing procedure).

Confirmation of a plan does not discharge guarantors or those
otherwise liable for the debtor's obligations. § 524(e). As to
whether a plan could effectively provide for discharging the liability of someone other than the debtor, such as a guarantor of the
debtor's obligations, see p. 359, *supra. Compare Union Carbide Corp.
v. Newboles,* 686 F.2d 593 (7th Cir. 1982) and *Underhill v. Royal,* 769
F.2d 1426 (9th Cir. 1985), *with Republic Supply Co. v. Shoaf,* 815

11 U.S.C. § 524. Effect of discharge

(e) Except as provided in subsection (a)(3) of this section, discharge of a debt of the debtor does not affect the liability of any other entity on, or the property of any other entity for, such debt.

11 U.S.C. § 1142. Implementation of plan

(a) Notwithstanding any otherwise applicable nonbankruptcy law, rule, or regulation relating to financial condition, the debtor and any entity organized or to be organized for the purpose of carrying out the plan shall carry out the plan and shall comply with any orders of the court.

(b) The court may direct the debtor and any other necessary party to execute or deliver or to join in the execution or delivery of any instrument required to effect a transfer of property dealt with by a confirmed plan, and to perform any other act, including the satisfaction of any lien, that is necessary for the consummation of the plan.

11 U.S.C. § 1143. Distribution

If a plan requires presentment or surrender of a security or the performance of any other act as a condition to participation in distribution under the plan, such action shall be taken not later than five years after the date of the entry of the order of confirmation. Any entity that has not within such time presented or surrendered such entity's security or taken any such other action that the plan requires may not participate in distribution under the plan.

11 U.S.C. § 1144. Revocation of an order of confirmation

On request of a party in interest at any time before 180 days after the date of the entry of the order of confirmation, and after notice and a hearing, the court may revoke such order if and only if such order was procured by fraud. An order under this section revoking an order of confirmation shall—

(1) contain such provisions as are necessary to protect any entity acquiring rights in good faith reliance on the order of confirmation; and

(2) revoke the discharge of the debtor.

F.2d 1046 (5th Cir. 1987), *Levy v. Cohen,* 19 Cal. 3d 165, 561 P.2d 252, 137 Cal. Rptr. 162 (1977) and *Stoll v. Gottlieb,* 305 U.S. 165, 170–71 (1938).

Unlike a corporation or partnership debtor, an individual debtor is not discharged in Chapter 11 from any debts that are nondischargeable under Section 523. § 1141(d)(2); see pp. 319–27, *supra.*

When the plan involves a liquidation of all or substantially all the estate and the debtor does not thereafter engage in business, confirmation does not have the effect of discharging claims in a corporate or partnership case. § 1141(d)(3). Under these circumstances the plan is the functional equivalent of a Chapter 7 case, in which corporations and partnerships do not receive discharges. Confirmation of this kind of plan for an individual debtor, however, will have a discharge effect unless a ground of objection to his discharge exists under Section 727(a).

The Code contains a variety of other provisions relating to postconfirmation matters. In a broad exercise of federal power, Section 1142(a) mandates the debtor and any successor to carry out the plan "[n]otwithstanding any otherwise applicable nonbankruptcy law, rule, or regulation relating to financial condition." Furthermore, to implement plans the court may order the debtor or any other party to execute instruments and perform any act necessary for consummation. § 1142(b). When old securities are to be surrendered or conditions are to be satisfied before a creditor or owner may participate under the plan, five years is given for compliance; default results in disallowance of the right to participate. § 1143. Finally, confirmation may be revoked, but only for fraud, provided that the request for revocation is filed within 180 days after confirmation. § 1144.

Chapter 11 contains some useful exemptions from the securities laws that should be noted briefly. Securities of a debtor (or of a related company in a joint plan) may be issued under a plan in satisfaction of claims or interests without registration under Section 5 of the Securities Act of 1933, 15 U.S.C. § 77e, or under a similar state or local law requiring registration or licensing. § 1145(a)(1), (2). The Code also provides that unless an entity purchases a claim against or interest in the debtor with a view to distributing securities received under the plan in exchange for the

11 U.S.C. § 1145. Exemption from securities laws [omitted]

11 U.S.C. § 1146. Special tax provisions

(c) The issuance, transfer, or exchange of a security, or the making or delivery of an instrument of transfer under a plan confirmed under section 1129 of this title, may not be taxed under any law imposing a stamp tax or similar tax.

claim or interest, that entity is not an "underwriter" within the meaning of the securities laws with respect to any securities of the debtor or a related company he received under the plan. § 1145(b)(3), (b)(1)(A). Moreover, the offer or sale of securities under a plan is deemed a public offering. § 1145(c). As a result of these provisions, the creditor or recipient normally will be able to freely resell the shares or other securities he receives under a plan despite otherwise applicable restrictions imposed by the securities laws and rules.

Finally, the issuance or transfer of a security under a plan and the delivery of a deed or other instrument of transfer pursuant to a plan may not be subjected to any stamp tax or similar tax imposed by a state or local taxing agency. § 1146(c).

I.R.C. § 1398. Rules relating to individuals' title 11 cases

(a) Cases to which section applies. — Except as provided in subsection (b), this section shall apply to any case under chapter 7 (relating to liquidations) or chapter 11 (relating to reorganizations) of title 11 of the United States Code in which the debtor is an individual.

10

Taxes

The interface of bankruptcy law with tax law is a complicated subject from the perspective of either discipline. Federal, state, local, and foreign taxes can affect transactions among debtors, secured creditors, unsecured creditors, and shareholders in Chapter 7, 9, 11, 12, and 13 cases. The brief discussion that follows seeks to highlight some of the more important aspects of the tax considerations in a bankruptcy case. A discussion of the rapidly changing aspects of federal tax law is, however, beyond the scope of this book.

§ 10.01 SPECIAL PROVISIONS ON STATE AND LOCAL TAXES

Some provisions in the Code that indirectly affect tax policy have been discussed previously — for example, priority of tax claims, nondischargeability of tax claims, and payment of priority tax claims in reorganization cases.

Further important and complex special tax provisions are contained in Sections 346, 728, 1146, and 1231, which treat with state and local taxes only. Among other things, these provisions deal with the status of the estate as a separate taxable entity, the treatment of tax attributes of the estate and the debtor, and the taxation of income from the discharge of indebtedness in a bankruptcy case. For federal tax purposes the Internal Revenue Code ("I.R.C."), Title 26 of the United States Code, contains some counterparts to these state and local tax provisions. For example, under Bankruptcy Code § 346(b)(1), in a case under Chapter 7, 11, or 12 concerning an individual, the bankruptcy estate of the individual is a separate taxable entity for purposes of state and local taxes. Section 1398 of the I.R.C. provides a similar rule for

I.R.C. § 1399. No separate taxable entities for partnerships, corporations, etc.

Except in any case to which section 1398 applies, no separate taxable entity shall result from the commencement of a case under title 11 of the United States Code.

11 U.S.C. § 1146. Special tax provisions

(d) The court may authorize the proponent of a plan to request a determination, limited to questions of law, by a State or local governmental unit charged with responsibility for collection or determination of a tax on or measured by income, of the tax effects, under section 346 of this title and under the law imposing such tax, of the plan. In the event of an actual controversy, the court may declare such effects after the earlier of—

(1) the date on which such governmental unit responds to the request under this subsection; or

(2) 270 days after such request.

11 U.S.C. § 505. Determination of tax liability

(a)(1) Except as provided in paragraph (2) of this subsection, the court may determine the amount or legality of any tax, any fine or penalty relating to a tax, or any addition to tax, whether or not previously assessed, whether or not paid, and whether or not contested before and adjudicated by a judicial or administrative tribunal of competent jurisdiction.

(2) The court may not so determine—

(A) the amount or legality of a tax, fine, penalty, or addition to tax if such amount or legality was contested before and adjudicated by a judicial or administrative tribunal of competent jurisdiction before the commencement of the case under this title; or

(B) any right of the estate to a tax refund, before the earlier of—

(i) 120 days after the trustee properly requests such refund from the governmental unit from which such refund is claimed; or

(ii) a determination by such governmental unit of such request.

federal taxes.[1] Under Section 346(c)(1) of the Bankruptcy Code, the commencement of a bankruptcy case does not effect a change in the status of a corporation or partnership for the purposes of state or local taxes. I.R.C. § 1399 accomplishes the same result for federal tax purposes.

In some respects the Bankruptcy Code and the I.R.C. deal with the same subject matter but provide different rules for state and local taxes on the one hand and for federal taxes on the other. For example, the treatment of discharge of indebtedness income for the purpose of state and local taxes under Section 346(j) of the Bankruptcy Code differs substantially from the corresponding rules for federal tax purposes under I.R.C. §§ 108 and 1017.

Of course, in some circumstances a rule provided in the Bankruptcy Code with respect to state and local taxes will have no counterpart in the I.R.C. For example, Section 1146(d) permits the bankruptcy court to determine the tax effects of a Chapter 11 reorganization plan with respect to state and local taxes. There is no comparable provision in any statute with respect to federal taxes, and in fact 28 U.S.C. § 2201 appears to prohibit the court's making this determination.

§ 10.02 PROCEDURAL TAX PROVISIONS

Certain important provisions of the Bankruptcy Code apply to federal taxes and to the Internal Revenue Service, notwithstanding the I.R.C. For example, Section 505, entitled "Determination of Tax Liability," grants the bankruptcy court wide authority to rule on the merits of any tax claims, including federal tax claims. The provision applies in Chapter 7, 11, 12, and 13 cases. § 103(a). Broadly drafted, the section authorizes the bankruptcy court to determine the amount or legality of any tax, any fine or penalty relating to a tax, or any addition to a tax, whether of the debtor or of the estate and whether or not it was previously assessed or paid, but not if the issue was contested in and adjudicated by a judicial or administrative tribunal before the commencement of the case. § 505(a).

---

[2]Unfortunately, in a Chapter 12 case there is a different taxable status of the estate for federal and state tax purposes.

11 U.S.C. § 505. Determination of tax liability

(b) A trustee may request a determination of any unpaid liability of the estate for any tax incurred during the administration of the case by submitting a tax return for such tax and a request for such a determination to the governmental unit charged with responsibility for collection or determination of such tax. Unless such return is fraudulent, or contains a material misrepresentation, the trustee, the debtor, and any successor to the debtor are discharged from any liability for such tax—

(1) upon payment of the tax shown on such return, if—

(A) such governmental unit does not notify the trustee, within 60 days after such request, that such return has been selected for examination; or

(B) such governmental unit does not complete such an examination and notify the trustee of any tax due, within 180 days after such request or within such additional time as the court, for cause, permits;

(2) upon payment of the tax determined by the court, after notice and a hearing, after completion by such governmental unit of such examination; or

(3) upon payment of the tax determined by such governmental unit to be due.

The court may also determine the right of the estate to a tax refund, but not unless administrative remedies are, in effect, exhausted first. § 505(a)(2)(B). Specifically, the trustee or debtor in possession must request the taxing authority to determine the amount of the refund, and it is given 120 days in which to act. After the taxing authority makes its determination, or after the 120-day period expires, the bankruptcy court is free to decide the amount of the refund due the estate. § 505(a)(2)(B). This 120-day period compares with the normal period of six months provided by Section 6532(a) of the I.R.C.

As a matter of federal bankruptcy law and federal tax law, the trustee or debtor in possession is responsible for filing all federal, state, and local tax returns and for paying all taxes incurred by the bankruptcy estate. §§ 346(c)(2), (f); I.R.C. § 6012(b)(3); 28 U.S.C. § 960. Thus, before distributing property to creditors in a Chapter 7 liquidation case or under a Chapter 11 plan, the prudent trustee will determine the estate's tax liability for postpetition taxes.

By requesting a determination of any unpaid tax liability of the estate under Section 505(b), the trustee or debtor in possession can bind the taxing agency. This is done, initially, by submitting the tax return and requesting a determination. The taxing authority then has 60 days to give notice whether the return has been selected for examination. If an examination is made, the taxing agency has an additional 120 days, for a total of 180 days after the date of the request, to complete the examination and notify the trustee of any tax due. § 505(b)(1)(B). The court may extend the 180-day period for cause.

If a time period expires without governmental action, then the trustee, the debtor, and any successor to the debtor are discharged from liability for the tax (other than as shown on the submitted return) unless the return was fraudulent or contained a material misrepresentation. If the taxing authority timely determines a tax to be due and owing, the trustee may elect to pay the amount thus determined, or, if he contests the finding, the amount may be determined by the bankruptcy court after a hearing. § 505(b)(2), (3). In either event, as long as the return is not fraudulent and contains no material misrepresentation, the liability for the tax is discharged. If the trustee merely files a return without requesting

I.R.C. § 6901. Transferred assets

(a) Method of collection. — The amounts of the following liabilities shall, except as hereinafter in this section provided, be assessed, paid, and collected in the same manner and subject to the same provisions and limitations as in the case of the taxes with respect to which the liabilities were incurred:

(1) Income, estate, and gift taxes. —

(A) Transferees. — The liability, at law or in equity, of a transferee of property —

(i) of a taxpayer in the case of a tax imposed by subtitle A (relating to income taxes),

(ii) of a decedent in the case of a tax imposed by chapter 11 (relating to estate taxes), or

(iii) of a donor in the case of a tax imposed by chapter 12 (relating to gift taxes),

in respect of the tax imposed by subtitle A or B.

I.R.C. § 368. Definitions relating to corporate reorganizations

(a) Reorganization. —

(1) In general. — For purposes of parts I and II and this part, the term "reorganization" means —

(A) a statutory merger or consolidation;

(B) the acquisition by one corporation, in exchange solely for all or a part of its voting stock (or in exchange solely for all or a part of the voting stock of a corporation which is in control of the acquiring corporation), of stock of another corporation if, immediately after the acquisition, the acquiring corporation has control of such other corporation (whether or not such acquiring corporation had control immediately before the acquisition);

(C) the acquisition by one corporation, in exchange solely for all or a part of its voting stock (or in exchange solely for all or a part of the voting stock of a corporation which is in control of the acquiring corporation), of substantially all of the properties of another corporation, but in determining whether the exchange is solely for stock the assumption by the acquiring corporation of a liability of the other, or the fact that property acquired is subject to a liability, shall be disregarded;

[Continued]

a determination of tax liability, however, a solvent debtor will remain liable for the taxes as a transferee of assets of the estate. *See generally* I.R.C. § 6901.

§ 10.03 CERTAIN FEDERAL TAX PROVISIONS

As noted, many important federal tax aspects of bankruptcy cases are governed entirely by provisions of the I.R.C. A confirmed Chapter 11 plan of reorganization, for example, will generally have tax implications for the corporate debtor as well as for the debtor's creditors and shareholders.

§ 10.03(a) Tax-free Corporate Reorganizations

At the outset, it is necessary to determine whether the confirmed plan of reorganization qualifies as a tax-free reorganization under Section 368 of the I.R.C. A corporate debtor in Chapter 11 is eligible to conclude a tax-free reorganization by way of a merger or consolidation, a stock-for-stock swap, a stock-for-assets swap, a division, a recapitalization, or a mere change of identity or form, the same as any other corporation under Section 368(a)(1)(A)–(F) of the I.R.C.

Additionally, a transaction in Chapter 11 qualifies as a tax-free reorganization if the debtor transfers all or part of its assets to another corporation, provided that in pursuance of the reorganization plan, stock or securities of the transferee corporation are distributed in a manner that qualifies under I.R.C. § 354, 355, or 356. I.R.C. § 368(a)(1)(G).[2] In this context the term "securities" is used in the tax sense to connote long-term bonds or notes with original maturities of five years or longer.

As a general rule, when stock or securities are distributed under I.R.C. § 354 to shareholders or to creditors who are security holders in exchange solely for stock or "securities" in the debtor, then no gain or loss will be recognized at the creditor or shareholder level. Thus stock or securities distributed to the debtor's sharehold-

---

[2]If the reorganization qualifies under more than one subparagraph of I.R.C. § 368(a)(1) (or under I.R.C. § 332 or 351), it is treated as a "G" reorganization. I.R.C. § 368(a)(3)(C).

(D) a transfer by a corporation of all or a part of its assets to another corporation if immediately after the transfer the transferor, or one or more of its shareholders (including persons who were shareholders immediately before the transfer), or any combination thereof, is in control of the corporation to which the assets are transferred; but only if, in pursuance of the plan, stock or securities of the corporation to which the assets are transferred are distributed in a transaction which qualifies under section 354, 355, or 356;

(E) a recapitalization;

(F) a mere change in identity, form, or place of organization of one corporation, however effected; or

(G) a transfer by a corporation of all or part of its assets to another corporation in a title 11 or similar case; but only if, in pursuance of the plan, stock or securities of the corporation to which the assets are transferred are distributed in a transaction which qualifies under section 354, 355, or 356.

ers or holders of long-term debt in a reorganization under Section 368(a)(1)(G) of the I.R.C. will not result in tax at the shareholder or security holder level. A taxable event would occur, however, if identical stock or securities were distributed to creditors holding short-term debt or trade debt.

But the stock or securities distributed will be taxable if their principal amount exceeds the principal amount of the securities surrendered or if securities are received and no securities are surrendered. Similarly, the transaction will be taxable at the shareholder or creditor level to the extent securities, stock, or other property received is attributable to accrued interest. If other property or money is distributed in addition to the stock or securities, gain is recognized at the recipient's level in an amount not in excess of the value of that additional consideration. No loss from the exchange or distribution, however, may be recognized.

§ 10.03(b) Treatment of Tax Attributes

Often it is important to determine whether the debtor's tax attributes (including its net operating loss) will carry over to the successor to the debtor under a plan of reorganization. The subject is dealt with generally by Sections 381 through 383 of the I.R.C., a matter beyond the scope of this book.

§ 10.03(c) Discharge of Indebtedness

Tax attributes, including the net operating loss, can be adversely affected by the discharge or forgiveness of indebtedness in a bankruptcy case, particularly under a Chapter 11 plan. As a matter of federal tax law, the amount of indebtedness forgiven in a Chapter 11 case as the result of a confirmed plan does not give rise to taxable income. I.R.C. § 108(a)(1). The debtor's tax attributes, however, will be reduced to the extent debt is forgiven in the bankruptcy case, I.R.C. § 108(b), in a fixed order prescribed by I.R.C. § 108(b)(2).

§ 10.03(d) Conclusion

The foregoing tax issues become even more complicated when transactions concern related corporations or involve multiple

debtors, as frequently occurs in parent and subsidiary bankrupt-cies. Discussion of the tax consequences of these transactions is beyond the scope of this book. *See generally* I.R.C. §§ 108(e)(4), 267(b), 368(a)(2)(C) and (D).

Finally, it is important to remember that provisions of the tax law are subject to revision by Congress on what appears to be an almost annual basis. In particular, general provisions relating to treatment of tax loss carryovers were enacted in 1986 by Congress and may be subject to significant revision in the future.

Table of Cases

(References are to section numbers)

Table of Statutes, Rules, and Regulations

(References are to section numbers)

United States Code

Bankruptcy Rules

Official Bankruptcy Forms

Internal Revenue Code

See 26 U.S.C. entries, above

Uniform Commercial Code

Uniform Fraudulent Conveyance Act

Uniform Fraudulent Transfer Act

Federal Rules of Appellate Procedure

Federal Rules of Civil Procedure

Federal Rules of Evidence

Index of Subjects

(References are to section numbers)

D

Debtors
  See also Estate
  duties and benefits of, generally, 1.04,
    7.01
  landlord or contract vendor, as, 5.04(j)
  exemption rights, 2.01(d)(2)(A), 4.04,
    7.02, 7.03
  forfeiture clauses, 5.04(b)
  individual debtors. *See* Individual
    debtors
  utility service, 5.05
  voluntary petitions of, 3.02(b), 7.01,
    7.10(b)
Debtor in possession, 2.03(b), 9.02(a)
Default on secured debts, 5.04(e),
    5.04(h), 9.04(d)(l)(C)
Definitions
  adjunct, 2.01
  antecedent debt, 4.03(c)(1)(Ɔ)
  arising under, 2.01(c)(2)(B)
  bankruptcy cases, 2.01(c)(1)(B)
  case, 2.01(c)(1)(B)
  cash collateral, 5.02(b)
  claim, 5.01(a), 6.01
  consumer debt, 7.10(c)
  contingent claim, 3.02(c)(1)
  core proceedings, 2.01(a)
  corporation, 3.01
  cram down, 7.10(f)
  creditor, 4.03(c)(1)(C), 6.01
  custodian, 4.02, 4.03(g)
  debtor in possession, 9.02(a)
  discharge, 7.05
  disposable income, 7.10(f)
  estates, 4.01(c)
  executory contracts, 5.04(a)
  interest in, 4.01(a)
  municipalities, 3.01
  noncore proceedings, 2.01(d)(2)(B)
  perfection of a transfer, 4.03(c)(2)
  person, 3.01
  preferences, 4.03(c)
  proceedings, 2.01(c)(2)(B)
  property interests, 4.01(c)
  regular income, 3.01
  related proceedings, 2.01(a),
    2.01(d)(2)(B)
  similarity, 9.03(c)
  statutory lien, 4.03(e)
  transfers, 4.03, 4.03(c)(1)(A)
  utility service, 5.05
Defrauded seller's rights, 4.03(e)

Deposits with debtors, 6.04
Discharge of claims
  assets, prior bankruptcy, 7.08(j)
  Chapter 7, under, 6.04, 6.05, 8.06
  Chapter 11, under, 9.06
  core proceeding, as, 2.01(d)(2)(A)
  defined, 7.05
  educational loans, 7.08(h)
  effect of discharge, generally, 5.01(d),
    7.05, 7.10(g)
  fiduciary capacity, and, 7.08(d)
  fraud, 7.08(b), 7.08(d), 7.10(g)
  governmental penalties, 7.08(g)
  hearings, 7.08(k), 7.09
  individual debtors, generally, 5.01(d),
    7.05, 7.07, 7.08(g), 7.08(k),
    9.06
  injuries, 7.08(f)
  nondischargeable debts, generally,
    7.05, 7.08, 7.10(g)
  objections to and revocation of, 7.07
  partnerships, 8.07, 10.03(c)
  reaffirmation agreements, 7.09
  scheduling, timeliness of, 7.08(c)
  spousal and child support, 7.08(e)
  taxation, 7.08(a), 10.03(c)
Dischargeability complaint, 7.08(k)
Discriminatory treatment of debtors,
    5.05, 7.06
Disposable income, defined, 7.10(f)
Distribution of estate, generally, 6.01-6.06
  partnerships, 8.06
District courts, 2.01(c), 2.01(d)(2),
    2.01(d)(3), 2.02(a)
Drunk-driving judgments, 7.08(i)
Due-on-sale clause, 5.02(e)

E

Educational loans, 7.08(h)
Elected trustees, 2.03(a)
Eligibility
  generally, 1.04, 3.01
  Chapter 11 reorganizations, generally,
    9.01(b)
  Chapter 13 rehabilitation, generally,
    7.10(a)
  corporations, 1.04
  partnerships, 1.04, 8.01
Embezzlement, 7.08(d)
Emergency Rule, 1.03, 2.01(a), 2.01(i)
Employee benefit contributions, 6.04